Also by RICHARD D. WHITE, JR.

Roosevelt the Reformer:
Theodore Roosevelt as Civil Service Commissioner

KINGFISH

RANDOM HOUSE NEW YORK

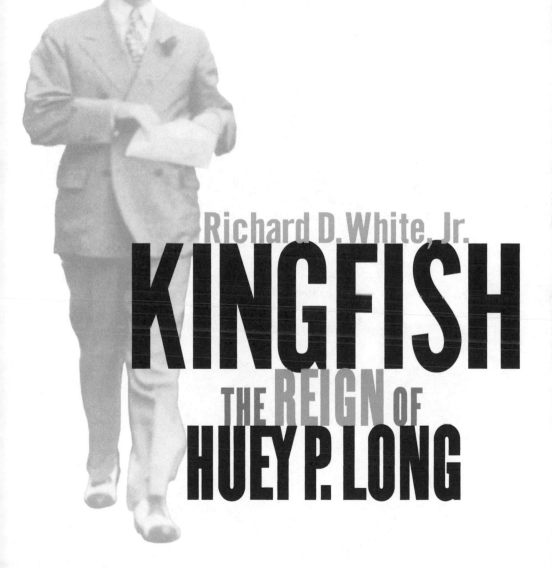

Richard D. White, Jr.

KINGFISH

THE REIGN OF

HUEY P. LONG

Published in the United States by Random House,
an imprint of The Random House Publishing Group,
a division of Random House, Inc., New York.

RANDOM HOUSE and colophon are
registered trademarks of Random House, Inc.

ISBN 1-4000-6354-X
Printed in the United States of America

Book design by Barbara M. Bachman

CONTENTS

INTRODUCTION

"Listen, there are smarter guys than I am," Huey Long once admitted, "but *not* in Louisiana." At the time Huey made the boast, many Louisianans agreed with his oversized opinion of himself, that he was the fastest-thinking, fastest-talking politician in the state and, if not the smartest, indeed the most shrewd and powerful. From 1929 until his violent death in 1935, he seized more control over an American state than any politician before or since. By the end of his tempestuous reign as governor of Louisiana and later as United States senator, he dominated almost every aspect of government in his native state. He used political whim to hire thousands of state government workers, from cabinet secretaries to laborers shoveling gravel onto highways, while thousands of local government workers, including schoolteachers, sheriff's deputies, and courthouse clerks, fell under his political mastery. He orchestrated elections, padded voting lists, and directed the counting of ballots. He assaulted freedom of the press by proposing a gag law that prohibited newspapers from printing "malicious, scandalous, or defamatory" stories about him. He deployed the state militia as his personal police force and declared martial law in cities that refused to submit to his mastery. He packed the courts with his loyalists to ensure that his increasing power went unchecked. Most blatantly, he dominated the state legislature and ordered it to slavishly pass hundreds of bills that increased his power, destroyed his enemies, and stretched the very limits of constitutionalism.

Paradoxically, Huey Long did more good for the people of Louisiana than any politician before or since. In the midst of the Great Depression, he built nine thousand miles of new roads and more than a hundred bridges over swamps and rivers, pulling Louisiana from the horse-and-buggy days into the age of modern transportation. He gave free schoolbooks to students, allowing thousands of poor children to attend school, and his adult night schools taught 175,000 illiterate Louisianans to read, including many poor blacks. He doubled the number of beds in the state's charity hospitals. He raised the state university to national stature in size and scholarship. He lessened the burden on poor farmers by giving a homestead property tax exemption and allowed thousands of them to vote when he abolished the poll tax.

Huey possessed enormous talent but grievous flaws. Both saint and sinner, he mixed frankness with hypocrisy, first-rate brains with buffoonery, compassion with savagery. Controversy followed him everywhere and scandals "swarmed about his head like mosquitoes." Ambitious, aggressive, uninhibited, exceedingly colorful, and mesmerizing, he received no lukewarm descriptions. To thousands of ill-housed, ill-fed, and ill-clothed Louisianans, Huey incarnated the savior of the common man and the liberator of the downtrodden. He promised hope in a land of hopelessness and brought humor to a saddened people. When he poked fun at the poor folk, they felt he was also poking fun at himself, and they loved it. They supported him staunchly, almost blindly, not worrying that he had built a ruthless political machine or that he allowed some corruption in state government or even that he pocketed some money himself. Seeing a man whose "musical heart loved the songs of the common people," the country people idolized him. "They did not merely vote for him, they worshiped the ground he walked on," a newspaperman observed. "He was part of their religion."

While thousands revered Huey, thousands more despised him. His enemies called him a clangorous demagogue and loudmouthed blatherskite and branded him an ill-balanced and domineering radical whose populist notions were not only impractical but ridiculously unattainable. Huey demanded that he rule and rule absolutely, and to do so he crushed anyone who stood in his way. His Machiavellian lust for power led him to ruthlessly destroy his enemies' political careers, ruin their businesses, raise their taxes, and fire their relatives from government jobs. He took a savage delight not merely in beating opponents but in humiliating them. His reign of power eventually split the state of Louisiana into a bifactional political battleground where those who wanted to sanctify him squared off against those who wanted to crucify him. There was no middle ground—a person had to be either for or against Huey.

Once he had grabbed tight control of Louisiana, the ambitious Huey was elected to the United States Senate, where his wild antics, uncouth manners, and long-winded filibusters made him the most entertaining show in Washington. He led a controversial crusade to limit the income of millionaires and redistribute their wealth to the poor. He proposed that Congress give a $30 pension for all needy persons over sixty, limit work hours to thirty a week, and give a free college education to deserving students. By 1935, he had organized his followers into the Share Our Wealth Society with eight million members nationwide. Although economists discarded his notion to redistribute wealth as rash and impractical, a vast and growing number of poor Americans believed his plan was a workable answer to the Depression. Disregarding fiscal realities, he defended himself with the Scriptures. "I never read a line of Marx or Henry George or any of them economists," he admitted. "It's all in the law of God." With his radical proposals and rude demeanor, Huey became Franklin Roosevelt's archenemy and most vocal critic of the New Deal. By 1935, he had announced he was running for president.

How could Huey Long do so much good and so much harm for so many people in such a short time? Today it is difficult to understand how one man could capture such absolute control over a modern, democratic state. Many factors contributed to his rise to near-absolute power. He possessed unflagging energy, razor-sharp political savvy, absolute brilliance, and, most important, an unquenchable thirst for power. He also had help from others, including a horde of bootlicking followers who did his bidding without question, disorganized opponents who never fully recognized his cutthroat ambition, and a Depression-weary population searching for someone to promise them a better life.

Huey defied description. While his critics portrayed him as a demagogue or dictator, neither term completely captured his penchant for up-lifting Louisiana's poor while simultaneously crushing the rich and powerful. He cast aside the demagogue label as easily "as an actor wipes off greasepaint" and bristled when opponents called him a dictator. While he openly admitted that his methods were harshly authoritarian, he insisted that Louisiana remained a democracy. "A perfect democracy can come close to looking like a dictatorship," Huey explained to a newsman, "a democracy in which the people are so satisfied they have no complaint." One observer coined a new term, *heterocrat,* meaning an absolutely different type of leader who resists stereotype. Huey himself recognized that he belied simple description, that he was truly one of a kind. "Just say I'm *sui generis,*" he once told an interviewer, "and let it go at that."

In the end, Huey Long's reign of power resembled that of a Shakespearean tragedy. He began with aspirations of populist greatness and, according to one critic, "the heights were there for him to climb, but he deliberately turned away, in willful ambitious pride, and sought to build a lower kingdom of his own." Addicted to power, he sadly wasted his enormous talent and the opportunity to be a great democrat. A more foreboding tragedy was that Huey not only destroyed many of his enemies, he came close to destroying republican rule. According to novelist Robert Penn Warren, he exploited one of the great flaws of democracy, for, ironically, democracy itself allowed an ambitious and remorseless leader like Huey to exploit the weaknesses and fears of the people and, ultimately, to employ democratic means to achieve undemocratic ends. Even a Louisiana State University faculty member fell for his political legerdemain. "There are many things Huey has done that I don't approve of," the professor told a writer. "But on the whole he has done a great deal of good. And if I had to choose between him without democracy and getting back the old crowd, without the good he has done, I should choose Huey. After all, democracy isn't any good if it doesn't work. Do you really think freedom is so important?"

KINGFISH

CHAPTER 1

1927
A WEDDED MAN WITH
A STORM FOR A BRIDE

Huey Long climbed onto a large bale of fresh-picked cotton and gazed out at a crowd of farmers attending a country fair. For a few moments he stood motionless, his shoulders hunched like a boxer waiting for the first bell to ring. Leaning forward to talk to the men in the front row, Huey began speaking in a whispery voice so quiet that the crowd shuffled closer to hear him. After a couple of minutes, he slowly raised his voice, a little louder each minute, until he roared to the gathering throng. He threw off his coat, rolled up his shirtsleeves, and slackened the red silk tie hanging around his neck. His voice booming across the dusty fairgrounds, Huey pummeled his audience with old-fashioned soapbox oratory and hell-for-leather political bluster. He whooped and hollered, pounded his fist, and punched in the air at imaginary enemies. His face turned the color of a ripe tomato. Twirling his arms above his head in the sweltering Louisiana heat, perspiration pouring down his cheeks, he quickly captivated the audience with spellbinding charisma and homespun guile.

It was the summer of 1927 and Huey was running full speed for governor of Louisiana. At every stop on the campaign trail, he treated his listeners to a boiling mixture of snake-oil salesmanship, burlesque tap dancing, evangelicism, and blistering billingsgate. He would preach to the crowd, holding a Bible in his hand in holy uplift and quoting from memory lengthy passages of the Scriptures. From Galatians he taunted his adversaries. "Am I therefore become your enemy because I tell you the truth?" More often though, Huey spewed a torrent of abuse upon his foes. He branded his political opponents with epithets like "low-down vile and slanderous men," "thieves, bugs, and lice," "grafters and money boodlers," "graveyard robbing politicians," and "blackguards in full-dress suits." His audience, mostly rural folk who took their politics raw like corn whiskey, could not get enough. "You tell 'em, Huey," the farmers yelled back. "Go get 'em."

Huey's crowd of farmers looked up at a man in his thirties, of medium height, approaching pudginess with a round face, puffy jowls, and skin glowing pink like a fresh sunburn. An unruly mop of chestnut-colored hair topped his head, with a curly forelock that tumbled down. An oversized nose jutted from his face and his brown eyes were large, round, and expressive, shifting from jest to rage in a twinkling. When he walked, he jostled along "like a saddling pony." As Huey dazzled his audiences, at times he appeared almost childish, spoiled, and "like an overgrown small boy with very bad habits indeed." In an instant, however, his face could turn exceedingly hard and cruel.

A dominating egotist, Huey hungered for the spotlight and could not bear to share it with another. "The only kind of band in which Huey Long could play," one newspaper editor wrote, "was a one-man band." A skillful speechmaker, he craved the microphone. "I can't remember back to a time when my mouth wasn't open whenever there was a chance to make a speech," he remarked. He could not stand to be ignored by the newspapers, admitting that "I don't care what they say about me as long as they say something." He knew that Louisiana voters would cast their votes for a known thief before they would vote for a name they did not recognize. Desperately wanting to be noticed, he dressed in a dazzling mix of pastel suits, purple shirts, flaming red flowered ties, and two-toned wing tips that provoked one onlooker to describe him as an explosion in a paint factory. "Drama was his natural art," a supporter wistfully remembered, "an actor whose stage was his work, whose scenery, the people about him."

Perpetually in motion, Huey wielded his "energy of ten men" as one of his most effective weapons. If he could not whip his political opponents with his brilliance or cunning, he simply wore them out by working harder, traveling more miles, making more speeches, shaking more hands, and twisting more arms. "He never relaxed," observed a campaign worker. "He got along with little or no sleep when he was under pressure. He awakened associates at all hours of the night to talk over a new notion which had come to him in bed." Always mesmerizing, he cast a spell upon his listeners. While he spoke at the parish fair that summer, a man who hated him stood to the side of the crowd, then disappeared. Later, one of Huey's supporters saw the man and asked why he left. "I left because I was afraid. That guy was convincing me. I had to get out."

HUEY LONG WAS BORN on August 30, 1893, in Winn Parish, Louisiana, amid the red-clay hill country dotted with longleaf pine and where a dark and relentless poverty sapped the lives of the straitlaced Baptists who struggled to survive there. The people there were so poor that, according to a wry local joke, they made a living by taking in each other's wash. Many of them lived in clapboard cabins with dirt floors and subsisted off small worn-out farms, cut-over timber lands, and paltry cotton patches. The parish seat, Winnfield, languished as a mud-pathed village of about two thousand residents, with two hotels, a lumber mill, seven other buildings, and neither running water nor electricity. The town was notable only for "large numbers of hogs and children, and by a scarcity of Negroes."

A year before Huey was born, his parents, Hugh and Caledonia Long, moved from Tunica, Louisiana, to Winnfield. Hugh bought 320 acres of scrub land, which he cultivated with cotton and corn and where he let his hogs run wild in the woods. After 1900, Winnfield became a railroad hub, with four lines passing through the town, and the site of a roundhouse and repair shops. The railroad built a depot on the Long farm and within ten years the town grew to about three thousand inhabitants. Hugh sold part of the farm in lots. On one side of his farm the business section rose and on the other side residences sprang up. Although far from wealthy, Hugh became one of largest landowners and livestock holders in Winnfield. He grew and raised most of what the family consumed, and when they needed cash, he sold a pig or cow. In 1907, he built a large home in Winnfield, with two stories, ten rooms, electric lights, indoor plumbing, high ceilings, and large columned verandas on three sides. Two big white oaks sat in the front yard and celery and asparagus sprouted in a bed at one end of the front porch.

Hugh Long turned forty when Huey was born in 1893. By then, Hugh's hair was an iron gray and his face brown and wrinkled like a walnut shell. A gangly six-footer, he glared at people through the same penetrating brown eyes that all nine of his children would possess. Hugh loved to talk in a booming voice and could be found sitting in front of Bernstein's store in Winnfield under an ancient chinaberry tree, amusing the townsfolk with his dry wit. Hugh was eccentric, gentle, even weak, had only an elementary education, and bragged of voting for the Socialist candidate for president, Eugene Debs.

Huey's mother, Caledonia, like his father, came from Pennsylvania Dutch stock. A slender, hazel-eyed, and raven-haired woman who weighed less than a hundred pounds, Caledonia was disciplined, self-educated, and had a photographic memory that Huey would inherit. She insisted her children read the Bible and attend the First Baptist Church of Winnfield. She had a preacher baptize Huey in a neighbor's fishpond but the boy rebelled against his Baptist upbringing. Caledonia, who refused to whip her children, tried to manage Huey, the most unruly and headstrong of her nine offspring, but her efforts proved futile. Even before he could walk he demanded that he control everything and everyone around him. Always inquisitive, as a toddler he wandered off and on one occasion crawled beneath a steam locomotive and delayed a train departing the Winnfield station. As a rebellious teenager he smoked, drank, chewed tobacco, and cussed like a field hand.

Caledonia passed on her charitable spirit to Huey. Known throughout the parish as a generous and compassionate woman, she frequently sent her son to deliver food and clothing to less fortunate families. From his parents, Huey inherited a belief that the wealth of the land should be shared and that "none should be too poor and none too rich." Caledonia insisted that Huey and the other children read avidly. If one of the youngsters was reading, the mother would not assign the child chores. The clever Huey learned to always have a book in his hands, whether or not he read it. At an early age he memorized long passages from the Bible, pored over Shakespeare's *Julius Caesar, Hamlet,* and *The Merchant of Venice,* and once bet a friend $10 that he could recite Bunyan's *Pilgrim's Progress.* He admired Dumas's *The Count of Monte Cristo,* where the lead character metes out harsh revenge to his enemies. John Clark Ridpath's *History of the World* also made a lasting mark upon young Huey. In future years while stumping around the state, he quoted Ridpath, who stressed the crucial role of powerful leaders in world affairs and deplored the social evil ingrained in concentrated wealth.

Huey was bright, outspoken, aggressively self-confident, and forever seeking the center of attention. "If he couldn't pitch, he wouldn't play," a childhood friend remarked. With a hot temper that fit his rust-colored hair, Huey could rage quickly into a tantrum, his bright, darting eyes revealing his anger. He quarreled often with his brothers and sisters, who were all smart and competitive. Of the four Long brothers and five sisters, three of the boys became attorneys, the fourth, George, a dentist and later congressman, and the girls received degrees in education from Louisiana Normal College in Natchitoches, one becoming a professor.

While in high school, Huey learned to set type and wrote short items for two local newspapers, the *Baptist Monthly Guardian* and the *Southern Sentinel.* When he was a junior, he competed on his high school debate team that traveled to Louisiana State University for the state rally. While in Baton Rouge, Huey stayed at the home of T. H. Harris, the state superintendent of education. "The boy was a perfect portrait of the man to follow," Harris later recalled. "He came swaggering into the house, leaving the baggage for others to bring in, and introduced himself to Mrs. Harris. . . . He was always late for meals, left his clothes all over the bathroom floor, and had everybody in the house awake by five or six in the morning."

Huey received an early education in Louisiana's freewheeling politics. He grew up in a household where the family argued politics each night at their large and noisy dinner table. When he turned seven, his father ran as an independent Democrat and finished a distant third in a state Senate race and ten years later finished sixth in a race for Winnfield's five aldermen. As a boy, Huey often walked into Winnfield, where he listened to the parish's rabble-rousers standing on the courthouse steps and sounding off at a political system that disenfranchised the poor population. In 1908, fourteen-year-old Huey campaigned at a polling precinct for Theo Wilkinson, who lost the race for governor to the New Orleans machine candidate, J. Y. Sanders. From the start, politics surged through Huey's veins. "All I remember is that the first time I knew anything about it, I was in it."

Huey never had much patience for school. In 1910, just before his seventeenth birthday, Winnfield High School expelled him. He was already showing an obsession to be in charge and to control those around him. "We had formed a secret society. . . . We wore a red ribbon," he recalled later. He belonged to "a sort of circle that was to run things, laying down certain rules the students would have to follow." If the students obeyed faculty rules, then Huey and his followers kept them off the baseball team or the debating team. The faculty told Huey that his antics were out of order but he continued to defy their authority. After he published a circular attacking the teachers, the principal expelled him. Even after being expelled, he did not give up. He hand-delivered a petition around Winnfield and convinced a majority of the citizens to sign it. They fired the principal.

Huey did not try to finish high school. He left Winnfield in July and took a job as a traveling salesman selling Cottolene, a lard substitute made from cottonseed oil. His salary was $19 a week. He traveled across the South, hawking his product and distributing pie plates and cookbooks and holding baking contests in cities and towns. Selling Cottolene door-to-door, Huey soon became a persistent and skillful salesman who combined his wit and outgoing personality with iron-willed determination to make a sale. He often turned to the Scriptures to persuade his customers. "I used the Bible on them, showing where the Lord had forbidden the Israelites to use anything from the flesh of swine food, and how cottonseed oil, seeing it was a vegetable product, was just bound to be pure." When quoting the Scriptures failed to produce a sale, he was more aggressive. "If I couldn't convince the woman no other way I'd go right into the kitchen and bake a cake for her, or cook supper for the family," he recalled. "I had to persuade those womenfolks that you could bake a cake with something else besides cow butter and fry meat in something else besides hog lard." Years later, many housewives remembered young Huey, his red curls tousled, barging into their farmhouse, rolling up his sleeves, and scattering flour about the steamy kitchen as he baked a cake or fried some chicken.

After only a few months, Huey was fired in November 1910 when business slumped. He next took a job in Memphis selling cured meats, lard, and canned goods for an Austin, Texas, food wholesaler. He met his quotas but ran through his expense account by staying in the most expensive hotels and eating lavishly and, "after being given a few warnings, which I did not heed, I was summarily discharged." With no job and less than a dollar in his pocket, Huey was evicted from his Memphis hotel room. "I went from park to depot and depot to railroad yards, sleeping wherever I might be permitted to lay my head."

In late September 1911, Huey's mother persuaded him to move to Shawnee, Oklahoma, where his older brother George was a dentist. Caledonia always wanted Huey to become a minister and managed to convince him to enter Oklahoma Baptist University. He lasted only one semester, rarely attended classes, and confessed to his brother that he was not cut out to be a preacher. He decided to become a lawyer. With a hundred dollars provided by George, Huey headed for law school at the University of Oklahoma in Norman. On the way, however, he spent New Year's Eve in Oklahoma City and lost his money at the roulette wheel of a local gambling parlor. The next morning he wandered the streets, broke, and on an impulse walked into the offices of the Dawson Produce Company. Huey introduced himself and asked to be hired as a salesman to work the Norman area while he attended law school. His brassy confidence impressed the manager, K. W. Dawson, who gave him a job at 5 percent commission. Huey needed to get from Oklahoma City to Norman but did not have the cash for a train ticket. At nine that night, with the thermometer dipping near zero and "a wind howling across the plains of Oklahoma that cut like a knife," he began walking. Five hours later, at two in the morning, he finished the eighteen-mile trek and arrived, chilled to the bone, in Norman. For the following semester Huey attended law school part-time and sold fruit and vegetables for Dawson. He showed up for only a few classes and quit selling groceries the following May. He received three Cs and an incomplete in the four courses he took. He also continued to gamble, spending most of his weekends in Oklahoma City at the dice and poker tables. "I didn't learn much law there," Huey recalled years later. "Too much excitement, all those gambling houses and everything."

By late summer of 1912, Huey was again on the road, this time selling for the Faultless Starch Company. Still not twenty, he rose quickly to regional sales manager, responsible for a four-state area and several salesmen, including his younger brother, Earl. Despite his youth and lack of experience, Huey was already a sales dynamo. "He's the damnedest character I ever met," his Faultless supervisor recalled. "I don't know if he's crazy or a genius."

Huey enjoyed traveling the dusty back roads of the South and sharing seedy hotels and boardinghouses with other salesmen. Frank Odom, a fellow salesman who sold a laxative pill called Nature's Remedy, met Huey in 1913 and recalled that Huey's pants were too short, he quoted the Bible continuously, and he would talk to you till midnight. By this time, Huey had become a smooth-tongued hawker who charmed housewives and country storekeepers. The skills he honed as a salesman were not much different from those needed for a successful politician. He tailored his language to his customers, sensed when he had their attention, and if he did not, would use his wit and charm to win them over. He met thousands of people as he traveled throughout Louisiana, staying overnight with farmers and establishing a friendship, and with his extraordinarily keen memory, never forgot them. Years later, during campaign speeches in the remote regions of the state, Huey would point to a former customer in the crowd and tease him for losing his hair or gaining a few pounds.

IN OCTOBER 1910, while still selling Cottolene and holding baking contests to advertise his product, nineteen-year-old Huey Long spotted a petite, dark-eyed, black-haired young woman among the seven hundred contestants who entered a bake-off in Shreveport's West End neighborhood. Rose McConnell had baked a bride-loaf cake made with sugar, flour, egg whites, vanilla, milk, and, of course, two-thirds of a cup of Cottolene. Taking a liking to her, he ensured she won first prize. Fifteen months older than Huey, Rose worked as a stenographer for a local insurance company. Unlike Huey, Rose was quiet, shy, calm, and tactful. He believed she was the most beautiful girl that he had ever seen and "outshines these girls up here by forty acres or more." To Rose, Huey was clever and quick-witted. They both loved music and began a stormy courtship that endured for the next two and a half years.

During his Christmas vacation of 1912, Huey returned to Shreveport to visit Rose and propose to her. She turned him down but he persisted, writing her constantly. Finally, during the following spring she relented and on April 12, 1913, took the train to Memphis where he was living. The couple married there in a small ceremony at the Grayoso Hotel. Huey borrowed $10 from Rose to pay the Baptist minister.

In the spring of 1914, Faultless Starch laid Huey off, but he soon got another job, with the Chattanooga Medicine Company. He sold patent medicines, including a laxative called Black Draught and the notorious Wine of Cardui, an elixir for menstrual cramps and other gynecological ailments. Although the American Medical Association denounced Wine of Cardui as a "vicious fraud" that same year, the product sold well and women loved it. Its main ingredient was forty-proof alcohol. Huey lost his job at Chattanooga Medicine in the fall. Meanwhile, the beginning of World War I cut off cotton exports and much of the South fell into a depression, lessening the chance for a salesman to earn much money in the region. With a wife to support, he looked for a more promising and dependable profession. His brother Julius suggested Huey return to his law studies. Julius, who received a law degree from Tulane after a year of study, persuaded him to follow the same path.

In September 1914, Huey and Rose moved to New Orleans, where he registered at Tulane's law school. The couple found a two-room apartment renting for $15 a month at 1215 Carrollton Avenue. For the next nine months he and Rose lived off $50 a month provided by Julius, plus $250 Huey borrowed from his friend S. J. Harper, a Winnfield cotton broker and state senator. After attending class all day, Huey returned to the dingy flat near the edge of the Mississippi River where he studied late into each night. Rose kept "his nose to the grindstone" and transcribed the notes he dictated from his classes. "We had a typewriter," he recalled later. "Immediately after reading a book, I would set my wife down at the machine, where I would dictate to her, and I would extract that book from hell to breakfast while it was fresh in my mind, and I would practically memorize that extract." Throwing all of his energy into the law, he dropped to a weight of 112 pounds and he couldn't sleep. "I would read until about five or ten minutes after midnight," Huey remembered, "and then I would trot about a half a mile up to a little beer stand and get half a gallon of beer and come back and drink that beer and lie down and slide off to sleep that way."

By April 1915, Huey felt he had learned enough law and, besides, he was broke. By then he had completed only two Tulane law courses, corporation law and federal practice. He failed two other courses and did not show up for the final exam in four others. He also attended lectures given by Tulane noted political science professor Charles Dunbar but later claimed he learned nothing about how politics really works. His lackluster academic record, however, did not reflect his overall energy. He cared less about formal academic grades than in learning the practical applications of the law. "Whenever I saw one of the professors leave the school to go to town," Huey recalled, "I would get on the streetcar with him, and I would talk law to him all the way to town." He posed detailed, realistic questions in class and cornered professors in hallways to quiz them on the finer points. "When the bell rang he always had one more question to ask," a classmate remembered.

The bar exam was scheduled in June but Huey was impatient and penniless. Instead of waiting a month, he petitioned the chief justice of the Louisiana Supreme Court, Judge Frank Monroe, to take the bar exam early. Yielding to the irrepressible law student, Monroe allowed an unusual special exam to be administered. On May 15, Huey went before a panel of attorneys and passed his oral bar exam with little difficulty. Now a twenty-one-year-old member of the Louisiana bar, he climbed aboard the train that evening and headed back to Winnfield with only enough money in his pocket to pay for his ticket.

By the time Huey got on the train, he already had decided that the law was only a stepping-stone to a much greater ambition. As he struggled to build a successful law practice over the next few years, he was obsessed with an overriding, burning passion to run for public office. "I was born into politics, a wedded man with a storm for a bride," he once admitted. Even before he finished his law studies he began plotting a political future that would not begin for another three years, when he was elected state railroad commissioner in November 1918. Not long after he was married, he told Rose that he first planned to win a minor state office, then become governor of Louisiana, then United States senator, and finally president. "It almost gave you the cold chills to hear him tell about it," Rose remembered years later. "He was measuring it all."

WITH A PILE OF "Long for Governor" campaign posters heaped in the back seat of his Ford coupé, Huey crisscrossed Louisiana during the summer and fall of 1927. He bounced along the dirt roads that meandered through the rolling hills of the north Louisiana farmland, passing majestic white-columned plantation houses surrounded by live oaks draped with Spanish moss, sharp contrasts to the nearby weatherbeaten one-room cabins inhabited by sharecroppers and farmhands. He drove through the southern Acadiana region, settled by refugee French Cajuns after the British expelled them from Nova Scotia in 1755. He skirted the flooded rivers and bayous of the Mississippi Delta, a region that seemed unable to make up its mind whether it was earth or water. He crossed lush cypress swamps on rickety bridges and steam ferryboats. When it rained, the unpaved roads he traveled turned into impassable quagmires, and when it didn't, the scorching sun baked the country lanes into dust-choked paths cursed with axle-deep, bone-jarring potholes. Journeys across Louisiana tortured both car and driver, but the state's wretched roads did not hold back the headstrong and indefatigable young politician. Huey Long was running for governor and nothing was going to slow him down.

Day in and day out, Huey campaigned across the state. He stopped at every crossroad village and country store, buttonholed any farmer or one-horse merchant he spied, and, on almost every tree and telephone pole he passed, tacked his campaign poster. In the towns, he dropped by the local barbershop and placed a poster in the window so that men waiting for a haircut had little else to do but stare at Huey's smiling face. On Sundays, he put his circulars in buggies while people attended church, and sometimes he stopped at a Baptist church during a service and asked to sing in the choir.

Huey never seemed to stop campaigning and his unflagging energy attracted attention. "All over the neighborhoods flew the news of my working through the nights," he wrote later. When Huey gave a speech in the rural parts, he would recognize people in the crowd whom he had met during his salesman days. "He would mention that one was getting fatter, or about how so-and-so borrowed a dollar from him," recalled a follower. "He saw to it that he was never a stranger in their midst." When Huey passed through rural parishes, as counties are called in Louisiana, late in the evening, at times he knocked unannounced on a farmer's door and asked to spend the night. Rising early before breakfast, he helped with the chores and washed the dishes, and when he left, paid the family a dollar. Deep down, Huey knew that the farmer and his family would never forget his surprise visit and that whenever they voted in the future, their support for him would not waver.

On a Thursday in the middle of September, a typical day on the campaign trail, Huey canvassed the northeastern parishes of the state. He passed through miles of rolling hill country studded with longleaf and loblolly pine and dotted with small sawmills that turned out rough-cut lumber, stacked in glistening piles to dry out in the sun. Starting at ten that morning, he delivered a rousing thirty-minute speech in Delhi, a small lumber town in Richland Parish. He then drove ten miles north to the village of Epps, where he bellowed another speech at noon, jumped back in his Ford and rushed forty miles to Forrest for a speech at one, then drove thirty-three miles to Pioneer for a two o'clock speech. From Pioneer, he drove nine miles to Oak Grove, the West Carroll parish seat and home of several large cotton gins and a lumber plant, and gave a speech at three o'clock in the town square. From there it was another eleven miles to Kilbourne, just below the border with Arkansas, for a rally at four-thirty. After a final twenty-mile dash to Lake Providence in East Carroll Parish, Huey delivered his seventh speech at eight that evening on the courthouse steps. At each stop he pumped hands, slapped backs, kissed babies, and entertained his audiences with fire and brimstone. A stiff belt of bourbon provided his only comfort at the end of the long day.

In October Huey raced across southeastern Louisiana giving spirited performances in villages like Amite, Bogalusa, and Denham Springs. When he passed through Independence, a small town settled by Italian immigrants at the turn of the century, he dropped by Garafola's store, where he ate bread and cheese and drank the sweet strawberry wine favored by the locals. He met with the town mayor, Charles Anzalone, who promised to deliver 90 percent of the Italian farmer vote. From Independence, Huey sped south along Highway 51 between Hammond and Ponchatoula, passing acres of newly planted strawberry fields. Highway patrolmen clocked him doing forty-eight miles per hour in a thirty-mile zone, but when the officers realized whom they had stopped, they gave an angry Huey a warning. Still furious when he spoke in Hammond that night, Huey attacked one of his opponents, the current governor of the state, and charged that the "highway coppers are so numerous now that a fellow driving a car has to stop and ask them to move out of the way."

HUEY LONG TOOK DEVILISH delight in shattering political traditions. Before he ran for governor, the Delta planters, wealthy businessmen, and New Orleans political bosses would meet in secret to pick the next Democratic candidate for governor. Louisiana was a one-party state and the only election that made any difference was the Democratic primary. Even primary elections were of little consequence, however, as the powerful politicos decided the results beforehand and controlled the voting by methods both fair and foul. Before Huey, milquetoast candidates waged dull and meaningless gubernatorial campaigns. Giving listless speeches, they made few promises, and when elected, carried out fewer. The candidates visited only the larger cities and token parish seats and ignored the rural and impoverished regions of the state.

Shunning the support of the political bosses, Huey waged an unorthodox campaign. He was confident that he could get his political support directly from the people and ran his campaign without the blessing of the state's Democratic wheelhorses. He spent little time in large courthouse towns and parish seats and focused instead on the "scattered people of the hills and hollows." In the past, candidates for governor pursued local political bosses, who controlled the voters in their parishes, but Huey did the opposite. "In every parish there is a boss, usually the sheriff," he told a friend. "[The boss] has forty percent of the votes, forty percent are opposed to him, and twenty percent are in-betweens. I'm going into every parish and cuss out the boss. That gives me forty percent of the votes to begin with and I will hoss trade them out of the in-betweens. . . . I always hit the big man first."

Huey introduced political cunning and crudity that was unheard of in Louisiana gubernatorial races. Traditionally, politicians acted as gentlemen who refrained from attacking their rivals, but he refused to campaign in the more polite and chivalrous manner of his opponents. He ignored what he called the "burglars code among politicians" that prevented candidates from attacking each other. With no hesitation, Huey attacked his political rivals "until the leaves on the trees shivered down." He also delivered his attacks by a more unconventional method, becoming the first politician in Louisiana to broadcast his speeches over the radio. By 1928 a large portion of the state's population could sit in their parlors, tune their polished wooden boxes to the powerful Shreveport station, KWKH, and listen to Huey launch his tirades. On the road, he employed two new sound trucks with huge loudspeakers attached to their roofs. One of the sound trucks always stayed ahead of him, arriving in the next town an hour early with music blaring and drumming up a crowd. Huey knew that soapbox speaking was still important in rural Louisiana, where few people read newspapers and political rallies provided rare entertainment.

In his speeches across Louisiana, Huey offered the people a "wagon load of promises." He pledged to provide free textbooks to schoolchildren, remove the tolls from the state's bridges, make the state penitentiary self-supporting, place union representatives on state boards, and increase worker's compensation benefits. He promised to allow unlimited hunting and fishing year-round and to abolish the state Conservation Commission, that "coon chasin' possum watchin' brigade. . . . I'll cut the tail off the Conservation Commission right up behind the ears." With a hoofer's knack for burlesque, the former traveling salesman sold his platform the way he once sold patent medicine.

As he ground away the miles of this campaign, Huey tailored his speeches to the local audience. In Alexandria and Shreveport, he promised to open the nearby Red River to navigation and bring shipping and commerce to the region. In Pineville, a small town near Alexandria, Huey had his father sit on the stage while he spoke, hoping to present more of a family image. In Baton Rouge, he promised to support the state university located there. When he spoke in New Orleans, he promised free bridges to connect the city with traffic arteries along the Gulf coast and to replace the city's expensive synthetic gas supply with cheaper natural gas. When he spoke in the Baptist north, his rhetoric was straitlaced and dry to alcohol use. In the south, he pitched a different story. "I want every man in this audience who ever took a drink to vote for me," Huey urged the mostly Catholic and decisively wet crowd at the Eunice Fair.

During one of Huey's early campaign trips through the Acadian south, a local political boss warned, "Huey, you ought to remember one thing in your speeches today. You're from north Louisiana, but now you're in south Louisiana. And we got a lot of Catholic voters down here."

"I know," Huey answered, and for the rest of the day he started his speeches by saying, "When I was a boy I would get up at six o'clock in the morning on Sunday and I would hitch our old horse up to the buggy and I would take my Catholic grandparents to mass. I would bring them home, and at ten o'clock I would hitch the old horse up again, and I would take my Baptist grandparents to church."

Later that night, the political boss complimented Huey as they headed back to Baton Rouge. "Why Huey, you've been holding out on us. I didn't know you had any Catholic grandparents."

"Don't be a damned fool," shot back Huey. "We didn't even have a horse."

HUEY LONG IGNORED the sweltering heat as he strutted down Alexandria's DeSoto Street at the head of a loud and colorful parade. It was Wednesday, August 3, 1927, and he officially launched his campaign for governor with circuslike fanfare. Unofficially, he had been campaigning hard for the last four years, but the Alexandria rally kicked off the final five months of frantic campaigning in the race for governor. Flanked by mounted policemen, Huey marched beneath a huge banner stretched between two telephone poles proclaiming, "Everyone Is a King but No One Wears a Crown," a phrase he borrowed from one of the few men he admired, William Jennings Bryan. Seven hundred of Huey's most loyal supporters from New Orleans, each paying $3.75 for the round-trip train ride, joined the parade. The New Orleans crowd also brought a fifty-piece brass band led by Emil Tosso of the Orpheum Theater to liven things up and play an afternoon concert on the oak-shaded lawn of the white-columned Bentley Hotel, where Huey headquartered his campaign on the second floor.

At eight that evening, three thousand people squeezed into the

Bolton High School auditorium, while another six thousand stood outside listening to loudspeakers. KWKH, which was owned by Huey's
friend W. K. Henderson, broadcast the event live across the state. Colonel
Swords Lee, Huey's wealthy cousin, opened the meeting with a rousing
introduction of Huey.

Arms flailing above his head as he bounded onto the stage, Huey
began his speech by attacking the debauchery of traditional Louisiana
politics. He railed against the injustices of poverty and informed his audience that "we must bear in mind that sixty-five percent of the people own
less than five percent of our wealth." He promised an education for "every
white child in Louisiana," free schoolbooks, free bridges, better highways, and cheap natural gas for New Orleans. He opposed any new taxes
and complained that "a man buying a plug of tobacco pays a tax every
time he spits." He concluded with a promise—already broken—to wage a
gentlemanly campaign and refrain from personally attacking his opponents.

Huey had run for governor once before, just after his thirtieth birthday. On election day, January 15, 1924, a heavy downpour inundated the
entire state and lowered the turnout of rural voters, who were most likely
to vote for Huey. He finished third in the Democratic primary. Henry
Fuqua won with 82,556 votes, Hewitt Bouanchaud got 82,287 votes, and
Huey, 73,762. Huey carried all the northern parishes except three and received majorities in twenty-one parishes, but his 12,000 votes in New Orleans were not enough. With the New Orleans vote excluded, he would
have won. His first campaign was poorly financed and inefficiently run
and he still appeared a little rough around the edges. "His pants didn't
meet his shoes, he wore a high stand-up collar," recalls a state senator
who saw Huey in Alexandria mingling with delegates at an American Legion convention. "He looked like a dressed-up country boy."

On the day after he lost the 1924 race, Huey bought a new suit and
began campaigning again. For the next four years, he never slowed down,
vowing that his 1928 campaign would be efficiently run and victorious.
In his new campaign he worked hard to build political support across the
state. His campaign manager, Harvey Ellis, wrote U.S. senator Ed Broussard and urged him to back Huey. Four months earlier, Huey campaigned
for Broussard, a south Louisiana Creole, who ran against ex-governor J. Y.

Sanders. Huey covered the state for Broussard, making four speeches a day. Broussard won by 3,479 votes and the *New Orleans Times-Picayune* credited the race to Huey. Despite his vigorous support for Broussard's reelection, the senator afterward gave him only a weak endorsement, as did the other U.S. senator, Joseph Ransdell, whose reelection Huey had supported in 1924. In spite of failing to get enthusiastic senatorial support, Huey continued to entice other political heavyweights and wealthy supporters.

Huey was able to raise more campaign funds in 1928 than he had in 1924. Harvey Couch, a utilities and railroad millionaire from north Louisiana, contributed several thousand dollars and served as Huey's go-between with the business community. Nicholas Carbajal, a wealthy New Orleans Italian-American, contributed $10,000, and W. K. Henderson, the rich Shreveport ironmonger and maverick radio station owner, gave $10,000 more, as well as free airtime on his KWKH station, and provided the amplifiers for the sound trucks that rambled across the state announcing Huey's arrival. Wearing a hefty diamond on his tie, a brown derby cocked to the side of his head, and colorful socks embroidered with New York governor Al Smith's name, the eccentric Henderson shared Huey's habit of crusading against the powerful. W.K. fought the proliferation of chain stores—"bloated plutocrats," he called them—as relentlessly as Huey fought his own nemesis, the "petroleumites" of the huge Standard Oil Company.

Huey's cousin Swords Lee, a wealthy lumberman, contractor, and political boss from Rapides Parish, gave $30,000 to the campaign. Lee believed that if Huey won he would receive lucrative road building contracts from the state. Colonel Robert Ewing, a wealthy newspaper publisher who saw himself as a political kingmaker, provided a sizable sum, as did the Fisher family, which ran a shrimping empire in south Louisiana. Even Huey's younger brother, Earl, now selling shoe polish and hoping for a political appointment, contributed several thousand to the campaign. Huey's biggest financial backer, however, was one of New Orleans's wealthiest businessmen, Robert Maestri. The son of an Italian immigrant and poultry peddler, Maestri owned huge tracts of property and over five hundred houses, many of them on the edge of Storyville, once the city's haven of prostitution. His enemies nicknamed him "Red

Light Bob" because many of his properties rented not by the month but by the hour. Impassive yet amiable and reliable, the rich Italian devoted himself to Huey for years to come. Unlike other contributors, Maestri appeared to expect nothing in return from Huey. Rising out of poverty, he was sympathetic to the underdog, especially one like Huey who challenged the ruling political bosses. Maestri contributed at least $40,000.

Huey's 1928 campaign was not only better funded than in 1924, it was much better organized. He hired a campaign staff to fill each day's schedule with his speaking events and to spend campaign funds where they mattered most. He kept a huge card catalogue of the addresses of thousands of his followers across the state and set up a network of his own political bosses in each voting precinct who made sure the people made it to the polls and "voted right."

At the time, it was customary for Louisiana's gubernatorial candidates to campaign alone, but Huey selected his own slate of running mates from different parts of the state. The Long ticket included Columbus Reid for attorney general, John S. Patten for superintendent of education, and H. B. Conner for treasurer. Conner, a three-term legislator from Concordia Parish, was a past Masonic grand master and added statewide popularity to Huey's ticket. All these men were die-hard Long loyalists. Huey added Cajun support to the slate by putting Paul Cyr, a French Catholic dentist from the heart of Acadiana, on the ticket for lieutenant governor. Forty-nine, with a grayish front hair lock teased in an upward curl, Cyr was a feisty two-hundred-pounder known as the "Wild Bull of Jeanerette." Huey liked having the muscular Cyr near his side in case a political gathering turned rowdy and fists began to fly.

AT THE BEGINNING of the 1928 governor's race, the state's political leaders regarded Huey Long as a threat to their entrenched power and no longer dismissed him as a loudmouthed upstart. Four years before, Huey had shocked many observers of Louisiana politics, including the large daily newspapers, with his strong showing. The wealthy Delta cotton planters, sugarcane growers, lumbermen, and New Orleans ward heelers detested Huey and were determined to fight and defeat him. Fearing his aggressive campaign style, Huey's foes knew that they must act quickly to choose their own candidate. On July 8, 1927, a blisteringly hot day, former governors John Parker, Ruffin Pleasant, and J. Y. Sanders, along with representatives of the Standard Oil Company, gathered in Alexandria to select their own gubernatorial hopeful. The New Orleans political machine also attended, traveling from New Orleans in fifteen Pullmans. That night, three thousand citizens sweltered in the same Bolton High School auditorium in which Huey would announce his candidacy. Jammed to the limit, the auditorium teemed with delegates yelling under a huge banner proclaiming "It Won't Be Long Now."

All of the speakers attacked Huey. Former governor Pleasant called Huey "a coward with the conduct of an egg-sucking yellow dog, and a man who lies with a craven heart like a white-livered popinjay." Shreveport mayor Lee Thomas, for years one of Huey's more vitriolic archenemies, threatened to run for governor just to stop him, calling Huey "quixotic and notionate" and claiming that he was one of the Grand Genii of the Ku Klux Klan. Known as "Wet Jug" due to his bald head and large ears, the heavyset Thomas belonged to the old school of fire-breathing politicians. "A great many citizens I know are opposed to a man of the destructive and Bolshevistic type for governor of this state," declared Thomas. "They sincerely believe that the election of [Huey Long] would be more injurious to the welfare of this state than the locusts of Egypt or the Mississippi floods which have devastated our rich alluvial soil."

Wet Jug hoped to get an endorsement for governor but received little support. Most of the political bosses knew that Thomas was no match for the aggressive Huey. Another who failed to win approval at the Alexandria meeting was the current governor, O. H. Simpson, who had announced three days earlier in Baton Rouge that he would seek reelection. Simpson, a dumpy little man who wore a wrinkled white suit and floppy black bow tie, had been clerk of the state House of Representatives for twenty years and later was lieutenant governor. In October 1926, after Governor Henry Fuqua died in office, Simpson became governor; he served for two years as the state's lackluster chief executive. On September 24, 1927, Simpson opened his own campaign in Washington, Louisiana, blandly announcing to his followers, "I love this place. I love the woods and streams and the fields close by. I love these people." A weak campaigner who read his stuffy speeches mechanically, Simpson also drank heavily and spent much of his time at the racetrack. The Alexandria bosses considered him unelectable and spurned him.

The *New Orleans Times-Picayune*, which supported Simpson, criticized the Alexandria meeting, saying it did not officially represent the state's Democratic Party because only delegates from northern parishes and New Orleans attended the event. Huey also attacked the conference, calling it a "stench in the nostrils of the good people and . . . an effort to put out a band-box candidate, hand-picked by a set of plunderbunders."

The Alexandria gathering eventually chose Riley Joe Wilson as their candidate for governor. A rugged square-jawed man who resembled a middleweight prizefighter, Wilson overcame poverty as a Winn Parish youth to become a teacher, district judge, and, in 1915, congressman. A little-known north country Protestant who was serving his seventh term in the House of Representatives, Riley Joe was one of the more senior members of the House and ranking minority member of the Flood Control Committee.

On August 11, 1927, Wilson officially opened his campaign with a huge barbecue in his hometown of Ruston, the parish seat of Lincoln Parish in the north-central cotton belt of the state. Unfortunately, Riley Joe campaigned little better than the dull Simpson. Inarticulate, colorless, and "embalmed in the House of Representatives for fourteen years," Wilson performed so poorly that the party bosses later would send him back to Washington for the final months of the governor's race.

Huey Long was delighted. He knew that both Simpson and Wilson were weak and vulnerable and neither would be able to match his energy or fend off his vicious and relentless attacks. Smelling the blood of his political prey, Huey wasted no time in pouncing mercilessly upon his two hapless opponents.

CHAPTER 2

1927
I WAS BORN BAREFOOT

"One day you pick up the papers and see where I killed four priests," Huey Long joked to a crowd at the Ascension Parish fair in Donaldsonville in 1927. "Another day I murdered twelve nuns, and the next day I poisoned four hundred babies. I have not got time to answer all of them." Everywhere Huey campaigned, the newspapers followed. He made good copy and the papers gave him wide coverage, although most of the reporting soundly denounced him. The *New Orleans Item* accused him of making campaign promises he could never keep and "pledging himself to cure the blind, the deaf and the deformed." One writer facetiously described Huey's attacks on his opponents as "pentecostal fanfaronades against plunderbunds of political corruption."

Huey constantly battled the press. In his unsuccessful 1924 race for governor, he did not have a single Louisiana daily newspaper behind him, and of the more than one hundred weeklies, only a handful endorsed him. Four years later, Huey's relations with the press had not improved, and his constant attacks on the newspapers made them criticize him more intensely. "There is as much honor in the New Orleans *Item* as there is in the heel of a flea," Huey yelled in one speech. In another, he mockingly portrayed the *Alexandria Daily Town Talk* as the *Alexandria Bladder*. On one occasion, Huey's hostility for the newspapers led to fisticuffs. He encountered Dolph Frantz, the editor of the *Shreveport Jour-*

nal, on a Shreveport street. "I am tired of your lies," Huey yelled at the editor. "The men clinched and rolled from the sidewalks into the gutter," reported a New Orleans newspaper. "Mr. Frantz was bleeding about the mouth but not seriously hurt when the combatants were separated by bystanders."

Despite his frequent bouts with the press, Huey needed newspaper support to help him win the governorship in 1928. He turned to two of his former enemies to get it. One of them, wealthy newspaper publisher Colonel Robert Ewing, had opposed Huey viciously in the governor's race of 1924. Sporting a bristling white mustache and barking in a clipped brogue, Ewing resembled an "angry schnauzer." The sixty-eight-year-old newspaperman, son of a wealthy Scottish cotton broker, managed the *New Orleans Chronicle* at the turn of the century, later bought the *New Orleans States* and *Shreveport Times,* and expanded into the *Monroe Morning World* and *Monroe News-Star.* Ewing was affluent, politically connected, "wringing wet," and his newspapers covered a large portion of the state. Huey needed Ewing on his side. To win him over, Huey courted the support of Ewing's friend John Sullivan. Sullivan managed the New Orleans Fair Grounds racetrack and lobbied for the liquor dealers. He also gambled notoriously. Six-foot-two, handsome with wavy hair, Sullivan led the New Regulars, a fractious group of maverick New Orleans politicians who had opposed Huey in his 1924 bid for governor. "To get Ewing, we would have to take Sullivan first," Huey admitted. In the middle of 1927, after Huey promised to back Sullivan and reward his New Regulars with patronage jobs in New Orleans, Ewing agreed to support Huey's ticket. Ewing and Huey did not like each other, but Ewing believed that if Huey won he could influence the young and inexperienced governor.

Huey's pact with Sullivan disrupted his political camp. In May 1927, Harvey Ellis resigned as campaign manager because of the Long-Sullivan partnership. An upstanding attorney from Mandeville, Ellis tried to run a clean campaign and earlier urged Huey to "cut out the rough stuff" and send personal notes to influential voters that he offended. Ellis believed that Sullivan was crooked and stood for three things, "racing, gambling, and whiskey." Huey tried to placate Ellis, claiming to have made no promises to Sullivan to protect gambling. "I never saw or bet on a horse race in my lifetime," he wrote to his campaign manager. Nevertheless, Ellis resigned. Huey replaced Ellis with Sheriff Charles Pecot of St. Mary's Parish, but managed his own campaign. He wrote all of his own speeches and circulars and personally made all of the decisions, from major platform strategy to buying campaign buttons.

Once Sullivan agreed to back Huey, Colonel Ewing's *New Orleans States* endorsed him in December 1927. The large New Orleans daily papers often chose different candidates during elections in order to increase controversy and boost circulation. The *Times-Picayune,* which opposed the New Orleans political bosses, backed Governor Simpson, while both the *Item* and the *Morning Tribune* supported Riley Joe Wilson. Because each newspaper gave one-sided coverage to its own candidate and ignored the other two, citizens needed to buy different papers to keep up with the campaigns.

Of the state's small weekly papers, only the *Hammond Vindicator, Bogalusa News, St. Tammany Farmer, Lafourche Comet,* and *Donaldsonville Chief* endorsed Huey for governor. Dozens of others bitterly fought him. In November, the *Houma Courier* described one of Huey's speeches as "disgusting buffoonery" and said that "a thousand people witnessed a cheap vaudeville performance, the chief actor in which [Long] was uncouth in manner and speech, preaching demagoguery of such arrant type that almost every utterance was an affront to an intelligent audience." The *Shreveport Caucasian* ridiculed Huey as the "honorable huey promising long" and thereafter spelled his name in lowercase letters.

THROUGHOUT THE WINTER and spring of 1927, as Huey Long campaigned across Louisiana, cold torrents of rain pelted the South. Powerful winds drove the rain sideways and thunder rattled windows and shook houses. Day after day, for months on end, the water fell in frigid, gray sheets, changing country roads and cowpaths into bottomless morasses and fields into un-plowable, un-plantable swamps. The Mississippi River, the people's wellspring in normal times, now loomed as the enemy. The angry river roared past, a swirling brown cataract that kept rising until it was higher than any old-timer could remember. By April, the huge earthen levees and piles of sandbags could no longer harness the torrent and the river broke through the dikes in several places, flooding vast expanses of the fertile Mississippi River valley. The massive flood did not spare Louisiana. Pouring through crevasses in levees, the foul and swirl-ing inland sea soon covered more than six million acres of flat Louisiana bottomland and left 278,000 people homeless.

On Good Friday, the storm intensified and dumped fifteen inches of rain on New Orleans in eighteen hours, the heaviest rain ever recorded in the city. The downpour covered many streets with four feet of water. As the rains continued, the rising river threatened the city, perilously situ-ated below sea level and protected only by a ring of levees. City leaders ar-gued that it was necessary to blow up other levees below New Orleans to create an outlet for the river and relieve the pressure on the city. Wanting to demonstrate that the city remained safe for business investment, they urged Governor Simpson to order engineers to blast away the levee. Meanwhile, the people of St. Bernard and Plaquemines Parishes des-perately fought the plan. Destruction of the levee below the city would inundate their two parishes and ruin the livelihoods of the mostly French-speaking Cajuns who had hunted, trapped, and fished there for generations.

Even though the river receded and the danger to New Orleans passed, city leaders forced the governor to ignore the pleas of the St. Bernard and Plaquemines citizens and destroy the levee. On Friday afternoon, April 29, at a sharp bend in the river twelve miles below the city near Poydras in Plaquemines Parish, engineers exploded thirty-nine tons of dynamite. The river surged through the crevasse, flooding St. Bernard and Plaque-mines. Ten thousand residents, now refugees, watched helplessly as their land and homes disappeared beneath the swirling brown river. The water did not recede until July.

The trappers and fishermen of St. Bernard and Plaquemines never forgave the political leaders of New Orleans for destroying the levee and devastating their lives. In every election for years to come, the French Catholics of the two southernmost river parishes viciously fought the Old Regulars and the Bourbon aristocracy. They also overwhelmingly sup-ported an unlikely ally, an irreverent Baptist from north Louisiana named Huey Long.

AT THIRTY-FOUR, Huey campaigned more vigorously and colorfully than either Riley Joe Wilson, fifty-nine, or O. H. Simpson, fifty-seven. On a sultry Saturday night at the end of August, 2,500 spectators watched Huey perform at Baton Rouge's Community Club. With theatrical coolness, he opened a wooden crate and dumped a stack of schoolbooks onto a table. These, he pointed out loudly, were a few of the textbooks that the state Department of Education recently discarded. Waving a book above his head, Huey charged that since Louisiana switched textbooks so often, the books could not be passed on from child to child and a family had to buy new ones each year. Louisiana paid $2 for each book, he added, while neighboring Texas paid only 90 cents and gave them free to the schoolchildren.

Promoting his free schoolbooks and other benefits, Huey tried to go everywhere and meet everyone. Where he didn't go, he mailed circulars, over a million of them during the last four months of the campaign, which outlined his platform and attacked his opponents. He personally composed these well-written broadsides, each averaging from a thousand to eighteen hundred words. His style had improved since his race four years earlier, when he distributed a circular that displayed his belligerence, if not his long-windedness. "Our present state government has descended into one of deplorable, misunderstood orgy of frequent corporate dictation," Huey had written, "mingled with bewildering cataclysm of various criminations and recriminations amongst the personal satellites of the governor and the beneficiaries of the immense public plunder he has dispensed." According to the New Orleans Times-Picayune, "there was a warlike spirit in the polysyllabic Huey."

Huey had learned a lot from his unsuccessful bid for governor and now was a much improved candidate four years later. His speeches were better written, more focused, and more powerfully delivered than those of 1924. He spoke of practical, tangible goals, such as better roads, better education, and free bridges, and provided clear-cut examples and simple statistics that discredited the vague promises offered by his unimaginative opponents. A new magnetism seemed to engulf him. Dazzling his listeners, he thrived on big, noisy crowds, and his leather-lunged oratory made them noisier. Always in motion, he learned to flash his natural charisma, sharply target his speeches to the local audience for maximum impact, and use his homespun humor to win over his country listeners. He spiced his speeches with rib-tickling homilies like "as slick as polecat grease," "more trouble than a boat can haul," "as hungry as a seed tick," "as crooked as a boar shoat's tail," and "a neck like a cushaw and a head like a gourd." He once described a man so mean that "he sleeps on a grindstone and has razor soup for breakfast."

On a Sunday night at the end of August 1927, Huey began his fight to win New Orleans with a mass meeting at the corner of Canal Street and Claiborne Avenue. Five thousand spectators crowded around and thousands more listened to the speech broadcast across the state by radio. Huey needed New Orleans and worked hard to shore up the city and increase his support. John Sullivan opened the rally, followed by John Overton, a prominent Alexandria lawyer and one of the state's best orators. Huey and Overton had been political allies since 1918, when he stumped for Overton's unsuccessful bid for the U.S. Senate. That same year Overton helped Huey win his first election as a state railroad commissioner. Attacking Wilson with biting ridicule, Overton accused "Prince Riley" of being crowned by the political aristocracy of the state and claimed Wilson's platform "sounded like a funeral dirge."

In a frenzy of red hair and flailing arms, Huey leaped to the rostrum and launched a barrage at the New Orleans political machine. Ignoring his earlier promise not to attack the character of his opponents, he assailed Governor Simpson for claiming the "right to be a candidate because a man died," a reference to Simpson having succeeded to the office when the previous governor died. Huey struck at Simpson's Conservation Commission, where "they are hiring men to watch coons on the streets of Shreveport and New Orleans." But Huey, who seemed to change unexpectedly from saint to sinner and back again, ended his New Orleans speech on a more inspiring note with a quote from his favorite poem, William Ernest Henley's "Invictus." "It matters not how strait the gate, how charged with punishment the scroll," he recited passionately. "I am the master of my fate, I am the captain of my soul."

A month later, Huey campaigned through the southwestern part of the state. On one hot afternoon, he sat on the back of a farm truck under the shade of the moss-hung live oaks of the Crowley courthouse square during the annual Rice Carnival. Riley Joe Wilson also showed up and the two candidates debated each other. They had planned to speak on the courthouse steps but the scalding sun drove the speakers off the platform to the nearby truck under the shade trees. Appearing drained by the scorching weather, Wilson gave a brief, wilted speech promising little change and firmly defending the status quo. He praised the level of education in 1927 and insisted that a good education was available to all children. Riley Joe denounced Huey's promise of free schoolbooks, saying he opposed any new taxation to pay for them.

The sweltering heat seemed to inflame Huey. Thrusting his red-beet face at his audience, sweat pouring from his brow and down his cheeks, he attacked Riley Joe, sitting stone-faced behind him on a folding chair. "Wilson is a candidate because he answered the call of the Alexandria convention," he roared, "where assembled the lords, dukes, nabobs, satraps and rajahs, who journeyed in special trains and were attended by bland masters." Jerking his arms up and down like pump handles, Huey loudly suggested Riley Joe had a role in the Great Flood of 1927. "Wilson," he shouted, "has been in Congress fourteen years, and this year the water went fourteen feet higher than ever before, giving him a flood record of one foot of high water a year."

Huey kept on the attack when the three candidates spoke at the Tri-Parish Fair in Eunice, an Acadian rice and cotton hub in St. Landry Parish. When Simpson and Wilson adopted his plan to span the state's rivers with free bridges, Huey made it clear that he had the idea first and his opponents had "jumped on the wagon after it was greased." After Simpson claimed that wealthy gamblers were backing Huey, he countered that four slot machines operated on a state-run ferry near New Orleans. Huey charged Simpson with recently doubling the size of the highway commission, hiring 1,737 highway workers in the past year to increase patronage and squandering $5 million of public money to help his own reelection. At one point, Huey attacked Major Frank T. Payne, the head of Simpson's Highway Commission, for ordering forty highway workers to cut weeds on a thirty-mile section of road. Ridiculous, howled Huey, cutting weeds in October that frost will kill in November.

The Eunice Fair was one of the few times Huey and Simpson appeared together. Huey tried to arrange a direct confrontation with Simpson, but the governor understandably avoided face-to-face encounters. Early in November, he learned that Simpson planned to speak in the lumber town of Colfax, parish seat of Grant Parish. To the governor's surprise, Huey showed up at the rally and ambushed him. Barging onto the speaker's platform, Huey first attacked Simpson for failing to provide a pension for old soldiers, an emotional issue in rural Louisiana, where the memories of the Lost Cause still lingered. "The old Confederate veterans may be denied their pension," he declared, "while the thin gray line is steadily perishing." When Simpson proposed to tax horse racing to fund public schools, Huey saw an opening and pounced again. "Let's see who it is that is so close to the races," he hollered, adding that he had never been to a horse race, had never bet on races, and had never asked racing interests for a single favor. Spinning around, he asked the flabbergasted governor, "How about you?"

FILLED WITH MUSTY ANTIQUE FURNITURE that smelled like wet horse hair, the Choctaw Club was one of New Orleans's seedier private fraternities. A three-story Creole-style building fringed with filigreed wrought iron balconies, the Choctaw offered no dining room, contained no bar where its patrons could drink highballs, nor provided any of the amenities available at the city's more posh retreats like the Pickwick or Boston Clubs. The Choctaw members were not the fashionable elite from uptown or the Garden District. Instead, they were a rougher crowd, mostly heavyset, cigar-smoking men who, if necessary, could use their fists to settle their frequent arguments.

One block down from the mayor's office in marble-columned Gallier Hall on Lafayette Square, the Choctaw served as the true heart of New Orleans politics. The Choctaws, also known as the Old Regulars and the Ring, had served as the Crescent City's most intimidating political machine since 1897. They ran the city crookedly and incompetently, but provided some social services that the state did not. On a scale that resembled New York City's Tammany Hall, the Choctaws dominated New Orleans politics and ruled each of the city's seventeen political wards with heavy hands. The Choctaw bosses were a Runyonesque bunch, men like Ulic Burke, the First Ward commissioner who later challenged Huey to a duel, Captain William Bisso, a local tugboat company owner who always wore a pink rosebud in his lapel and a glittering diamond horseshoe stickpin in his tie, and James Comiskey, Third Ward boss and notorious liquor dealer. Through the ward leaders and about 2,100 other members, they controlled elections with ruthless, often corrupt, and sometimes violent effectiveness. By the 1920s, the Ring controlled 35,000 votes. According to one observer, "if they like you, they would steal the election." Another critic was more blunt, recalling that "they were a bunch of bums." Elections were preordained, as the Old Regulars selected their own henchmen as voter registrars who padded the rolls generously with the names of dead people, imaginary people, and people who had moved elsewhere but somehow showed up to cast their ballot on election day.

Taxing gamblers and prostitutes to fatten their machine coffers, the Old Regulars controlled a vast patronage stockpile. City policemen, firemen, and street maintenance men all owed them their jobs and most of the state government jobs in the city fell within their control. The city sewerage and water board alone had over four thousand jobs and men got those jobs only with the blessing of the Choctaws.

Huey Long knew that he would never win New Orleans until he controlled the political bosses who ran the city. The Choctaws not only held a firm grasp upon New Orleans but also held the trump card in statewide gubernatorial and congressional elections. The city had 20 percent of the state's voting population and elected twenty House members and eight senators. Although few Old Regulars ran for statewide election, they nevertheless wielded considerable influence in deciding the state's political future. When the Old Regulars collaborated with the wealthy plantation owners along the fertile Mississippi bottom land, their candidate became nearly unbeatable. From 1900 to 1924, the Choctaws delivered the deciding votes for Governors William Heard, Newton Blanchard, J. Y. Sanders, Ruffin Pleasant, and Henry Fuqua. Any candidate for governor of Louisiana who did not carry New Orleans had little hope of victory, a fact well known to an upstart young politician named Huey Long.

IT WAS LUNCHTIME and a crowd of visitors attending a bottlers convention filled the plush lobby of New Orleans's Hotel Roosevelt. A group of Orange Crush salesmen were relaxing in the hotel grill after finishing their fried oyster sandwiches when they heard yells and scuffling outside the door. Rushing into the lobby, they were surprised to see an elderly overweight gentleman grappling with a younger man on the marble floor.

Many of the onlookers recognized the two men fighting. The older gentleman was J. Y. Sanders, sixtyish and the former governor of the state, and the younger was the red-haired Huey P. Long.

An old-fashioned Southern orator full of clichés about the Lost Cause and the virtues of white supremacy, Jared Y. Sanders was a household name in Louisiana politics. Supported by the New Orleans Ring, he served in the state House of Representatives from 1892 to 1904, as lieutenant governor from 1904 to 1908, governor from 1908 to 1912, and U.S. congressman from Louisiana's Sixth District from 1917 to 1921. A fire-breathing Protestant who fought liquor and gambling, Sanders ran unsuccessfully for the U.S. Senate in 1912, 1920, and 1926. While governor, Sanders accomplished little and succumbed to the conservative backroom politics of gentlemanly know-nothingness that kept Louisiana mired in the nineteenth century. His refusal to improve the state's archaic highways earned him the nickname "Gravel Roads" Sanders.

Huey claimed he had opposed Sanders in every election since 1908, including the 1926 Senate race when he campaigned across the state for incumbent Senator Ed Broussard and against that "long-legged sapsucker" Sanders. Sanders now was bent over by age, prompting Huey to call him "Old Buzzard Back." J.Y. detested Huey, writing that "when it comes to arousing prejudice and passion, when it comes to ranting and raving, when it comes to vituperation and vilification, when it comes to denunciation and demagoguery, there is one who stands out by himself alone. [Huey] has many imitators but no equals." Any meeting between the two men usually turned ugly.

Ugly indeed was the scene on Tuesday, November 15, 1927, when Huey and Sanders clashed in the Hotel Roosevelt lobby. Huey had just arrived in New Orleans for a week of campaigning and headed to his headquarters on the hotel's twelfth floor. Unexpectedly he ran into J.Y., who was just leaving the dining room. When he spotted Huey, Sanders yelled across the marble-columned lobby that he was a "damned liar." Huey jumped on the ex-governor, punched him, and turned and ran to the elevator at the other end of the hotel. Sanders, portly and puffing and bent over with age, chased Huey to the elevator and squeezed in before the doors shut. The two men wrestled on the floor as the boy operating the elevator watched in stunned silence. Bystanders broke up the scuffle. Neither man was injured and both claimed victory. J.Y. declared that Huey crouched in the elevator like a "terror-stricken kitten" and Huey's opponents branded him as a coward who fled from the sixty-year-old ex-governor. Later that afternoon Huey strutted through the lobby viciously chewing on a six-inch cigar and flaunting a part of J.Y.'s shirt cuff ripped off in the elevator. That evening, he still waved J.Y.'s torn cuff and bragged of his elevator triumph as he spoke to a huge crowd in Palmer Park on Carrollton Avenue.

ON A THURSDAY EVENING in early November 1927, Huey stood under a gnarled live oak next to the winding waters of Bayou Teche in the quaint, tree-shaded town of St. Martinville. Campaigning in the heart of Acadiana, he gave the most forceful and polished speech of his campaign. He reminded his audience of folklore close to the hearts of all Cajuns. "And it is here under this oak where Evangeline waited for her lover Gabriel, who never came," he began. "This oak is an immortal spot, made so by Longfellow's poem, but Evangeline is not the only one who has waited here in disappointment. . . .

"Where are the schools that you have waited for your children to have, that have never come?" Huey asked. "Where are the roads and the highways that you send your money to build, that are no nearer now than ever before? Where are the institutions to care for the sick and the disabled? Evangeline wept bitter tears in her disappointment, but it lasted through only one lifetime. Your tears in this country, around this oak, have lasted for generations. Give me the chance to dry the eyes of those who still weep here."

Huey campaigned tirelessly as election day approached. On a chilly December 13, he delivered nine speeches in the small lumber towns of Webster Parish. He kept attacking with biting humor. When he read that Riley Joe claimed to have gone barefoot as a child, Huey fired back. "I can go Mr. Wilson one better. I was *born* barefoot."

HUEY ENDED HIS CAMPAIGN on Saturday night, January 14, 1928, with a packed rally at the Lafayette Theater in New Orleans. He estimated that he had delivered six hundred speeches, traveled fifteen thousand miles, and addressed 300,000 people during the campaign. From New Orleans he took the train north to await the election results at his family home in Shreveport. Tuesday morning, January 17, dawned bright and clear, with no hint of rain. As the election returns began to pour in later that evening, the first results from New Orleans revealed Huey did poorly in the Crescent City. The Wilson camp and the Old Regulars, bolstered by a *New Orleans Item* prediction of their victory, were confident that Huey would again finish a poor third and receive fewer votes than in 1924. Indeed, the New Orleans tally was Wilson, 38,244 votes, Simpson in second with 22,324, and Huey a distant third with 17,819. The country vote began to come in late that night and into the next morning and showed a heavy turnout in the rural parishes. The north country tallies showed Huey with a large majority but the Wilson supporters remained unshaken, as they had expected the northern parishes to support Huey just as they had in 1924.

The votes from Acadiana, however, shocked Huey's opponents. Huey swept the French parishes as handily as he swept the north country and with more than enough votes to pass Wilson. Overall, Huey carried forty-seven of the state's sixty-four parishes and six of the eight congressional districts. In some French parishes he racked up surprising majorities of 60 to 70 percent. When the statewide votes were tallied, Huey polled 126,842 votes to Wilson's 81,747 and Simpson's 80,326. For the first time, a Protestant politician successfully invaded predominantly Catholic south Louisiana. Huey's support came not from the truly poor, as sometimes believed, but small independent farmers and merchants. The poll tax prohibited many of the state's poor from voting, and sharecroppers, who were controlled by the planters, were not yet a voting force.

Huey performed weakly in the cities, failing to win his hometown Shreveport and the state capital of Baton Rouge. He was furious that Sullivan and Ewing delivered few New Orleans votes. Harvey Ellis, his former campaign manager who resigned over the Long-Ewing-Sullivan pact, wrote Huey to rub it in. "What did I tell you?" chided Ellis.

Because no candidate received a majority of the votes, state law required a second Democratic primary between the top two finishers, Huey and Riley Joe. The Choctaws and many other observers assumed that Simpson and his supporters now would back Wilson, giving Riley Joe more than enough votes to win. Huey, knowing he needed Simpson's votes, took the first train south from Shreveport with his wife, Rose. He arrived in New Orleans on Thursday morning and immediately began to bargain with Simpson's supporters. Simpson could not be located and was rumored to be on a prolonged drunk. Wilson's campaign began to collapse on Saturday when the *Times-Picayune,* which backed Simpson, refused to endorse Wilson and became the first major paper to call for Riley Joe to withdraw from the race. At the same time, Paul Maloney, an ambitious New Regular who ran Simpson's New Orleans campaign, sensed that the political winds had shifted in Huey's direction and abandoned Wilson. The year before, Huey backed Maloney's unsuccessful bid for New Orleans mayor and now his support paid off. With these defections and other backroom deals, Simpson shifted his support to Huey. Simpson later accepted a $5,000-per-year state attorneyship from Huey and became secretary of the Long-controlled state Senate. On Sunday evening, Riley Joe met with his supporters in New Orleans and decided not to run a second primary. He conceded later that night.

With Wilson's surrender, Huey Long stood as the only remaining Democratic candidate and, facing no realistic Republican opposition in the one-party state, was now the next governor of Louisiana. As word of Huey's victory spread across the city, hundreds of his supporters began filling the lobby of the Roosevelt Hotel. As the night wore on, the crowd became noisier and drunker, slapping each other on the back and hollering in triumph. In their midst was Huey, with his tousled hair falling down upon his red face and bloodshot eyes and his sweat-soaked shirt pulled open at the neck. He shouldered his way through the crowd, pumping the hands of his followers, and in his tired, hoarse voice kept repeating to each of them, "We'll show 'em who's boss. You fellows stick by me. . . . We're just getting started."

CHAPTER 3

1928
SCHOOLBOOKS, SCANDALS, AND SKULDUGGERY

Huey Long disliked the citizens of Baton Rouge as much as they disliked him. He ridiculed the inhabitants of the state capital as little more than a bunch of bridge clubbers, stuffed-shirted Episcopalians, and pie-eating bureaucrats. After Baton Rougeans refused to vote for him at the polls, he threatened to make "the grass grow in Third Street," the city's main thoroughfare. And so, during his inauguration on a steamy May 21, 1928, Huey chuckled when he turned the straitlaced capital city into his own hillbilly country fair. Fifteen thousand of Huey's faithful poured into Baton Rouge in four separate trains, a stream of cars, several buckboard wagons pulled by haggard mules, and a few lone souls plodding into the city on foot.

Most of the crowd arrived in the long line of dusty cars and trucks, their once black paint bleached an ashen gray by the scorching Louisiana sun. The old flivvers carried hard-boned dirt farmers who wore red galluses over their best Sunday shirts and black felt hats to shield them from the sun. They brought their wives, in threadbare calico dresses and straw sunbonnets, and wide-eyed children overwhelmed by the drumbeats of marching bands and the sweet-numbing taste of ice cream bought from hawkers on the street corners. They strolled by the neat cottages of the city's residents, who peeked through their shutters in horror, and through the downtown past the J. C. Penney Company, where tropical suits "carefully tailored of Palm Beach cloth" were on sale for $13.75.

The toilworn country people who descended upon Louisiana's state capital brought hopes that the new young governor who was to be sworn in on that scalding day would make a difference in their lives. Huey Long promised to lift their state out of its medieval conditions and end the poverty, corruption, and despair that had ruled Louisiana for generations, and the country people poured into Baton Rouge to see him begin his crusade.

Waving his arms wildly at the crowds from the window of a seven-passenger Lincoln, Huey paraded victoriously through the streets of the capital. "It seemed as if over half of his body was through the window of the car," remembered one spectator. Led by mounted city police, a brass band, and a troop of Boy Scouts, his inauguration parade left from the old LSU campus, circled east on North Boulevard under arches of live oaks, past the governor's mansion, and then to the Gothic-looking state capitol. Dressed in a gray three-piece suit, Huey stepped onto the inaugural stand located on the north side of the capitol, now draped in red, white, and blue bunting. Just after noon, he placed his right hand on the Bible and Chief Justice Charles O'Neill administered the oath of office. After a seventeen-gun salute, Huey pulled three typewritten pages from his breast pocket and began reading his short speech. He said little of the coming days of his administration, but promised a better, more prosperous life for the people of Louisiana. He also promised to stamp out the incompetence and corruption that had riddled state government for years. "Our face is to the rising, not the setting, sun," he began. "I will eliminate all means and avenues of waste, extravagance, and plunder . . . and without ambition for ever again holding another public office."

A carnival spirit swept over Baton Rouge as Huey's supporters celebrated his inauguration. To cool off the spectators sweltering in the blazing sun, he ordered buckets of water with tin dippers placed on the grounds around the capitol, where he erected a dance pavilion for country music and jazz bands. At two that afternoon, the New Regular Democratic Organization Band treated the crowd to a concert, and at five the Standard Oil Refinery Band performed at Victory Park. That evening at eight-thirty, ten thousand people attended a reception for Huey and Rose at the old LSU campus pavilion, decorated in a canopy of Spanish moss. Clear weather prevailed throughout the day, but by seven that evening it began to rain. At nine, a fierce thunderstorm swept through Baton Rouge, soaking the decorations. Thirty minutes later, the rains stopped and the inaugural ball began in a large open pavilion, where Robards Serenaders of Ponchatoula and Sou Generes of Baton Rouge entertained the revelers.

Baton Rouge survived the unusually boisterous inauguration. Traffic clogged the city streets but police reported no serious crimes. The worst incident of the day occurred when a galloping horse crashed into a parked car on Third Street near the old LSU campus. The horse was killed and its rider, Mrs. S. J. Hunt of the Hollywood section of town, suffered a broken wrist and ankle.

The local paper, the *Baton Rouge Advocate,* gave the inauguration wide coverage. The *Advocate,* one of the few Louisiana dailies that tried to avoid partisan politics, ran a heartwarming picture of Huey, Rose, and their three children sitting on a porch swing at their Shreveport home. The oldest child, named Rose after her mother, was eleven and son Russell was ten. When Russell was born, his mother originally named him Huey P. Long III, but his father arrived shortly after his birth and changed his name to Russell. "I hated being Little Huey all my life," he told Rose. "It's better for the boy to have his own name so if things go bad for me, he can have his own name to make it on." The third child, a son named Palmer, was seven.

On the page opposite the Long family photograph, the *Advocate* also displayed a huge picture of Huey's secretary, twenty-two-year-old Alice Lee Grosjean, who was "pretty and popular" and staying at the Heidelberg Hotel. Alice Lee first appeared in Huey's public life in 1923. As he campaigned across the state during his unsuccessful run for governor, he was accompanied by his attractive auburn-haired and hazel-eyed private secretary. Alice quit school at fifteen to marry James Terrell, but the couple soon separated and divorced in 1928. Bright and discreet, Alice Lee became one of Huey's few trusted workers and the custodian of his campaign funds. Gossip spread about Baton Rouge that Alice Lee was more than a secretary. Some witnesses close to Huey claimed that Alice Lee was his mistress, while others maintained he kept her near him only because she was efficient and completely trustworthy. For years to come, Huey's closeness to his pretty secretary kept rumors flying.

IMMEDIATELY AFTER HIS ELECTION, Huey Long sent a forceful message that he was going to be not only governor of Louisiana but also its undisputed political boss. On February 16, 1928, three months before he took the oath as governor, state Democratic Party leaders met in New Orleans to plan a convention to select delegates for the presidential convention to be held the following summer in Houston. For years, the traditional method for selecting delegates had been by a statewide convention, but Huey decided otherwise. He discovered no requirement for a convention and learned that the party's central committee could select the delegates. Two days after the state Democratic leaders met, Huey called a quorum of the party's committee that he stacked with his own supporters. He chaired the meeting and ordered his own slate of delegates approved, naming Colonel Ewing as national committeeman and himself as a delegate-at-large. Huey's committee selected no Old Regulars or any of his enemies as delegates.

The Old Regulars and Delta planters were furious but powerless. Former governors J. Y. Sanders and Ruffin Pleasant, left off Long's slate, attacked Huey. Pleasant threatened to beat up the "cowardly" Huey and called him a "red-mouthed, white-livered, yellow-backboned enemy of our country." Harry Gamble, who served as Parker's campaign manager during that governor's election, led the fight for the old Democrats. Gamble, an anti-Long attorney from Natchitoches recently elected to the legislature, accused Huey of being another Mussolini. Soon after the inauguration, Huey removed Gamble from his position as state inheritance tax attorney and gave the job to his brother Earl.

Undeterred by Gamble's attacks, Huey fired back a statement from Shreveport on February 24 that made no excuse for his tactics. "They say that they were steam rolled," he wrote. "The only reason that the roller didn't pass over more of them was because there were no more in the way. I had promised my people that I would put this gang of bosses and plunder-bund pie eaters out of control of the Democratic Party just as quick as I could. We hesitated very little about it."

Sanders, Pleasant, and the old Democratic leaders drew up their own slate and in June both delegations took the train to the convention. In Houston, Huey ordered his delegates to pledge their allegiance to New York governor Al Smith, who also controlled the credentials committee. After the two rival Louisiana delegations argued to be seated, the committee members ruled that Huey's delegation was the official state representative and sent the Sanders group home.

Huey campaigned for Smith during the last days of the 1928 presidential campaign in order to ensure future federal patronage from the Democratic Party. In a speech in Alexandria in October, Huey denounced bigots who would vote against Smith because he was a Catholic, but said that Herbert Hoover was unfit because he was a Quaker. Huey also accused Hoover of favoring "Negro domination," adding, "We believe this is a white man's country and are not willing to turn it over to the Negroes." While Hoover won the presidency, Louisiana gave Smith his largest statewide majority.

HUEY KNEW HE MUST also strike fast to take control of the Louisiana legislature. A week before his inauguration, legislators arrived in Baton Rouge for their regular session. Huey was a step ahead and already hard at work when they arrived. He worked feverishly behind the scenes, pressuring party bosses and making deals to have his own supporters placed in committee leadership positions. Only eighteen of one hundred representatives and nine of thirty-nine senators had been elected as Long supporters, while a similar number opposed him. Huey concentrated on winning the remaining uncommitted members and promised them jobs, patronage, and other boodle. He showed a genius for persuasion and deal making and, according to a supporter, "knew how to trade a cat for a cow, the cow for an elephant, and the elephant for a farm."

For speaker of the house, Huey chose a newly elected legislator, John Fournet. Tall, strong, with a round face and thinning hair parted in the middle, Fournet was from Jennings in Evangeline Parish. A bright, witty Cajun, Fournet flashed a ring with an extraordinarily large diamond. Despite the legislator's lack of experience, the House members elected Fournet as Speaker, 72–27. For president pro tempore of the Senate, Huey chose another Frenchman, Phillip Gilbert. A paunchy little aristocrat from Napoleonville in Assumption Parish, Gilbert won easily, 27–10. As his floor leader in the Senate, Huey selected his boyhood friend O. K. Allen, who had just been elected to the legislature. Soon after, Huey appointed Allen as chairman of the Highway Commission and later picked his New Orleans benefactor Robert Maestri as head of the Department of Conservation.

In the past, the legislature picked its own committee chairmen and members, but Huey rewrote the rules. He called in Fournet and Gilbert and personally dictated the name of every member of every committee. Huey had them appoint Harley Bozeman, a boyhood pal and new legislator, as chairman of the important House Appropriations Committee. He ordered Old Regular legislators banished from powerful committee chairmanships and assigned them to meaningless committees where they could do him no harm. Loyal Longites took their place. He particularly angered the New Orleans delegation when he selected only two Old Regulars to sit on the New Orleans City Affairs Committee, while stacking it with thirteen trusted representatives from rural parishes.

WHILE STUFFY BATON ROUGE never endeared itself to Huey Long, New Orleans intoxicated him. Like Huey, New Orleans seldom slept. During the Roaring Twenties, the city that butted up against a wide crescent-shaped bend in the Mississippi River was America's bawdiest. While other cities tried to hide their share of illegal liquor, gambling, and prostitution behind the closed doors of speakeasies and after-hours clubs, New Orleans made no attempt to cloister its rampant vices. New Orleaneans treated Prohibition as just another minor annoyance, like their pesky mosquitoes, and a stiff drink could be bought almost anytime and anyplace on aptly named Bourbon Street in the Vieux Carré. In the cafés scattered across the town, illegal booze flowed as freely as the strong French coffee the natives preferred. Federal prohibition agents labeled New Orleans the "worst wet spot in the country," a city where newsboys sold three marijuana cigarettes for a dime. Gambling was widespread and open across the area. Dozens of gambling clubs operated in neighboring St. Bernard and Jefferson Parishes, while across the street from New Orleans's swank Roosevelt Hotel sat the 1-2-3 Club, where roulette wheels spun at all hours of the night. Although the infamous Storyville red-light district had been closed for over a decade, prostitution flourished across most parts of the city. As former mayor Martin Behrman remarked on prostitution's wide appeal, "you can make it illegal but you can't make it unpopular."

Deeply etched by racial and economic anguish, New Orleans was a city of extremes and contradictions. Great wealth resided next to woeful poverty and the highest society prospered amid the lowliest of vices. The city of a half-million residents embodied a sultry mix of different races, religions, languages, and cultures, and with its exotic Creole cuisine and steamy climate, oozed a sinuous mystique. Jazz music poured from honky-tonks and black music clubs like the Dog House on Rampart Street and Prima's Shim Sham Club in the heart of the French Quarter. The pulsing main artery of New Orleans was Canal Street. The noisy thoroughfare, whose wide middle ground was paved in red-and-white terrazzo marble, teemed with rattling streetcars, vegetable vendors, horse-drawn supply wagons, and newsboys singing out the headlines from the city's four daily papers. The romance of the "city that care forgot" lured novelists like William Faulkner and Sherwood Anderson and inspired great works like Oliver La Farge's Pulitzer Prize–winning *Laughing Boy* and Tennessee Williams's masterpiece *A Streetcar Named Desire*.

Each year, the New Orleans social scene swirled around Mardi Gras and its week of revelry, drinking, and parades of masked merrymakers. The Mardi Gras celebration of 1928 began on Thursday, February 15, with the great parade of King Momus, "God of Mirth and Dispeller of Doom." Perched atop his ornate float, Momus rode down Canal Street past the palacelike Saenger Theater, the posh Pickwick Club, Marullo's Physical Culture Gym for Ladies, and the American Drug Store, where huge double-dipped ice cream cones cost a nickel. The highlights of Mardi Gras were the exclusive balls where partygoers spared no expense on grand orchestras, ornate costumes, and sumptuous cuisine. Since the Civil War, the trendier Krewes hosting the balls always invited the governor of Louisiana as an honored guest. In 1928, however, Huey Long received no invitations.

The New Orleans uptown elite did host a banquet for the newly elected governor. The purpose of the dinner was to heal the wounds of the bitter campaign and to repair the serious rift that still existed between

Huey and the city's political leaders. Most of the attendees were bankers and businessmen who knew it was good business to deal with the new governor, even if they disliked him personally and disagreed with his politics. The political bosses of New Orleans, however, made no attempt to disguise their hostility toward Huey. The huge, white-haired, and spectacled mayor of New Orleans, Arthur O'Keefe, refused to attend the dinner, and all of his Old Regular lieutenants boycotted the event.

Gathering in the Tip Top Inn of the Roosevelt Hotel, over eight hundred of the city's aristocracy paid $5 each to be seen with the young man whose election they had fought vigorously just a month before. The new lieutenant governor, Paul Cyr, could not attend because an automobile had run over his twelve-year-old son and broken his leg. An unexpected guest was K. W. Dawson of Oklahoma City, who years before hired a penniless salesman named Huey Long to sell groceries. Dawson entertained his listeners by describing how Huey, during the worst of winter, walked eighteen miles from Oklahoma City to Norman.

Colonel Robert Ewing, confident that he would be able to exert a strong influence upon the new governor, presided over the testimonial. Near the end of the dinner, Huey took the rostrum looking uncomfortable and out of place in a tuxedo, high collar, and black bow tie. Huey spoke much more reservedly than he had on the campaign trail and refrained from attacking his opponents. In measured tones he promised his audience that he would create a state of utopia. "Unemployment in Louisiana will be virtually eradicated," he predicted. "Commerce will revive. Peace and prosperity will be here." He pledged to improve education, attack illiteracy, take better care of the unfortunate, and reform labor laws. He promised to provide New Orleans with state aid for roads and bridges, improve the port facilities, and bring natural gas to the city. Reserved and noncommittal, Huey renounced "all ambitions to sit in the national legislative halls at Washington . . . the governorship is the limit of my political ambition." He assured the New Orleans audience that "I have no ambition to build up any powerful faction in Louisiana politics" and pledged to "go into the governor's office as your servant."

When the dinner ended, the hosts presented Huey and his wife, Rose, who did not attend the all-male affair, with a chest full of expensive silver dinnerware. Robert Maestri, the New Orleans businessman who helped fund Huey's campaign, made a large donation for the dinnerware, but the uptown bankers and businessmen refused the check from the wealthy but socially unacceptable Italian. Instead, Maestri bought a $2,500 emerald and diamond stickpin for Huey, who took great pride thereafter in flashing the gaudy jewelry and bragging about its cost.

SELDOM SITTING IN THE HUGE leather chair behind his desk, Huey Long bounced back and forth under the whirling electric fan hung from the tall ceiling of his office. It was only nine in the morning but the sweltering Louisiana heat already began to wilt the starched seersucker suits of the men hustling in and out of the governor's office. As Huey dashed about and roared orders to assistants, beads of sweat dripped from his brow and a curly reddish forelock drooped defiantly just above his right eye.

It was Tuesday, May 22, 1928, the morning after the inauguration and Huey's first day at work as Louisiana's new governor and, like so many others to follow, a busy one. His first order of business was to "kick the rascals out" and take firm control of the state government bureaucracy. He assaulted the state's powerful boards and commissions, dismantling agencies over which he had immediate authority, firing old appointees, and selecting his own men for the jobs. With thousands of workers, the Highway Commission, the State Board of Health, the Hospital Board, and the Orleans Parish Levee Board were prime targets of Huey's political housecleaning. Before the day ended, he fired seventy-three New Orleans Dock Board employees and cashiered eighty out of one hundred Highway Commission speed cops, replacing them with his own men. Over the next few weeks, he removed from office every major and minor employee whose job he controlled, and by the time he finished, he commanded thousands of workers across the state and began amassing a powerful arsenal of spoils patronage and political support.

Huey ruthlessly took over the state boards and commissions. He required new appointees to sign undated letters of resignation. If the appointee ran astray, he merely filled in the date and accepted the resignation. He also settled old political grudges. He detested the president of the Board of Health, Dr. Oscar Dowling, who had served under five previous governors. Dowling's term of office did not expire until 1932 but

Huey was determined to remove him. He forced the legislature to pass a bill cutting Dowling's term short and, a week later, fired Dowling and appointed his own replacement. Huey dealt similarly with the powerful New Orleans Levee Board. To take control of the board, which maintained the dikes protecting the city from the Mississippi and had one of the largest employment rolls in the state, he pressured the legislature to dissolve the old board and create a new five-member body. Four of the new appointees were Long supporters and the vast Levee Board patronage fell into Huey's grasp. That summer, Huey grabbed control of the New Orleans Dock Board, another patronage stockpile, and fired another enemy in his "son-of-a-bitch book," Marcel Garsaud, general manager of the city's port authority.

Huey's crude methods shocked his opponents. Used to passive governors who seldom interfered with legislative prerogatives, his foes quickly realized that he ignored or rewrote the rules to force the legislature to carry out his political agenda. "I'd rather violate every one of the damned conventions and see my bills passed," he admitted, "than sit back in my office, all nice and proper, and watch 'em die." His relentless energy also astounded his opponents. With no hesitation, he dashed unexpectedly out of his office and up the sweeping spiral staircase to the capitol's second floor. He burst into the legislative chambers and brazenly accosted senators and representatives at their desks, ordering them to vote for his pet bills or against those of his opponents. Abandoning protocol and any separation of powers, he stomped through committee rooms and scattered committees with a nod of his head or the crooking of a finger. He entered the Senate and House, organized his own system of runners on the floor, and bullied the legislators with frowns, stinging jokes, and foul-mouthed threats. Many of the legislators loudly protested Huey's meddling but he ignored them. After he barged unannounced into a committee hearing one night, one irritated senator threw a copy of the Louisiana constitution at Huey's head. "Maybe you've heard of this book," shouted the senator. The governor picked it up, looked at the title, flipped it aside and shot back, "I'm the constitution just now."

Soon after the legislature arrived, Huey introduced several bills aimed to carry out his agenda and increase his control. Although he did not hold a majority of the legislators, he managed to get his legislation passed through a loose alliance of lawmakers from the rural north and Acadiana. He soon became impatient with the legislature when a backlog of routine legislation delayed his bills from being brought to a vote. To speed up the legislative process, he ordered his floor leaders to no longer fight his opponents' legislation but instead move every bill through the committees, limit floor debate to a minimum, and allow all legislation to pass as quickly as possible. To his delight, the legislature cleared the backlog in four hours. Later, when the huge pile of legislation reached the governor's desk for approval, Huey carefully sorted through each of the bills, signed his own legislation into law, and vetoed the objectionable bills by the score. Many of the bills he vetoed were pork barrel measures such as the construction of a road or a new schoolhouse in a particular legislator's district. In the past a governor routinely signed these bills, as they were a legislator's political lifeblood back in his home parish. Huey, however, signed only the bills proposed by his supporters and vetoed those of his shocked opponents.

One of the bills that Huey proposed and signed was Act 99 creating the Bureau of Criminal Identification. The BCI was independent of all sheriffs, police, and constables and possessed the unprecedented power "to make arrests anywhere in the State of Louisiana, without warrants, for all violations of the law." Huey personally framed the act, which called for the governor to chair the BCI's board of managers and select its members. Secretive and powerful, the BCI provided Huey with a hefty political weapon and signaled an ominous first step toward creation of a police state.

TO HUEY LONG, the ramshackle old governor's mansion typified everything that was wrong and backward in Louisiana. With paint peeling from its sides, the rambling old wooden frame house with square white pillars supporting broad galleries had been built by slaves before 1860. It once served as a public hospital and later as a boardinghouse. The mansion was "full of damn rats," Huey told one newspaperman; he complained to another that the creaking floors kept him awake at night. The roof leaked badly, the interior was damaged, and the walls were weakened and out of plumb. Laborers making repairs discovered that the house was infested with termites. Six months after his inauguration, Huey summoned a Baton Rouge building inspector to the property who concluded that "the structure is in a generally dilapidated condition and would need to be completely reconditioned."

Huey refused to move into the mansion and lived up the street in the Heidelberg Hotel, while Rose and the children stayed at their family home in Shreveport. Huey asked his treasurer, H. B. Conner, for funds to build a new mansion on the present site, but Conner told the governor he could provide the funds only after the legislature approved the expenditure. Huey ignored Conner's ruling and asked the state Board of Liquidation, the agency authorized to borrow money and incur debt, to grant a $150,000 loan to construct a new mansion. The board approved the loan but, agreeing with Conner, said that Huey first needed the legislature's approval. The loan approval from the board was all that Huey felt he needed. He phoned the warden of the state penitentiary at Angola and told him to send a gang of convicts to Baton Rouge. When the prisoners arrived, Huey led them from the capitol to the mansion and cheered them on as they demolished the old building.

Afterward, someone criticized Huey for tearing down the old mansion, saying the house had been good enough for former governors. "I can see where the criticism is sound," Huey replied. "It reminds me of the old man who keeps a boarding house. When one guest complains that the towel is dirty, he says, 'People have been wiping on that towel for a month without complaining. I don't see what's the matter with you.' "

The antique furniture, fine china, and expensive silverware that were in the old mansion disappeared, although the sergeant-at-arms of the House later testified that the silver was engraved with the name "Huey P. Long" and shipped to Shreveport.

THE LOUISIANA RAILROAD COMMISSION regulated intrastate railroads, pipelines, and public utilities and was one of the most powerful bodies in the state. To Huey Long, the commission was the perfect place for him to run for his first public office and launch his political career. In 1918, ten years before he became governor, twenty-five-year-old Huey entered the race for railroad commissioner representing the twenty-eight parishes of north Louisiana. In the first primary against four other candidates, he finished second behind the popular incumbent, Burk Bridges. Huey was confident that he could upset Bridges. "I can beat that old man," he boasted. Stumping tirelessly across the north country, he surprised Bridges in the second primary and won by 636 votes. Huey carried only four of the parishes in the runoff but amassed huge majorities in the rural areas.

Before Huey became a member, the Railroad Commission had been a stagnant three-member body that was slave to the state's wealthy interests. As soon as he took office, Huey rebelled against the wealthy businessmen who had controlled the commission's decisions and demanded that freight rates be lowered to help the small farmers. After he became commission chairman in 1922, he injected new energy and independence into the agency, later renamed the Public Service Commission. During his ten-year tenure, he worked to increase the commission's—and his own—power. He crusaded for lower utility rates, forced the railroads to extend their service to small villages and hamlets, and demanded that the Standard Oil Company end the importation of Mexican crude oil and use more oil from Louisiana wells.

Once he became governor, Huey turned against the commission. He stripped much of its authority in order to attack two of its members who were his bitter political opponents. One of them, Francis Williams, a big, red-haired New Orleans politician, had been elected to the commission in 1922. Francis was a charismatic and eloquent speaker and, like Huey, hated the New Orleans Ring. Francis and his loosely knit New Orleans political organization, the Independent Regulars, backed Huey in his unsuccessful 1924 race for governor. However, Francis's Independents garnered few New Orleans votes and Huey never forgave him for the weak political support. Soon after taking office, Francis joined forces with Huey to outvote the third member and elect Huey chairman of the commission. For two years the two men cooperated in fighting for lower utility rates across the state.

Their friendship soured after 1924 when Huey refused to support Francis in the race for New Orleans mayor and instead backed another maverick politician, car dealer Paul Maloney. Francis and Huey openly broke in December 1926 when a new public service commissioner, Dudley LeBlanc, took office. A feisty little Cajun with round spectacles, Dudley once sold Battleax Shoes at the same time Huey sold Cottolene, and the two drummers often crossed paths. From the first, Huey hated Dudley. During the Public Service Commission meeting at the end of 1926, Francis and Dudley joined together and voted Huey from his chairmanship, replacing him with Francis. From then on, Huey rarely attended commission meetings.

Now governor in June 1928, Huey punished Dudley and Francis by vetoing all of the commission's funding. He saw no contradiction in crushing the same agency in which he launched his own political career. He also admitted that he enjoyed retaliating against his enemies and firing people not decidedly on his side. "No music ever sounded one-half so refreshing," he admitted, "as the whines and moans of pie-eaters when shoved away from the pie."

Other political opponents suffered Huey's wrath during his first months in office. One of them, District Judge H. C. Drew, had been elected to the state Court of Appeal. Drew decided to resign his district judgeship three months early so that the post would be vacant for more than a year, thereby requiring an election to fill the vacancy. Huey wanted to appoint his own replacement and simply refused to accept Drew's resignation. Once the vacancy had less than a year left, Huey ordered the state Supreme Court, then stacked with loyal Long supporters, to select another Longite, Judge J. F. McInnis. Refusing a resignation had never been done before, but Huey used a simple administrative act to have his own man appointed.

Despite his relentless drive, Huey lost some of his early political battles. At first, he failed to convince the legislature to remove Dr. Valentine Irion as chairman of the "coon chasin'" Conservation Commission. The legislature rejected Huey's attempt to pack the powerful state Court of Appeal with his own appointees by increasing the number of judges from nine members to fifteen. The legislature also rebuffed his attempt to gain control of the Orleans Parish Courthouse Commission and the governing board of the state-run Charity Hospital in New Orleans.

Late that summer, an undaunted Huey replaced four members of the Charity Hospital board and gained a majority of the votes. At the next meeting of the board, held in his tenth-floor corner suite in the Roosevelt Hotel, he ordered the new board to fire the superintendent, Dr. William Leake, who had run the hospital since 1921. The previous board unanimously reelected Leake in March 1928, but the doctor's father was Hunter Leake, an anti-Long attorney for Standard Oil. For that reason alone, Huey found Dr. Leake unacceptable. Huey replaced Leake with Dr. Arthur Vidrine, a bright but inexperienced young surgeon from Ville Platte. A huge 230-pound man with a puffy face and grayish hair, Vidrine was a Rhodes Scholar and World War I veteran who completed his internship only four years before.

In little time, Huey used his political skulduggery to go through the list of government employees, replacing dozens of officeholders of questionable loyalty with his own supporters. None of his enemies were too weak and no political job too unimportant to receive attention. A drawbridge tender in Plaquemines Parish lost his job when the governor, passing through the area, discovered the man was a friend of a wealthy state senator who opposed the Long organization. That first winter, Huey forced Dr. V. L. Roy to resign as president of the State Normal School in Natchitoches. Roy, who had served as president of the college for eighteen years, claimed Huey fired him for refusing to campaign for a judge running for the state Supreme Court and to support a referendum on constitutional amendments. "On election day the Governor called me on the telephone," Roy explained, "and told me that one of the ballot boxes near the State Normal School 'wasn't going right' . . . to go out and get busy. I was incensed. I never heard such a request being made of a college president."

Nor was Huey averse to nepotism. He appointed his brother Earl as inheritance tax collector earning $15,000 a year. During his campaign, Huey promised to abolish the tax collector position and use the money to build a hospital for tuberculosis patients near Lake Pontchartrain. After his brother's appointment, a New Orleans newspaper published Earl's photograph, with the ridiculous caption, "New Lakefront TB Hospital." Within months of taking office, Huey placed at least twenty-three of his relatives on the state payroll, including Earl as tax collector, a sister on the faculty of a state college, two brothers-in-law in good jobs in his new Bureau of Criminal Identification and Shreveport's charity hospital, plus other state jobs for an uncle and eighteen cousins. He appointed his cousin T. W. Tison to replace Dr. Roy as college president in Natchitoches at a salary of $7,200 a year, close to the $7,500 Huey drew as governor.

Huey liked to joke about giving state jobs to his kin. "Look at old Jess [Jess Nugent, a distant relative and vice chairman of the Highway Commission]," Huey boasted to one of his staff. "He's the best employee in the whole state. He does his work better than anybody we got." Finally, somebody asked what Jess did. "Not a goddamn thing," Huey snapped back. When newspapers published the names of the relatives he hired, he laughed and confessed the list was incomplete, bragging that he would have placed more of his kinfolk on the payroll if some of them were not being housed and fed at the state penitentiary.

OF ALL OF HUEY'S campaign promises, none was more important than to provide free schoolbooks to the state's children and to stop "the fleecing of the barefooted Louisiana schoolboy." Seymour Weiss, the manager of the Roosevelt Hotel, remembered when Huey penciled his proposal for free schoolbooks on the cardboard backing from one of his starched shirts.

On Huey's first day of work as governor, Superintendent of Education T. H. Harris, whom Huey stayed with eighteen years before as a high school debater, paid a call on the new governor. Like Huey, Harris wanted to improve education in the state. The two men agreed to increase the funding for education, including providing free schoolbooks, by raising the severance tax on oil taken from Louisiana wells. The new severance tax would raise $2 million and allow them to abolish the unpopular tobacco tax, which previously provided $1.5 million for education. Huey summoned one of Louisiana's sharpest lawyers, George Wallace, to draft the severance tax legislation calling for a graduated levy of between 4 and 11 cents per barrel of crude. Wallace, who shared Huey's talent for devising clever legislative maneuvers, was from Winn Parish and had known Huey since childhood. His father, J. T. Wallace of Winnfield, defeated Huey's father for the state Senate in 1900. Wallace, who was often incapacitated by liquor, drafted many of Huey's bills and became one of his trusted inner circle.

On Friday, May 25, 1928, Representative J. E. McClanahan proposed the new severance tax before the legislature. A new member of the House from Caldwell Parish, McClanahan served as the anti-Long sheriff of his parish only a few months before. Sensing Huey's growing power,

McClanahan switched allegiance and would serve as his loyal floor leader until Huey appointed him warden of the state penitentiary. Legislators debated the severance bill into the summer, passing it in early July. A month later Standard Oil filed suit claiming the severance tax was unconstitutional, and as schools opened in the fall, the lawsuit held up the money for the free schoolbooks. Huey was furious.

Until the courts settled Standard Oil's suit, Huey could not use the new severance tax to fund the schoolbooks. He convened the Board of Liquidation and obtained an authorization for $500,000 to buy the books, with the loan to be repaid when the courts resolved the lawsuit. Huey took the authorization to a New Orleans bank to get the loan, but the bank declared that such a loan was illegal because there was no guarantee the court would rule against Standard Oil. Unfazed, he reminded the bankers that the Board of Liquidation already owed their bank $935,000, which the legislature previously ordered paid. "It ain't going to be paid," he threatened. "Your attorneys ruled those loans illegal, and if it's illegal to make them, it's illegal to pay them. We'll keep the $935,000 and buy the books and have $435,000 to spare." Huey stormed out of the bank, marched down the street to the Roosevelt Hotel, and ordered a sandwich in the restaurant. As he sat alone at his table and waited, a banker rushed in to tell him he could have the loan immediately. "Take back the sandwich," he ordered. "Fry me a steak."

"IT'S THE GREATEST CESSPOOL of hell that has ever been known to the modern world," Huey Long bellowed as he described the vice-ridden region around New Orleans. The area that stretched south from the city's border into Jefferson and St. Bernard Parishes served as the mecca for Louisiana's legion of bootleggers, smugglers, and gamblers and had been the scene of nefarious misdeeds for hundreds of years. At the southern tip of Jefferson Parish was Barataria Bay, where Jean Laffite and other pirates used the maze of bayous and waterways as a smugglers' paradise. Many of their descendants still did so. Since the 1880s, the Sicilian Mafia controlled much of the illegal gambling in St. Bernard and Jefferson, where lavish gambling houses such as Club Forest and O'Dwyer's operated openly and profitably.

In the summer of 1928, New Orleans civic leaders asked the new governor to crack down on gambling in the city and surrounding parishes. Huey, who as a youth challenged his luck at the roulette table and dice dens, did not have strong hostility toward gambling, but recognized the opportunity to gain political support from some of the more stalwart New Orleans citizens. He issued a statement directing officials in St. Bernard and Jefferson to halt gambling in their parishes and warned the city to enforce its own laws. "We are not going to stand for open lawlessness in the New Orleans area during the four years I am Governor."

On August 18, he ordered raids upon the Jai Alai and Arabi Clubs, both busy gambling halls on notorious Friscoville Avenue in St. Bernard Parish. Huey did not obtain search warrants, nor did he turn to local police and sheriffs who had jurisdiction over the area to carry out the raids. Instead, he used the Louisiana National Guard as his own personal police force. In the middle of the night, with rifles at the ready, Huey's guardsmen bashed in locked doors and marched into the casinos. They broke tables and chairs, ripped out roulette wheels and slot machines, and searched private citizens. Their first raid confiscated $25,000. Three months later, at one in the morning on November 12, he ordered his national guardsmen to raid Beverly Gardens, a gambling house in Jefferson Parish just across the border from New Orleans, and nearby Fagot's Grocery Store, where a gambling den operated on the second floor. The troopers seized $18,000 in cash and burned $3,000 worth of gambling equipment. "We found cases of dice, not a straight pair in the lot," Colonel E. P. Roy reported. "All those places were crooked." Huey's attacks delighted his supporters. Just after the raids, the *Baton Rouge Advocate* reported that his friends presented him with a luxurious new seven-passenger automobile, "sagebrush green in color."

Huey didn't let up. Just before Mardi Gras, on February 9, 1929, he ordered raids in Jefferson Parish. In the middle of the night his troopers marched into Rudy O'Dwyer's Original Southport Inn and seized five dice tables, three roulette wheels, and several thousand dollars in cash, while a hundred well-dressed patrons stood by with their hands in the air. On February 13, just after midnight, his troopers hit the Tranchina Night Club, six miles from New Orleans, and nearby Suburban Gardens across from the racetrack. Just before the raids, however, Huey attended a party given in the French Quarter studio of wealthy bachelor and hotelman Alfred Danzinger. Danzinger served plenty of illegal booze and entertained his guests with a hula dancer named Helen Clifford. Huey, who never held his liquor well, flirted with a woman and bragged about the upcoming raid. "Cabaret girl tipped off gambling raids," read the next morning newspapers, adding that the girl Huey flirted with had warned the gambling hall proprietors. When Huey's troopers arrived at the scene, no gambling was in sight.

Huey's attack on gambling and his heavy-handed use of the National Guard outraged many citizens. When anti-Long Attorney General Percy Saint learned of the raids, he declared the use of the National Guard illegal and marching into "the teeth of the law." Huey denounced the attorney general's ruling. "Nobody asked him," he snapped back. "I warn the gamblers now, right in the city of New Orleans and elsewhere that Attorney General Saint's opinion will do them no more good than it did the gamblers at Jai Alai and the Arabi Club in St. Bernard Parish and Beverly Garden and Fagot's Grocery in Jefferson Parish."

The gambling raids provided a political opportunity for Huey. Now elected, he no longer needed the support of John Sullivan and Robert Ewing. They had failed to deliver the New Orleans vote, yet now they demanded more patronage jobs for their cronies. Ewing irritated Huey, seeing himself as a sort of prime minister and assuming Huey would come to him for advice on major political decisions. The gambling raids provided the last straw to the breakup. The raids hurt Sullivan directly, as the gambler maintained close ties with the Jefferson Parish gambling bosses. In his *New Orleans States*, Ewing struck at Huey, decrying the gambling raids and calling Huey a "boon companion of indicted criminals, a chronic distorter of facts, a habitual double crosser, a traducer of character, a beneficiary of funds contributed by gamblers, a tyrant suffering from delusions of grandeur, and the singing fool of New Orleans cabarets." Huey had already decided that he needed to create his own separate New Orleans political organization, detached from Ewing, the Old Regulars, Sullivan's New Regulars, and Frances Williams's Independent Regulars. The break became obvious when Huey branded Ewing and Sullivan with derogatory labels. He called Ewing "Colonel Bow Wow" due to his schnauzerlike appearance and clipped barking voice and tagged Sullivan as "Bang Tail," a reference to the notorious gambler's frequent visits to the racetrack.

AT FIRST, HUEY'S free schoolbooks angered the state's Catholics because a Louisiana law forbade state funds from being spent on sectarian or private schools. They complained they were being discriminated against because only the public schools received the free books. Not wanting to antagonize Catholic voters, Huey ordered the legislature to pass a bill that called for the books to go directly to the children, not the schools. To him, providing the books to all children, regardless of religion, would be a secular act. The state superintendent of schools, T. H. Harris, opposed giving the free books to Catholic schoolchildren and told Huey his bill was unconstitutional. "I am a better lawyer than you are," Huey shot back at Harris, "and books for children attending private schools go in the act." The bill passed.

In the northwest corner of the state, Huey faced another problem with his free schoolbook plan. The more affluent people of his hometown of Shreveport, in Caddo Parish, never accepted him into their city's higher society, and most of its citizens fought his election as governor. Along with neighboring Bossier Parish, they fought the free schoolbook plan and obtained a restraining order from a Baton Rouge judge forbidding the distribution of the textbooks in their two parishes. "This is a rich section of the state," Shreveport mayor "Wet Jug" Thomas announced. "We are not going to be humiliated or disgraced by having it advertised that our children had to be given the books free."

In December 1928, Huey struck back at Caddo and Bossier during a six-day special session of the legislature. At the time, the U.S. Army was investigating possible locations for a new air base and Shreveport was among the fifty communities around the country being considered. The air base would become the home of the Third Attack Wing, with 200 officers, 1,500 enlisted men, and over 200 aircraft, and would add $5 million to the Shreveport economy. In order to compete for the base, Shreveport needed the governor's approval to give eighty acres of state land to the army for the airfield. A delegation from Shreveport, including Huey's friend W. K. Henderson and Robert Ewing's son John, expected the governor's immediate approval, but they underestimated his capacity to hold a grudge. Huey refused to sign the authorization for the air base until Shreveport accepted the textbooks. Desperate for the base, the leaders of Caddo and Bossier surrendered to the governor and agreed to take the free schoolbooks. "I didn't coerce them," Huey boasted later. "I stomped them into distributing the books." That following spring, after several pro-Long justices were elected to the Louisiana Supreme Court, the high court justices denied the complaints of Caddo and Bossier Parishes and voted 4–3 to uphold the free schoolbook law.

During the school year, Huey ordered over 600,000 new textbooks to be printed and distributed to Louisiana's schoolchildren. With many families previously unable to afford to pay for books, the free textbook plan increased school attendance by 15,000 pupils. That fall, as children returned to school from summer vacation, Huey received a letter scribbled in pencil from a child in Forest Hill. "Dear Governor Long," the letter read. "I surely appreciate the free text books. You are the only governor of Louisiana who has done what you said you would do. I am thirteen years old. I am in the eight [sic] grade. I expect to finish school. Sincerely yours, Helen Edwards."

"I HOPE THAT NATURAL GAS can be brought to New Orleans peacefully," Huey Long warned the political leaders of New Orleans, "but if the gentlemen who are banded to keep it from coming here want a rough-house, they want to remember that I can stand more rough-house than they ever saw." For several years before Huey's election, the Old Regulars and city bankers had allowed the New Orleans Public Service Incorporated, or NOPSI, to be the only provider of gas, electricity, and streetcar service in the city. NOPSI had conspired with the business and political leaders to allow only expensive artificial gas to be brought into New Orleans, even though cheap, efficient natural gas was available across Louisiana. The arrangement was profitable for all parties, except the city's consumers. While politicians had promised to bring natural gas to the city in the past, none had seriously attempted to confront NOPSI's monopoly.

During the testimonial dinner given in February 1928, Huey repeated his campaign promise to bring natural gas to New Orleans and, once in office, did not hesitate. "It is plain to me that New Orleans is being fought from within," he told a newspaperman. "Those who have been elected to protect and serve the people have failed in their duties for the past many years." The Old Regulars fought his natural gas proposal. Semmes Walmsley, the Choctaw commissioner of finance and soon to be mayor, condemned Huey's proposal. "It is impossible to hasten this development," Walmsley declared. "It must be taken in a sane, orderly, and scientific manner and we certainly do not propose to use any half-baked methods."

Huey's opponents underestimated the new governor's determination to get his way. He ordered his lieutenants to introduce a series of bills before the state Senate, including a constitutional amendment authorizing the New Orleans city government to spend up to $50 million to purchase NOPSI and bring natural gas to the city. Another bill permitted the city to operate the utilities. The Old Regular political bosses knew that if the bills were enacted, they would destroy their profitable monopoly. Huey did not favor a government takeover of the utility but his bills provided the threat he needed. When NOPSI and the Old Regulars refused to negotiate, he maneuvered his takeover bills quickly through the Senate committees and onto the floor, where they passed. He then delayed passage in the House while public sentiment built against NOPSI, and waited for his opponents to act. Before long, the Old Regulars and NOPSI realized they were beaten. Walmsley wired Huey that they were ready to negotiate. On July 7, less than two months after he proposed his takeover bills, the New Orleans City Council passed a motion that adopted the rate prescribed by Huey, and NOPSI agreed to bring natural gas to the city at a price lower than that of the artificial gas. Two days later, Huey ordered the House Judiciary Committee to kill his bills taking over the utility.

IT TOOK ONLY a few months for Governor Huey Long and Lieutenant Governor Paul Cyr to despise each other. On the campaign trail in 1927, they maintained a cool but harmonious relationship. Once the two men took office, Huey decided he no longer needed Cyr, while Cyr realized that Huey would not endorse him in the next race for governor. Under Louisiana law, a governor could not succeed himself and Cyr at first assumed he would be next in line. When Huey refused to support him, the feisty "tooth puller from Jeanerette" was furious. In December 1928, the

smoldering hatred between the two men exploded when they became involved in one of Louisiana's most notorious murder cases.

On a steamy night in July 1928, James LeBoeuf, a forty-five-year-old
electrician, took his wife, Ada, boating on a lonely part of Lake Palourde
near Morgan City. Ada was an enticing dark-haired woman and mother of
their four children. While paddling their pirogue across the lake, the
LeBoeufs met another boat carrying two men, Dr. Thomas E. Dreher and
Jim Beadle, a local trapper and Dreher's handyman. As the boats pulled
alongside, Beadle raised a shotgun to his shoulder and fired two charges
of buckshot into LeBoeuf's chest. Beadle and Dreher tied railroad angle
irons to the victim's head and feet and dumped his body into the water.
After Ada reported her husband missing, the local sheriff began a search
and a few days later fishermen found the body. The sheriff arrested Mrs.
LeBoeuf, Dr. Dreher, and Beadle. Dreher confessed and admitted that he
and Ada were lovers and hired Beadle to kill her husband. During the trial
in Franklin, a jury convicted the three defendants of first-degree murder.
Beadle, who turned state's evidence, received life imprisonment and Mrs.
LeBoeuf and Dr. Dreher were sentenced to hang.

Shortly after Huey became governor, the condemned couple appealed the death sentences to the Louisiana Supreme Court, but the court
denied their writ and affirmed the sentences. In a 2–1 vote, the state
Board of Pardons also rejected their plea for clemency. Attorney General
Percy Saint and trial judge James Simon voted to uphold the death sentences, while the third member, Lieutenant Governor Cyr, voted to spare
their lives. Cyr was a friend of Dr. Dreher and from the same southwestern region of the state, where Cajun sympathy for the condemned couple
was growing. The imminent first hanging of a white woman in Louisiana
history received wide coverage.

Appalled at the crime, Huey signed the warrants for the death penalty.
"Never had a more conscienceless murder been known," he wrote. Meanwhile, Attorney General Saint changed his vote during the next Pardon
Board meeting and the board recommended commutation to life imprisonment. Huey erupted and called the board's reversal a "mockery against
decency and civil order in this state." The board's vote, however, was not
binding, as the final decision rested with the governor. Huey ignored
the second Pardon Board vote and ordered the execution. The *New Or-*

leans *Times-Picayune* endorsed his decision, while Ewing's *States* recommended clemency. Cyr threatened that if Huey left the state, he would assume the duties of governor and reverse the decision. "How long," roared Cyr, "have I been humiliated by having to deal with this man."

Huey scheduled the hanging for January 5, 1929. On the night before, the state Supreme Court met again, this time to review a last-minute request from Dreher and LeBoeuf to stay the execution and empanel a lunacy commission to decide if they were sane. For five hours, the justices quarreled over the case behind closed doors and when they emerged they continued a heated argument. Chief Justice O'Neill and Judge Brunot were yelling angrily at each other and friends stepped between them before blows were struck. Just before eleven, Brunot telephoned the sheriff in Franklin and told him the court had voted 4–1 to uphold the death sentences. O'Neill, the one dissenter in the decision, wrestled the phone from Brunot and ordered the sheriff to stay the execution. O'Neill was from Franklin and was a friend of both Dr. Dreher and Lieutenant Governor Cyr. With conflicting orders from the Supreme Court, a confused Sheriff Pecot had no idea what to do the next day.

When Huey learned of the episode at the Supreme Court, he had little choice but to intervene. The next morning, only an hour before Dreher and LeBoeuf were to be hanged, he issued a reprieve to allow the court sufficient time to issue a consistent legal opinion. A week later, the justices met again, overrode O'Neill's objection, and issued a writ that allowed the hanging to proceed. Just after noon on Saturday, February 1, 1929, in the ivy-clad St. Mary Parish jail that overlooked nearby Bayou Teche, Charles Dreher and his lover, Ada LeBoeuf, stepped onto a makeshift gallows and were hanged.

The hanging of the two lovers also killed the fragile friendship between Huey Long and Paul Cyr. From then on, the governor and the lieutenant governor of the state of Louisiana, two cussedly stubborn and vindictive men, never exchanged a friendly word.

CHAPTER 4

1929
ENOUGH MONEY TO
BURN A WET MULE

Whenever Huey Long stood on the front steps of the state capitol and looked northward toward the Standard Oil refinery, the unearthly scene made his blood boil. Above his head, heavy pitch-black smoke billowing from nearby stacks darkened the noonday sun, while beneath the skyline bright orange pyres of flame erupted from tall vents. Day and night, the smoke and fire created an infernal aura to the landscape and etched a sharp contrast to the picturesque oak-shaded streets only a few blocks away. Since 1909, the Standard Oil Company's refinery, the world's largest, had dominated Baton Rouge. Stretching for several miles along the east bank of the Mississippi River, the refinery sprouted a forest of smokestacks, sheet metal sheds, and a plantation of massive red tanks brimming with petroleum from the Gulf oil fields. When the wind blew from the northwest, the mothers of Baton Rouge ordered their children inside to escape the stench and oily grit that drifted down upon the city.

Ever since 1918 when he took his first public office as a state railroad commissioner, Huey had attacked Standard Oil relentlessly. He had personal reasons for hating the giant oil company. As a young attorney he invested $1,050 in a local independent oil drilling business that subsequently struck oil. His stocks soared at first, but Standard Oil later refused to accept any oil from independent producers, and many of them were put out of business. Huey's stocks plummeted and he lost his investment. "Do you think I can forget that?" he later remarked. "Do you blame me for fighting the Standard Oil?"

To Huey, the oil giant represented all that was evil in American business, a huge monolithic corporation run by millionaires that used its vast financial resources to crush the little man. As public service commissioner, he failed in his attempt to have Standard Oil declared a public utility, thereby placing the price of its oil under state regulation. He had also tried to force the company to stop importing Mexican crude oil and instead refine more Louisiana oil. During his first campaign for governor, Huey denounced "the Invisible Empire of the Standard Oil Company," a reference linking the giant oil company with the Ku Klux Klan. "This octopus is among the world's greatest criminals," he now roared as governor. "It was thrown out of Texas following its raid on Spindletop. It was ousted from Kansas. It was forced to terms in Oklahoma." In another tirade, he charged that the state's farmers produced $180 million in crops a year while Standard Oil's Baton Rouge refinery, pumping up to 100,000 barrels of oil each day, earned $216 million a year in profits. Even so, he added, the state's farmers paid forty times more in taxes than Standard Oil.

Huey needed money to pay for his new roads, expansion of the state's hospitals, and other campaign promises. His ambitious programs had quickly exhausted the state treasury. Originally, he planned to fund the free schoolbooks with an increase in the oil severance tax, but an unexpected ruling by the Supreme Court rescinded the increase. He was able to provide free schoolbooks by forcing the banks to provide a loan, but he still needed new sources of revenue. To him, the obvious target was the rich vault of the Standard Oil Company.

On Monday, March 18, 1929, Huey called a six-day special session of the legislature to give him the authority to raise more funds. Although special sessions irritated some legislators who lost time from working at their home professions, he never hesitated in calling them to Baton Rouge. Three months before, in December 1928, he convened a six-day special session and succeeded in convincing the legislature to authorize bonds for his $30 million road building program. That session went well, as Huey worked with his floor leaders to persuade each house to suspend its rules by a two-thirds vote and allow bills to be quickly introduced, read once, and passed with little debate. He personally orchestrated every step of the legislative process. When the vote was taken, he discovered that two members who promised to support him had disappeared. Needing their votes to get the two-thirds majority, a furious Huey learned where the men were hiding and ordered them brought to the floor by state policemen.

Huey was still confident he could control the legislature during another special session and get it to approve his ambitious plans for new revenue. At an earlier meeting in New Orleans, he boasted that he held the legislature "like a deck of cards in my hands" and could deal the deck as he pleased. He also believed he had the people on his side. Earlier that winter, Louisiana voters approved his $30 million road building bond referendum by a three-to-one margin.

WHEN THE LEGISLATURE convened at eight in the evening on Monday, March 18, 1929, the sun had set and the night air had cooled. Legislators liked to meet at night to escape the Louisiana heat and after they had eaten their dinners of fried catfish or étouffée at nearby hotels. When they met they were stuffed and relaxed and many of them had a bottle near their desk so they could sip some whiskey as they carried out the state's business. The atmosphere was usually slack. "Jim Buie always had three or four bottles of beer on his [House] desk," remembered one legislator, "and would sit there guzzling it."

The session started off on a sour note when Rabbi Walter Peiser of Baton Rouge refused to offer the opening prayer. Feeling "coarsened and cheapened" by Huey's actions, the rabbi said that he could not in good conscience "call down the blessings of God on such a Governor . . . who is unworthy of the high office he holds." The legislators were also edgy. Huey had given them only two days' notice before they had to report to Baton Rouge, the shortest notice ever given for a special session in the state. When the legislators arrived, they expected to conduct only routine business during the session. They soon were surprised to learn that Huey's purpose for calling the special session was much more controversial and that he proposed a radically new processing tax on refined oil. Unlike the severance tax that imposed a levy on crude oil extracted at the wellhead, an oil processing tax would impose a 5-cents-per-barrel levy on finished petroleum. He calculated that the new tax would yield $5,000 per day for the schools, nearly $2 million per year. The oil companies estimated the tax would cost them over $3 million. During the first regular session held the previous December, Huey considered levying a similar 5-cent processing tax but withdrew the proposal when it became obvious there was too much opposition. This time he believed he had enough votes. He also hoped that the oil companies would not offer stiff resistance, and told one newspaper, "I am hoping that the oil trusts will not make any opposition to this form of license, as they have done to progressive measures heretofore."

Huey had lit the fuse of a political bombshell. Every legislator from oil-producing parishes knew that voting for a processing tax meant suicide in their next election. Small increases in the severance tax, while fought by Standard Oil and the other oil companies, had been more acceptable because the increases applied to a tax already on the books. An oil processing tax was a new source of revenue and a substantial burden on the oil industry. Other businessmen feared that Huey might expand occupational taxes in the future to include all types of business, not just oil.

The legislature, confused and surprised by Huey's new tax proposal, adjourned until the next morning. Overnight, his enemies began rallying for an attack. Standard Oil president Daniel Weller hurried from the company home office in New York and established headquarters in Baton Rouge's Heidelberg Hotel. He would stay in town throughout the special session, pressuring legislators to join the fight against Huey's oil tax. Huey claimed that Weller and Standard Oil brought enough bribe money to "burn a wet mule." And indeed, Weller's cash began to convince several balky legislators to turn against Huey. "You could pick up fifteen or twenty thousand dollars any evening," one representative admitted. Weller also knew that Standard Oil had the support of the citizens of Baton Rouge. He warned that Huey's new oil tax could cause Standard to shut down the refinery. Its loss would devastate the local economy of a city where, out of a population of thirty thousand, the refinery employed eight thousand workers. So dominant was the oil company that on refinery paydays, shops and banks along the city's bustling Third Street stayed open late into the night.

On March 19, the *Baton Rouge Advocate,* owned by the powerful Manship family and usually neutral in political affairs, began to oppose Huey in editorial after editorial. In a front-page article, the paper charged that all the "years of planning and building and hoping on the part of a farsighted citizenry have suddenly been jeopardized by the personal whim of a [governor] thrown by chance into a position where he can exercise that whim to the detriment of an industry he conceives to be antagonistic to him." The paper warned that Huey's "spite tax" would force Standard Oil to fire two thousand local workers. The *Advocate* concluded that "every daily newspaper in Louisiana, every chamber of commerce, every business executive . . . every man who has a payroll, every clear thinking worker who values his Saturday pay envelope, and every public servant who can see farther than the end of Governor Long's big stick," opposed Huey's new oil tax.

The first sign of serious trouble for Huey appeared when he failed to get two-thirds of each house to suspend the rules. He understood the legislative process better than most representatives and realized he no longer could move his oil processing tax quickly through the legislature. He needed a longer session to gather more votes. On March 20, Huey called for eighteen days to be tacked onto the current six-day session. He realized that the six-day session was a big mistake, as did his foes. "It sounded like Huey 'faw down and go boom,' " the *New Orleans States* reported sarcastically.

As Huey struggled to capture more votes, his bullying quickly upset many representatives, including several supporters. Rarely content to stay in his office to await the results of a vote, the impatient Huey charged through the capitol corridors, up the sweeping stairway into the House or Senate, where he paced up and down, inside the bar and in violation of the legislative rules. He barged into legislative committees, interrupting the proceedings to campaign for his bill. Shortly after the session opened, Representative Lavinius Williams, an anti-Long legislator from New Orleans, spotted Huey pacing the legislative aisles and prodding House members. As Huey glared at him from the aisle, Williams called for enforcement of House Rule 20 prohibiting visitors on the floor. "This House has stood for this indignity long enough," Williams declared. After

Williams's motion passed with loud applause, the sergeant-at-arms escorted the governor, his face burning red, from the floor of the House.

Lieutenant Governor Paul Cyr, still enraged at Huey over the executions of Ada LeBoeuf and Thomas Dreher, joined the mounting opposition. On March 21, Cyr took the Senate floor and accused Huey of abusing the office of governor and "feathering the family nest" by hiring his brother Earl as inheritance tax collector. Cyr also attacked Huey for leasing several million dollars' worth of south Louisiana land to a Texas oil company, a deal that would reap huge profits when wells were drilled and millions of barrels of oil discovered. The oil leases belong to the state, cried Cyr, and any revenues collected should go into the state treasury, not into the pockets of Huey's cronies. Cyr, besides being a dentist, was a surface geologist who had worked for Humble Oil and knew that huge petroleum deposits sat below salt domes from Plaquemines Parish to the Texas line. Cyr revealed that several independent oil developers who earlier contributed to Huey's campaign had received lucrative oil leases on state lands as a reward for their support. "[Huey is] the worst political tyrant to rule the state," Cyr bellowed.

Bombarded by his enemies and hostile newspapers, Huey lost his temper. On the morning of March 20, he threatened Baton Rouge newspaper publisher Charles Manship that if the city's newspapers did not "lay off me, I am going to publish a list of the names of people who have relatives in the insane asylum." Huey knew that Manship's brother was confined in a state mental hospital. That afternoon, the front page of the *Baton Rouge State-Times* revealed Huey's threat. "This, gentlemen, is the way your Governor fights," read the boldfaced headline. "I might say, however," Manship wrote in an editorial, "that my brother Douglas is about the same age as the Governor. He was in France in 1918, wearing the uniform of a United States soldier, while Governor Long was campaigning for office."

Undeterred by Manship's revelation of his contemptible tactics, Huey forged ahead. "Always take the offensive," he later offered. "The defensive ain't worth a damn." He continued to slander Manship's brother. "They say I made a terrible offense because they say the insanity of this young man, the brother of Manship, is due to shell shock in the World War. That ain't so—it is due to venereal disease, the record shows." Speaking to a crowd in Alexandria a few days later, Huey again went after the Manships. "Did you ever hear of shell shock causing syphilis?"

HUEY USED ALMOST EVERY ruse he could devise to force representatives to support his legislation. One of his targets was Cecil Morgan, a bright young attorney recently elected to the House from Caddo Parish. Huey and Cecil knew each other well. In 1921, two years after Morgan graduated from LSU Law School, Huey asked him to become his law partner. Morgan, then a Shreveport attorney struggling for business, declined because he disliked Huey's methods. "I couldn't do it," Morgan admitted later. "I didn't think he was ethical." During Morgan's first legislative session in 1928, Huey warned the young legislator that if he voted against his bills, including the highway bond issue, he would fire his father, an elderly state bank examiner. Morgan ignored Huey's threat and defiantly voted against the bills. Huey fired his father, despite bank examiners' guaranteed overlapping six-year terms. "I moved my family to Shreveport, bought them a small house," Morgan recalled. "I was unmarried then. I had to borrow money to do it. He hit me on my tenderest spot when he fired my father. . . . [Huey] was as cold-blooded in his desire for power as a human being could be."

Huey angered many legislators when he announced in a radio speech that any legislator who voted against the oil processing tax had been "bought." On the House floor, Gilbert Dupre, an elderly and deaf representative from St. Landry Parish who had served in the legislature since 1888, rose to defend his colleagues. Despite his age, the crusty Dupre soon would become one of Huey's most zealous antagonists. "This House is not a den of thieves," argued the proud old Creole. "There may be a lot of damned fools and there may be some damned rascals, but the majority are intent upon doing their duty."

On Friday morning, March 22, the *Shreveport Journal* called for a thorough investigation of Governor Long's behavior and, if necessary, "swift and determined action to oust him should be taken and he should be immediately impeached from office." The next day, Senator Charles Huson of DeSoto Parish sent Cyr a telegram urging the lieutenant governor to begin impeachment proceedings. Later in the week, Manship's *Ad-*

vocate declared that "Governor Long's tyranny over Louisiana should end" and called for impeachment to proceed "calmly and deliberately." Within a week, three large News Orleans newspapers, the *Times-Picayune, Item,* and *States,* joined the call for Huey's ouster. His opponents, including Cecil Morgan and several young legislators, closed ranks and enlisted other representatives who previously had been fence-sitters. Late at night, lights burned in office windows throughout Baton Rouge as politicians plotted their strategy either to defend Huey or to send him packing.

Huey, barricaded in his suite on the top floor of the Heidelberg Hotel, sensed disaster. From his twelfth-floor window, he could look out upon the Mississippi River. "The water is rising," he reflected. "It looks as if another flood might come." But it was not the mighty Mississippi that Huey worried about. His governorship was at stake. Only a handful of his supporters remained loyal. "My ground had begun to slip from under me," he wrote later. "Rats began to leave the apparently sinking ship. I had to draw back to find out where I stood."

On Sunday night, realizing that continuing the special session could lead to political disaster, Huey called Speaker Fournet and his other House leaders to his room in the Heidelberg. With no chance of passing the oil processing tax, he instructed his floor leaders to move for indefinite adjournment *sine die* when the House convened the following evening. A legislature that was not in session, Huey knew, could not impeach a governor.

ON MONDAY EVENING, March 25, hundreds of Baton Rougeans finished supper early and strolled to the antebellum state capitol perched on the bluff overlooking the Mississippi. They sensed something was going to happen and they were going to be there to see it. Those who arrived early quickly grabbed one of the few seats in the spectators gallery of the House. The rest of the crowd milled around the capitol grounds, waiting nervously for the session to begin.

An electric tenseness filled the air when Speaker Fournet called the House to order just after sunset. As soon as the clerk completed the roll call, Representative Cleveland Fruge, a Long supporter from Evangeline Parish, rose to speak. During the meeting the night before, Huey ordered Fruge to make the motion to adjourn *sine die*. Before Speaker Fournet could recognize Fruge, however, Cecil Morgan jumped from his seat to take the floor. Fournet ordered Morgan to be seated but the young legislator, quivering with excitement, refused. He declared loudly that one of the governor's former bodyguards had accused Huey of hiring him to assassinate Representative J. Y. Sanders, Jr. Like Morgan, Sanders was a fiercely anti-Long legislator and the son of the former governor whom Huey grappled with in the lobby of the Roosevelt Hotel a year before.

Speaker Fournet, pounding his gavel on his desk, ignored Morgan and recognized Fruge, who shouted his motion to adjourn over angry cries from House members and spectators seated in the gallery. Morgan stood trembling at his desk, waving an affidavit containing the bodyguard's accusation, and demanding that a committee investigate the murder charge against Huey. "Put Mr. Morgan in his seat," Fournet ordered. While Morgan still yelled his accusations, dozens of House members jumped to their feet and began to argue loudly with one another. When the sergeant-at-arms, Major Stewart, moved toward Morgan, twelve anti-Long members, including Representatives Mason Spencer and George Perrault, who each weighed over 250 pounds, stood in a circle around Morgan with locked arms so that the sergeant-at-arms could not reach him. "This is a dastardly outrage!" Morgan yelled. "You shall not vote me down until I have had my say."

Still banging his gavel loudly, Fournet tried to end the ruckus and called for a vote on Fruge's motion to adjourn. House members rushed back to their seats and pressed the buttons on the electric voting machine. The colored lights above the speaker's chair flashed and the machine tallied sixty-seven green lights in favor of adjournment and thirteen red lights against. Fournet announced that the motion to adjourn passed, dropped the gavel on his desk, and hurried from the chamber. Many members who voted against adjournment looked up and saw that their votes were incorrectly tallied as green votes. A howl of protest arose that made the statehouse walls tremble. "You goddamn crook!" someone screamed. "Oh, God, don't let them get away with this," another shouted. The protesters were all on their feet, in the aisle, on their desks, clamoring toward the speaker's chair and shouting angrily that the vote was fixed, while Huey's supporters surrounded the speaker's platform and defended it like a child's castle. "Blood and fire shone from every pair of eyes and the most trivial untoward incident might have caused them to run amuck," Huey wrote afterward. Fights broke out all over the chamber. Members wrestled on the floor. Inkstands, huge law books, and other debris flew through the air like missiles.

Clinton Sayes, a hot-tempered anti-Long representative from Avoyelles Parish, climbed across the tops of desks and tried to capture the speaker's platform. A group of Long supporters, including floor leader Lorris Wimberly and former Tulane football player Lester Lautenschlaeger, cut off Sayes. "The bald headed wild fellow, Sayes, wanted to do physical harm to somebody and ran across desks," Lautenschlaeger remembered. "It looked as if he had a pistol. I ended up between him and the platform by Fournet and grabbed Sayes. He would not be calmed down."

As Lautenschlaeger and others pounced upon Sayes, another anti-Long, Harney Bogan, leapt from the top of a desk into the pile of wrestling representatives to rescue Sayes. He pulled Sayes out with blood pouring from his bald head. Depending on the source, Sayes received his wound either from a Long supporter wearing brass knuckles, a blow from a heavy cane, a diamond jutting from a ring on Wimberly's finger, or the blade of a ceiling fan that struck Sayes in the head when he climbed on top of his desk. Nevertheless, enough blood had spilled for the infamous night session to be dubbed "Bloody Monday."

Finally, Spencer, the huge, hulking anti-Long legislator from Madison Parish, climbed atop the press table and bellowed a call for order. Hearing Spencer's booming voice, most of the brawlers paused for a moment. "Let us be sane," Spencer roared. "Let there be silence, and let the House be polled by oral roll call." To Spencer's surprise, the House fell silent. Seizing the opportunity, he polled each member by name and a great roar erupted when he announced there were seventy-nine votes to remain in session and only nine votes to adjourn. Even with order somewhat restored, the House realized that it could not conduct any level-headed business that night and adjourned until the next morning.

Huey, looking "as if a threshing machine had passed over him," left his office in the capitol and headed to his suite atop the Heidelberg Hotel. He was forlorn and distraught, for instead of facing a legislature that he firmly controlled only three months before, he now confronted what he described as "a few hundred highly intelligent animals temporarily bereft of reason and milling wildly about." He miscalculated his power and failed to send the unmanageable legislators home. He originally counted over fifty votes for adjournment, more than enough for passage, but once Cecil Morgan rose to announce the bodyguard's accusation, he lost control. Ominously, he was losing supporters fast. As legislators departed the capitol that Monday night, several who previously supported Huey announced they were shifting allegiance. One of them, elderly Representative R. Miles Pratt, until that time a staunch supporter of the governor, declared he was "against Long from now until hell freezes over."

ON TUESDAY MORNING, March 26, an eerie, uneasy calm hung over the capitol. As legislators walked across the grounds and through the large crowd milling about the statehouse, many waistcoats bulged from loaded revolvers stuck inside men's belts. "I'll bet there were five hundred pistols in that crowd," one senator remembered.

Speaker Fournet opened the session with an apology to the House members for anything he may have done the night before to cause the fracas. He explained that the voting machine, an archaic and unreliable contraption powered by wet-cell batteries, had malfunctioned and still showed the tally from a previous vote. Most representatives accepted the explanation and those who didn't were not worried about punishing Fournet. They instead had turned their wrath on only one person, Huey Long.

Throughout the night before, Huey's more militant opponents gathered to draw up a formal bill of impeachment. The "Dynamite Squad," so named because it aimed to explode Huey's legislation, included Cecil Morgan, Mason Spencer, J. Y. Sanders, Jr., George Perrault, and about a dozen other newly elected representatives. All were from the old aristocratic families and friendly with the Old Regulars. "Those boys were not amateurs," remembered a Long loyalist, "very skilled and smart." Now, after Bloody Monday, the Dynamiters no longer were content to destroy Huey's legislation, but saw his impeachment as their only goal. They were nervous. "During the impeachment, our group was very cautious," Cecil Morgan remembered. "We always ate together and never went out alone at night." Throughout Monday night and into Tuesday morning the squad met in J. Y. Sanders's office on the third floor of the Romain Building, devising their strategy and outlining the bill of impeachment. After drafting nineteen charges of misconduct, the Dynamiters walked the few blocks to the capitol, bleary-eyed and weary from no sleep and just in time for the House to reconvene.

As each House member took his seat, he found sitting on his desk a petition listing the nineteen impeachment charges. Although most legislators knew what was coming, many of them still were awestruck when they heard one of the Dynamite Squad read solemnly, "whereas, Huey P. Long, Governor of the State of Louisiana, has been guilty of high crimes and misdemeanors in office, incompetency, corruption, favoritism, oppression in office, gross misconduct . . ." The nineteen charges that followed were a patchwork of complaints, ranging from frivolous and absurd to serious and felonious. The bodyguard's accusation that Huey planned to murder J. Y. Sanders, Jr., was, of course, the most serious of the impeachment charges. However, even Dynamite Squad members admitted there was little likelihood of the bodyguard's charges being true. Huey had fired the bodyguard, a slow-moving and dull-witted former prizefighter named Battling Bozeman, before the affidavit was signed, and vengeance was Bozeman's likely motive. The affidavit was a wild, rambling testimony so full of inconsistencies that the Dynamiters had no intention of entering it into the House proceedings. "No, I didn't believe Battling Bozeman's story," Mason Spencer admitted later. "But what a wonderful witness he made." Spencer and most other legislators believed that while Huey was a tyrant, he was incapable of murder. Later, the House dropped the murder charge, as well as frivolous complaints that accused Huey of carrying a concealed weapon, violently abusing citizens visiting him on public business, gross misconduct in public places, repeatedly appearing on the floor of the House of Representatives, purchasing a $20,000 ice machine for Angola Penitentiary without advertising for bids, fondling a New Orleans nightclub stripper, and uttering "blasphemous and sacrilegious expressions by comparing himself to the Savior."

Other charges, much more serious, provided the grounds for impeachment and, if he was convicted by the Senate, Huey's removal from office. The more serious accusations alleged that Huey illegally influenced the judiciary, offered bribes to legislators, used the militia unlawfully to pillage private property, and improperly spent state money. Huey's opponents later tacked on a twentieth, catchall charge that accused the governor of "incompetency, corruption . . . and gross misconduct."

With charges now pressed, the anti-Long forces were overjoyed. An air of celebration spread over Baton Rouge, for most of the capital city steadfastly detested Huey and his cohorts. "It was so bad during the impeachment that we fellows couldn't even get a shave and a haircut in Baton Rouge," one pro-Long legislator recalled. "That's how bitter they were." The state's large daily newspapers, all of which were now rabidly anti-Long, had a field day. The *Times-Picayune* exhorted impeachment, saying Huey was "temperamentally and otherwise unfit to hold the office" and "a cruel political tyrant," while the huge headline of Colonel Ewing's *States* declared that the "Crooked Game of Long Is Blocked." Evoking the memory of the Lost Cause, the *States* applauded the legislators who fought against Huey on the House floor, the "sons of men through whose veins coursed the good red blood of their fathers who, back in the dark days that tried men's souls when alien tyrants were despotically striving to enslave them, rose in their might and rid themselves of such tyranny." Forecasting the governor's demise, the *States* declared that Huey, "like Aesop's fox, is now gnawing at his own tail to release himself."

That Tuesday afternoon, placards sprouted about the city announcing a mass meeting to protest Huey's "radical legislation" and his "attack on the prosperity and credit" of the state. At eight that night the anti-Long forces gathered at the city's Community Club pavilion for a huge rally. Six thousand attended the impromptu carnival, where fireworks exploded, pistol shots rang into the night, and the sixty-piece Standard Oil Band, poorly disguised in its street clothes, entertained the throng with lively medleys. From New Orleans came a trainload of Old Regulars, eager to see the downfall of their hated governor. From the stage, a host of anti-Long speakers beat their breasts and vented fire-breathing attacks on Huey, declaring him "too weak and unlearned" to be governor and calling him a dictator with scheming designs for the purpose of satisfying a personal grudge and getting revenge. One of the speakers, Mrs. Ruffin Pleasant of Caddo Parish, the dark-haired, round-faced wife of the ex-governor, discarded her ladylike demeanor and viciously attacked Huey. "Glib are the utterances that slip from the Governor's oily tongue," the childlike Mrs. Pleasant declared, "but his selfish acts utterly belie them."

On a balcony across the street from the rally, a somber Huey stood in a darkened doorway where he could not be seen and listened intently to the speakers.

CHAPTER 5

1929
BOUGHT LIKE A SACK
OF POTATOES

Nervous, depressed, and sleeping little, Governor Huey Long at first brooded over the mounting calls for his impeachment. His brother Julius, who drove from Shreveport to help with Huey's defense, said he found him lying on a bed sobbing. But Huey, like a fighter shaking off a lucky punch, quickly regained his confidence and bounced back with as much energy and aggressiveness as ever. "Huey was wild up in his rooms in the Heidelberg Hotel," a legislator observed. "He couldn't find out what had happened. The corridor was lined with guards. Huey was pacing the room, shirt off, a pistol stuck in his back pants pocket, like a wild man."

On March 27, 1929, just two days after Bloody Monday, Huey began attacking his impeachers with a massive circular campaign, a tactic he used successfully during his campaign for governor to publicize his platform. Over the next few weeks, he dictated each circular to Alice Lee Grosjean and sent it to the Franklin Press in New Orleans for printing. Besides assailing his enemies and defending his governorship, the circulars had an extra, more practical application in rural Louisiana. "Don't use any of that damned smooth stuff [paper]," Huey ordered the printer. "Use some that they can use on their backsides after they get through reading it."

Huey ordered his circulars sent out immediately across the state. The mail was too slow for him. As soon as the printers bundled the circulars, they rushed them to state workers driving Highway Commission trucks and state policemen on motorcycles, who then raced across the state, flooding the countryside with thousands of copies of his latest message. The circular campaign alone, totaling 900,000 copies, cost $40,000, and Bob Maestri, to Huey "the greatest of all friends in foul weather," financed much of his counterattack.

Huey's circulars assailed Standard Oil. "This is the fight of my life," he wrote in the first one, titled *The Cross of Gold: Standard Oil Company vs. Huey P. Long.* "They are laying their lines to try and ruin me. But we will have the entire state plastered with this literature before we are through. I never have rested since I became Governor. I will not now." In a later circular, he swore, "I would rather go down to a thousand impeachments than to admit that I am the Governor of the state that does not dare to call the Standard Oil Company to account so that we can educate our children and care for the destitute, sick, and afflicted. . . . If this state is still to be ruled by the power of the money of this corporation, I am too weak for its governor." In yet another, he asked, "Has it become a crime for a governor to fight for the school children and the cause of suffering and destitute humanity?"

Still trying to build popular support, Huey called his own mass meeting at the Community Club on the night of April 3. "Watch out for the lying newspapers," he warned his followers in a circular. "They may announce that this meeting will be called off or they may say that the Governor has resigned. Pay no attention to anything they say. Come to Baton Rouge. Don't take time to dress up." To build the crowd, he ordered hundreds of highway workers and other state employees from across the state to attend the rally. Owing their jobs to Huey, they quickly headed to Baton Rouge. Huey sent dozens of telegrams to his local political bosses drumming up support. The mayor of Pineville, Rolo Lawrence, received one of Huey's three-page messages ordering him to "bring the boys to Baton Rouge." Lawrence sent five cars filled with supporters to the state capital.

By sunset, "the city was swamped," Huey recalled. "Even the streets could hardly hold the crowds . . . it was a panic, and very few of the laborers or farmers had taken time to change from their working clothes to come to the capital." His opponents held a parade that ended in front of the Heidelberg Hotel, and his supporters held another that ended just up the street. Several fights erupted and, according to Lawrence, the clashes "could have been a riot." At eight o'clock, John Overton, the Alexandria attorney and gifted stump speaker, stepped onto the Community Club stage to open Huey's rally. "As I see him there now," Overton bellowed Tennyson-like from loudspeakers, "with his rapier flashing, fencing off the enemies to the left, to the front and to the right, when this smoke of battle shall have cleared, as in the beginning, I will be standing or lying by the side of Huey P. Long."

After Overton and other speakers finished, Huey took the rostrum and spoke for two hours. To one critical newsman, his speech combined the talents of "an unscrupulous Bryan and a political Barnum." With impassioned oratory, he accused Standard Oil of plotting his overthrow and appealed to the people to come to his defense. "The buzzards have returned," Huey roared. "They want to gloat and gulp at the expense of the poor and afflicted." Near midnight, he ended the speech with his favorite quotations from "Invictus," ". . . I am the master of my fate, I am the captain of my soul." His supporters said it was his finest performance. "I saw people in front of the old capitol on their knees praying for Huey during impeachment . . . country people," a follower remembered.

Each evening, Huey caucused with his defense team in the nearby Louisiana National Bank building where they took over an entire floor. He was tireless as he prepared for the impeachment proceedings, sleeping "only in snatches and seemed to subsist primarily on strawberries and cream." Early in the week, Earl Long called a local Baton Rouge businessman, L. P. Bahan, and ordered thirty-four typewriters brought to the capitol. Soon, a secretary was busy at each typewriter as Huey walked along the line dictating telegrams to each girl off the top of his head. Bahan did not charge Huey and afterward got all of the state's typewriter business.

To fund his defense and buy votes to stop his impeachment, Huey turned to Robert Maestri, the New Orleans millionaire, who delivered $130,000 from unknown sources and with no strings attached. Standard Oil and Huey's other opponents also brought huge sums of cash to Baton Rouge for bribes. They offered a huge sum to buy Jules Fisher, a pro-Long senator from the Jefferson Parish shrimping family, while William Boone, a senator from Claiborne Parish, claimed he turned down $50,000 to impeach Huey.

Both sides used other ruses besides money to coerce legislators. The president pro tem of the Senate, Phillip Gilbert, opposed Huey at first, but a last-minute plan to build a road from Sicily Island to Winnsboro in Gilbert's district was the reported payoff. The Long forces enticed Senator James Anderson, a Baptist minister, to a Baton Rouge hotel room for a compromising encounter with liquor and a prostitute. Facing political blackmail, "Preacher" Anderson joined Huey. Huey's opponents were no less nasty. Anti-Long forces, led by New Orleans attorney Esmond Phelps, threatened Representative Lester Lautenschlaeger that if he did not support impeachment, he would lose his job as backfield coach of the Tulane football team. The coach received a telegram dismissing him after he announced he would remain neutral until he heard all of the evidence. Tulane officials rehired Lautenschlaeger only after the other coaches threatened to resign. Henry Larcade, a pro-Long Senator from Opelousas, felt the pressure in his hometown. During the impeachment session, anti-Longs tacked up notices in all businesses around Opelousas that read, "If Henry Larcade votes to acquit he will be tarred and feathered if he returns to Opelousas." When Larcade returned home from Baton Rouge, he carried two pistols. His wife made him promise to get out of politics and he burned all his papers. "Until impeachment, I never knew how low humanity could sink," one observer recalled.

A FEW DAYS BEFORE the impeachment proceedings began, Huey telephoned his wife, Rose, in Shreveport and told her to buy two or three expensive but conservative dresses and come to Baton Rouge. When the hearings began on April 3, 1929, Rose, a shy woman who disliked public occasions and society events, sat quietly in the first row of the House gallery in a new, white frock dress. Huey showed up wearing a white suit and a black bow tie and smoking a large cigar. Despite the steamy weather, spectators filled the gallery, and the aisles and corridors were "packed with perspiring humanity."

The twelve House members who would question witnesses sat at two long oaken tables in a small well in front of the speaker's rostrum. Six

questioners were Dynamite Squad members and six were Huey's supporters. Joining Huey at his defense table was a team of skilled lawyers,
including George Wallace, John Overton, Huey's brothers Julius and Earl,
State Senator Harvey Peltier, Representative Allen Ellender, and Leander
Perez, a brilliant young attorney from Plaquemines Parish. Another
member of the defense team was O. H. Simpson, the former governor
whom Huey defeated the year before, considered one of the ablest parlia-
mentarians in the state. An early casualty of the team was Huey's boyhood pal Harley Bozeman, who was a newly elected legislator from Winn
Parish and Huey's floor leader. Harley supported Huey but angered him
when he recommended that Huey resign as the impeachment crisis
worsened. He never forgave Bozeman. To Huey, his friend's recommen-
dation showed a lack of courage and loyalty. The following winter, he
forced Harley to resign as chairman of the lucrative Louisiana Tax Commission, where he earned $400 a month. From then on, the two men
were bitter enemies.

The first witness called was Representative Adolphe Gueymard of
Iberville Parish, who testified that Huey offered him jobs with the Highway Commission or as manager of the penitentiary at St. Gabriel if he
supported the oil processing tax. Other witnesses followed with similar
stories. Representative J. O. Fernandez, an Old Regular from New Orleans, testified that Huey offered him a bribe, and a parish sheriff testified that Huey bragged about bribing Representative W. H. Bennett of
East Feliciana Parish. "I bought and paid for him like you would a sack of
potatoes," Huey reportedly boasted.

As witness after witness took the stand and testified to outrageous
episodes of Louisiana politics, the impeachment hearings at times
seemed vaudevillian. One journalist described the proceedings as "a fight
to death between the gorillas and baboons." Alfred Danzinger, a New Orleans hotelier who was a friend of Huey's, offered some spicy testimony
when he described a hula girl sitting on Huey's knee at the party he held
in his French Quarter studio. The testimony infuriated old Judge Dupre,
who vainly tried to listen to the witnesses with a huge, old-fashioned
horn-shaped hearing contraption. The legislator accused Huey of spending state money in a whorehouse. "You talk about appropriating money

for the halt, the sick and the blind," Dupre shouted, "but you appropriate money for the Governor to raise hell in brothels!" The hula dancer, Helen Clifford, later took the stand. "I wore a straw skirt," the dancer told the gawking legislators. "I was bare except around my chest." After Clifford testified that Huey had been "very frisky" at the party, legislators requested her phone number.

Humorous testimony occurred when Huey's bodyguard Joe Messina took the stand. Messina, a dark, squat Italian who carried a blackjack and bulky pearl-handled revolver, was listed on the Highway Department payroll as a "license checker." When questioned about his duties, the slow-witted Messina admitted that he never worked at his highway job but if called upon, "could tell a 1928 from a 1929 plate."

One of the few legislators who rose to defend Huey was George Delesdernier, a nice, gaunt old Cajun from a family of trappers from Pilottown in the remote, roadless part of Plaquemines Parish. Delesdernier argued that a special session could not impeach the governor because impeachment was not an agenda item in Huey's original call for the special session. One of the impeachers attacked Delesdernier's logic. "Do you think that the Governor would ever call a special session to impeach himself?" A few days later, Delesdernier gave one of the more outrageous speeches given in the House. At times rambling incoherently, he compared Huey to Jesus Christ. "Today there is a creature relieving the sick and the blind, aiding the lame and the halt, and trying to drive illiteracy from the state," Delesdernier declared. "He is being shackled with paper to a cross. The cross was manufactured, one of the uprights, out of a saintly piece. The horizontal part of the cross is from the beams of the moon, and this divine creature is being shackled with paper." While House members protested and yelled cries of blasphemy and sacrilege, Delesdernier continued to preach. "Mr. Chairman," he concluded, "take my life but give me my character!" He then fainted and lay motionless on the floor while the House voted on a motion. Afterward, Delesdernier's friends splashed water on his face and carried him from the chamber.

Although the House impeachment proceedings often seemed ridiculous, they did include serious testimony. Much of the case against Huey rested on whether he misspent state funds. To investigate his financial

dealings, the House called Seymour Weiss, the manager of New Orleans's swank Hotel Roosevelt and Huey's unofficial business manager,
to testify.

THE CLOSE FRIENDSHIP BETWEEN Huey Long and Seymour Weiss appeared unlikely, for the two men were opposites in many ways. The son
of a Jewish storekeeper, Seymour was born in Abbeville, a small town in
southwestern Louisiana. In 1917, at twenty, he moved to New Orleans,
where he worked as a clerk in a downtown shoe store. Later he became
manager of the barbershop in the Roosevelt Hotel, an influential job that
allowed him to become well acquainted with the city's politicians, salesmen, investors, and gamblers. Seymour rose quickly at the Roosevelt,
from assistant manager, to manager, president, and, by 1931, principal
owner. Tall, slender, and ramrod straight, his blond hair already thinning,
Seymour had blue eyes that revealed intuitive intelligence and a burning
desire to succeed. Well mannered, dressed in expensive three-piece suits,
a silk handkerchief perfectly peeking from his left breast pocket, he enjoyed being surrounded by luxury. To his employees, he was a kind boss,
unfailingly pleasant, always requesting, never ordering. "Seymour Weiss?
He was a prince," bartender Joe Scaffidi later said of him.

Weiss met Huey in 1927 during the race for governor and quickly became his most trusted adviser. Huey depended on Seymour to oversee his
private finances and manage the thousands of dollars of campaign funds
that were piled in the Roosevelt's double-door cast-iron safe. Seymour
was absolutely loyal to Huey and in return became a very rich man. Soon
after they met, Seymour joined a partnership with Huey, O. K. Allen, and
Shreveport millionaire Harvey Couch in a limestone quarry in Winn
Parish. The quarry was an excellent investment, as it supplied much of
the roadbed for Huey's huge highway building program. Seymour and
Huey also were founding partners of the Win or Lose Oil Company, a
holding corporation that bought and sold lucrative state oil leases.

Seymour was a good listener, quiet, and a perfect counterpoise to
Huey's explosive personality. Along with Huey's wife, Rose, Seymour was
one of a few who could actually calm Huey down, or get away with telling
him when he was wrong or when he dressed outrageously. On one formal
occasion Huey accented his swallowtail coat and striped pants with a

monstrous, flaming red tie. "Jesus Christ," Weiss moaned when he saw the outfit. "You can't go down there like that." Huey changed the tie. The friendship between the brash young politician from the Baptist north country and the restrained, urbane hotel manager from southern Louisiana never wavered.

On April 4, 1929, the House of Representatives called Seymour Weiss to testify. The Dynamite Squad accused Huey of misusing state funds during a four-day conference of state governors held in New Orleans the previous November. Seymour handled the arrangements and paid the bills—always in cash. Fourteen governors attended and enjoyed New Orleans's finest, including theater at the Saenger on Monday night and dinner at Antoine's on Tuesday. The House appropriated $6,000 for the festivities but Weiss's testimony did not account for several thousand dollars of expenditures. On the stand, Seymour was polite, bland, and businesslike, but he stubbornly refused to divulge the details of entertainment expenses. The impeachers, probing for fraud, knew that the unaccounted extra expenses were for liquor and women. Dupre was especially incensed as Weiss refused over and over to answer the questions. "There is an insect here from New Orleans," the old legislator muttered. "He is a contemptible specimen of manhood, who has set himself up here to protect the Governor."

The impeachers pressed on, for they knew that Huey purchased a brand-new Buick, a sporty red two-door coupé, at about the same time as the governor's conference. On the day after his secretary, Alice Lee Grosjean, cashed the $6,000 check for the conference, Huey sent one of his assistants, Frank Odom, to pick up the new car from Barns Buick and pay cash for it. One of the Dynamiters, Mason Spencer, considered use of state funds to buy the car as the worst impeachment offense. Spencer and other legislators grilled Seymour about the missing cash throughout the day, called him again on the following morning, and again eleven days later, but Seymour refused to answer their questions. Although some legislators accused the obstinate Weiss of contempt, they gave up and dismissed him.

A WEEK AFTER the House impeachment proceedings began, Huey left town. While the House debated the charges against him, he took to the road to appeal his case directly to the people. To him, the most effective way to put pressure on legislators was to convince them that the voters back in their home parishes steadfastly supported him, and if a legislator voted for impeachment, then his own political career was over. At Greensburg on April 12, Huey began a three-week speaking tour that was just as energetic and combative as his campaign for governor. While speaking in Bogalusa, he asked all those in favor of impeachment to stand. Huey knew that any anti-Long listeners would be embarrassed, if not pummeled, if they were to stand among a pro-Long crowd. Few ever stood. When the newspapers described the reception Huey received, they reported the crowds to be decidedly pro-Long. The turnouts were heavy. In Lake Charles on April 24, he spoke to a roaring crowd of ten thousand.

Delivering as many as seven speeches a day, Huey aimed much of his wrath at Standard Oil. While speaking to a crowd in Alexandria, he accused the oil company of bribing the publisher of the *Alexandria Daily Town Talk,* R. C. Jarreau. Huey proclaimed that "bird Jarreau's buying him a limousine, I hear." Jarreau was in the audience and yelled out that the governor was a liar. The crowd became unruly and interrupted Huey's speech for five minutes. The air was tense as Long's supporters and opponents glared at one another. "I can't begin to get over to you the tension gripping the state," Representative Norman Bauer recalled.

Besides Standard Oil, Huey aimed his ire at other opponents. As he spoke in the towns of the southern Cajun country, he attacked a local favorite and his bitter enemy, Lieutenant Governor Cyr. "He rode into office on my coat tails," Huey announced in Abbeville, "and electing him was like trying to pull an elephant through a snowstorm." While in Opelousas he attacked another native son, old Judge Dupre. "Some people claim to be honest just because they're deaf," Huey shouted, referring to Dupre's lack of hearing. Back in Baton Rouge the following day, Dupre learned of the attack and took the floor of the House. The old man was furious and challenged Huey to a duel. His voice trembling with anger but strong enough to ring through the House chamber for all his seventy years, Dupre lashed out at Huey. "The Governor of this state went to my home town yesterday and wickedly and maliciously and deliberately slandered me," Dupre declared emotionally. "I fight in the open, and I carry no concealed weapons," lifting his coattail to show he was unarmed. "But I'll fight anyone at the drop of a hat. Governor Long has the wrong sow by the ear. . . . Governor Long is dancing over a volcano. He has called us 'jackasses.' I do not understand this man. I certainly never before heard of a man who would ridicule another man's infirmity in order to slander him."

Soon afterward, another elderly gentleman, seventy-eight-year-old judge J. E. Reynolds, threatened to punch the governor in the nose after he orchestrated the judge's defeat for the state Supreme Court. "What's the matter with all these old boys?" Huey asked. "Ain't there somebody younger than seventy to take a poke at me?"

ON THE AFTERNOON OF April 6, shortly after Seymour Weiss finished his tightlipped testimony, Representative George Perrault of St. Landry Parish, a brawny man who always carried a loaded pistol in his briefcase, rose from his seat in the House. Perrault called for the House to vote on the impeachment charge that Huey attempted to blackmail Charles Manship. Perrault declared that he could not believe "that any man here, be he lawyer or be he layman, can deep down in his heart approve the act of Governor Long in placing before the people of the world the misfortune of Douglas Manship," and concluded that, "it is difficult to believe that so ruthless, so heartless a character should occupy the high office of Governor of this state. And it is your duty to do your utmost to see that he does not much longer hold it." The House voted 58–40 to impeach Huey on the blackmail charge.

For the next two weeks the House debated and voted on the remaining six charges against Huey, which included accusations of bribery and misspending state funds. The members also filled the air with old-fashioned oratory. Leading the charge against Huey, Judge Dupre rose in a burst of antebellum eloquence. "By the graves of my ancestors, one of whom honored this state as its chief executive, by my sire who distinguished himself as a member of the Confederate Congress, by my eldest brother who gave up his life for the Lost Cause, by the grave of my only son, for the love and dignity of this great state, for the rising generation and those who are to follow us, I ask you, I beseech you, I implore you, to give [Huey Long] his just deserts and send him to the bar of the Senate which he has sought to corrupt in advance of trial, and let him defend himself there if he can do so."

J. E. McClanahan of Caldwell Parish was one of a few legislators defending Huey. "[I am] ashamed of Louisiana," cried the boisterous legislator. Quoting from an article in *The New Republic,* McClanahan argued that "when the impeachment process becomes a tool for persecution, it will have become one of the most vicious of political devices." McClanahan ended his speech emotionally. "I want to remind you of the assassination of Caesar by Brutus. Brutus said he did not love Caesar less, but loved Rome more. But after the truth had been known, you know what happened to Brutus."

On April 26 the House impeachment hearings ended. Of the original charges, seven were passed by the House and would be sent to the Senate for trial. The legislators charged Huey with attempting to blackmail Charles Manship; attempting to bribe legislators; not accounting for state money he had spent, specifically on the new automobile; illegally removing an official of the state training school; using mansion funds for personal purposes; using state money to purchase a private law library; and permitting a construction company to build defective culverts. On the final day of the proceedings, the House voted on an eighth, catchall charge accusing Huey of forcing appointees to sign undated resignations, insulting citizens, discharging a college president, appointing a corrupt parole officer, and demonstrating that he was incompetent and temperamentally unfit for his office.

The last charge passed 55–39 at three o'clock that afternoon after a bitter two-hour debate. "Why, you wouldn't convict a nigger foot chicken thief on such evidence," Speaker Fournet argued. "The purpose of this bill is that if you can't catch him on one charge you think you can, catch him on another." Before Fournet could finish, one of the Dynamite Squad, Representative Harney Bogan, rushed into the chamber with blood pouring from his mouth and a gash in his cheek. Bogan had been in the capitol lobby talking with Robert Maestri when Huey's brother Earl Long approached. "Why are you talking to that sonofabitch?" Earl asked Maestri. Bogan slugged Earl and the two men clinched and grappled on the floor, where Earl sank his teeth into Bogan's cheek and bit him on the ear. Bystanders pried them apart. "I just tore Harney to pieces," Earl bragged later.

Huey was in his hotel room when he learned of the fight. "I bet Earl bit him, didn't he? Earl always bites."

JUST AFTER NOON on April 27, 1929, the clerk of the Louisiana legislature, his arms loaded with copies of the bulky impeachment documents, walked down the winding capitol staircase to Huey Long's first-floor office and placed the pile of papers in the governor's hands. Huey had been expecting the clerk and, leaning back in his leather chair, laughed cockily. He knew that the impeachment documents contained a meticulous compilation of the eight charges against him, but he also was aware that the legalities of the proceedings now had become much less important than the politics. The Louisiana constitution was vague enough to allow almost any infraction to be grounds for impeachment. "They can impeach you because they don't like the way you part your hair," Huey noted, and a Memphis newspaper editorial agreed, surmising that "some legislator will discover that Governor Long has been guilty of the heinous offense of having at one time played the saxophone." While the House impeachment proceedings offered entertaining melodrama and humor, they now were of little consequence to Huey's future as governor. Under the state constitution, the House could only impeach, an act similar to an indictment. The Senate was where the real trial would take place, and only the Senate, by two-thirds vote, had the power to remove a governor from office. Now that the House had completed its deliberations and forwarded the charges, all eyes turned to the deliberations that would begin across the hall in the Senate chamber.

On May 14, the Senate convened to try the impeachment charges. Presiding over the trial was Chief Justice Charles O'Neill, who swore Huey in as governor almost exactly a year before. Huey and O'Neill had been bitter enemies since they fought over the Dreher-LeBoeuf murder case. Huey referred to the chief justice, who walked with a limp, as a "crooked-leg sonofabitch." When Long's supporters protested that O'Neill was prejudiced against Huey and suggested he recuse himself, the feisty O'Neill fired back, "Don't they think that I'll give the thieving sonofabitch a fair trial?"

On the first day of the Senate trial, Huey strutted into the chamber wearing his immaculate white suit, smoking another huge cigar, and took his seat at a table on the front row amid his battery of attorneys. The Senate was packed. At the rear of the chamber, carpenters built wooden bleachers to accommodate over one hundred spectators, and tickets were issued for each seat.

Huey's attorneys argued that the impeachment was illegal. They based their defense on the fact that any charge filed after April 6, the date set for adjournment of the special session, was invalid. After that date, according to his attorney Leander Perez, "the legislature would stop being a lawmaking body and become just a crowd of men." Because the Senate needed to examine and debate a number of complex charges, spectators expected the trial to be a long, dragged-out affair. They eagerly anticipated an entertaining spectacle similar to that of the House, with more scenes like Bloody Monday's fistfights, Helen Clifford's hula dance testimonial, and Earl Long trying to bite off Harney Bogan's ear. To the surprise of almost everyone, the spectacle in the Senate was a short one.

Two days after the Senate convened, at ten o'clock Thursday morning, Phillip Gilbert, president pro tempore of the Senate, rose from his seat, walked up the aisle, and, in his clipped French accent, began addressing his colleagues. The rotund little Cajun announced that he had a petition signed by a group of fellow senators who agreed that the charges against Huey should be dropped. In the petition, the senators declared that any charge filed after April 6 was invalid. The signers swore that they would not vote for Huey's impeachment, no matter what testimony followed and no matter what evidence was presented. Fifteen out of thirty-nine senators, one more than needed to kill the two-thirds vote for conviction, signed the document.

Huey had shocked his opponents again with his political skill. He had known that his only chance of survival was in the Senate, and he knew exactly how many votes he needed and which senators he could coerce to support him. While the House proceedings dominated the headlines, Huey used promises, threats, bribes, liquor, women, and any other stimulant he could devise to secure the votes of the fifteen senators, and with their signatures now in hand, he had survived his closest call with political extinction.

Gilbert's petition, thence emblazoned in Louisiana history as the notorious Round Robin, stunned the Senate, paralyzed Huey's opponents,
and elated his supporters. Quietly, the senators realized there was nothing more they could do, adjourned *sine die,* and abruptly ended the impeachment proceedings.

AFTER BARELY ESCAPING IMPEACHMENT, Huey immediately began
punishing his enemies and rewarding his friends. He ordered his local
political bosses to begin recall movements against nine legislators who
opposed him. The impeachment charges still stood in the House and his
enemies could again try to oust him during the next regular session. Before the legislature met in 1930, he needed to weed out as many enemies
as he could. The most serious recall efforts targeted George Ginsberg and
Horace Wilkinson. During a speech at Alexandria's Bolton High, Huey
attacked Ginsberg, mocking the legislator as "George J-J-Jackass Ginsberg." The next day somebody, probably Huey, ordered a bale of hay delivered to Ginsberg. Because recalls were difficult to execute, none of the
attempts to remove his enemies succeeded. When his opponents retaliated and initiated recall efforts against the Robineers and other pro-Long
legislators, Huey agreed to a truce and both sides canceled their recalls.
The truce, arranged by his millionaire friend Harvey Couch, included a
promise from Huey not to pursue the oil processing tax or increase business taxes, while the state's leading businessmen promised to use their
influence to stop any renewal of impeachment proceedings.

Nevertheless, Huey continued his reprisals, firing dozens of relatives
of anti-Long legislators who still held state jobs. He was "vindictive beyond description," remembered Ginsberg, who sat in the House for six
weeks with a gun on his hip. "Huey ruined me. I was director of Commercial Bank. His examiners closed it. Did the same to Perrault in St.
Landry." Three years later, when Ginsberg faced reelection, "Huey really
unloaded on me," and spent $25,000 to defeat him. Huey failed to recall
Senator Donald Labbe but later went to Lafayette and spoke against him
at the courthouse. He accused Labbe of accepting a new Ford from Standard Oil and, according to Maxime Roy, "killed him as dead as a door
nail." Labbe, who always opposed Huey, remembered that "you couldn't
be independent. You had to be for him or against him." Labbe realized

Huey's opposition was too strong. "I didn't run in 1932. He would have beat me."

While punishing his opponents, Huey rewarded his supporters. Each of the fifteen Senate Robineers received a lucrative reward such as a state job, a judgeship, or state contracts. He appointed Lester Hughes as a $350-per-month attorney for the Highway Commission. He gave a similar highway job to William Boone, a superstitious senator who would not sign the Round Robin as the thirteenth signer but signed as the fourteenth. "Preacher" Anderson, the senator found in an embarrassing position with a young woman, became chief enforcement officer of the Highway Commission, and Senator Thomas Wingate, a cousin of Huey's from Vernon Parish, got another highway job. Robineer T. A. McConnell became chairman of the fish and oyster division of the Conservation Commission. Huey appointed Senator Phillip Gilbert as judge in the Twenty-third District, Fred Oser as a New Orleans city judge, and Hugo Dore as a judge on the Circuit Court of Appeals. Other loyal legislators were rewarded. Fournet, besides being speaker, also became a Highway Commission attorney, and Representative J. E. McClanahan was appointed warden at the state penitentiary.

Round Robin signers who did not receive state jobs got their rewards in other ways. Senator F. E. Delahoussaye, from Iberia Parish, who carried the nickname "Barrel Head" because he demanded his payment on the barrelhead, probably received his reward in hard cash. Henry Larcade signed the Round Robin to get roads built around his Opelousas hometown. Larcade, from an area in Acadiana noted for bootlegging, supplied Huey with whiskey. "I quit doing it because Huey drank too much. Would drink heavily at night till he passed out. Half pint would put him out."

Huey's rampant awarding of state jobs to his legislator friends later backfired. In February 1930, the state Supreme Court ruled that elected officials could not legally hold state jobs, throwing sixteen of his legislators off the state rolls. Undeterred by the ruling, Huey reinstalled all of them, one by one, into less visible positions of affluence and opportunity.

HUEY CONTINUED TO SHOW a special loyalty to the senators who signed the Round Robin. When Lester Hughes's nine-year-old son died of leukemia, Huey drove from Baton Rouge to New Orleans to the Hotel Monteleone, where he stayed up all night comforting Hughes and his family. He found a Gideon Bible and read from it as the sun rose.

Later in the month after the impeachment trial had ended, Huey invited all of the Robineers to join him on a short vacation. The men piled into huge black Packards and Cadillacs and raced southwest from New Orleans along the winding clamshell road that skirted the bank of Bayou Lafourche. Several hours later the road came to an abrupt halt at the village of Golden Meadow. There, in front of Picciola's general merchandise store, they boarded a fishing boat. It was a steamy day and the sun screamed down, sweat already soaking the men's shirts. As the boat shoved off from the dock, Huey and the Robineers howled and shot pistols in the air. Many of them were already drunk. Chugging south through the bayous, the boat ended up at Grand Isle, the remote spit of land that juts out into the Gulf of Mexico, where, according to Sidney Marchand, "the mosquitoes were as big as grasshoppers." For the next few days, Huey treated the Robineers to a hunting and fishing party where everyone picked apart fresh-caught crabs boiling in huge cauldrons, soaked up his beer and whiskey, and tried to wash away the bitter taste of politics.

CHAPTER 6

1930
GREEN SILK PAJAMAS
AND A KIDNAPPING

A new intensity burned in Huey Long's piercing brown eyes. After he barely survived impeachment, he no longer seemed the same; his attitude was different. He became more grim and cynical, more secretive, and confided only to a small, tight group of trusted friends. "He didn't put his cards on the table as he used to," his sister Lottie remembered. Huey still laughed and joked, but when he made important political decisions, he was dead serious. Increasingly mistrustful, he vowed never again to underestimate his enemies. During the spring after the impeachment, he seldom appeared without several burly bodyguards, including one carrying a sawed-off shotgun in a brown paper bag. "Very effective at close range," one bodyguard snarled. "Kill a man at seventy-five yards."

Colder and more ruthless, Huey moved decisively to control every aspect of state government. "Forgetting nothing and forgiving no one," he intimidated both foes and friends by threats or reprisals that he carried out with cold-blooded aplomb. He summarily fired enemies from state jobs, made punishing thrusts at their relatives, raised their taxes, and crushed their businesses. Even distant relatives of opponents lost their jobs. "Everybody who ain't with us is against us," he forewarned. No longer content merely to win the battles with his enemies, he had to annihilate them. "I used to try to get things done by saying 'please,' " Huey said after surviving impeachment. "That didn't work and now I'm a dyna-miter. I dynamite 'em out of my path."

Now more than ever, acquiring absolute power consumed Huey. A man in a hurry, he employed almost any means to achieve his ends. "I want power so that I can do all the things I want to do," he admitted to a friend. "Give me that militia and they can have all the laws they want." Much of his power rested on patronage, the thousands of state and local government jobs controlled by a governor. He increased his control of ex-isting boards and bureaus, abolished the contrary ones and then created new ones to do his bidding, while steadily increasing the state payroll with his supporters. With the Depression putting thousands of Louisian-ans out of work, state jobs became even more precious and patronage an increasingly powerful political tool. Huey hired extra game wardens, bridge tenders, state policemen, and added thousands of jobs with his huge road building program, with every new job securing at least one new vote. By 1931, Louisiana employed over 22,000 men working on highways, more than any other state in the country.

Huey demanded that his organization be financially self-sufficient and not dependent upon contributions from traditional political factions like the New Orleans Ring or business interests like Standard Oil. He funded his political organization with money given by wealthy supporters like Robert Maestri and Abe Shushan, and from the collection of "deducts" from state workers. State employees paid 5 to 10 percent of their salaries, a total of $1 million a year, for the upkeep of his political machine. If they re-fused to pay, the "come or quit" employees lost their jobs. When the squeeze was put on them for more contributions, they uttered the expression "de ducks are flying" and shelled out for tickets to the machine-controlled base-ball park or took out another subscription to the machine-owned news-paper. Contractors doing business with the state had to kick back 20 percent of their bids. In return, they received sweetheart deals that returned huge profits. At this time, Huey revived an archaic practice of farming out state prisoners from Angola as cheap labor for private contractors. As early as April 1929, Angola prisoners worked on a rice farm near New Roads. He or-dered the prisoners back into their striped cotton convict uniforms, a prac-tice abolished years before.

Huey replaced anti-Long workers with crude and brutal finality. During the spring of 1930, he appointed Robert Maestri as chairman of the powerful Conservation Commission. However, the incumbent, Dr. Valentine Irion, refused to step down. When Huey issued an order suspending Irion, the doctor took the case to court. In November 1929, after the state Supreme Court refused to allow Dr. Irion's petition to go to the U.S. Supreme Court, Irion's employment was terminated. Learning of the court's decision, Huey mobilized eighty National Guard troopers to oust Irion at bayonet point. "If I can't get him out any other way," he declared, "I'll get a corkscrew and screw him out." Before the soldiers arrived, Irion resigned. A few hours later, one of Huey's legislators appeared at the Conservation Commission offices in New Orleans and gathered the employees about him. The message he delivered from the governor was short. "You're all fired—now!"

THE GERMAN CRUISER *Emden*, a massive white warship bristling with mighty cannon, slowly steamed up the Mississippi toward New Orleans. The Mardi Gras celebration was in full fury and the pride of the Prussian fleet arrived to visit the Crescent City as a part of the festivities. On Saturday, March 1, 1930, the *Emden* docked alongside the pier at the foot of Canal Street. The next day, the cruiser's captain, Lothar von Arnauld de la Periere, donned his full-dress uniform festooned with jangling medals and epaulettes, strapped on his gilt-handled sword, and, following accepted protocol, headed for the Roosevelt Hotel to pay his official call on the senior American dignitary, Governor Huey P. Long of Louisiana. At the hotel door, Seymour Weiss greeted Captain von Arnauld, who was accompanied by the stuffy German consul wearing a monocle, top hat, and tails. Seymour escorted the two men to the twelfth floor and into the governor's suite. The Germans were shocked when they faced Huey, dressed only in green silk pajamas, a blue and red lounging robe, and bright blue bedroom slippers. The night before obviously had been a long one, with Mardi Gras going full speed, and Huey, probably hungover, saw no need to put on special airs for the Germans. After an icy greeting, the German captain and diplomat clicked their heels, wheeled about, and quickly departed.

Seymour tried to smooth things over. After some persuasion and hot coffee, he convinced Huey that this time he had gone too far by insulting the Germans. The next morning, Seymour insisted that Huey return the German captain's call with an official visit to the cruiser. Seymour dressed him in a borrowed swallow-tailed suit with, according to Huey, "a collar so high I had to stand on a stool to spit over it." To replace his ubiquitous straw boater, Alfred Danzinger lent him a more formal gray fedora. Seymour, dressed in the uniform of a Louisiana National Guard colonel, escorted Huey to the cruiser and they arrived uncharacteristically on time. The visit to the *Emden* appeared successful, as Captain von Arnauld seemed satisfied and told reporters that he found the governor to be "a very intelligent, interesting, and unusual person." While Huey likely redeemed himself with the German captain, his disdain for protocol persisted. Three months later, on June 5, he received Major General Frank McCoy, commander of the U.S. Fourth Army, clad only in his underwear. A few weeks later, while campaigning across southern Louisiana, Huey had his French audience chuckling when he told them that his bad behavior would continue. "I have too much Cajun blood in me to be dignified."

ON A COOL MORNING in late October 1929, Huey strode briskly through the lobby of the Roosevelt Hotel after finishing his breakfast in the coffee shop and ran into Rudolph Hecht, president of Hibernia Bank. A pillar of the New Orleans community, Hecht was one of the few businessmen friendly with Huey.

"Governor, hell's broke loose," the banker said. "The biggest crash of everything that you have ever seen. It is going to be sixty days before this country will get back to normal." Hecht was alarmed, but he underestimated the seriousness of the stock market crash that had just occurred, when sixteen million shares were sold at plummeting prices.

Precipitated by hectic stock speculation, lowered foreign trade, and overproduction of farm products, the Great Depression had begun. The stock market crash ushered in staggering levels of unemployment, failing businesses and banks, drastically lower agricultural prices, and, for the next decade, economic disaster. At first, Louisiana appeared little affected, as the state had suffered for decades from its own form of chronic economic depression. Hopeless poverty always had overshadowed the state's pastoral beauty. By early 1930, however, even Louisiana began to feel the effects of the national crisis. Manufacturing in New Orleans declined by 50 percent, while the state's small farmers and small-town merchants suffered terribly. Over the next three years, Louisiana's annual per capita income declined from $415 to $222 and farm income fell from $170 million to $59 million.

Louisiana's banks were especially vulnerable to the failing agricultural economy. During the early months of the Depression, Huey learned that a run had begun on the Bank of Lafayette and Trust Company, an important bank in the southwestern Louisiana sugar belt. Huey drove from Baton Rouge to New Orleans, where he met with the bank president in the Roosevelt Hotel. "Governor," the banker pleaded, "I've never been for you politically, but if you'll help save this bank I'll be for you for life." Picking up the telephone, Huey called officials of the Federal Reserve Bank in New Orleans and delayed some of the fund clearances levied on the Lafayette bank. This bought some time but the bank was still in danger.

Late that night Huey and Seymour Weiss drove to Lafayette and arrived at the bank the next morning just before its scheduled opening. Already a line of depositors waited at the door to withdraw their funds. Relaxing in the bank president's chair, his feet propped up on the desk, Huey called in the first person who came to withdraw his funds. The customer, a local lumberman holding a check to withdraw $18,000, was surprised to come face-to-face with the governor. "The state of Louisiana has $265,000 in this bank, and here's the state's check for it," Huey told the customer. "There ain't but about that much cash in the bank, and I was here before you were. You insist on drawing out your $18,000, and I'll insist on drawing out the state's $265,000—and I get first draw, so there'll be nothing left to pay you. You agree to leave yours in, and I'll leave the state's money in, and nobody'll be hurt. I'm staying right here till closing time at noon, in case anybody else wants to draw out." The customer and those in line behind him had little choice but to leave their funds in the bank and depart. By the end of the day, Huey's brilliantly simple action gave the bank enough time to secure more loans and stave off the run.

ON ALMOST ANY NIGHT that he stayed in New Orleans, Huey Long held court in the Blue Room nightclub of the Roosevelt Hotel. Blanketed in a painted ceiling of blue with a splattering of glittering stars, the Blue

Room was the place to be. Top names like Phil Harris and Sophie Tucker performed there live and broadcast their entertainment out to millions of listeners on WWL, the powerful New Orleans radio station that located its studio in the hotel. Often standing at the bar near the stage, Huey swayed back and forth to the beat of the music, his eyes dreamily closed, and for a few brief moments he drifted away from the hectic world of Louisiana politics.

Huey was at home in the Roosevelt. To him, the plush hotel symbolized power and money, the place in New Orleans where politicians, gamblers, and movie stars hung out to be seen by newshawks bustling in and out of the spacious lobby. Opulent and expensive, the Roosevelt flaunted walls covered with French, African, and Italian marble, ornate cornices adorning thirty-foot-high ceilings, and massive columns of gilt and gold. During the afternoon, the hotel's well-dressed patrons enjoyed bridge tournaments in the palmed foyer, shopped in the hat shop, got doted on in the beauty parlor and the exotic Turkish bath, and dined on spicy Creole cuisine in one of three excellent restaurants. Although the Roosevelt had no air-conditioning, it advertised that its Fountain Grill was cooled by "refrigerated air."

Huey's uptown enemies, however, seldom met in the Roosevelt. Instead they preferred the quiet elegance of the St. Charles Hotel, where on weekends they could listen to a four-piece combo, the Rhythm Aires, play the best music in New Orleans. Located on the streetcar line that rattled along the city's most picturesque, oak-shaded avenue, the hotel was a hotbed of anti-Long forces. On June 18, 1930, three hundred of his enemies defied the sweltering heat and met in the St. Charles to devise a strategy to unseat him. Mostly politicians, business leaders, and corporation lawyers, they formed the Constitutional League of Louisiana, devoted to preventing "Governor Huey P. Long from treating the organic law of the state as a scrap of paper." The first announcement of the league accused Huey of demoralizing the state government bureaucracy with "the mirth and abandon of a king's jester." At the first meeting in the St. Charles, the league named former governor Parker as its president.

Wealthy cotton planter, former friend of Theodore Roosevelt, and "quintessential southern progressive," John M. Parker remained a popular figure in Louisiana and national political circles. Like Huey, Parker hated the New Orleans Ring and spent most of his political career fighting it. In 1920, Huey campaigned energetically for Parker for governor and helped him carry the north Louisiana district by only 761 votes. Despite his progressive reputation, Parker turned out to be as conservative as his predecessors and accomplished little to improve the backward conditions plaguing Louisiana. Huey and Parker soon broke when Huey, then chairman of the Public Service Commission, demanded that Governor Parker declare oil pipelines as public utilities and falling within the rate controls of Huey's commission. Parker, yielding to oil industry pressure, quashed Huey's suggestion, and the two men became bitter enemies. In 1921 Parker failed in an attempt to have Huey impeached from the commission.

In the first fifteen minutes of the meeting at the St. Charles, Parker and the Constitutional League collected over $100,000 in contributions to fight Huey. They planned to use the money to finance campaigns of anti-Long legislators and to buy radio time calling for the governor's ouster. Soon after, the league published a list of Huey's twenty-three relatives on the state payroll and revealed that his cousin Otho Long had a state contract to supply the tires for all of the Highway Commission's cars and trucks. The league filed a lawsuit objecting to Huey giving state jobs to friendly legislators. Seemingly amused by the assaults, Huey dubbed the league the "League of Notions" and the "Constipational League." After Parker attacked him in a radio speech, Huey labeled the former governor as "old sack of bones Parker in the radio croak hour."

On a Wednesday night in the middle of June, the league held a mass meeting in Baton Rouge at the Community Club pavilion. Parker and the new mayor of New Orleans, Semmes Walmsley, led the speakers. Walmsley called Huey a "self seeking demagogue, a despot, a tyrant, usurper, madman, a man who is reckless and ruthless, black-jacking and blackmailing individuals and communities, a cur who is too low to face his accusers." Six thousand attended the rally, carried statewide on the radio. Huey, not to be outdone, held a counter-rally that began a half hour earlier at the old LSU campus on Third Street. "There is not a thief or safeblower at Angola penitentiary who can hold a candle to Mayor T. Semmes Walmsley," shouted Huey. Throughout the night, fistfights broke out along the city streets as drunken Long supporters collided with drunken anti-Longs.

Besides the League, Louisiana's daily newspapers relentlessly attacked Huey. The *Hammond Daily Courier,* for example, published bitterly satirical editorials that referred to him as "Screwy P. Swong," and the *Baton Rouge State-Times* called him "a little sniveling demagogue from Winn." Huey fumed when the *New Orleans Times-Picayune* attacked him for putting pro-Long legislators on the state payroll and drawing double salaries. Huey responded with another surprise move. He created his own newspaper.

STARTING A NEWSPAPER was not a new idea for Huey. In September 1917, while still a struggling young attorney, he investigated launching a newspaper in Winnfield. He contacted a printer to see what a four-page, seven-column weekly paper would cost but soon dropped the idea. As governor, Huey finally realized his ambition on March 26, 1930, when he published his first issue of *Louisiana Progress.* The newspaper was an overnight success. He had no difficulty getting readership or financing, for he required all of his state workers to contribute part of their salary for a subscription. Money from the "deducts" also helped support the *Progress,* and Huey assigned female state workers from the Levee Board, Dock Board, and Board of Health to work on the paper. Pa-Poose Root Beer and the Winnfield Rock Quarry, owned by Huey, O. K. Allen, and millionaire friend Harvey Couch, were among the businesses that bought ads.

Huey hired John Klorer, the tall balding night editor of the *Times-Picayune,* to manage his new newspaper. The *Progress* claimed a circulation of 125,000 weekly, including 30,000 copies sold in New Orleans. The first issue announced that Louisiana would prosper only if the state "buries the fossils, runs out grafters, runs over obstructionists, exposes liars, keeps its ears and eyes open, its tongue ready with opinion, its hands ready with the ballot." The front page displayed a large cartoon of Huey handing free schoolbooks to children.

Huey described his newspaper as "a weekly newspaper which proposes to cover truth and the full truth about Louisiana affairs, its public business, its public officials, etc." He used the *Progress* as his personal soapbox to attack the state's large dailies. "If the daily papers had their way there wouldn't be any free school books, paved roads or night classes for illiterates in Louisiana," an early *Progress* editorial spouted. "These daily newspapers have been against every progressive step in this state and the only way for the people of Louisiana to get ahead is stomp them flat." In yet another assault, Huey asked, "How long does it take you to read a New Orleans newspaper? Fifteen minutes by the clock, unless you read all the ads, then it takes you an hour. It is a well-established newspaper precedent that a daily should contain twice as much reading matter than it does advertising. New Orleans' papers have twice as much advertising as they have reading matter. . . . The only reason you read them is because you don't want to miss what they are saying about me."

The tabloid rhetoric of the *Progress* ushered in new levels of pugnacity to Louisiana journalism. The paper charged the New Orleans Ring with reopening the city to prostitution, with a banner headline blaring, "Red Lights Blaze as Vice Dens Pay $75,000 Monthly." The paper also accused the Choctaws of politicizing Tulane and turning the university into a "swill trough." Mayor Walmsley replied that Huey's assaults on the city government and Tulane were the "utterances of an insane man." The *Progress* blasted the "four oracles of New Orleans—the pompous *Times-Picayune*, the slip-shod *States*, the smart-aleck *Item* and the baby-faced *Tribune*. . . . They don't know what the truth is . . . double-crossing polecats . . . guzzling like bleary eyed hogs from a trough filled with malice, lies, and hypocrisy."

After the *Times-Picayune* lacerated Huey for rewarding pro-Long legislators with state jobs and drawing double salaries, he retaliated in the *Progress* by denouncing Arthur Hammond, the brother of the *Times-Picayune*'s Esmond Phelps, for serving as an attorney for both the state Dock Board and the Levee Board at a salary of over $700 a month. Hammond, the *Progress* charged, had been "luxuriously reclining, fed with the amber ladle of the levee board and at the same time sitting at the pie counter of the port." Huey promptly fired Hammond from both positions. A few days later, the *Progress* charged that the "the swindling newspapers" of New Orleans were bought off by advertising money from the big interests. "Those papers don't care what happens to the city," the

Progress wailed. "They're out for what they can get. It's like a burglar who knows how to blow a safe but couldn't open one with the combination."

Huey's *Progress* personally attacked the editors of the large dailies. On May 8, 1930, the *Progress* targeted *New Orleans Item* editor Marshall Ballard. Nicknamed "Lie-to-'em" Ballard by Huey, the editor had published caustic editorials censuring Huey. Huey dug deep to slander Ballard. In 1924, the wife of *Item* publisher James Thomson ran for Congress and Ballard supported her candidacy with his editorials. Colonel Ewing supported her opponent and as the contest got nasty, Ewing published a cartoon in his *States* showing Ballard as a narcotics addict. Huey's *Progress* now depicted *Item* characters with grotesque hypodermic needles protruding from their bodies and announced that Ballard is "full of hop."

Huey was not content with blasting the large daily newspapers with mere words. He vowed to put them out of business. During the regular legislative session in the summer of 1930, he proposed a 15 percent tax on all gross revenues received by Louisiana newspapers from advertising sales. Another bill allowed the state to use a court injunction to halt the printing of any newspaper that was "obscene, lewd, or lascivious" or was "malicious, scandalous, or defamatory." The outraged publishers of the dailies fought back and denounced Huey's proposed legislation as "an opinion-smothering gag law" and a "padlock" on the freedom of the press.

On June 21, 1930, forty-six newspapermen from across the state met in Baton Rouge to develop a strategy to fight his anti-newspaper bills. Charles Manship, the publisher of the Baton Rouge newspapers and Huey's archenemy, convened the meeting. The publishers put heavy pressure on the legislature and their efforts paid off. On June 26, the Ways and Means Committee of the House voted against the newspaper advertising tax, despite Huey's last-minute attempt to salvage the measure by lowering the tax rate from 15 to 5 percent. The newspaper gag injunction bill also died a quiet death in the Senate Judiciary Committee. A year later, the U.S. Supreme Court ruled in a five-to-four decision that a Minnesota gag injunction law, similar to Huey's, was unconstitutional.

AS THE SUMMER HEAT descended in a steamy, suffocating haze upon Baton Rouge, Huey Long arrived in the capital city for another regular legislative session. Seeing the governor barrel into town in his limousine, local citizens braced themselves for more legislative fireworks. Bloody Monday was still fresh in their minds as they watched the legislators step from the trains arriving at the depot just below the bluff where the state capitol sat. On May 11, 1930, the legislature convened and the session began almost as unruly as the 1929 special session. Tempers from the last session still flared as representatives argued in every corner of the capitol and an occasional fistfight erupted. Huey ordered several hundred of his state workers, the "payroll" they were called, to descend upon the capitol and act as his own personal lobbyist army. Loud and combative, they disrupted an already unruly legislature and added hostility to the atmosphere. Even committee hearings were quarrelsome. When Huey showed up at a Senate Penitentiary Committee meeting early in the session, the committee members ordered him to leave. "Huey Long, self-appointed emperor of Louisiana, trying to emulate the caesars, came to the Senate penitentiary committee yesterday," the *Shreveport Journal* reported. "He came and he saw but he failed to conquer."

Huey's enemies had lost the impeachment battle but they had not given up and looked for other ways to defeat him. To get at Huey, they lashed out at John Fournet and began a movement to unseat "the Governor's creature in the Speaker's chair." Ex-governors Parker and Sanders and other Constitutional Leaguers arrived in town to lead the fight against the speaker. When anti-Long representative Joe Hamiter made a motion to remove Fournet, Huey rushed about the capitol corridors, grabbing legislators and threatening them if they did not support the speaker. The House voted 55–44 to retain Fournet. Huey won the battle but was angered by the attempted attack on one of his lieutenants. He retaliated by removing opponents from all committee chairs, including Judge Dupre as chair of the powerful Judiciary Committee, a seat he had occupied for years. Huey ordered the pesky old Creole banished from any leadership job. He replaced the judge with Allen Ellender, a short-statured representative from Terrebonne Parish and a staunch supporter. The removal of Dupre outraged many of the House members, who passed a resolution condemning the governor's interference. A couple of days later, the crusty old Dupre, who delighted in describing Huey's harangues as "heifer manure," resigned all of his committee assignments in protest and accused Huey of having a "malformed or diseased mind." The *Progress* announced that Dupre was acting like a "blubbering two-year-old."

Huey worked hard to strengthen his support in the Senate. He pressured senators to elect a pro-Long member, Alvin O. King of Lake Charles, as president pro tempore to replace Phillip Gilbert, who had been appointed to the bench. Huey's strong-arm tactics worked, as seven senators who voted for his impeachment now joined him. These included J. O. Fernandez, an Old Regular from New Orleans who testified during the impeachment trial that Huey tried to bribe him. Known as "Bathtub Joe" because he got rid of unwelcome callers with the excuse he was taking a bath, Fernandez sensed Huey's resurgence and switched allegiance. Fernandez planned to run for U.S. Congress in the next election and negotiated a deal with Huey. Huey also increased his support in the House, where he convinced fourteen representatives who voted for impeachment to switch to his side.

Huey was confident he could recapture much of the control he possessed before Bloody Monday. While his earlier effort to recall anti-Long legislators collapsed, his subsequent campaign to win local elections succeeded and his candidates won twenty-one seats in the lower house in the 1930 election. Huey now could count on a majority of the House to support his less controversial bills, but he still lacked the two-thirds majority necessary to pass constitutional amendments and bond issues. He would need two-thirds to finish building his roads.

HUEY LOVED TO STOP his car and watch the road graders and cement mixers grinding away, smell the fresh-laid asphalt, and admire the brand-new highways stretching in a straight line off in the distance. Back at his desk in the state capitol, he kept a running tally of the highway mileage added each month. To him, modern roads were much more important than merely a means of transportation. They provided symbols of his success as governor. Roads were tangible, something he could see and feel. He liked to get out on the fresh-paved roads and experience the progress firsthand. Speed limits never deterred the hot-footed Huey, and the smoother the pavement covering his new highways, the faster he could race across the state in his huge blue Cadillac limousine.

When Huey took office in 1928, Louisiana funded its pitiful road system with a 2-cent gasoline tax, road district property taxes, and a few thousand dollars of federal aid. At that time, the state had just over 300 miles of paved highways and 5,728 miles of gravel "gumbo" roads. Most were in terrible condition. "The trip on the river road from New Orleans to Baton Rouge took four or five hours," a journalist remembered, "and you usually had four or five punctures on the way." In 1928, Huey had funded his $30 million road building program by selling bonds secured by a small increase in the gasoline tax. Now, two years later, he proposed to spend $68 million to complete a modern highway system. His long-term goal was for the state to possess 2,500 miles of concrete roads, 1,300 miles of asphalt, and 9,600 miles of gravel under state maintenance. Before the regular session convened in 1930, he toured the state and inspected the first set of roads completed. The concrete highways built with the 1928 bonds resembled a spiderweb, running a few miles out from parish seats and then ending abruptly in a pre-Long gravel road. Huey designed the incomplete highway pattern to whet the appetite of the voters for good roads in their parishes. "We had started on the road system by scattering the work through the parishes, putting five, ten or fifteen miles to the parish," Huey wrote. "When the people once knew the pleasure of traveling over paved highways their support for a program to connect up the links was certain. Our enemies were quick to see the plan and attacked us bitterly for it. We persisted in our plan. None ever worked better." Huey knew the political value of roads, especially with isolated truck farmers and sharecroppers who lived far from railroad lines and needed the roads to deliver their goods to market.

Huey appointed his friend O. K. Allen as head of the Highway Commission and ensured that contracts went only to his loyal followers. Pro-Long legislator and shrimpmonger Joe Fisher sold more than fifty thousand cubic yards of clamshells to the Highway Commission at a rate double the market value. Even more blatantly, Huey, O.K., Seymour Weiss, and Harvey Couch took over a failing Winnfield gravel business and created the Louisiana Quarry Company. They charged the Highway Commission $1.65 for soft, substandard crushed rock while better quality rock was available for $.63. According to Huey's brother Julius, they even padded the bill by watering the rock to increase its weight. Because Huey wanted to increase the mileage constructed, the highways were never more than eighteen feet wide, although twenty-two feet was the safe minimum. Highway engineers provided no drainage, laid no foundations, and poured slabs directly on the ground, allowing erosion to soon wash the roads away. Little money went to maintenance, and future governors would inherit the problem of repairing the poor roads. Nevertheless, his paved roads were better than none at all and enormously popular. Huey was not concerned that the quality of his new roads was poor, the price inflated, and the program riddled with corruption. He ignored accusations of graft in the Highway Department. "We got the roads in Louisiana, haven't we?" he snapped back at a reporter. "In some states they only have the graft."

To fund the completion of the roads, Huey was forced to issue state bonds to satisfy the Louisiana constitution, one of the longest and most unmanageable in the nation, which required that a pay-as-you-go taxation scheme finance road construction. The $68 million highway plan funded by new bonds required the people to approve a constitutional amendment to allow the state to go deeper into debt. Huey knew the voters would support him. But first, two-thirds of both houses of the legislature was needed before the amendment could go to the people. On June 17, 1930, Huey's paved roads constitutional amendment fell seven votes short of the two-thirds majority in the House. Initially Huey counted on the New Orleans delegation to support his road bill. However, Mayor Semmes Walmsley opposed Huey. Walmsley, who five months earlier defeated Francis Williams by fewer than ten thousand votes, met with the Choctaw leaders and they agreed to oppose all of Huey's bond proposals. They sent orders to the New Orleans delegation to abandon the governor and to vote against his road bill. Without the New Orleans votes, it was impossible for Huey to muster two-thirds. He retaliated by attempting to cut off New Orleans's ability to borrow money or collect taxes.

Failing to get the two-thirds vote, Huey countered by proposing a convention to change the state constitution and allow him to borrow money for his roads. Ironically, he needed only a legislative majority to call a constitutional convention. He planned for the convention to convene on January 12, 1931. Huey's opponents immediately attacked his proposal. "God forbid," declared the *Shreveport Times*, "that this mad scheme of the demonical despot who held the state up to the ridicule of the nation and scared away investment capital, be put over." His enemies feared that he would use the convention not only to give him the power to borrow more funds, but also to remove the constitutional prohibition against a governor serving two consecutive terms. If so, he could run for reelection and perpetuate himself in office.

On June 25, the House approved Huey's proposal for a constitutional convention by fourteen votes. The Senate refused to go along, however. A few anti-Long senators, knowing that Huey probably had a majority, began a filibuster. His perennial enemy Lieutenant Governor Cyr presided over the Senate and refused to recognize anyone except anti-Long legislators. When the legislature adjourned by law on July 10, sixty days after convening, Huey's constitutional convention and his plan to complete the roads had died.

YEARS BEFORE, WHEN Mark Twain first steamed past Baton Rouge on a paddle wheeler and spied the whitewashed Louisiana state capitol perched above the Mississippi River, he took an instant dislike to the Gothic-and-gingerbread edifice. He imagined that the turreted eyesore came from reading too much Sir Walter Scott. Built in 1847 and rebuilt after Union soldiers set it ablaze, the four-story "eclectic hodge-podge of Norman and Moorish architecture" had other detractors besides Mark Twain. Huey Long was among them, decrying the state capitol as a dowdy old antique ready for demolition. To him, the old capitol was a reminder of hundreds of years of conservative politics, aristocratic rule, and a state mired in hidebound tradition. More to the point, it had provided the stage for his impeachment trial and he wished to erase it from sight and memory.

Besides his road building program, Huey's other main goal during the 1930 regular session was to build a modern state capitol. He asked the legislature for $5 million to build one, and for several days the members of the House hotly debated the proposal. The opponents of a new capitol argued that it was too costly. Mason Spencer, the huge anti-Long legislator who calmed the House with his bellowing voice on Bloody Monday, rose on the floor to argue against the new capitol. Spencer, whom Huey called "pot-gut Spencer, Louisiana's laziest white man," broke the tension in the chamber when he proposed legislation ordering state workers to collect all of the driftwood floating down the Mississippi River and sell it for extra money. Spencer's prank bill passed. Afterward, a reporter asked Huey what he would do with the old capitol once a new one was built. "Turn it over to some collector of antiques," he fired back.

Huey was sure he had two-thirds of the votes in the House to build the new capitol but when the vote was taken, the lights on the board showed that he was several legislators short. He ordered Fournet not to announce the vote. After asking several of his supporters why they voted against his bill, Huey learned that his brother Earl had fought the new capitol behind the scenes. Criticizing the proposed capitol as a "monument for someone's vanity," Earl suggested to House members that the governor actually opposed the capitol. Outraged at his brother, Huey forced all of his loyal representatives to vote for the new capitol and soon had the two-thirds he needed to pass the bill.

Although Huey had enough votes in the Senate for his new capitol, the filibuster still raged there over his proposed constitutional convention. The filibuster lasted until the end of the session when the legislature adjourned on July 10. All of his major bills died, including his call for a constitutional convention, funding for his road building program, and the new state capitol. Later that summer, Huey was his most vengeful as he vetoed dozens of bills passed by his opponents. He slashed $6,400 from Lieutenant Governor Cyr's funds and $29,980 from Attorney General Percy Saint, another of his bitter enemies. He again vetoed funding for the Public Service Commission to punish Dudley LeBlanc and Francis Williams. About this time Huey charged that Williams employed his father, cousins, and uncles on the Public Service Commission, and Williams retaliated by publishing a list of dozens of Huey's relatives who were on the state payroll. A few weeks later, as Huey walked through Union Station in New Orleans, he ran into L. F. Sherer, a staff member of the now fundless Public Service Commission who knew the governor well. As Huey passed by, Sherer held out his hat, closed his eyes, and pretended to be a blind beggar. Without breaking his stride or saying a word, Huey flipped a shiny new dime into Sherer's hat.

ON JULY 16, 1930, Highway Department trucks and state police cruisers carted the latest edition of Huey Long's *Louisiana Progress* across the state.

When the paper arrived on doorsteps that morning, the huge banner headline across the paper shocked many of its readers. Huey was running for United States senator. His announcement puzzled many Louisianans, since he still had two years left as governor and had pledged during his inauguration to serve "without ambition for ever again holding another public office." More recently he denied "all ambitions to sit in the national legislative halls at Washington." Now Huey explained that he was running for the Senate to use the campaign as a referendum for his bond issues for roads and a new state capitol. Because the legislature denied the people the chance to vote on his plans, he decided to bypass the legislature, go directly to the people, and use the Senate campaign to allow them to show their support of his programs. If he lost, Huey promised, he would resign as governor.

By jumping into "the fight for Huey Long's political life," he took a calculated risk. "Huey Long has piled all his chips on the table to bet on one throw of the dice," one anti-Long newspaper observed. "Win this time and we are through with him." Huey knew that if he lost the race, his political career was probably finished. But his political ambition had begun to expand beyond Louisiana and he judged that the timing was right to run for the Senate. He could not run for governor again and his opponent in the Senate race, the incumbent Joseph Ransdell, was old and vulnerable. Huey did not wish to wait until he finished his term as governor in 1932 and run against the other more formidable senator, Edwin Broussard.

Huey announced that, if elected senator, he would remain as governor until he completed his term. Ransdell's term would expire in March 1931 and Huey's would end in May 1932. During that fourteen-month period, the Senate slot would remain vacant although, as Huey pointed out, the Senate would be in session for only four of those months. He added that there was precedent for holding two offices, as other governors in recent years, including David Hill of New York, Robert LaFollette of Wisconsin, and Hiram Johnson of California, waited until their gubernatorial terms expired before taking their seats in the Senate. When newspapers criticized Huey for planning to leave the Senate position vacant until he finished his term, he attacked the incumbent. "I will have to stay out of the Senate four months," he contended, "leaving the place just as vacant for that four months as it has been for the last thirty-two years." He added that he would not collect his Senate salary until after arriving in Washington. This would prevent him from violating a provision of the Louisiana constitution that prohibited a person from holding both federal and state offices simultaneously. Huey assured his supporters that he would not leave them to be destroyed by the lieutenant governor and that "Cyr will never be governor of this state for one minute."

Huey's opponent, Senator Joseph Ransdell, was a seventy-two-year-old slow-witted attorney from East Carroll Parish. Tall and thin, his gaunt face adorned with a white goatee reminiscent of the Civil War era, Ransdell was a relic of past politics. He had been in Washington for thirty-two years, serving as a congressman since 1899 and senator since 1912. Ransdell was backed by the New Orleans Ring and the anti-Long Constitutional League. At a New Orleans banquet for flood control congressmen on July 14, Huey introduced Ransdell as "one of my oldest and dearest friends." Huey's earlier promise to refrain from personal attacks on his opponent did not last long. Soon after his announcement to run, Huey, who was four years old when Ransdell was first elected to Congress, charged that the old senator was senile and too old to purchase life insurance. He began poking fun of Ransdell's goatee by branding the gruff politician as "Old Feather Duster" and "Old Trashy Mouth."

Huey's run for the Senate ignited a firestorm. All eighteen of Louisiana's daily newspapers, not surprisingly, supported Ransdell and berated Huey. "You are being asked to help send to the United States Senate a man without a scintilla of respect for worthy womanhood," the *Shreveport Times* declared, calling Huey a "reprobate of the first water, a man possessing neither culture nor refinement, a man whose every public or private act is offensive to good taste—a blasphemer, a ruffian and a cad." Colonel Ewing's *New Orleans States,* which supported Huey in 1928, now opposed his race for Senate. "[Huey Long] is the liar, crook, petty larceny thief and scoundrel," the *States* reported, "who is now Governor of Louisiana and seeks to perpetuate his evil power by not only controlling the governorship but by representing this great state in the United States Senate, which would be a disgrace and dishonor." The *Shreveport Journal* claimed that Huey treated the state constitution as "merely a scrap of paper," and that "the people, like a bunch of dumb, driven sheep, stand for it."

Huey mobilized an efficient and well-financed campaign. To fight the New Orleans Ring, he formed his own political organization, the Louisiana Democratic Association, and named Dr. Joseph O'Hara, head of the state Board of Health, as president, and his benefactor Bob Maestri, now conservation commissioner, as its New Orleans leader. He bought two new shiny green sound trucks at $30,000 each to canvass the state and ordered convicts at the state penitentiary to paint his campaign signs. By now, Huey was expert at canvassing the state. With an almost mystical memory for detail, he knew the parishes better than any of his local workers and could recall an incredible number of citizens by name and how they stood and precisely how many voters turned out for him in each precinct in the last election. Huey stayed "three or four curves ahead of you," a supporter remembered.

With plenty of campaign funds, Huey flooded the state with over two million copies of vicious broadside circulars attacking Ransdell. One of the circulars, titled "Landmarks of Senator Ransdell's Progress," declared that in the thirty-two years Ransdell had been in Washington, he had been responsible for numerous "improvements" in New Orleans, including losing the U.S. Mint, losing the Federal Reserve Bank, closing down the United States Navy Yards, abandoning the United States Army military post at Jackson Barracks, and losing a station on the Transcontinental Air Mail Route. "We have not yet lost the Post Office," Huey's circular concluded.

Just before noon on Saturday, August 2, 1930, Huey began his speech making in the easygoing Cajun town of St. Martinville with a loud parade. One of his sound trucks blared Rudy Vallee's "The Maine Stein Song" from huge loudspeakers on the truck's cab. Standing under the legendary Evangeline Oak next to the Bayou Teche, he launched a two-pronged attack that he repeated throughout the campaign. He assailed the legislature for failing to pass his road bonds. "If the good roads plan were passed, work and employment could be had for thousands of our idle laborers," Huey said, "and good roads could be had for everybody and no one would be charged a dime for it." His other target was his old enemy, the New Orleans Ring, "that gang of ballot-box stuffers who have been voting the St. Louis Cemetery Number One and St. Louis Cemetery Number Two for the past thirty-five years." Soaked with perspiration from the summer heat, he asked his audience, "Are the New Orleans Ring politicians and their lying newspapers going to run the state, or will the people be allowed to vote on the matters which affect their welfare?"

Huey beamed with confidence, knowing that his popularity was high outside the cities and a landslide victory would increase his power over any recalcitrant rural legislators. During a speech in south Louisiana, he appeared unconcerned over his own Senate race. Standing on a stage with his candidate for Congress, Numa Montet, Huey told his audience, "If you don't think you can vote for both of us, vote for Montet. He needs your vote more than I do." Huey was always able to think on his feet. While he was speaking later on the courthouse steps in Jennings, a train passed by and for a few moments its whistle drowned him out. When it stopped, he grabbed the opportunity and yelled, "Is that what you want, for the big businesses to use a train to shut me up?"

As always, Huey drew large crowds. In a campaign stop in the town of Plain Dealing in Bossier Parish, he arrived early, just as the sun was rising. The town had a population of twelve hundred and, according to one spectator, one thousand of them showed up for the dawn rally. Standing in the old cotton market in the center of town, he stared out over the crowd. Holding a Bible in his hand, he waited for a couple of minutes and finally raised his hand. "Is there a single person in this audience who can tell me the name of my opponent?" he asked. "I'll tell you. It's Old Feather Duster Ransdell. When I get to Washington you'll always know the name of your U.S. Senator."

As the summer wore on, the campaign became, according to the *New York Times*, "as amusing as it was depressing" and soon deteriorated into one of the nastiest that Louisiana had seen. In August, Huey's opponents accused his campaign workers of purging the voter lists of Ransdell supporters in St. Bernard Parish. In its many outrageous cartoons, the *Louisiana Progress* pictured Ransdell as a cadaverous bungler asleep at the switch, as a charter member of the "old gang" of sapsuckers who milked the state and gave nothing in return, and as a groveling tool of the bloated Ring. When Ransdell campaigned in Opelousas he shared the platform with Huey's nemesis, feisty old Judge Dupre. Breathing fire, Dupre called Huey "a stench in the nostrils" of the people of Louisiana, "a liar, a briber, an embezzler of the people's money," and a "sinuous and slimy person." In August, Mrs. Ruffin Pleasant, the wife of the ex-governor, smeared Huey in a Shreveport newspaper. Huey was "common beyond words," she railed. "He has not only common ways, but a common, sordid, dirty soul." She described Huey as possessing the qualities of lower animals, "the greed and coarseness of the swine, the cunning of the fox, the venom of the snake, the cruel cowardice of the skulking hyena."

Near the end of the campaign, a rally for Huey in New Orleans threatened to clog the city's streets. When he sent his state police to direct traffic, anti-Long New Orleans police officers raced into the area and soon the air was thick with fists, clubs, jackboots, and blackjacks, as blue-shirted city police and gray-clad state troopers slugged it out. When the New Orleans police jailed a state police sergeant, Huey vowed to march on the city jail and free his trooper.

Using no notes, Huey gave one of his more energetic speeches in Shreveport, standing on the courthouse steps in front of the Confederate statue. "If you believe that Louisiana is to be ruled by the people, that the poor man is as good as the rich man, that the people have the right to pass on issues themselves, if you believe that this is a state where every man is a king but no man wears a crown, then I want you to vote for Huey Long for the United States Senate." According to a reporter at the scene, Huey not only gave a masterful performance but did so while being dead drunk.

SIX DAYS BEFORE the Senate election, in the middle of the night on Thursday, September 3, 1930, six armed men barged into a room of Shreveport's Gardner Hotel and kidnapped two men sleeping there. The armed men belonged to the Louisiana Bureau of Criminal Identification, Huey's personal police force. One of the BCI officers was David McConnell, Huey's brother-in-law, and another was Huey's cousin Wade Long. The kidnapped men were Sam Irby, an uncle of Huey's secretary, Alice Lee Grosjean, and James Terrell, Alice Lee's ex-husband. Both Irby and Terrell had inside knowledge of Huey's political and private affairs and if persuaded to talk, could reveal embarrassing details that could damage his upcoming election for senator. Huey was not going to let that happen.

The kidnapping episode began the day before when the anti-Long attorney general, Percy Saint, started an investigation into corruption within the state Highway Commission, an agency known for widespread graft and kickbacks. The investigation was an attempt to slander the governor just before the Senate election. Saint announced that his key witness would be Sam Irby, who had worked for the Highway Department before becoming business manager of Huey's *Louisiana Progress*. After Huey fired him, Irby threatened to get even. Knowing that he had become Huey's marked man, Irby flew from New Orleans to Shreveport to hide out in a hotel under an assumed name. Later that day, James Terrell joined him and that night the BCI men barged in.

Irby and Terrell disappeared, and for the next couple of days rumors flew concerning their whereabouts. Some reports suggested they were being held at Angola penitentiary, but according to Huey's radio speech on September 5, they were locked in the Jefferson Parish jail. Many believed their bodies lay on the muddy bottom of a remote Louisiana bayou. The kidnapping, according to an angry Mayor Walmsley, was "the most heinous public crime in Louisiana history." Irby's lawyer, Senator Pike Hall, filed a habeas corpus motion against the governor on the following day. Federal agents began to investigate the disappearance and a U.S. marshal delivered a subpoena ordering Huey to appear before the federal district judge to explain the disappearance of the men. As the marshal entered Huey's twelfth floor suite in the Roosevelt Hotel, William Wiegand, a reporter for the *New Orleans Item*, pretended to be with the marshal and followed the officer into the room. When Huey recognized Wiegand, he called the reporter a sonofabitch and the two men immediately started punching each other. Huey's bodyguards grabbed Wiegand but he broke away and landed one last punch. According to witnesses, the younger Wiegand "knocked Huey groggy with a magnificent right to the chin." The following day, Huey complied with the court order and appeared in a New Orleans federal court to explain the situation, but offered little to clear up the mystery and denied knowing the whereabouts of the two missing men. He lied.

What Huey did not reveal was that earlier, after the three BCI officers kidnapped Irby and Terrell, he and his cronies met in a hotel room to decide what to do with them. His impetuous brother Earl offered an immediate solution: "Let's take the son of a bitch [Irby] and kill him." Huey wheeled around and kicked his brother. "Get out of here," he roared. "I don't want to be a U.S. Senator or anything else if I have to murder somebody." Huey sent Abe Shushan, one of his wealthy supporters, and Joe Fisher, a loyal legislator from Jefferson Parish, to borrow a boat from Frank Ehret, another loyal Jefferson Parish politician. They steamed south through the bayous, taking Irby, Terrell, and their BCI captors to remote Grand Isle. Once on the island, Huey's men planned to hold the two abducted men until after the election. Irby was a terrible drunk and they kept him quiet with plenty of bootlegged liquor.

In the midst of these far-fetched events, Lieutenant Governor Cyr arrived in New Orleans hoping to see Huey meet his demise with a charge of kidnapping. Huey earlier infuriated Cyr by facetiously saying he could not allow Cyr to succeed him. "I won't [run for the Senate] if I have to let that good friend of mine, the Lieutenant Governor, get the office," Huey taunted. "I love him too much to impose the duties of governor on him." Walking through the plush lobby of the Monteleone Hotel, Cyr came face-to-face with one of Huey's supporters and the two men waged a short but violent fistfight beneath the hotel's ornate crystal chandelier.

On Sunday night, two days before the Senate election, the mystery of Irby and Terrell ended, not in a gruesome tale of murder but more like a phony dime novel. In a radio broadcast from his Roosevelt Hotel room, Huey surprised his listeners when he introduced Irby to his audience. Irby denied that he and Terrell were kidnapped and declared they had been on a fishing trip to Grand Isle. There was little doubt that Huey had either threatened the two men, paid them to keep quiet, or both. As soon as the radio interview ended, Huey's men whisked Irby away so he could not be interviewed by the press or local law enforcement officers. Fisher, Shushan, and John Klorer, the editor of the *Louisiana Progress,* threw Irby into the back of a limousine and sped from the Roosevelt. Federal agents and city police gave chase, but Huey's men lost them in the back streets of Harrahan, a suburb just across the border of Jefferson Parish. Later, after the election, Irby recanted the radio interview and told a different story, that he and Terrell were indeed kidnapped, taken to Grand Isle, tied to a tree, and attacked by the island's notorious mosquitoes. By that time, the election was past and, amazingly, neither the press nor the public paid much attention to the two men's story.

ON TUESDAY, SEPTEMBER 9, 1930, Huey Long won the Democratic primary election for U.S. senator, trouncing the incumbent Senator Ransdell, 149,640–111,451. Huey carried fifty-three of the sixty-four parishes. As expected, Huey won by a landslide in the rural regions, where 60 percent of Louisianans lived. However, he faltered in the larger cities. He lost New Orleans by 4,600 votes, but raised his raw vote in the Crescent City from 17,819 in 1928 to 35,599. He also lost his hometown of Shreveport. And in the state capital, the hatred between Huey and Baton Rougeans showed in the ballot box, where Ransdell won handily, 7,578 to 1,567.

While Huey lost New Orleans, both of his pro-Long candidates won congressional seats in the city over their Choctaw opponents. Bathtub Joe Fernandez upset incumbent First District congressman James O'Connor, and Paul Maloney, whom Huey previously backed for mayor, won the Second District congressional seat. Another Longite, Numa Montet, won the Third District. In a race for the northern member of the Public Service Commission, the Long candidate, Harvey Fields, defeated Huey's boyhood friend and now bitter enemy, Harley Bozeman.

Bathtub Joe won the closest race. The deciding votes came from St. Bernard and Plaquemines Parishes, the remote bayou regions south of New Orleans notorious for bootleggers, moonshiners, and corrupt elections. The sheriff of St. Bernard, Dr. L. A. Mereaux, ruled the parish like his own personal duchy. In neighboring Plaquemines, Leander Perez, the brilliant attorney with bushy eyebrows and rimless glasses who defended Huey during the impeachment, was building an empire of enormous wealth and political power that would go unchallenged for the next forty years. Huey's totals attested to the electioneering shenanigans of that region. St. Bernard, which had only 2,454 registered voters, tallied a preposterous 3,979 votes for Huey and 9 votes for Ransdell. Next door, Plaquemines gave Huey 1,315 votes and Ransdell 73. Fernandez got a similar "landslide" from the two parishes, just enough to overcome the overwhelming New Orleans vote amassed by the Old Regular incumbent, O'Connor.

The *Baton Rouge State-Times* reported that the ballot returns from St.

Bernard and Plaquemines Parishes had an "extremely bad odor about them." In one St. Bernard precinct, the official record indicated that voters marched to the polls in alphabetical order. The parish rolls listed the names of Clara Bow, Babe Ruth, Jack Dempsey, and Charlie Chaplin, none of whom was ever known to have set foot there, but who indeed voted. "They had trees registered down there," one of Huey's bodyguards remembered. "That was a parish, the Free State of St. Bernard."

After the election Huey immediately began signing his name "Huey P. Long, Governor and Senator-Elect."

CHAPTER 7

1931
SELL THEM PLUGS

"I can't lead a normal life," Huey Long once admitted to his wife, Rose. Obsessed with his frantic pursuit of political power, he devoted little time or interest to being a dedicated husband and father. Even when he spent some time with his family, his mind continued to dwell on politics. During a stay in New Orleans, a busy Huey took his teenage son, Russell, to the Orpheum Theater to see a movie. Soon after the lights in the theater darkened and the movie began, Russell discovered that his father's seat was empty. Huey had slipped away, hustling down Canal Street to the Roosevelt to meet with his cronies. After the movie, Russell caught a streetcar and returned home alone.

Always in motion, impatient, seldom sleeping, addicted to a life of hotel rooms, restaurant meals, bootlegged liquor, and the big-city nightlife of New Orleans, Huey was incapable of sitting quietly in the state capital of Baton Rouge. His health deteriorated. At one point he tried to clean up his lifestyle, cut back on his drinking, and lose some of the weight that steadily swelled his girth. To attack his "bay window," as he called his paunch, a delivery truck backed up to the governor's residence one afternoon and unloaded a rowing machine, a medicine ball, and other exercise equipment. Those close to him, however, saw little change either in his appearance or his fast living.

In early 1930, workmen completed the new governor's mansion

that he had ordered to replace the old frame building a gang of convicts had demolished the year before. The new mansion, costing a sizable $150,000 during the Depression years, provided a stunning example of Georgian architecture. Three-storied and buttressed with four thirty-foot-tall Corinthian columns, the stuccoed mansion immediately reminded onlookers of the White House in Washington. Inside, Huey ordered the most expensive appointments, including Chippendale and Duncan Phyfe furniture, fine damask and velvet drapes, crystal chandeliers, and hand-printed French wallpaper.

At first Huey and Rose followed the protocol expected of a governor and his wife. On May 27, 1930, they held their first open house in the new mansion. Huey dressed for the occasion in an expensive white suit, Rose in an ecru lace evening gown with jade fan and green accessories, and their thirteen-year-old daughter, Rose, in a pink frock. Huge baskets of red and white peonies, pink gladiolas, and large roses decorated the mansion, while chefs from the Roosevelt Hotel in New Orleans prepared banquet tables brimming with spicy Creole dishes. Tuxedoed Seymour Weiss, who arrived in a big van from the Roosevelt bringing china, silver, food, and servants, hovered over the spectacle, ensuring that the affair went perfectly. Guests listened to serenades by the LSU cadet band seated on the front terrace beneath a fancy marble great seal of Louisiana depicting a pelican feeding her young. Visitors wandered through the upstairs and peeked into the pastel bedrooms and the six bathrooms, each painted a different color.

Huey was never comfortable playing host at social occasions and he held few formal events while governor. One of the few occurred the following winter when Huey and Rose gave a formal dance at the mansion, complete with a string orchestra in the huge reception room, to honor the two daughters of Alexandria attorney John Overton. Although Huey officially moved his living quarters from the Roosevelt to the mansion in December 1930, he continued his hotel living, preferring to relax in his top-floor suites of the Heidelberg and Roosevelt and listening to dance bands and prizefights on the radio.

The only time when Huey did not order people around was during one of his infrequent visits to his home, where Rose Long was in complete charge. "She had the Indian sign on him," a supporter remem-

Huey P. Long, 1893–1935.

The Kingfish.

WINNFIELD, LOUISIANA

Huey during his early years in high school.

Huey stands on the railroad tracks near Winnfield. As a rebellious teenager, he smoked, drank, chewed tobacco, and cussed like a field hand.

Huey, Rose McConnell, and an unidentified friend during their courtship.

Huey left Winnfield at seventeen to become a salesman. He traveled the South, first selling Cottolene, a lard substitute, then hawking packed foods, vegetables and fruit, and patent medicines. He was a natural salesman, a fast-talking, smooth-tongued drummer who could quickly charm a housewife into a sale.

Huey and Rose Long at the time of their marriage in 1913. He was broke and borrowed $10 from his wife to pay the Baptist minister.

CAMPAIGNING FOR GOVERNOR

Huey (far right) speaks to a crowd in Amity, Louisiana. One of his sound trucks sits to the left. While the stifling Louisiana heat and humidity sapped most politicians, the energetic Huey seemed to thrive under the oppressive conditions.

COURTESY OF THE STATE LIBRARY OF LOUISIANA

Huey as a state railroad commissioner, about the time he unsuccessfully ran for governor, in 1924.

COURTESY OF THE STATE LIBRARY OF LOUISIANA

Huey was one of the first politicians to take advantage of the enormous power of the radio to transmit his message to thousands of voters.

COURTESY OF THE STATE LIBRARY OF LOUISIANA

At his inauguration, Huey is seated beside O. H. Simpson, the outgoing governor, whom he defeated.

Paul Cyr was elected lieutenant governor on Huey's ticket in 1928. Soon after their inauguration, the men became bitter enemies.

Huey Long, his wife, Rose, and their three children at the time of Huey's election as governor.

GOVERNOR OF LOUISIANA

The old state capitol, where Huey was inaugurated. He hated the old capitol, regarding it as an archaic symbol of the past.

COURTESY OF THE STATE LIBRARY OF LOUISIANA

Huey stirs a pot of greens as Seymour Weiss, the manager of the Roosevelt Hotel and Huey's closest confidant, looks on.

COURTESY OF SECRETARY OF STATE W. FOX MCKEITHEN, LOUISIANA STATE ARCHIVES

Huey cuts the ribbon to open one of the many highways he constructed across the state.

COURTESY OF SECRETARY OF STATE W. FOX MCKEITHEN, LOUISIANA STATE ARCHIVES

Huey with a tour
of dairy farmers in
front of the Bentley
Hotel in Alexandria,
Louisiana.

Huey appointed
Alice Lee Grosjean,
his private secretary,
as secretary of state.

The new governor's mansion, erected by Huey after
he summarily ordered prisoners to demolish the old
mansion.

SURVIVING IMPEACHMENT

Huey looks confident before his impeachment trial in the state Senate. John Overton sits to Huey's left. After he was acquitted, Huey took revenge upon his enemies.

COURTESY OF THE STATE LIBRARY OF LOUISIANA

Representative Cecil Morgan rose on the House floor to accuse Huey of plotting murder and launched the effort to impeach Huey.

COURTESY OF THE STATE LIBRARY OF LOUISIANA

Huey harangues his audience.

COURTESY OF THE STATE LIBRARY OF LOUISIANA

"The Truth Shall Make You Free"

Haven't we fiddled long enough while Rome is burning down?

Hear the facts about New Orleans and Louisiana

Huey P. Long

Governor of the State of Louisiana

·At the

MUNICIPAL AUDITORIUM

THURSDAY NIGHT, MAY 8TH,

8:00 O'CLOCK

We have all slept here longer than Rip Van Winkle.

Progress   *versus*   *Decay*

Paved Roads, Paved Streets, Farm Roads, a Free Bridge over the Mississippi River, the Intracoastal Canal, Employment for our people, the State and City working together with progress and prosperity for both.

versus

Partisan Politics, Bickerings, Quarrels, Obstruction and a lot of useless tomfoolery.

"Am I therefore become your enemy because I tell you the truth?"

Galatians, 4th Chapter, 16th Verse

Come to the Auditorium Thursday Night and hear the Governor's plan as endorsed by:

The New Orleans Association of Commerce (unanimously).
The Young Men's Business Club (unanimously).
The Motor League of Louisiana (unanimously).
The New Orleans Realty Board (unanimously).
Police Juries, School Boards, Farm Bodies, and Labor Organizations.

41

Campaign poster for the Senate election.

The First Tree Sitter

People,—Isn't it time to get rid of the old time, moth eaten practices of the past? We can't wake up this old crew,—but we can elect a virile man who has done real work, and who now is trying to give us 3000 miles of good concrete roads and a free bridge over the Mississippi River.

Huey used his own newspaper, *Louisiana Progress,* to attack his opponents bitterly. This cartoon insulted Joseph Ransdell during the *1930* Senate race.

COURTESY OF LOUISIANA STATE
UNIVERSITY, LLMVC

Huey presents his credentials as a new senator to Vice President Charles Curtis on January *25, 1932.*

COURTESY OF THE STATE
LIBRARY OF LOUISIANA

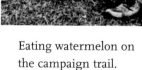

Eating watermelon on the campaign trail.

COURTESY OF THE STATE
LIBRARY OF LOUISIANA

Oscar Kelly Allen, Huey's handpicked successor as governor. Friendly and harmless, O.K. followed Huey's orders like an obedient cocker spaniel.

COURTESY OF THE
STATE LIBRARY
OF LOUISIANA

Huey and Hattie Caraway on an Arkansas ferry crossing the Black River from Newport to Batesville.

Huey and his son Russell. Russell would be elected to the U.S. Senate in 1948 upon the death of John Overton.

Huey raises his arms in his classic campaign style while giving a speech for Hattie Caraway in Russellville, Arkansas, on August 4, 1932.

LSU'S BIGGEST FAN

Huey at the LSU railroad station next to the cadet train before leaving for a football game.
COURTESY OF THE STATE LIBRARY OF LOUISIANA

Huey with LSU president James Monroe Smith. A court later sentenced Smith to prison after he embezzled half a million dollars' worth of the university's bonds.
COURTESY OF THE STATE LIBRARY OF LOUISIANA

Huey leading the LSU band through New Orleans during Mardi Gras.
COURTESY OF LOUISIANA STATE UNIVERSITY, LLMVC

Huey with LSU cheerleaders at Tiger Stadium.
COURTESY OF LOUISIANA STATE UNIVERSITY, LLMVC

CRUSHING ALL OPPONENTS

Huey with James Farley, Franklin Roosevelt's campaign manager during the presidential campaign of 1932. The two men soon became bitter political enemies.

The towering capitol that Huey built on the bank of the Mississippi.

Governor O. K. Allen signs a bill to construct a bridge across the Mississippi as Huey and New Orleans mayor Semmes Walmsley (far right) look on.

Louisiana national guardsmen stand watch at the Baton Rouge Airport on January 26, 1935, after routing several hundred anti-Long demonstrators.

Huey leads a protest
parade of veteran
bonus marchers
through New Orleans.

Huey with Milo Reno, leader of
the Farm Holiday Association, on
April 8, 1935, in Des Moines.

Huey and John Overton attend a hearing in New Orleans on election
corruption. Congressional investigators dropped charges that Huey illegally
engineered Overton's election to the Senate.

A contented Huey poses with several New Orleans Old Regular bosses after they surrendered their political power to him.
COURTESY OF THE STATE LIBRARY OF LOUISIANA

The national media lampooned Huey, as in the unflattering cartoon at left from *The Forum*.
COURTESY OF *THE FORUM*

The real Huey was no cartoon character, but a shrewd, determined politician.
COURTESY OF SECRETARY OF STATE W. FOX MCKEITHEN, LOUISIANA STATE ARCHIVES

On the night he was shot, Huey oversees proceedings in the Louisiana House of Representatives, as speaker Allen Ellender motions in the background.

Carl Weiss was a brilliant young doctor and a happily married man with a young child when he allegedly assassinated Huey Long.

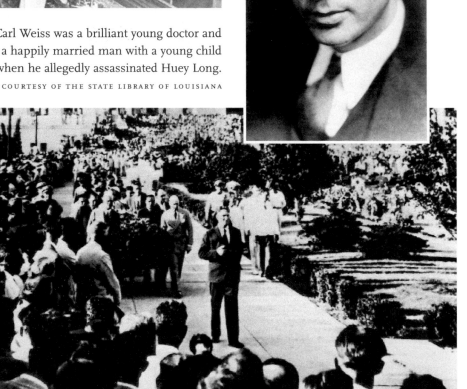

The Reverend Gerald L. K. Smith leads the casket at Huey Long's funeral on September 12, 1935. Smith's impassioned funeral oration brought many of the mourners to tears.

bered. An LSU football player who lived in the mansion during the fall of 1931 recalled, "Mrs. Long was very much the boss," and a friend agreed that she "was the only one who could calm Huey." Like Huey, Rose avoided the governor's mansion and spent most of her time in Shreveport or, after they moved their home, in New Orleans. In early 1932, Huey moved his law practice from Shreveport to New Orleans and Rose and the children moved to a plush new home on New Orleans's Audubon Boulevard near Tulane. Her reluctance to stay in Baton Rouge was probably due to Huey's rumored relationship with his secretary, Alice Lee Grosjean.

In October 1930, Secretary of State James Bailey died with three years remaining in his term. Huey surprised even his closest confidants when he appointed his twenty-four-year-old secretary, Alice Lee, to the vacant cabinet post. As secretary of state, she would fill the highest office ever held by a woman in Louisiana. Huey's appointment of Alice Lee set "many a gossipy tongue to wagging," a New Orleans newspaper reported. "When I came up from New Orleans this morning I didn't have the slightest idea I'd have a new job," Alice Lee told a newspaper reporter, adding, "I'll probably have a little time now to go to dances, play some golf and tennis." A year later, Huey planned a dance at the mansion in honor of Alice Lee but canceled the event at the last minute when Rose became sick with the flu.

HUEY LONG AND Semmes Walmsley were cut from very different cloth. While Huey hailed from the impoverished, dirt-poor north Louisiana town of Winnfield, the gregarious and cultured Walmsley grew up in the most fashionable uptown section of New Orleans amid the luxury of a thirty-room mansion surrounded by an imposing cast iron fence and a grove of lush palms and live oaks. A six-foot-two, bald, and likable man in his early forties, Walmsley graduated from Tulane Law School, joined a prestigious law firm and the exclusive Boston Club, and settled comfortably into his mansion on Prytania Street. Walmsley, however, was unlike other uptown elites and, like Huey, was a savvy politician who could roll up his sleeves at meetings in the seedy Choctaw Club and make deals with ham-fisted ward heelers. In 1930, Walmsley swept fourteen of the city's seventeen wards and won the mayoral victory over Francis Williams. As mayor he became the nominal leader of the Old Regulars, who won all of the seats on the City Commission. The Choctaws gave Walmsley a new Pierce-Arrow sedan as a token of their political alliance.

Walmsley immediately became a bitter enemy of Huey Long. During the first of many disputes, the new mayor called Huey a madman, anarchist, liar, tyrant, usurper, and self-seeking demagogue. Walmsley's hatred, however, created a problem in the New Orleans political ranks after Huey won the Senate election in September 1930. New Orleans bankers and businessmen knew that Huey now held a tight grip on the legislature and believed that a war between the mayor and the governor would only worsen economic conditions. New Orleans needed financial help from the state government to solve its growing problems, especially its decrepit streets and sewers, a burdensome debt of the port, and a city that owed over $3 million. Led by banker Rudolph Hecht, city leaders pressured Walmsley to make a deal with Huey.

On Thursday, September 11, just two days after Huey won the Senate election, Walmsley met with Huey in his twelfth-floor suite of the Roosevelt. Other Choctaw political leaders, bankers, lawyers, businessmen, and the Old Regular clerk of the City Council traveled along with the mayor. Walmsley and his allies were ready to barter but Huey was obstinate, knowing that he held the high cards. He controlled the legislature, a large number of patronage jobs in the city, and, only two days before, his candidates for Congress, Bathtub Joe Fernandez, Paul Maloney, and Numa Montet, had defeated the Ring candidates.

Huey had a stranglehold over the Old Regulars, knew it, and drove a hard bargain. "He is always trying to trade us a biscuit for a barrel of flour," Walmsley complained later. Huey refused to give up any patronage or elected offices to the Choctaws. Getting nowhere, Walmsley finally gave up. "We've accepted your proposition," said the mayor. "We're ready to go through." Leaning back in his chair and puffing on a huge cigar, Huey accepted Walmsley's surrender. The Old Regulars agreed to support Huey's entire program, including building his huge network of modern highways, constructing a new state capitol, and dropping any impeachment charges still pending in the legislature. Huey agreed to help repair the city's streets and sewers and refinance the port, but he refused to give the Choctaws any political concessions that would diminish his own power. He was confident that he could control and, if necessary, conquer the disorganized Choctaws. "It has been my good fortune to have blind men like these in politics," he wrote later. "They cannot see something after it has passed over them, and they have been knocked down by it a half-dozen times."

Once Huey made his deal with Walmsley, all of the New Orleans state legislators shifted to the Long camp. Other delegates, including some fence-sitters and those who voted for impeachment, conceded and joined Huey. With a twist of vengeance, Huey ordered the Old Regulars to strip John Sullivan, the traitor who had returned to the Old Regulars as lowly Third Ward leader, of any Ring office. Bang Tail Sullivan, the maverick politician, gambler, and onetime Long supporter, faded into obscurity.

The alliance among Huey, Walmsley, and the Choctaws created an unprecedented concentration of power, patronage, and political muscle. The new pact worried opposition leaders like Gus Williams, a rebellious New Orleans politician who opposed both Huey and the Ring. "By joining forces they hope to secure a policy of political life insurance," Williams remarked, "and at the same time create a monster political machine that will, at the people's expense, supply them and their henchmen with political graft for a generation to come."

Overnight, Huey's victories altered the Louisiana political landscape. His power grew while his enemies were weakened. On the day after he won his landslide in the race for Senate, the Constitutional League, formed by ex-governor Parker almost exactly a year before to "prevent Governor Huey P. Long from treating the organic law of the state as a scrap of paper," disbanded. When wealthy businessmen realized it was better to join Huey than fight him, they no longer funded the league and it collapsed.

JUST FIVE DAYS after Mayor Semmes Walmsley and the New Orleans Ring surrendered to his demands, Huey Long called a special session of the legislature. With newfound political clout, he struck quickly to consolidate and strengthen his power. Starting at eight in the evening on September 16, 1930, the representatives convened for five days in Baton Rouge. The session opened with an air of eerie peacefulness, a far cry from the fistfights and billingsgate that had dominated recent sessions. With the legislature more firmly under his control, Huey ordered his bills introduced and voted on before his confused opposition could reorganize. On Thursday, September 18, the House passed his $68 million road construction bill with only twelve opposing votes. The legislature approved increased school funding, a one-cent gasoline tax increase to refinance the port of New Orleans, $5 million for a new capitol building, and $7 million for a bridge spanning the Mississippi at New Orleans. When the House voted on Allen Ellender's motion to expunge all the impeachment charges, only twenty-one legislators voted against the resolution.

A small number of legislators, including J. Y. Sanders, Jr., Mason Spencer, and Cecil Morgan, refused to succumb to Huey. The most stubborn opponent was Huey's unrelenting nemesis, Judge Gilbert Dupre. Although elderly and deaf, Dupre could read a speaker's lips and followed the House proceedings by looking over the shoulder of newspaper reporters and reading their notes. The eccentric old French aristocrat "slept in his clothes and shaved every night before retiring," one legislator recalled, supposedly "so he would be prepared if he died in his sleep." Dupre was also unbending and combative, perpetually sparring with Huey's floor leaders. One day he ended a quarrel with Representative J. E. McClanahan with the challenge, "We'll order pistols and coffee for two."

Huey, who took a curious liking to Judge Dupre because of his feistiness, enjoyed getting the old man's goat. On one occasion, as Dupre was talking, Huey came up from behind and mimicked the old legislator. Soon it dawned on Dupre that people were smiling at the wrong time. "He turned and put his finger in Huey's face," a House member remembered, "and ordered him off the floor of the House and threatened to get a horse pistol and shoot him."

Before the House voted on the proposal to construct a new state capitol, Huey walked to the back row of the chamber where Dupre sat at his desk and wrote on the old man's pad, "Are you going to vote for the new Capitol?" Dupre shouted back an angry "No!" Huey took the pad and wrote again, "Die, damn you, in the faith!" According to Huey, Dupre just smiled "and almost came over" to vote for the bill. Soon after, Huey ordered one of his workers, E. J. Oakes, to climb onto the capitol roof and remove a couple of slates precisely above Dupre's desk. Every time it rained, which happened often in muggy Baton Rouge, a steady trickle dribbled down upon the old fire-breather.

In the midst of the special session, the legislature adjourned early in the afternoon so the members could board a train for New Orleans. Later that evening they attended a testimonial banquet for Huey in the Roosevelt's ritzy Venetian Room. The guests included Mayor Walmsley, the Old Regular captains, and the uptown elite, many of the same men who refused to attend the banquet held for Huey soon after his election. Six hundred men and one woman, Rose Long, filled the smoky hall stuffed with flowers and sumptuous food. Walmsley appeared to bury the political hatchet when he gave Huey a warm and enthusiastic introduction. "Even in the hour of our defeat," the mayor remarked, "we feel that he has stretched to us the hand of friendship for the good of the state."

Taking the rostrum after the glowing introductions, Huey delivered a three-hour speech promising to provide the city with $700,000 to repair New Orleans's decrepit streets and antiquated sewers, construct a huge $3 million modern airport on the edge of Lake Pontchartrain, and build a $7 million span across the Mississippi to be aptly named the Huey P. Long Bridge. Huey thanked the previous speakers for the praise they gave him but suggested they might have gone too far in their glowing testimony. He then told them the story of a man in Winn Parish who died, leaving behind a wife and mother-in-law. At the funeral the preacher described in great flowery detail the attributes of the deceased. Each time the preacher added another tribute to the dead man, the mother-in-law stood, walked over to the casket, peeked in, and returned to her seat. After she did this several times, the minister turned to the woman and asked her if there was anything he could do to relieve her grief. "I just want to stand here, Parson," the woman replied, "to be sure that the man you're talking about is my son-in-law."

AT ABOUT THE TIME of his Senate election, Huey acquired a new nickname. He began calling himself the Kingfish. Taken from the character who was the leader of the Mystic Knights of the Sea in the popular radio comedy *Amos 'n' Andy*, the nickname sarcastically fit Huey. He liked the appellation's "homespun majesty" and often answered the telephone simply with "This is the Kingfish!" The nickname also helped lighten his more serious business of controlling Louisiana. "It has served to substitute gaiety for some of the tragedy of politics," Huey wrote later. "I have made no effort to discourage it." His critics, however, saw his new nickname as a choice opportunity to belittle him. *Vanity Fair*, for example, said that the Louisiana kingfish has a "big mouth, feeds off suckers, thrives best in mud and slime, and is very hard to catch."

On November 4, 1930, after the special session of the legislature concluded, the voters of Louisiana overwhelmingly passed all of Huey's constitutional amendments, including his new road building program. During the following summer, he forced Walmsley and the Ring to allow him to select his own candidates in eight state House races and three Senate races, all in the New Orleans area, leaving the remaining nine House and five Senate contests to the Choctaws. With these New Orleans representatives added to his roster of pro-Long rural and Acadiana legislators, Huey now maintained a majority control over the legislature and close to the two-thirds vote necessary for funding bills and changes to the state constitution.

On the day after the people passed his constitutional amendments for roads and the new capitol, the *Times-Picayune* warned that Huey had been given greater control of the state than any of his predecessors and he should be held responsible in the future. Huey's critics previously concentrated their attacks on his unconventional, unethical, and illegal methods to ramrod through his legislation. Now, some of the newspapers who opposed him struck a more ominous note. They saw him amassing an unprecedented amount of power over most aspects of Louisiana government and realized that his iron grip on the legislature and the state government bureaucracy posed a bigger, more fundamental threat, a threat to basic democratic governance. Papers across the nation began to take notice of Huey and his domination. In a full-page Sunday spread, the *Kansas City Star* labeled him as a ruthless politician and described Louisiana as a "political dictatorship." Other observers agreed. Katherine Anne Porter viewed Huey as "the worst sort of Fascist demagogue" and H. L. Mencken described him as a "backwoods demagogue of the oldest most familiar model—impudent, blackguardly, and infinitely prehensile."

HUEY LONG, who never finished high school and completed only a few college law courses, always regretted that he had never been able to attend

LSU. Years before as a teenager, he won a scholarship to the university during his high school debates but could not attend because the scholarship did not include books and living expenses. "I remember to this day how, at the age of sixteen or seventeen, I harbored an ambition to attend the old Louisiana State University," he told an audience during his Senate campaign. Missing the chance to attend the university, he now would try to experience college life as governor.

By June 1929, shortly after surviving impeachment, Huey began to intervene in LSU affairs. The LSU board had selected General Campbell Hodges as the university's new president, but when Huey learned that Hodges helped found the Constitutional League and that his brother was Riley Wilson's campaign manager, he sent for the general and told him not to bother coming to LSU. He told the board that he would select the next university president. Before the matter reached a boiling point, President Hoover appointed Hodges to a federal post and LSU selected a less controversial president. Nevertheless, Huey's interest in LSU continued to deepen. By 1930, he realized that by making the state university a showcase he could promote himself, confiding to one of his supporters that he would take over LSU like "any other damned department."

In the fall of 1930, Huey drove to the southern edge of Baton Rouge to LSU's campus to pay an unannounced visit to the university's president. When he arrived in David Boyd Hall he could not find the president. Down the hall he found Fred Frey, who had become dean of students only two months before. When Huey asked for the president, Frey informed him that President Thomas Atkinson was at home recovering from a mild heart attack. An impatient Huey began to rap his walking cane loudly on a conference table. "This is a hell of a note," he barked at Frey. "I come out here to talk to the president and I have to talk to some damn kid." Frey, a little miffed by the governor's comment, snapped back that he was two years older than the governor. Huey broke out laughing and the two men got along fine from then on.

After President Atkinson retired for reasons of bad health on November 17, Huey took an active role in most important decisions at LSU, calling Frey and other school officials several times a week to get a status report on his pet projects. He personally oversaw the replacement of Atkinson. At a meeting of the LSU board at the governor's mansion, he chose James Monroe Smith as president. Born in Winn Parish, Smith taught at Southwestern Louisiana Institute in Lafayette and had served as dean of the college of education since 1923. With a doctorate in education from Columbia University, Smith was neither ignorant nor incompetent; he proved to be an efficient administrator, but unfortunately he was weak and corrupt. Nicknamed "Jingle Money," Smith was exactly the college president that Huey wanted. "There's not a straight bone in Jim Smith's body," Huey said, "but he does what I want him to, so I think he's a good president." When asked about Smith's qualifications, he remarked that Smith had "a hide as thick as an elephant's." On one occasion, Dr. Smith, wearing a threadbare old suit, went to a meeting at the mansion. Huey handed Smith a wad of cash and ordered him to "go out and buy yourself some clothes and try to look like a president."

When Huey first visited LSU after becoming governor, he found the university to be a third-rate, aimless Southern college with sixteen hundred students, ranked eighty-eighth in size among the nation's universities, and miserably underfunded. Despite the Depression and scarce funds, he began an overnight modernization. Pumping thousands of state dollars into the university, he quickly brought LSU up to the highest national standards and equipped the school with a faculty that included some of the nation's most noted scholars. Over the next few years, the university enjoyed an intellectual renaissance, attracting excellent young writers like Robert Penn Warren and Cleanth Brooks, establishing the LSU Press, publishing the *Southern Review,* and awarding its first doctorates. The university produced landmark research in agricultural science, petroleum geology, and aeronautical engineering and operated a sugar school that attracted students worldwide. In December 1930, Huey announced that he was building a new LSU medical school in New Orleans. The blueprints were completed a month later, contracts were let in March, construction began in April, and students started classes in October. To Huey's delight, the LSU music department produced grand opera accompanied by its own huge symphony.

By 1937, when most of Huey's innovations were complete, LSU ranked twentieth in the nation in size and eleventh among state universities. Enrollment leaped from sixteen hundred to seven thousand students and the faculty size nearly tripled to four hundred professors. In the center of campus he constructed the half-million-dollar Huey P. Long Field House with a spacious dance hall, a soda fountain, and a huge pool 180 feet long. When he asked if his pool was the largest in the country, the architect told him that a West Coast university had a pool 10 feet longer. Huey ordered the LSU pool torn up and lengthened until it was indeed the nation's longest. With almost brick-by-brick scrutiny, he supervised the construction of the magnificent new campus, including the first women's dormitory and a fine arts building with a huge theater decorated in flashy Art Deco. According to one legend, Huey was inspecting the near-complete women's dormitory and noticed workers about to pour the new concrete sidewalks. Suddenly Huey jumped between the workers and ordered them to stop. Wait a year, he shouted, and then pour the sidewalks on top of the paths where the students naturally walked. The gently winding sidewalks of LSU still survive as a testimony to his lively and creative mind.

Second best never satisfied Huey. When he first visited LSU, the school band had twenty-eight members. He created the largest marching band in the nation, 250 strong, with the most expensive uniforms he could buy. Unknown to Huey, however, some of the band members who swelled the ranks could not play their instruments and were recruited only for their ability to march in a straight line. He personally chose the majorettes and cheerleaders. When he became impatient with the growth of the band, he replaced the band director with his friend Castro Carazo, the Roosevelt Hotel's orchestra leader. Castro remembered that Huey liked "Smoke Gets in Your Eyes" and "That Lonesome Road," but nothing could top "Harvest Moon," a simple sweet dance tune that made Huey look "dreamy and blissful . . . with his eyes closed." Together they composed two Tiger classics, "Touchdown for LSU" and "Darling of LSU." Huey promised to make Castro director of the Marine Band when he became president.

Other priorities fell by the wayside. In 1931, LSU spent $14,345 for its band, while giving only $837 to its law school and $493 to its graduate school. To Huey, quantity implied quality, such as large marching bands, more athletic scholarships, more grand pianos, a longer swimming pool, but not intellectual freedom or a better library. As he heaped vast amounts of cash upon his favorite university, graft and incompetence inevitably occurred. When workers completed LSU's huge, expensive swimming pool, they discovered the new pool had no drains. When he ordered several of the finest pianos delivered to LSU's new music building, the piano manufacturer, Werlein's, had to kick back $5,000 from the $45,000 total. By 1933 more than half the student body was on the state payroll. Many jobs and scholarships were based not on need but on political loyalty of a student's father. When criticized for holding a Senate seat while remaining governor, Huey fired back, "Hell, I've got a university down in Louisiana that cost me fifteen million dollars that can tell you why I do like I do." In December 1931, a newspaper accused Huey of politicizing the university. "I didn't," Huey retorted sharply. "I just Longized it." By this time, some professors began to feel Huey's political pressure and were careful what they said in the classroom. "We were all so scared we couldn't say anything," a psychology professor remembered. "I'll bet there wasn't 'dictatorship' mentioned in sociology, government, anything."

While Huey showed little concern with either corruption or restricted academic freedom at LSU, deep down he loved his university and its student body. When LSU students delivered a copy of the *Gumbo*, the yearbook they dedicated to him, he sat on the edge of his bed and cried. In his own peculiar way, he looked upon the students at LSU as his own. After a young LSU coed was thrown from a horse and badly injured at the university riding academy run by President Smith's wife, Huey shot off a curt telegram to the LSU president—"Sell them plugs."

COTTON WAS THE lifeblood of rural Louisiana. From the red hills dotting the northern parishes to the edge of the sugar bowl in southern Acadiana, endless fields of cotton spread across the landscape like a snowy blanket. In early spring, as soon as the danger of frost had passed, farmers planted the cotton from seed. From late August until late December, hundreds of farmhands invaded the fields to pick the lush bolls that blossomed atop the plants. For the small dirt farmer of the hill country, cotton farming was a struggle. In a good year, six acres of hardscrabble land produced five or six large bales totaling about three thousand pounds. If the farmer could get 10 cents a pound for his crop, the $300 he cleared barely fed his family and maybe allowed him to buy a new pair of shoes, coveralls, and a calico dress for his wife.

On August 8, 1931, the U.S. Department of Agriculture issued its annual cotton crop forecast. The farmers of the cotton growing states dreaded the August report, for it usually confirmed a dangerous increase in production and a ruinous decrease in prices. The report was worse than expected and forecast sixteen million bales for the 1931 crop year, the third largest yield in history. The bumper crop, added to a huge on-hand surplus of eight million bales from the previous year, foretold catastrophe for cotton farmers. Twenty-four million bales would be available for 1931, but the annual worldwide cotton consumption was only twelve million. With twice the amount of cotton needed on the market, prices plummeted. Cotton prices, averaging 40 cents a pound in 1920 and dropping to 20 cents a pound in 1927, now averaged an unthinkable 4 cents a pound by the late summer of 1931. The cotton industry, a victim of enormous surpluses, an economy mired in depression, and shrinking world markets, now searched for answers to stave off economic disaster.

The U.S. Department of Agriculture recommended that farmers immediately plow under every third row of cotton to eliminate the surplus, but state governments and farmers rejected the federal plan as impractical. The federal government then declared that it was the obligation of the governors of the cotton growing states to take action.

Of the governors, only Huey Long immediately responded. His plan was not the only one for dealing with the crisis but it was the simplest and most drastic. He called for a one-year ban on all cotton production. Huey believed that a one-year moratorium would create a flurry of buying that would double the price and enable farmers to earn enough in 1931 to cover the banned year of 1932. If the people adopted his plan, he predicted the South would see 20-cent cotton in three weeks. "Hold your cotton," Huey urged Southern planters, "and my cotton holiday plan will boost the price so you won't lose any money and won't have to make a crop in 1932." He appealed with biblical logic. "The Lord told us to lay off raising these crops one year out of seven to let the people have time to consume them."

On August 16, Huey telegraphed senators, governors, and congressmen from the cotton states and invited them to a conference in New Orleans five days later. Of the twelve governors invited, only the governors of Arkansas and South Carolina showed up, but the others all sent representatives. When the delegates met at the Roosevelt Hotel in New Orleans, Texas proposed to reduce cotton production by 50 percent in 1932, but the attendees voted the plan down. Instead, they overwhelmingly endorsed Huey's plan. The ban would not be binding unless those states producing three-fourths of the cotton also passed similar legislation. This stipulation meant that Texas, which harvested one-third of the total crop, had to agree or the plan failed. However, Texas governor Ross Sterling opposed Huey's plan. "It's Governor Long's baby," Sterling declared, "let him wash it first."

At ten in the evening on Tuesday, August 25, Huey convened the Louisiana legislature for a six-day special session. Wearing a white cotton suit, he took the rostrum and personally guided the proceedings. He had two of his opponents propose the cotton holiday legislation to show that his plan had wide endorsement, including that of Mayor Walmsley and most of Huey's enemies. Only one representative spoke against the cotton holiday plan. Old Judge Dupre rose from his seat and argued that the plan to ban cotton production was unconstitutional. One of Huey's supporters jumped up to challenge Dupre, turning to his colleagues and asking, "Hell, if the government can tell a man what he can't drink, why can't they tell him what he can't plant?" Two days later the House passed the plan, 77–0, and the Senate followed the next day, 32–0. Dupre abstained. That night, at 1:30 in the morning, Huey signed the bill in his bedroom in the governor's mansion, sitting on cotton bedsheets and wearing a cotton nightshirt. "Now I can take this damned thing off," he told his aides as soon as the photographers departed, and climbed back into his silk pajamas.

Huey used the radio to sell his plan across the South, broadcasting from KWKH in Shreveport and WWL in New Orleans and buying time in Memphis, Little Rock, and on the Dixie Radio Network, a CBS affiliate. His broadcasts irritated Texas governor Sterling. "[Long] may be able to demand that his legislature vote whatever he wants," Sterling complained, "but we are a little more democratic in Texas." Sterling called a special session of the Texas legislature on Tuesday, September 8, and a week later the Texas House defeated the Long plan, 92–38. After the vote, one Texas legislator called Huey an "arrogant jackass who brays from Louisiana," and a political mule "without pride of ancestry or hope of posterity." When Huey learned of the Texas vote, he called Sterling a "dirty millionaire" and accused the Texas legislature of being "paid off like a slot machine."

Huey's proposal was popular across the South and he received over sixteen hundred letters of approval. Although he failed to implement his plan, his actions on a regional level strengthened his political stock and embellished his image far beyond the Louisiana border.

ON JANUARY 9, 1931, one of the few pro-Long newspapers in Louisiana, the *Bogalusa News,* proposed that Huey Long run for president. He liked the idea. His spirits were the highest since his inauguration, for he now was seeing his pet projects accomplished. A month earlier, state workers finished his brainchild, the concrete-paved Airline Highway stretching across southern Louisiana. Cutting thirty-eight miles off the journey from Baton Rouge to New Orleans, the Airline was a modern, arrow-straight roadway that replaced the old, winding path over clamshells, potholes, and fathomless mud. Huey now could speed in his limousine back and forth between the two cities, whizzing past cypress swamps and cane fields, and complete the eighty-mile, one-way trip in exactly an hour. To Huey, who hated antique reminders of Louisiana's past, the Airline Highway symbolized the state's entry into the modern, progressive, and faster-paced world. Soon, he would have built nine thousand miles of new highways across the state. A yarn traveled around Shreveport that Huey laid so much concrete around Winnfield that "cats go for miles for a place to scratch."

In February, Huey received another boost to his spirits. In an extravagant ceremony in New Orleans's Municipal Auditorium with seven thousand attending, Loyola University granted him an honorary Doctor of Laws degree. He recently had his staff compile the eight constitutions of Louisiana, and Loyola used the compilation as the reason to give him the degree. Huey earlier had approached Tulane for the degree but the Tulane board, whose members were steadfastly anti-Long, rebuffed him.

Huey was busy. At noon on Thursday, February 12, in the midst of another Mardi Gras, the assistant secretary of the navy hosted Huey on the battleship USS *Wyoming* in New Orleans. Huey, having learned his lesson in naval protocol, made his visit appropriately dressed in a blue business suit. His attire changed abruptly a month later on March 26, when he donned a Cleveland Indians baseball uniform in the Roosevelt Hotel. He convinced the team to continue spring training in New Orleans instead of going to the West Coast as planned. In the spring, he dedicated another symbol of progress, the new Baton Rouge Airport, and officiated at the air races following the ceremony.

Political events were going Huey's way. On March 25, he announced his support for his friend and longtime supporter, John Overton, who was running for the Eighth District congressional seat. Earlier, one of his bitter political enemies, Congressman James Aswell, died and the seat became vacant. The courtly, white-haired Aswell, whom Huey called "Chicken Jim," had served in the House since 1913. On April 14, Overton, the urbane lawyer from Alexandria who defended Huey during impeachment, easily defeated Claybrook Cottingham, the president of Louisiana College. Another death provided more political power for Huey when, on June 5, Colonel Robert Ewing died. Ewing, the newspaper publisher who backed Huey for governor in 1928 and then became a bitter enemy, was recently the Democratic national committeeman. The Party chose Huey Long to replace Ewing.

ONE OF HUEY'S PASSIONS was football and he yearned to create the best LSU team that state money could buy. Winning on the football field was another symbol of LSU's rise to national prominence as a university, as well as a personal tribute to his own success and power. "I don't fool around with losers," he told a friend. "LSU can't have a losing team because that'll mean I'm associated with a loser." In December 1930 he called LSU coach Russ Cohen to the governor's mansion and gave him a new three-year contract and a $500 raise to his $7,000-per-year salary, probably the highest in the South. Huey demanded that his coaches recruit top athletes from across the country. During one four-month period, he had four star players live in the mansion and fed them steaks and milk shakes twice a day to fatten them up. "There was no training table then," one of the players remembered. "We were paid fifty dollars a month and blew a lot of it on the horses." At night, Huey took his players to the huge ballroom of the mansion, where he set up chairs and ran between them to demonstrate football plays he designed.

Before a game with Vanderbilt, Huey invited dozens of LSU students to his suite at the Heidelberg Hotel and handed out $7 loans to finance a five-train excursion to the game in Nashville. He also paid for the school's mascot, Mike the Tiger, to make the trip. No one ever asked where Huey got the thousands of dollars to pay for the trip. On another occasion, as he entered the stadium for a game against Tulane he spotted a supporter's son wearing a large Tulane button. He told the boy that if Tulane won, he would give him the new flowered silk tie he was wearing. Tulane won and the boy got the tie. Before a game with Southern Methodist, he discovered that the Ringling Brothers Circus was in Baton Rouge and the circus parade would interfere with the game. When the circus owners refused to move the event to New Orleans, he threatened to invoke a seldom-enforced law requiring animals entering the state to be free of pests and insects. The circus managers surrendered to Huey's demand when they realized he would force them to dip their tigers, lions, and elephants.

Huey did not hesitate in telling the coach how to do his job. At halftime during LSU's 27–12 win over Arkansas in Shreveport, he walked into the locker room unexpectedly and gave the Tigers a "talking to" as Coach Cohen stood by speechless. After LSU lost a game to TCU in Fort Worth, Huey blamed the loss on his absence and told the students back at LSU that "from now on the coach is going to be my assistant." During another of his pep talks, with LSU losing at halftime, he gave his Tigers extra incentive. "If you win," the governor of Louisiana promised, "I'll give every slap damn one of you a job on the Highway Commission." LSU came back and won.

Before a Thanksgiving game against Tulane, Huey arrived at the stadium an hour and a half early, entered the dressing room, and gave the Tigers another long pep talk. During the game, 25,000 fans watched as Huey, dressed in a flashy brown suit, brown hat, brown shoes, and carrying a gold-headed malacca walking stick, ran up and down the sidelines, intermittently cheering and cussing the LSU players. At one point, he ran up to Cohen and collared the coach. "Next time one of those Tigers tries to pass and finds his receiver covered," he urged, "have him run with the ball the way Don Zimmerman of Tulane did against Georgia." Cohen nodded but never turned his head from the play. Huey decided to signal plays to the quarterback with his hat, held a certain way or dropped on the ground, "and when I grab the coach around the neck that means a forward pass." The coach complained afterward that he grabbed him so many times he had a sore neck for a week. When the game turned against LSU, Huey went to the end of the field and squatted cross-legged on the turf like a spoiled child, angrily pulling up great handfuls of grass.

One coach refused to let Huey interfere. During the Sugar Bowl game against Oregon State in December 1934, LSU was losing 13–0 at halftime. When he tried to enter the locker room to give his usual pep talk, Coach Biff Jones met him at the door and refused to let him enter. "All right," Huey growled, "but you had better win this one." Jones, a six-foot-three, two-hundred-pounder, lost his temper. "I don't have to win this one," the coach snapped back. "Win, lose, or draw, I'm going to resign at the end of this game." After Huey left, Jones went back to his players. "I've never asked a personal favor of you but I am now," the trembling coach told the team. "I want to win this game more than anything in the world." An inspired LSU team fought back and won, 14–13, and Jones resigned the next day.

NO ONE IRRITATED Huey Long more than Paul Cyr. After the *Louisiana Progress* attacked Cyr for abandoning Huey, the lieutenant governor sent a telegram to the editor of the *Progress,* John Klorer, and called him a "liar and a poltroon." The bitter exchange was just enough to rekindle the smoldering animosity between Louisiana's two highest ranking officials.

On March 4, 1931, Senator Ransdell's term expired and the Senate office became vacant. Huey, whose gubernatorial term would not end until May 1932, refused to assume the Senate office until his successor as governor was in place. Hostile newspapers, Huey's opponents, and especially the lieutenant governor demanded that Huey step down and go to Washington and take his seat. Throughout that spring and summer of 1931, Dr. Cyr threatened to take the oath of office as governor.

Huey had been reluctant to leave the state since February 1929 when he and Cyr split over the Dreher-LeBoeuf murder case. He feared that Cyr would decimate the Long political machine if he became acting governor in his absence. "Governor, Senator-Elect, and a Prisoner in His Own State," read the headline of a St. Louis newspaper on March 22, 1931. On one occasion, Cyr learned that Huey had spent the night in Jackson, Mississippi, and headed for Baton Rouge to take over. Huey rushed back, crossing the state line in time to send a telegram saying he was safely back on Louisiana soil just before Cyr entered the capital city to seize the governor's office. After Huey sent national guardsmen to surround the capitol with machine guns, Cyr gave up.

That fall, Huey canceled plans to travel to West Point for the LSU football game. He blamed Cyr, who refused to sign a document promising not to take the oath of office if Huey left the state. Cyr gave a verbal promise not to take power but Huey would accept only a written one. For months, Huey had planned to accompany the LSU student body on a cross-country train excursion throughout the Northeast on their way to the military academy, but he did not make the trip. On November 7, 1931, a furious Huey stayed in Louisiana while seventeen hundred LSU students traveled to West Point and watched Army beat LSU, 20 0.

Dr. Cyr filed suit in early October to oust Huey as governor. On October 14, the dentist declared himself governor and had a Shreveport justice of the peace give him the oath of office in the Caddo Parish courthouse. Cyr insisted that Huey had vacated the office upon being elected senator. "I want Huey Long to get out of office as soon as possible," said Cyr, "so I can go in and straighten up this state and put an end to this debauchery." When Cyr arrived in Baton Rouge and threatened to take over the mansion, Huey raced from New Orleans to the capital. Chick Frampton, a *New Orleans Item* newspaper reporter, was with Huey. As they left, the governor stuck a gun in his belt. "Huey was deathly opposed to guns and he didn't drive much," Frampton remembered. "We got in that low-slung, special-built Cadillac and we drove to Baton Rouge in less than an hour and my heart was in my mouth, with Huey driving ninety and a hundred. I thought he was crazy."

When Huey arrived in the capital, he ordered the National Guard to mobilize. Troops again surrounded the capitol with strict orders not to admit the lieutenant governor. Within a few days, state police replaced the guardsmen. "It was an armed camp," recalled one of Huey's supporters. "Doc carried a gun and Huey carried a gun." Huey, taking no chances, also ordered the four LSU football players who were living at the mansion at the time to stay home from class and "throw Cyr out on North Street" if he showed up. Dr. Cyr realized he was beaten again and returned to his home and dental practice in Jeanerette.

Huey was not finished with Cyr, however. He argued that Cyr, by taking the oath of governor, had vacated the lieutenant governorship and since his oath for governor was illegal, he held neither job. "Taking the oath of office as governor ends Dr. Cyr," Huey declared. "He is no longer Lieutenant Governor, and he is now nothing." Huey appointed one of his loyal legislators, Senator Alvin O. King, as lieutenant governor and ordered that Cyr no longer receive a salary from the state.

On November 3, Huey traveled to Shreveport and argued for an hour and a half to convince a Shreveport court that Dr. Cyr's claim to the governorship was baseless. Huey contended that several other governors had delayed their Senate appointment while finishing their gubernatorial terms. He also argued that the courts could not remove a governor and that the qualifications for a U.S. senator could only be determined by the U.S. Senate. He was persuasive, for two weeks later Caddo district judge T. F. Bell dismissed Cyr's suit to oust Huey as governor.

Huey Long and most other Louisianans agreed with the pro-Long *Bienville Democrat* that Cyr "had about as much chance being installed or elected governor of Louisiana as a Texas billy-goat had of making a nonstop jump to the planet Mars."

CHAPTER 8

1932
WITCHES BOUND
AT THE STAKE

O f all of Huey Long's supporters, none was more loyal than Oscar Kelly Allen. Silver-haired, friendly, and harmless, O. K. Allen followed Huey's orders like an obedient cocker spaniel. In late 1931, Huey neared the end of his four-year term as governor and, needing to pick a successor who would blindly carry out his bidding, turned to his old friend Oscar to run for governor in the upcoming January 1932 election. Allen, eleven years older than Huey, grew up in poverty on a farm three miles from Hugh Long's spread in Winnfield, taught in a country school, and later managed a sawmill and opened his own small store. Voters elected him Winn Parish assessor in 1916. In 1918 he borrowed $500 from a Winnfield bank to help finance Huey's first campaign for railroad commissioner and from then on he was completely devoted to Huey. O.K. was elected to the state Senate in 1928 at the same time Huey became governor. Shortly afterward Huey appointed him chairman of the Highway Commission.

Mild, modest, and dignified, O.K. was forgetful and did not remember people's names. He suffered both from heart disease and his huge, overbearing wife, Florence. "Between Huey and his wife," Allen's secretary, Richard Leche, remembered, "old Oscar really used to catch it." Huey dominated O.K., often bullying him in front of others. "Huey used to cuss him unmercifully," Leche recalled. During a caucus of Long supporters, Huey exploded at O.K. and shouted, "Oscar, you sonofabitch, shut up!" Despite Huey's abuse, O.K. remained steadfastly loyal and over the next few years their friendship made Allen a rich man.

Along with O. K. Allen running for governor, Huey's "Complete the Work" ticket included John Fournet running for lieutenant governor, Gaston Porterie for attorney general, and a full slate of his supporters for the other elected officers. Because several of the offices up for election sat on the powerful state Board of Liquidation, Huey ensured that he controlled every contest. He selected Allen Ellender, the representative from Terrebonne Parish, to succeed Fournet as speaker of the house and also serve as campaign manager for the ticket, although Huey continued to decide upon the smallest of details.

When Huey picked Fournet to run for lieutenant governor he created a nasty split within his own family. His brother Earl wanted to run for the post and asked Huey for his endorsement. Huey and Earl had always had a love-hate relationship. As children, they were close, slept in the same room, and played together, but the brothers constantly competed. Tall, lean, and graceful, Earl was slower mentally but stronger physically than Huey and aspired to follow in his brother's footsteps. "Huey was fond of Earl but Earl tended to be jealous of Huey," a Long supporter remembered, adding that the brothers split and reconciled several times. "Those Longs are like a bunch of quail. They flutter up and beat at each other but when it's over they settle back together." When Huey chose Fournet, Earl blew up and decided to run anyway. Huey's older brother Julius campaigned energetically for Earl and the entire Long family backed Earl.

When the race for governor started in summer 1931, Allen faced three opponents. George Guion, an upper-class lawyer from New Orleans with little political experience, ran on an honest-government platform. Guion had little chance, for Huey still controlled the New Orleans vote after Walmsley and the Old Regulars surrendered to him a year before. Lieutenant Governor Paul Cyr also entered the governor's race. Huey pretended he was surprised when Cyr announced, remarking that Cyr "should run for a race he could win, such as justice of the peace in Jeanerette." Cyr realized he had no chance of winning, withdrew, and endorsed Guion.

The third opponent to enter the race for governor was Huey's antag-onist Dudley LeBlanc, the flamboyant Frenchman who served on the Public Service Commission without pay because Huey kept vetoing the commission's appropriations. LeBlanc had a small following in Acadiana but his only organized support was Francis Williams's weak New Orleans faction.

As soon as the campaign began, Dudley launched attacks that were almost as vicious and colorful as Huey's. "Why, if I had a cow as stupid and dumb looking as O. K. Allen," Dudley declared, "I'd take him out and cut his head off." LeBlanc accused Ellender, who owned a large farm, of selling "inferior potatoes to the penitentiary at superior prices." Most of Dudley's ire, though, was aimed at Huey. He claimed he was running for governor to rid "this state of Long and all of his blood-sucking, tax-eating, bribe-giving, and bribe-taking crowd." Dudley branded Huey as a "cow-ardly slacker" for not serving in the military during World War I. "I now call upon those buddies who fought with me in the trenches for fourteen long months to go to the polls and vote for me," LeBlanc urged his audi-ence. Dudley bent the truth, as he was drafted into the army in 1918 for only five months and never went overseas. LeBlanc "wasn't even kicked by a mule or bit by a horsefly," Huey charged back.

While O.K. was the candidate for governor, the race was still about Huey. Earl called his brother the "yellowest physical coward that God had ever let live" and dared "big-bellied Huey" to meet him face-to-face in front of the Roosevelt Hotel. Huey struck back. "[Earl is] my brother but he's crooked. If you live long enough he'll double cross you. He'd double cross Jesus Christ if he was down here on earth."

The campaign was even uglier when Huey and Dudley hurled racial epithets at each other. In December, in a speech in Colfax, a lumber town in Grant Parish, Huey claimed that LeBlanc "operates a nigger burial lodge and shroud and coffin club. He charges for a coffin and he charges $7.50 for a shroud. I am informed that the nigger is laid out, and after the mourners have left, LeBlanc takes the body into a back room, takes off the shroud, nails them up into a pine box, and buries them at a total cost of $3.67 and a ½ cents." In a speech a couple of nights later, LeBlanc called Huey and O.K. "nigger lovers." After LeBlanc promised a $30-a-month old-age pension for every Louisianan over sixty, Huey claimed, "LeBlanc is going to pay pensions to Negroes, too, because don't you think he is going to overlook his lodge brothers. It will cost twenty million dollars a year to pay the Negroes' pensions alone, and you white people will be working the year around to pay the pensions to Negroes."

On December 10, Huey and Dudley treated the people of Bunkie, a small town west of Baton Rouge, to an evening of political fireworks. As Huey campaigned there for Allen, LeBlanc showed up and the two politicians parked their sound trucks about seventy yards apart on the main street, turning up their amplifiers until the loudspeakers shook, shouting invectives, racial insults, and charges at each other for over two hours. "You pronounce LeBlanc's name by trying to grunt like a hog," Huey yelled, "and changing your mind when you're half way through."

The newspapers of Louisiana loved the political carnival, as it sold more papers. Near the end of 1931, the *New Orleans Item,* in a circulation battle with the *Times-Picayune,* broke ranks and shifted support to Huey and Allen. *Item* publisher James Thomson felt that an alliance with Huey would boost circulation. On January 12, 1932, a week before the election, Huey ceased publication of his *Louisiana Progress* and required all state employees to subscribe to the *Item.* Soon after, the *Item* reporter Chick Frampton, who was friendly with Huey, accepted a position in the state attorney general's office for $300 a month.

LeBlanc tried to imitate Huey and started his own newspaper, the *Louisiana News.* First published from Lafayette in May 1932 and costing 25 cents a year, Dudley's *News* was created for the purpose of "the exposure of political crooks." Because he was unable to force state workers to subscribe, LeBlanc's paper never achieved success. While he pictured himself in the same role as Huey, Dudley possessed neither the guile nor determination of Huey. The Louisiana political arena was too small for two such characters and Huey shared his stage with no one.

The campaign was hectic. On New Year's Eve, Huey raced across the center of the state giving ten speeches in one day for Allen. Over the course of the campaign, LeBlanc delivered nearly five hundred speeches, nine on the day before the election. Dudley's energetic campaigning was no match for Huey, however. On January 19, the voters of Louisiana delivered a landslide victory to Allen. O.K. received 214,699 votes; LeBlanc, 110,048; and Guion, 53,756. Allen won fifty-four of the sixty-four parishes and captured 70 percent of the New Orleans vote, thanks to the support of the Old Regulars.

One reporter described the election as "ignorant and meaningless a campaign as was ever staged in Louisiana history." Rumors of corruption at the polls were rampant. An eighteen-year-old voter in New Orleans, A. O. Rappelet, claimed to have gotten his political initiation when he voted for the Long ticket twenty times on election day. In notoriously crooked St. Bernard Parish, controlled by pro-Long Sheriff Mereaux, Allen received 3,152 votes, the other candidates no votes, despite the fact that the parish had only 2,194 registered voters. Earlier in the campaign, Mereaux came to the Roosevelt where Huey asked the sheriff how many votes the opposition would get. Mereaux answered about two. When St. Bernard went unanimously for Allen, Huey called up Mereaux and asked, "What the hell happened to those two fellows?" The sheriff answered without hesitation: "They changed their minds at the last minute."

The voters swept most pro-Long legislators into office. Twenty-eight of eighty-six members of the House who sought reelection were defeated, most of them anti-Longs, while other anti-Long representatives decided not to run for reelection when they discovered that Huey's machine was just too powerful. To the displeasure of most of the Long family, Huey's candidate, John Fournet, defeated his brother Earl for lieutenant governor.

SOME OF HUEY'S OPPONENTS chose not to challenge his increasingly powerful and well-financed political machine. One of his diehard enemies who decided not to run was the venerable Judge Gilbert Dupre, the contrary, deaf old legislator. Dupre decided to abandon the House seat he had held since 1888 when he learned that his son-in-law, Dr. Octave Pavy, would oppose him in the upcoming election. Dupre knew he had no chance. The ruling Creole families of St. Landry Parish, including the powerful Pavys, switched allegiance to Huey after he promised to build a state road through Opelousas, their quaint French-American parish seat. Penniless, Dupre looked for employment. In a sad twist of politics, Huey took pity on his old nemesis and hired Dupre as a columnist for the *Louisiana Progress*. Dupre's articles were as vitriolic as his former speeches in the House, although he now aimed his attacks at Huey's opponents instead of Huey. His columns stooped to antebellum racism, claiming in one that LeBlanc "associated with Negroes." Heralded by the *Progress* as "one of the most capable barristers of the state," Dupre later defended Huey's attempt to tax the state's large newspapers. "Whether the papers should be taxed is debatable," Dupre wrote. "But to argue that taxing them was an assault on freedom of the press is rot pure and simple."

On Thanksgiving Day 1931, shortly after he went to work at the *Progress,* Dupre was back in Opelousas and while crossing the main street ran into his friend Charlie DeJean, a forty-year-old salesman. DeJean stopped Dupre and wrote on the deaf man's pad, "You thought Allen was a crook three months ago. What do you think of him now?" Dupre, still proud and stubborn at seventy-two, exploded at DeJean's suggestion that he was a hypocrite. The judge walked back to his home a couple of blocks away and stuck his .38 revolver in his belt. He returned to the town square, rounded a corner near the courthouse, and again ran into DeJean. Dupre pulled out his revolver and shot Dejean in the stomach. The man died on the spot.

Huey felt sympathy for Dupre and hired Austin Fontenot, the Long leader in the parish and a shrewd attorney, to defend the old man. Dupre claimed self-defense, arguing that "I couldn't physically fight a man of that size." A parish court acquitted Dupre of the murder. Huey later appointed Fontenot district attorney to replace another St. Landry enemy, Lee Garland.

ON A WINTRY AFTERNOON late in January 1932, Senator Jim Watson of Indiana, the stodgy and stiff Republican leader of the United States Senate, relaxed near his desk. Watson was startled when a stranger spun him around, slapped him sharply in the chest with an open hand, and introduced himself. "Jim, I want to get acquainted with you!" Staggered by the blow, Watson asked, "Well, who in the hell are you?" The stranger loudly answered so all around could hear, "I am Huey Long."

Several days before, Huey decided that the time was right to take his seat in the U.S. Senate. With O. K. Allen elected to succeed him as governor, Huey could depart Baton Rouge and proceed to Washington. He left Lieutenant Governor King, earlier selected to replace Paul Cyr, in Baton

Rouge's Heidelberg Hotel to act as governor until Allen's inauguration in May. Just before nine in the evening on January 23, Huey boarded the *Crescent City Limited* in New Orleans's Louisville & Nashville Station and headed north. Wearing a flashy polka-dot tie and a gigantic gladiola in the lapel of his swanky charcoal suit, Huey refused to let a driving rainstorm dampen the spirit of his departure. The Kingfish was in a gay mood and a party atmosphere filled the private Pullman coach that took him to Washington. He invited a large following along for the ride, including his wife, Rose, Seymour Weiss, O. K. Allen, John Fournet, a handful of Old Regulars, and New Orleans mayor Semmes Walmsley. When the train stopped in Atlanta, Huey stepped from the coach for some fresh air. He looked surprisingly relaxed. "I'm going to get an education in Washington," he told a reporter standing on the platform. "This is the first time in five years that my blood pressure has been normal. Why, I've been sleeping with four telephones in my bedroom."

At four in the morning on January 25, Huey arrived in Washington and checked into the Mayflower Hotel with several of his ever-present bodyguards. Later that day, after smacking Senator Watson on the chest, he took the oath as United States senator. Although he occupied the seat once used by venerable Senator John C. Calhoun, Huey was unimpressed by the Senate's tradition and flouted its hidebound protocol. On his first day, he sauntered onto the floor wearing a gray double-breasted suit and smoking a large cigar, a violation of the Senate's no-smoking policy, and placed the smoldering stogie on a senator's desk while he held up his right hand to take the oath of office. On that day, he snubbed another old enemy, the senior senator from Louisiana, Edwin Broussard. Huey had stumped for Broussard in 1926 against J. Y. Sanders but since that time the two hated each other. In 1931, Broussard demanded that Huey resign as governor and take his seat in the Senate, dubbing him "the worst Governor Louisiana ever had." Normally the senior senator would introduce a new senator from his home state to his colleagues. Neither Huey nor Broussard were on speaking terms, so Senator Joe Robinson of Arkansas escorted Huey into the chamber.

HUEY LASTED ONLY one day in Washington. On the day after he arrived in the Senate and took the oath, he climbed aboard the *Crescent City Lim-*

ited and rushed back to Baton Rouge. When he reached New Orleans, Huey appeared disgusted by his first venture to the nation's capital. Washington, D.C., was the "farthest spot from the United States I've seen," he remarked to reporters. "The Democrats seem like a whipped rooster with the victor pecking us on the head, and all standing there bleeding, taking it."

Huey claimed he returned to Louisiana to help move his family to their new home in New Orleans but he really hurried back to quell another revolt. Paul Cyr, the ousted lieutenant governor, tried again to seize control of Louisiana's government. When Huey arrived in Baton Rouge on January 28, he found that Cyr was back in town claiming to be governor. Cyr believed that Huey's absence from the state capital gave him the opportunity to take control and that Huey would not abandon the Senate. Cyr underestimated his bitter enemy and did not understand that despite his new responsibilities in the Senate, Huey's overriding priority would always be to maintain his control over Louisiana.

A week before, the Louisiana Supreme Court with four pro-Long members on the bench had decided, 4–3, that Cyr held no legal claim to the governorship, but Cyr ignored the court and established his "executive offices" in Baton Rouge's Heidelberg Hotel. He took the oath as governor for a second time. After Huey discovered Cyr's location, he called the manager of the Heidelberg and had the former lieutenant governor evicted. Cyr moved down the street to a seedier location, the Louisiana Hotel. With Huey in firm control of the capital, the dentist left Baton Rouge and returned to Jeanerette. Later, when Huey was back in Washington, Governor Alvin King ordered General Fleming, the head of the National Guard, to stay at the mansion in case Cyr tried again. Despite his duties in the Senate, Huey frequently would travel back to Louisiana to attend state legislative sessions, help his candidates win local elections, and ensure that his power over the state remained secure.

Before he returned to Washington, Huey and Rose completed their move from Shreveport to New Orleans. Their new home was a pink stucco Italian Renaissance mansion at 14 Audubon Boulevard near Tulane University. Bob Maestri bought the old Shreveport home and personally financed the $40,000 mortgage for the new one. The house in

New Orleans had come up for sale when its previous owner lost a fortune at the gambling table. That fall, Huey formed a new law firm with Senator Harvey Peltier of Lafourche Parish and the two attorneys opened an office on the eighteenth floor of the Canal Bank Building in New Orleans.

While in New Orleans, Huey also barged into the Mardi Gras celebration. He called President Smith of LSU and ordered the university band sent immediately to New Orleans. That night, Huey and the huge band, 250 musicians clad in purple and gold, surprised the thousands of revelers when they marched at the head of the Parade of Rex, King of Mardi Gras, down Canal Street. Huey, waving a baton wildly above his head, led the parade as drum major. When New Orleans police stepped momentarily in his path he shouted them out of his way. "Stand back," he roared. "This is the Kingfish!"

HUEY ARRIVED BACK in Washington in the middle of February and immediately began upsetting the staid Senate with his wild antics, loud outbursts, and outlandish dress. While his colleagues conformed to conservative striped blue suits, Huey romped about the Senate chamber in flashy brown tweeds, beautiful white shirts of the finest fabric with his monogram embroidered on one sleeve, a bright red silk necktie, and, according to one chastising reporter, "a handkerchief regrettably on the pink side." The courtly Senate had never observed such savage energy in its chamber, its members stunned as Huey "galloped about the Senate floor getting acquainted like a colt let out to pasture." Always in motion, his body was as restless as his mind. When not speaking he meandered around, sitting down in any convenient seat. If he was interested in the debate he moved to a desk near the speaker and stared intently up at him. If bored by the proceedings, he roamed the back of the chamber, spinning a pencil between his fingers and grabbing any senator who passed by and lecturing him on the latest controversy. Just being in the same room with Huey exhausted his colleagues.

By the time Huey arrived in Washington, the Seventy-second Congress had been meeting for two months. Over the next five months, he enraged his colleagues with an abysmal attendance record. He rarely attended any committee meetings and of the 137 days that remained in the session, he was absent for eighty-one. Later that year, Senator David Reed, a Pennsylvania Republican already repulsed by Huey's brash style, reprimanded him for repeated absences from the Senate.

When Huey did show up, he exasperated his colleagues with political bluster and radical motions. On April 4, 1932, he took the Senate floor and gave the first of many speeches calling for legislation to share the wealth, limit all fortunes to $100 million, and divide up the remaining millions among the poor. Titled "The Doom of America's Dream," this speech was an aggressive critique of President Herbert Hoover's feeble economic policy. He quoted labor leader Samuel Gompers and philosopher John Dewey and provided statistics arguing that corporate monopoly and maldistribution of wealth were the root causes of the Depression. He warned there must be a drastic redistribution of wealth. "There is no rule so sure as that one that the same mill that grinds out fortunes above a certain size at the top, grinds out paupers at the bottom," Huey declared. A week later Huey introduced an anti-monopoly bill in the Senate and proposed a 65 percent surtax on incomes greater than $2 million. All of his motions and resolutions gained little support from his colleagues and his bills to share the wealth never received more than twenty votes. The other senators began to shun him. "I don't believe he could get the Lord's Prayer endorsed in this body," one senator remembered.

TO HUEY AND MANY of his colleagues in the United States Senate, Joe Robinson was "cooler than a fresh cucumber and sourer than a pickled one." A short-statured but solid Southern aristocrat who always wore a funereal black bow tie, Robinson was the senior senator from Arkansas, minority leader, and powerful Democratic wheelhorse. Conservative, arrogant, and a stickler for the Senate's stuffy traditions, Robinson autocratically issued orders to the Democratic members and expected them to obey him blindly. He immediately detested the insubordinate new senator from Louisiana.

When Robinson and other conservative Democrats refused to support Long's amendment to limit annual incomes to $5 million, Huey attacked the Arkansas senator. As he had in past political fights, Huey continued to "always hit the big man first." Rising on the Senate floor, waving his arms and clenching his fists, he insisted that the Senate immediately remove Robinson as minority leader. While his colleagues sat appalled at their desks, he suggested that the Democrat Robinson join Republican Hoover's campaign as his vice presidential running mate. "Robinson and Hoover work together for the same things, with the same ideas, and with the same results." He blamed the Depression on a conspiracy among Robinson, Hoover, financier Bernard Baruch, and Eugene Meyer, governor of the Federal Reserve Bank.

Huey's cruel attack became more personal when he read a list of Robinson's Arkansas corporate clients that represented "every nefarious interest on the living face of the globe." He accused Robinson of getting rich from his Senate office. "The Bible tells us that where a man's treasure is, there is his heart. When a man comes into the Senate without enough clients to make a corporal's guard and winds up representing every big corporate interest, if that does not mean something, what does?" He even criticized Robinson's appearance, remarking that "Joe doesn't look really as well with his hair dyed." During Huey's tirade, Senator Reed of Pennsylvania motioned to invoke Senate Rule Nineteen prohibiting a senator from personally attacking another member. A few days later, Vice President Charles Curtis abruptly ordered Huey to take his seat after he made another personal attack on Robinson.

Huey ignored the censures and on May 12, 1932, launched one of his most vicious attacks on Robinson. "It was an epitome of bad taste—and bad psychology," Senator Hattie Caraway wrote. "[Huey] is making a spectacle of himself of which he will be ashamed as he gains in years and wisdom— If!" At the end of his harangue, a purple-faced Huey brushed back a lock of hair that kept falling in his face and turned to the presiding officer of the Senate. "I send to the desk, Mr. President, my resignation from every committee . . . that has been given to me by the Democratic leadership since I have been here." Huey's resignation of his committee assignments startled everyone. One newspaper reporter wrote that his act "makes one think of the schoolboy who won't play on the school ball team because the players won't let him pitch." Senator Robinson belittled his performance as a "comic opera performance unworthy of the great actor from Louisiana." The *Washington Post* called for Huey to resign from the Senate.

When Huey realized his motions and speeches produced little result, he began a new strategy to wear out his opponents. On May 16, he delivered a three-hour filibuster in which he told "some rather funny stories." With unlimited freedom to speak, Huey enjoyed his control over the Senate. "I am beginning to be convinced by the logic of my own argument," he declared. "I feel the urge to talk." As he gave his filibuster, he ignored the rule that a senator should stand formally by his desk when he rose to speak. Instead, he wandered into the center aisle that divided the semicircle of desks, approached the speaker's rostrum, and wove between the desks of his exasperated colleagues. Increasingly, he resorted to long-winded diatribes. In June, he delivered another filibuster, this time delaying a bill that increased income tax rates.

As word of Huey's antics spread, crowds began to fill the Senate galleries each time he took the floor. Often his humorous barbs caused the spectators to laugh loudly. On one occasion, after a particularly scathing attack on one of his colleagues had the gallery roaring, the presiding officer threatened to clear the galleries if the laughter continued. Senator Alben Barkley, however, argued for the show to continue. "When the people go to the circus," the caustic Barkley declared, "they ought to be allowed to laugh at the monkey." During many of these sessions, one of the spectators was a tall, gawky Texan in his early twenties named Lyndon Johnson. Just arrived in Washington as an aide to a congressman, Johnson begged the Senate doorkeeper to call him whenever Huey was about to speak. "For leading the masses and illustrating your point humanly, Huey Long couldn't be beat," remembered the future president. "I was simply entranced by Huey Long."

AT A MEETING OF the LSU Board of Supervisors in the fall of 1931, Huey stormed into the conference room and immediately ordered the board members to fire Professor John Uhler. A popular English instructor, Uhler recently had published the novel *Cane Juice* and Huey was furious. Set in southern Louisiana, *Cane Juice* portrayed a crude and stubbornly nonconformist Cajun student who struggled to survive in the fast-paced, somewhat debauched college life of LSU. The novel painted a realistic but less than complimentary picture of Louisiana, its backward culture, and the state university. *Cane Juice* made no mention of Louisiana politics nor Huey, other than a passing mention of the state's governor leading the

LSU band down the field during a football game. To most readers, the novel contained little that would have been considered outrageous or lewd, and it probably would have stirred little controversy outside Louisiana. Its most ribald scene occurred early in the book. "These Cajun boys and girls climbed up and down platforms, ate handfuls of brown, wet sugar, laughed and chattered and disappeared into dark corners and made love," wrote Uhler. "Immediately about them was rumble and roar of turning machinery and the fragrance of cane juice, and beyond was the silence of the swamp and the blackness of the night."

The tepid prose of *Cane Juice,* however, ignited controversy in the tinderbox of Baton Rouge politics. Father F. L. Gassler, the local Catholic priest who gave the invocation before the Bloody Monday House session, called Uhler's novel "slimy animalism and mental filth." In a letter to Uhler, the outspoken priest accused the professor of creating "an insult to the intelligence of its Creole inhabitants" and "a monstrous slander of the purest womanhood." Soon after Father Gassler's letter reached the LSU Board of Supervisors, Huey called the meeting of the board and demanded Uhler's ouster. A former army lieutenant who served in the trenches during World War I, Uhler refused to resign. A couple of days later, on orders from Huey, LSU president Smith fired the professor.

"I realize that behind my dismissal there are sinister and powerful influences, difficult to combat," Uhler told a newspaper writer after his firing. "I feel like one of the witches bound at the stake in Salem." Uhler did not mention Huey's name, but almost every person in Louisiana knew that the "sinister and powerful influence" to which Uhler referred was none other than the Kingfish.

Uhler's firing quickly became a national sensation. The professor, a lean, high-browed scholar with a pencil-thin mustache, received hundreds of letters of support from across the country. The American Civil Liberties Union, a prominent force after the 1925 Scopes monkey trial, agreed to take Uhler's case and sue the university. The ACLU, in an "emergency call for action," urged its members to write LSU president Smith, and letters protesting the firing began to pour into the university. H. L. Mencken sent the professor a letter saying he was lucky to escape "servitude in such a hole" as Louisiana.

Cane Juice, however, may not have been the chief reason for Uhler's firing. In 1930, LSU law student Kemble K. Kennedy published a scathing scandal sheet called the *Whangdoodle* that made vicious and obscene attacks on several LSU faculty members. The *Whangdoodle* was especially cruel with Uhler. "LSU professor dope fiend [Uhler] nabbed by Baton Rouge police," read a headline in the scandal sheet, adding that when police arrested Uhler, the professor was sleeping in the Istrouma Hotel with a woman of "ill repute . . . of the fifty-seven variety." After Uhler and three other professors filed a slander suit, a Baton Rouge court convicted Kennedy of criminal libel and sentenced him to a year in parish prison. The crusty dean of the law school, Robert Tullis, refused to grant Kennedy a law degree because of the *Whangdoodle*. However, Kennedy was one of Huey's pet students, having formed a pro-Long political fraternity, Theta Nu Epsilon, standing for "The New Era," that championed Huey's machine. Many of the TNE brothers got jobs at the Highway Commission. Huey reprieved Kennedy after serving a week of his sentence and ordered the state Tax Commission to give him a job in its New Orleans office. After Uhler sued Kennedy, the professor's name apparently found its way into Huey's "son of a bitch book" and the *Cane Juice* controversy provided Huey with a fitting excuse to fire Uhler. To Huey, Uhler was just another state worker and subject to firing by political whim. "Huey just made them and broke them," a faculty member recalled.

For six months letters of protest arrived in President Smith's office, including challenges from influential organizations such as the American Association of University Professors. At the same time, Uhler's colleagues rallied to the professor's side and called for him to be rehired. On April 5, 1932, six months after the dismissal, President Smith rehired Uhler, giving no reason for either the firing or the rehiring. It was Huey who probably yielded and ordered Uhler's reinstatement, as the Kingfish tired of seeing his precious university becoming a laughingstock across the country.

Cane Juice, a mediocre novel at best and originally turned down by several publishers, benefited from the windfall of national notoriety and, to Huey Long's chagrin, quickly sold fifty thousand copies.

CHAPTER 9

1932
HATTIE AND HUEY

On the same Monday in May 1932 that Huey Long launched his first filibuster on the floor of the United States Senate, one thousand miles to the south a pelting rainstorm swept through Baton Rouge and delayed Oscar K. Allen's inauguration as the next governor of Louisiana. When the storm passed, O.K. stepped to the rostrum on the capitol steps and took the oath of office as Huey's handpicked successor. After standing rigidly at attention while the Louisiana National Guard fired a seventeen-gun salute, Allen, a silver-haired and dignified man of few words, gave the shortest inaugural speech in Louisiana history.

Allen's inauguration also was the occasion for the dedication of the new state capitol. "That's some building," Huey boasted. "It only cost five million and I had it finished within a year of the day we laid the cornerstone." He helped design the soaring thirty-four-story capitol and approved every detail "down to the last brass cuspidor." Bragging that the five-hundred-foot building was the tallest state capitol in the nation, he spared no expense. Elaborate Art Deco marble friezes adorned the building and a finely chiseled Roman soldier stood resolutely beside the grand entrance. Carvings of Audubon, the naturalist, and Charles Gayarre, a historian of Louisiana, appeared alongside a bigger-than-life carving of Huey Long. The breathtaking lobby contained over thirty varieties of marble from all over the world, including floors of polished brown lava quarried from Italy's Mount Vesuvius.

The new capitol bred controversy. "Only an otiose soul, struck by a lopsided gleam of grandeur, could have inflicted such an anachronism on a peaceful ante-bellum community," one journalist wrote, "where one might expect a graceful, colonnaded structure reminiscent of old Creole days, a skyscraper, adorned with embellishments from New York's garment center, ravages the eye." Huey ignored the critics, adoring the modernistic spire that contrasted sharply to the old, medieval capitol that sat abandoned a few blocks away. To him, the new capitol was the perfect symbol of his power, success, and towering ambition.

HUEY NO LONGER served as governor but he held more political power than ever and continued to expand his domination over almost every facet of state government. His personal attendant, O. K. Allen, sat in the huge leather governor's chair, but each time Huey returned to Baton Rouge from Washington, the Kingfish took over and O.K. moved to a secretary's office. Whenever Huey and his bodyguards took the elevator to his private apartment on the capitol's twenty-fourth floor, they often crowded Allen off the elevator, leaving the governor of Louisiana standing sheepishly alone waiting for the next lift. Allen was so completely obedient to Huey that, according to Earl Long, a leaf once blew through a statehouse window onto the governor's desk and O.K. signed it.

To keep an eye on Allen and ensure that his enemies did not manipulate the pliant governor, Huey assigned Richard Leche as O.K.'s secretary. A tall, hefty attorney from New Orleans's Fourteenth Ward, Leche understood that his primary duty was to keep Huey informed of happenings in Baton Rouge. Leche phoned Washington several times each day, taking his orders from Huey, who continued to make the day-to-day decisions of running Louisiana.

Huey needed to make plenty of decisions, as his ambitious programs had depleted the state treasury. A modern highway system, a hundred new bridges, new schools, free textbooks, free reading classes for 175,000 illiterates, state charity hospitals doubled in size, a new governor's mansion, a new state capitol, and thousands of extra state workers to swell the patronage ranks had drained the state during the worst of the Depression. During 1931 alone, Huey spent $79 million, just $2 million less than Governor Parker spent in four years, and pushed the state debt from $11 million to over $100 million. He financed many of his expensive building projects by selling bonds, which forced the state deeper into debt. The deficit stimulated the economy and created jobs during the Depression but Louisiana's credit rating eventually fell so low that state-issued bonds no longer could be sold. Huey was bankrupting the state.

Huey's financial extravagance already had caused a rift within his cabinet. H. B. Conner, the state treasurer, had tried for four years to keep Huey within the law and sound economics. After Conner refused to borrow funds irresponsibly from the Board of Liquidation, Huey banned the treasurer from his political camp. "You'll never get a job in the state as long as I'm alive," he threatened. Conner, a sharp, popular accountant, left office in 1932 and soon was hired by a Louisiana accounting firm. Within a few days, Huey's henchmen visited the firm and ordered Conner's new boss "to fire the sonofabitch or you would not get any business." After getting five jobs and being fired from each of them shortly thereafter, Conner left his family in Baton Rouge and moved to Atlanta to take a federal job.

Now needing new sources of revenue, Huey ignored the economic and political consequences and ordered a series of new taxes to be levied upon the people of Louisiana. When the legislature convened on May 12, 1932, for its regular sixty-day session, he instructed Governor Allen to propose a constitutional amendment that would create the state's first income tax. Incomes over $2,000 a year would be taxed at one percent. Even the income tax would not generate enough revenue, however, and Huey looked for other sources to pay for road and bridge bonds and salaries for new state employees. He ordered another amendment that increased sales taxes on cigarettes, gasoline, soft drinks, dairy products, chain stores, and business franchises. He also drafted a tax on insurance premiums collected in the state, a tax on electric power companies, and a franchise tax on all corporations. As legislators worked through the bills, Huey stood nervously in the back of the House eating peanuts, and when a vote started he moved along the seats tapping men and telling them how to vote.

Huey's new taxes, normally inflammatory issues with any legislator, rolled through both houses, passing overwhelmingly and with little debate. His supporters chaired all of the important committees and Speaker of the House Allen Ellender and President Pro Tem of the Senate Frank Peterman, a short, bald, and slight senator from Alexandria, were staunch Long loyalists who made certain that only Huey's bills were brought to a vote. Having all of the New Orleans representatives support his bills and voting as a bloc ensured that Huey's legislation flowed smoothly through both houses.

Huey's opposition, depleted by the recent election, had little chance to thwart the new taxes. When now-senator J. Y. Sanders, Jr., still one of Huey's more vocal antagonists, introduced a bill to create a state civil service system modeled after that of the federal government, the proposal quickly died in committee. Another opponent, Representative Malcolm Dougherty of East Feliciana Parish, introduced a futile resolution in the House accusing Huey of "lobbying and meddling" with the business of the House and suggesting he return to his seat in the U.S. Senate. As Huey stomped angrily back and forth in the legislature corridor, House members defeated the resolution, 77–12. Meanwhile, on the other side of the capitol, the Senate Rules Committee, chaired by Huey's law partner, Harvey Peltier, granted ex-governors the privilege of the floor when the Senate was in session. Peltier's motion passed unanimously.

Huey's new taxes ignited loud but ineffective protests. His opponents, including many businessmen, feared that the new taxes would drive business and industry from the state. The Louisiana economy already suffered from the Depression, and New Orleans slipped from the second to the fifth busiest port in the nation during Huey's governorship. "I'll never invest another cent in Louisiana while that lying crook is in power," vowed a wealthy lumber and oil man. On June 13, Mrs. Ruffin Pleasant, the explosive wife of the ex-governor, testified before the House against the new taxes. "If this tax bill passes, it will mean nothing but your baring your backs to Huey P. Long," Mrs. Pleasant argued. "I appeal to the manhood and womanhood of the state not to come here and listen to the dictator who has come down here from Washington to run things." She concluded by labeling Huey's administration the "second regime of carpetbagging." Huey, standing in the back of the House when Mrs. Pleasant began, walked loudly out of the chamber in the middle of her testimony. He feared the temperamental Mrs. Pleasant. "She carried a pistol in her bag and threatened to shoot him," one of his bodyguards remembered. "I always sat right behind her at meetings."

Huey's opponents held an anti-tax rally in Baton Rouge at the old state capitol on June 13. Many protesters came armed. As expected, he called his own citizens' rally and ordered the New Orleans Ring to send twenty-one railroad cars filled with state and city employees. Both sides poured into the legislature to speak their piece. At the anti-tax rally that night, the irrepressible Mrs. Pleasant joined a chorus of anti-Longs attacking Huey's tax package. Their pleas fell on deaf ears as the Louisiana Senate passed all of the tax bills, with only five senators voting against them.

Before the session ended, Huey appointed his secretary of state, Alice Lee Grosjean, as supervisor of accounts. Supervisor of accounts was a powerful position that controlled the flow of funds into and out of the treasury and managed the collection of taxes across the state, and Huey needed one of his most trustworthy supporters in the job. Alice Lee seemed surprised at the appointment, having admitted to a reporter only a few weeks before, "I don't believe that a woman's place is in politics." When Mrs. Pleasant learned of the appointment, she exploded, describing Alice Lee as a "twenty-six-year-old girl who doesn't know the difference between single- and double-entry book keeping." During the next four years that Alice Lee served in the position, however, she proved to be an effective administrator and, overall, improved the management of the state's finances. Her performance was remarkable, considering the widespread corruption that riddled state government at that time. Mrs. Pleasant failed to mention that Alice Lee had recently held an even loftier position. A month before O. K. Allen took office, then-governor King traveled to Richmond, Virginia, to attend the National Governors Conference. At the time, there was no lieutenant governor nor president pro tem of the Senate, leaving Secretary of State Grosjean as next in line. For several days, no one in the state seemed to worry that Huey's former secretary, Alice Lee, served as acting governor of the state of Louisiana.

NOT ALL OF Huey's bills embraced new taxes. One of them spewed outright revenge. Huey was not satisfied when O. K. Allen soundly defeated

Dudley LeBlanc in the race for governor and continued his crusade to completely crush his enemy. Huey had shown his intense vindictiveness before. His harassment of Paul Cyr did not end until the lieutenant governor was gone from office, and his order to have John "Bang Tail" Sullivan banished from New Orleans politics revealed his lust for vengeance. His dislike for Dudley, however, was much more intense and personal. Huey intended to ruin LeBlanc not only politically, but professionally as well. Dudley, who described himself as the "Huey P. Long of southwest Louisiana," touched an unusually nasty nerve in Huey.

On June 7, 1932, Huey introduced a bill that strictly regulated the burial insurance industry and abolished "benevolent and cooperative associations." Every legislator realized that the bill had one purpose, to destroy Dudley's Thibodaux Benevolent Association and one of the more successful burial insurance enterprises in the state. Huey called Dudley's business the "crookedest scheme in Louisiana." Ironically, the association's records revealed that on August 1, 1922, a young attorney named Huey Long joined the association after giving a Fourth of July speech in Thibodaux.

The bill to destroy Dudley at first backfired. While Huey was in Chicago attending the Democratic National Convention, his enemies in both houses challenged the attack on Dudley. Representative George Perrault, one of the few remaining Dynamite Squad members, denounced the bill outlawing burial associations "as nothing more than an attempt to crucify LeBlanc" because he was "politically aligned against those who control the politics of the State." Representative D. F. Edwards, who originally promised Allen that he would vote to destroy Dudley's business, changed his mind after reading the bill. "I am going to be first of all a man and not a monkey," Edwards announced, "and am going to vote against it." Representative Joe Hamiter fought Huey's bill so viciously that, back in Jeanerette, Dr. Cyr named his two fighting gamecocks "Hamiter" and "Huey P. Long" and claimed to put gloves on the roosters' spurs to keep Hamiter from killing Huey P. Long.

On June 23, as representatives debated the LeBlanc bill, a fistfight erupted between two of Huey's supporters. One of them, Representative William Pegues, voted for postponement and asked his colleagues, "because a man is defeated politically, do you want to go out and cut his head off?" A fellow Longite, David Cole, jumped up and accused Pegues of straddling on the bill. The two men grappled in the middle of the floor; Pegues's shirt was ripped open and his chest bared. Both men came away with scrapes and bruises. The next day, Representative Horace Wilkinson jokingly proposed that all spectators to the House proceedings be charged a quarter for admission to view the "amusements" from the gallery.

Meanwhile, one of Huey's bodyguards, Louie Jones, assaulted Dudley's bodyguard, Joseph Boudreaux, in the marble lobby of the state capitol. Boudreaux had threatened to beat up Huey and vowed "to black both his eyes before he went back to the Senate." Jones, a short, muscular man known to be as deadly as a rattler, grabbed Boudreaux and dragged him outside onto the capitol steps. Jones claimed Boudreaux pulled a pistol. "I beat him to it with mine and knocked hell out of him," Jones recalled. He pistol-whipped Boudreaux and fractured his skull. A judge convicted Jones of attempted murder and sentenced him to prison. On Huey's orders, Governor Allen immediately pardoned Jones and later made him assistant superintendent of the state Highway Patrol.

The House voted to postpone the LeBlanc bill, but the next day Huey returned from the Chicago convention, entered the chamber, and took command. As he marched up and down the aisle wheedling legislators, the resistance melted and his bill passed, 62–28. Earlier, across the hall in the Senate, J. Y. Sanders, Jr., had led an effort that killed the LeBlanc bill. Now back in town, an iron-willed Huey reintroduced the bill and ushered it through the Senate, where it passed on July 7, the last day of the legislative session. The new vote was 31–3, with Sanders, Cecil Morgan, and Happy Sevier the only dissenters. That afternoon, Governor Allen signed the bill that put Dudley LeBlanc out of the burial insurance business in Louisiana. By 1934, LeBlanc had moved the Thibodaux Benevolent Association to Orange, Texas, just a few miles across the border.

HATTIE CARAWAY LOOKED out of place sitting at the desk next to Huey Long on the back row of the United States Senate. Matronly and fiftyish, her dark hair pulled back in a neat bun, she seemed as if she belonged on her front porch back in Jonesboro, Arkansas, knitting away in her favorite rocking chair. Huey liked Hattie. "Sitting there quiet as a mouse in her little black dress with the little black shawl over her shoulders," one observer recalled, "she probably reminded him of his boyhood Sunday school teacher." The two senators soon became good friends. Hattie was "this brave little woman" to him and he was a "poor lamb" to her. Huey amused her by bringing "color and quite a display of fireworks" to the stuffy Senate chamber, while Hattie enjoyed his "much slinging of arms" but complained that "my ear drums suffered."

Hattie and Huey first met when she accompanied her husband, Senator Thaddeus Caraway, to the cotton conference that Huey hosted in New Orleans in August 1931. Thad Caraway died unexpectedly that November and Hattie was appointed to take his place. She was sworn in three weeks before Huey arrived. Most Arkansas insiders expected Hattie to occupy her husband's Senate seat for only a few months, as the next election was scheduled for the following August. Six well-financed male opponents, including a former governor, a justice of the state Supreme Court, and a Democratic national committeeman, already had announced to run. Hattie, with virtually no money to campaign, agonized over whether to enter the race. She knew that no woman had ever been elected to the Senate for a full term. Despite little support, Hattie finally decided to enter the race. When her friends told her she had no chance in winning, she was heartstruck. "Guess my political life is nearly over," she lamented in May 1932. "I'm in for crucifixion." She sent out letters to drum up money but received no contributions. "I almost weep and then I rave," she wrote in her journal, "no wonder my hair won't stay in wave."

On May 21, Huey met Hattie on the Senate floor and told her that she had little chance of being elected. She returned to her desk, sat down with her head in her hands, and started to cry. Huey, seeing the little woman still dressed in mourning black weeping alone, was touched. Later that day he burst into her Senate office and urged her to run. "We'll put on a campaign they'll never forget," he promised, "because I'm coming to Arkansas to help you." He bounced around Hattie's office brimming with self-confidence. "We can make the campaign in one week. That's all we need. That won't give 'em a chance to get over their surprise."

Hattie was unsure if she should accept Huey's offer to help. While she agreed with his populism and other liberal causes, she worried that he was "just a bit radical" and disapproved of his crude style and methods. "Huey made a perfectly *mad* speech," she wrote in her journal that week.

"Being right next to him I had to sit through it." A month later, Hattie again disapproved of his methods. "Long is certainly cussing the Republicans now," she wrote. "I'm not enjoying that much either." She needed his help but she did not want him to control her vote. "Huey called today to donate to my campaign and work for me," she wrote. "I can't sell my soul and live with myself. It would mean nothing to me to sit here day after day and have no freedom of voting." Hattie finally agreed to accept his help on two conditions. First, he could not use the campaign to attack her fellow Arkansan, Senator Joe Robinson, and second, he could not control her vote in the future. Huey agreed.

Huey came to Hattie's aid for several likely reasons. First, the Arkansas campaign offered the opportunity for him to campaign outside Louisiana and speak to a national audience. "I can elect her and it will help my prestige," he told his aides. It also gave him the opportunity to go into the home state of his bitter enemy, Joe Robinson, and embarrass the senior senator. He kept his promise to Hattie, however, and refrained from any direct, personal attacks on Robinson. Huey also had a fondness for Hattie because she was one of only a few senators to vote for his bills, especially his unpopular motions to share the wealth. Hattie, like her late husband, voted the populist platform and irritated dyed-in-the-wool conservatives like Robinson. Finally, Huey seemed to have true sympathy for the widow in high-buttoned black shoes. Whenever he returned from one of his frequent trips back to Louisiana, he stopped by Hattie's desk and asked "how his pardner was and whether she was true to the Kingfish?"

THE FIRST DAY in August 1932 was already a scorcher when Huey departed Shreveport with his odd caravan of limousines, state troopers riding motorcycles, sound trucks blaring away, and vans carrying loads of campaign literature. They headed north, crossed the state line into Arkansas as the sun came up, and joined Hattie Caraway at Magnolia, the first stop on their campaign tour.

The people of Arkansas turned out in droves to see Huey perform, and he did not disappoint them. "I'm here to get a bunch of pot-bellied politicians off this little woman's neck," he bellowed. In Magnolia, the Kingfish wore a neatly tailored, expensive gray suit, white shirt, and flaming red necktie. As he spoke he bounced up and down, tugging at his trousers and hitching his belt, unaware that his gyrations pulled his shirt-tail out in front. Waving his arms and nervously running his hands through his unkempt hair, he soon perspired clear through his coat. After hearing him give his thunderous speech in Magnolia, a local politician sent a telegram to friends in Little Rock. "A cyclone just went through here and is headed your way," he warned. "Very few trees left standing."

As word of Huey and Hattie's "circus hitched to a tornado" spread across Arkansas, the crowds, large from the beginning, grew bigger at each stop, reaching a thousand in Newport on Wednesday, four thousand in Russellville on Thursday, and five thousand in Hot Springs on Friday night. In El Dorado, the swelling crowd forced the two senators to move from the courthouse steps to the local ballpark, where Huey parked his sound truck on the pitcher's mound and climbed onto the roof to speak. In Pine Bluff, they drew more than twenty thousand people, and in Little Rock's city park band shell on Sunday night, nearly thirty thousand attended the largest political gathering in the state's history. After his speech in Little Rock, supporters gave Huey a dinner in the city's best hotel, the Marion. He knew the hotel well, having lived there twenty-one years before when he sold packaged meats. Now, the waiters delivered his food wearing a Kingfish trademark, green silk pajamas.

Even when they did not stop to make a speech, Huey and Hattie attracted a crowd. Men and women lined roadways just to glimpse the caravan speeding by, hoping to spy Huey through the window of his huge blue Cadillac. For a hectic week, the two senators crisscrossed the state at seventy or eighty miles an hour. "The gravel roads were hell on cars," remembered Huey's bodyguard and driver, Murphy Roden. "We blew six sets of tires."

Huey and Hattie maintained a grueling schedule, speaking six times a day, with Huey doing most of the talking. The speeches took place on the shady side of a county courthouse, in a vacant lot, from the back of a lumber truck, and from a rickety platform of pine planks in a town square. When they arrived in Mt. Ida, they climbed onto the back of Mack Guinn's flatbed Chevrolet and spoke in front of an old pine desk, where a bucket and dipper replaced the usual pitcher of water. In eight days, they covered over two thousand miles and delivered two tons of circulars spouting Hattie's platform and Huey's plan to share the nation's wealth. Huey gave thirty-nine speeches to more than 200,000 Arkansans.

Weeks before the Arkansas election, state political leaders and the major newspapers forecast that Hattie would place dead last in the primary. But that prediction was before Huey entered the campaign. On August 9, Hattie stunned conservative politicians across the South when she won in a landslide. For the first time in U.S. history, a woman was elected to a full term in the Senate. Hattie won sixty-one of seventy-five counties, got 47 percent of the vote, and outdistanced her nearest opponent by more than two to one. There was no runoff. Hattie Caraway returned to the United States Senate, where she served three terms until 1945. She knew that without Huey Long's support, the results of the election would have been completely different.

HUEY DID NOT slow down. Without breaking stride, he led his caravan of limousines and sound trucks south from Arkansas and back into Louisiana for another election. He knew he must continue to have his friends elected to office if his political machine was going to survive. He now campaigned for seven of his incumbent congressmen, including two important New Orleans representatives, Paul Maloney and "Bathtub Joe" Fernandez. Scheduled for September 13, 1932, the Louisiana election included two other races that ranked high on Huey's political agenda. Huey picked Congressman John Overton, his longtime loyal supporter and impeachment counsel, to run against Louisiana's other incumbent senator and Huey's bitter enemy, Edwin Broussard. In 1926 Huey campaigned across the state for twenty-one days for Broussard's reelection when the senator was challenged by J. Y. Sanders, but their friendship soon turned bitter. Huey and Broussard had not spoken since Huey's first day in the Senate. Earlier in the summer, "Coozan Ed" announced that he would fight the Long ticket and urged defeat of all of Huey's candidates. Reelection normally would have been easy for Broussard, who had held the Senate seat since 1921, but this time both Huey and the New Orleans Ring opposed him.

Huey also targeted a minor local election in southwest Louisiana, where Dudley LeBlanc was up for reelection to the Public Service Commission. After ruining Dudley's funeral business, Huey now intended to ruin his political career. In normal years, Dudley would have expected to be reelected easily, but Huey ordered a supporter, Wade Martin, to enter the race. Martin, a hot-tempered, gun-toting Creole, was the former sheriff of St. Martin Parish and a local power in southwest Louisiana. Huey gave Martin $12,000 for the campaign.

During four hot weeks in August and September, Huey and his caravan of limousines and green sound trucks barreled across the state, stumping for Overton and Martin and pummeling Dudley. Huey distributed nearly one and a half million circulars promoting his ticket and attacking his enemies. Even by Louisiana standards, it was a nasty and sometimes hilarious campaign. In early September, Huey campaigned for Martin in Lake Charles and claimed Dudley was trying to save his "nigger coffin club." Meanwhile, LeBlanc took a monkey on a string with him on the campaign, telling people that this was the way that Huey would handle Martin after the election.

The election was also one of the most corrupt. Huey used almost any tactic he could devise that increased his edge at the polls. "I'm always afraid of an election," he once confessed. "You can't tell what will happen." In one New Orleans precinct, votes were tallied before the polls closed, while in another voting began before they opened. Huey ordered state workers to contribute to the pro-Long campaigns and if they didn't, they lost their jobs. His machine spent huge sums to pay the one-dollar poll taxes for impoverished small farmers. "Paying the poll taxes kept all of the politicians broke," one of his supporters remembered. "We had to raise two or three thousand dollars. We raised it ourselves." C. C. Barham, the pro-Long mayor of Dubach, used school buses to get voters to the polls. "I paid some poll taxes, twenty-five or thirty," Barham recalled.

To give his candidates an advantage, Huey ordered dozens of dummy candidates to run for senator, public service commissioner, and other offices. The purpose of the dummy candidates was to ensure the selection of loyal election commissioners. Election commissioners decided if voters were eligible and assisted voters in areas where illiteracy was high.

Each candidate had the right to nominate five commissioners, but since a total of only five could be selected, all of the nominated election commissioners' names were placed in a hat and five drawn. The numerous pro-Long dummy candidates each added their nominations to the hat, guaranteeing the selection of a pro-Long slate of commissioners. Once selections were made, the dummy candidates, whose $125 filing fee was paid by Huey, withdrew from the race on the last day. To Huey, every vote counted and his commissioners went to the homes of his supporters where they helped them vote and then carried the ballots back to the polls. In New Orleans, Overton had 1,119 election commissioners, Broussard had 61.

A few days before the election, Judge Benjamin Pavy of St. Landry Parish forbade any commissioners selected from dummy candidates from serving in his district. Huey's workers ignored the judge and their election commissioners participated anyway. After Pavy jailed the commissioners, Governor Allen immediately telegraphed a reprieve to set the men free.

The election involved dozens of candidates but the debate still raged around one person—Huey Long. His opponents aimed their wrath mostly at him while ignoring other candidates. Huey campaigned as if he were running for office, defending his people, his platform, and himself. Standing on the steps of the new state capitol on a steamy afternoon, he attacked his critics with a classic Kingfish performance. "They'll tell you what you've got to do is tear up Longism in this state," he began. "Get you a bomb or some dynamite and blow up that building yonder [the new capitol]. That's a good place to start. Then go out and tear up the concrete roads I've built. Get your spades and your shovels and scrape the gravel off of them roads we've graveled, and let a rain come on them. That'll put them back like they was before I come. Tear down the new buildings I have built at the University. Take the money away from the school boards that I've give them to run your schools. And when your child starts out for school tomorrow morning, call him back and snatch the free school books out of his hand that Huey Long gave him. Then you'll be rid of Longism in this state, my friend, and not till then."

Huey won and so did his candidates. On September 13, 1932, in an election filled with crookedness, Overton won by a vote of 181,464–124,935. The race for public service commissioner was much closer. Out of 115,831 votes cast, LeBlanc lost to Martin by fewer than 4,000.

"I ADVISE ANYONE who thinks he knows something about politics to go down in Louisiana and take a postgraduate course," Texas senator Tom Connally told his colleagues. Connally had just returned from Louisiana, where he investigated voting fraud in the recent Senate election. Connally's visit had been spurred by fellow senator Broussard, who charged that his opponent, John Overton, had won illegally. Now a lame duck, Broussard requested that the Senate convene a committee to examine the returns from all parishes that used dummy candidates and to investigate illegal campaign expenditures by Huey's machine.

On October 5, 1932, Connally, along with Senator Sam Bratton of New Mexico, held their first hearings in New Orleans's post office building. A handsome and stuffy conservative Democrat, Connally detested Huey Long and Louisiana and complained that he was "wallowing in the mud" anytime he came to the state. For two days, Broussard's attorney accused Huey's workers of illegally paying poll taxes, using dummy candidates, and other election tomfoolery. Huey, who represented Overton, argued that dummy candidates had been used for years in Louisiana elections. He offered examples of his enemies entering dummy candidates against him. "Cain has cried for the blood of Abel and he has got it on his own hands," he concluded loudly. Soon, Connally and Bratton had heard enough and returned to Washington to report their initial findings to the Senate. After the new year began, the Senate would decide whether to convene more formal hearings to investigate Broussard's claims that the Overton victory was fraudulent.

While the Senate investigated Louisiana's elections, other government agencies began to take a keen interest in Huey. His constant attacks on President Hoover's administration created other enemies besides his fellow senators. By the end of 1932, the Federal Bureau of Investigation's chief agent in New Orleans began sending frequent reports of Huey's activities to his boss in Washington, J. Edgar Hoover, who passed the reports to the White House. Eventually, Huey's FBI file filled two thousand pages.

Elmer Irey, the intelligence chief of the Bureau of Internal Revenue, began to investigate Huey's income taxes. Irey successfully developed the tax evasion case that sent Al Capone to a federal penitentiary in 1931. Former governor Parker, still looking for ways to oust Huey, was a frequent visitor to Irey's Washington office, dropping by and asking, "When are you going to do something about Long?" Irey earlier had sent his Dallas agent, Archie Buford, to look into the finances of Huey and his henchmen. Buford was appalled after visiting New Orleans. "Chief, Louisiana is crawling," Buford reported. "Long and his gang are stealing everything in the state . . . and they're not paying taxes on the loot." Irey concluded that "practically every contract let in Louisiana since Long became Governor had been graft-ridden."

When Henry Morgenthau later became treasury secretary, he ordered Irey to go after Huey and "let the chips fall where they may." Irey sent thirty-two of his two hundred agents to New Orleans, where they took over an entire floor of the Masonic Building. Hiring undercover agents to gather information, the agents began to target Huey's close supporters, including Joe Fisher, Seymour Weiss, and Abe Shushan. Their ultimate quarry, however, was the Kingfish. When Huey learned of the tax investigation, he appeared unconcerned and scoffed to a reporter that "my skirts are clear."

CHAPTER 10

1933

WHO IS THAT AWFUL MAN?

A few months before the 1932 Democratic National Convention, Huey Long traveled to New York City and stopped by the just completed Empire State Building to visit Al Smith, one of the front-runners for the Democratic presidential nomination. Huey already had decided to support Franklin Roosevelt for the presidency but wanted to stay on the good side of Smith. In 1928, he campaigned for the "Happy Warrior" but no longer thought the former New York governor had much of a chance against Roosevelt in the upcoming convention. In Smith's office, the two men relaxed and, after a couple of drinks, the conversation turned to politics. Leaning forward so that he nearly touched Smith, Huey insisted that the New York politician tone down his opposition to Prohibition so that he could support him for president. Holding a highball in his hand, Huey was getting tipsy. "Don't spoil my chances of putting you in the White House," he told Smith. The South was no drier than any other part of the country, he maintained, but Southerners supported the ban to keep liquor from blacks. "There are some people we don't want to get it," Huey said. Smith, the son of an Irish immigrant who prided himself on liberal racial views, left the room and phoned the man who set up the meeting. "John, come and get this fellow," Smith ordered. "Otherwise, I'm going to throw him off the roof."

Soon after his meeting with Al Smith, Huey focused on the presidential campaign. During the busy summer of 1932, while orchestrating the senatorial elections of Hattie Caraway and John Overton, he attended the Democratic convention as head of the Louisiana delegation. As usual, controversy was his companion. The previous February, he called a meeting of the state Democratic Central Committee, which, on his orders, re-elected him as national committeeman and selected New Orleans mayor Walmsley as state party chairman. His enemies refused to accept the Central Committee's decision and insisted, as they did four years earlier, that delegates be chosen at a state party convention. In June 1932, a week before the Chicago convention, a rival Louisiana delegation of anti-Longs met in Shreveport and picked John Ewing, the son of Colonel Robert Ewing, as national committeeman. The Shreveport delegation chose ex-governors Parker, Sanders, and Pleasant as delegates, prompting Huey to call them "just a bunch of exes." In late June, all of the Louisiana delegates, including Huey's entourage and the Shreveport group of anti-Longs, headed north.

WHEN HUEY LONG, dressed in a white double-breasted suit and a snappy straw boater, stepped from the train that brought him to Chicago for the Democratic National Convention, a reporter approached and asked him if he would accept the vice presidential nomination on a ticket headed by Franklin Roosevelt. The cherub-faced Kingfish smiled at first but suddenly turned cold and snarled back at the newspaperman. "Huey Long ain't vice to anybody or anything." Storming through the corridors of the Congress Hotel in his polished two-toned shoes, giving loud, impromptu speeches in the bar, butting into meetings unannounced and uninvited, he immediately became the most entertaining show in town. He was also the most combative, at first threatening to "kill" Virginia's governor, Harry Byrd, for not supporting his delegation, but soon after offering to support Byrd for vice president.

On Tuesday night, June 27, 1932, the delegates poured into the Chicago Coliseum for the first formal session of the convention. Both of the rival Louisiana delegations showed up and noisily claimed to be the exclusive representative of their state's Democratic Party. Later that evening, the two rival delegations argued their cases before the Credentials Committee. Mrs. Pleasant was in the audience and once again Huey ordered a bodyguard to sit behind her in case she pulled her pistol from her purse and tried to take a shot at him. First to speak was J. Y. Sanders, who delivered an uninspiring "magnolia-and-molasses" speech urging that the Shreveport delegation be seated. When Sanders finished, Huey and Walmsley had forty-five minutes to argue for their own delegation. After Walmsley laid out the legal framework, Huey followed and everyone expected one of his legendary harangues. At first he attacked Sanders and what he called the "poor fish" delegation. "I am the Democratic Party in Louisiana," he began loudly. "Every one of this Sanders bunch is a sore-head about the way he's been beaten by me. I beat them time and again." But Huey soon calmed down, gave a convincing argument based on solid legal precedent, and finished his surprisingly restrained speech with his audience swayed. Once having won his case before the credentials com-mittee, fifty-five to thirty-two, he needed only to win the vote on the con-vention floor.

The next night, June 28, Huey stepped to the microphone to argue his case before all of the delegates and the American people, who listened from across the nation to radio broadcasts on CBS and NBC. "The eyes of the nation were turned his way," a politician remembered, "and he loved it." The conventioneers were loud and unruly on the muggy evening and whiskey-fortified Al Smith supporters heckled Huey. Soon, though, the crowd began to quiet as they listened to the logical, calm arguments of the cream-suited politician from Louisiana. Huey abandoned his redneck rhetoric and no longer peppered his talk with "aints" and homespun homilies, nor did he windmill his arms above his head or jump around the stage. "He sensed the fact that it was time to cut out the horseplay and the oratorical nonsense," Roosevelt campaign manager James Farley re-marked. "He delivered a reasoned, common sense argument." Huey brought a pile of law books, holding one up and quoting the relevant cita-tions from memory, and carefully explained that Louisiana law permitted, but did not require, its delegations to be selected by convention. He in-sisted that his delegation had been selected absolutely legally. "Who is our delegation?" he asked, then answered that his delegates represented the existing Louisiana government, not the past, and listed among them the incumbent eight congressmen, both U.S. senators, the governor, and the mayor of New Orleans. "How could the convention refuse to seat these men?" he concluded. The conventioneers, listening intently to his speech, were firmly in the Kingfish's grasp.

When Huey ended his performance, the boos he heard when he started had turned into loud applause and cheering. The delegates voted shortly after his speech and seated his delegation, 638–514. Seeing the vote, he no longer needed to be restrained. He grabbed the huge wooden sign of the Louisiana delegation and waved it like a captured standard, then jumped onto a chair, "gesticulated wildly" and "yipped and yowled lustily." Afterward, the Roosevelt delegates congratulated him for the victory, for they desperately needed Louisiana's twenty votes. Clarence Darrow, the famed criminal lawyer, told Huey that his speech was one of the greatest summaries of fact and evidence he had ever heard. Will Rogers, the popular newspaper humorist, was also impressed. "By golly he made a good speech today," Rogers wrote. "He won his own game."

Huey stumped hard for Roosevelt. Described by one Roosevelt aide as a "perpetually erupting volcano," he darted up and down the aisles of the convention center, issued instructions to his followers in a roaring voice, and sparred with newspapermen or other delegates. "Wherever Huey appeared the temperature shot up several degrees," Jim Farley remembered, "and on one or two occasions he narrowly missed getting into fistic encounters."

Huey struggled to keep the Southerners in line, pressuring wavering delegations from Mississippi and Arkansas to stay with Roosevelt. During the fourth ballot, he stormed onto the floor and elbowed his way through the Mississippians, his reddish hair tousled and white suit soaked with sweat. He wagged a fist in Senator Pat Harrison's face and shouted, "If you break the unit rule you sonofabitch, I'll go into Mississippi and break you!" Harrison stuck with Roosevelt. Huey made the same threat to his Senate enemy, Joe Robinson, and the Arkansas delegates. Arkansas also held and on the fifth ballot Roosevelt broke his deadlock with Al Smith and John Nance Garner and captured the nomination.

Huey was pleased when Roosevelt accepted the Democratic bid for president on July 2, sensing that the New Yorker shared his philosophy for distributing the nation's wealth. In an earlier campaign speech, Roosevelt had called for changes that would aid "the forgotten man at the bottom of the economic pyramid." In his acceptance speech, the presidential nominee called for major economic change, telling a radio audience that "men and women, forgotten in the political philosophy of the government for the last years, look to us here for guidance and for a more equitable opportunity to share in the distribution of the national wealth." Huey liked what he heard and felt he could persuade Roosevelt to support his plan to limit incomes of the rich. "When I was talking to Governor Roosevelt today, I felt like the Depression was over," he told a reporter. "That's a fact. I never felt so tickled in my life."

Roosevelt, however, was not tickled with Huey. He feared the Kingfish and the economic radicalism he spouted. The president-elect worried that if the Depression was not curtailed soon, the American people, much like those in Germany and Italy, would lose patience with the democratic process and turn to radical leaders like Huey. "In normal times," Roosevelt wrote Henry Stimson, "the radio and other appeals by [the radicals] would not be effective. However, these are not normal times. The people are jumpy and ready to run after strange gods." Only a few days after the convention, Roosevelt conferred with one of his advisers, Rexford Tugwell. After they discussed the convention and coming campaign, their conversation turned to political extremism in America. "It's all very well for us to laugh over Huey," Roosevelt said, "but actually we have to remember all the time that he really is one of the two most dangerous men in the country. We shall have to do something about him." The second most dangerous man, Roosevelt admitted later, was Douglas MacArthur.

"I'M LEAVING STATE POLITICS for good," Huey announced in September 1932 during a speech in New Orleans. "I won't have time to fight precinct brawls and engage in a national campaign, too. I've done all I can for Louisiana. Now I want to help the rest of the country." While few believed that he had abandoned Louisiana politics, his ambitions now clearly extended beyond his home state. Confident that he now held a firm grip over Louisiana, he decided to "shove the boat away from shore." Only a few months before, the populistic Farmer-Labor Party met in Omaha and offered Huey their party's presidential nomination. They selected old Jacob Coxey, who led the unemployed "Coxey's Army" march on Washington during the depression of the 1890s, to be his running mate. Huey saw no future in the Farmer-Labor Party and turned the offer down.

Huey intended to spearhead the Roosevelt campaign. During the first week of October, he traveled to New York to meet with Jim Farley and offer his services. Huey told Farley to charter a special train, with loudspeakers mounted on top of the cars, that would carry him on a whistlestop tour of all forty-eight states. Beaming with excitement, he promised to give a dozen speeches a day and said he would offer an immediate cash payment to the soldier's bonus. He seemed unfazed by the cost of his proposed campaign, didn't bother to inquire whether Roosevelt favored a soldier's bonus, and ignored the obvious impression that Huey Long would be the center of the campaign, not Franklin Roosevelt. To Roosevelt's aides, Huey's campaign plan was grandiose, expensive, and completely unacceptable. Farley politely turned him down. At the time, Farley regarded Huey as "somewhat of a freak."

On Sunday, October 9, amidst the fall splendor of New York's Hudson Valley, Huey traveled to Hyde Park to visit Roosevelt at his estate. It was their first face-to-face meeting. Before the two men met, Huey told the press that Roosevelt had "the greatest heart for mankind I have ever seen." When Eleanor Roosevelt arrived from church, she met Huey at the door and escorted him into the house. "You know, there's a striking resemblance between Mrs. Roosevelt and Mrs. Coolidge," he confided to a reporter. He was in rare Kingfish form, wearing a loud plaid suit, orchid shirt, and pink necktie. At the large dinner table, he dominated the conversation and lectured the presidential candidate like a schoolboy. Roosevelt seemed amused but his mother, Sarah, was not. The family matriarch was less than tactful when she listened to Huey's outbursts at the other end of the table. "Who is that *awful* man?" she said in a whisper loud enough for everyone to hear, including Huey. "By God, I feel sorry for him," Huey remarked soon after leaving. "He's got more sonofbitches in his family than I got in mine." He was not impressed with Roosevelt. "He's not a strong man, but he means well."

Later that month, Farley persuaded Huey to make a less ambitious campaign tour for Roosevelt. During the last week of October, he took his fleet of sound trucks into the Dakotas, Minnesota, Nebraska, Iowa, and

Kansas. He paid for the political caravan with $69,000 from his Louisiana "deduct box." The grind of the campaign took its toll on the vehicles. "At Fargo I told him some of our cars were in bad shape," a bodyguard recalled. "He told me to go out and buy a new Ford for $750. I asked where I would get the money. He gave me a check on Chase National Bank. This was the only time I saw him use anything but cash."

Farley and other Roosevelt aides considered the Midwestern states that Huey canvassed either already lost or completely committed to Roosevelt. With little to lose, Farley did not worry about him antagonizing any voters. Soon, however, he received reports from campaign workers saying that Huey attracted enthusiastic, large receptions at all of his stops. Farley realized that Midwestern farmers, as Depression-weary as their Southern counterparts, responded warmly to Huey's homespun humor, biblical quotes, and promises to redistribute the wealth. A campaign worker wired Farley, "If you have any doubtful state, send Huey Long to it." Farley admitted later that "we underrated Long's ability to grip the masses with his peculiar brand of public speaking. He put on a great show." At the same time, Farley sent Walmsley to campaign in Pennsylvania, but the New Orleans mayor was ineffective and Roosevelt lost there. Later, Farley and other Roosevelt aides agreed that if they had sent Huey into the mining regions of Pennsylvania, Roosevelt could have won that key state by a comfortable margin. "We never again underrated [Huey]," Farley admitted.

On November 30, soon after Roosevelt won the presidential election, Huey stopped in Warm Springs, Georgia, to meet with the president-elect. On his way from New Orleans to Washington, he joked to the press that he was there to see Roosevelt "about a postmastership in Winship, Louisiana." The meeting between the two politicians was friendly but Huey soon tired of Roosevelt's evasiveness. He left Georgia puzzled and disturbed by Roosevelt's lack of commitment to any notion of redistribution of wealth. "When I talk to him he says, 'Fine, Fine, Fine!' " he complained afterward. "But Joe Robinson goes to see him the next day and again he says 'Fine, Fine Fine!' Maybe he says 'Fine' to everybody."

IN JANUARY 1933, Huey was back on the floor of the United States Senate, entertaining the packed galleries with rustic buffoonery, billingsgate, evangelical fervor, and, at just the right time, surprisingly shrewd common sense. To his Senate colleagues, however, he no longer was amusing. Flouting every senatorial custom and abusing the privilege of filibuster, he had become an outcast. "Imagine ninety-five Senators trying to outtalk Huey Long," Will Rogers wrote at the time. "They can't get him warmed up." Huey launched crude and insulting attacks on his colleagues. When they failed to support his bills to redistribute the wealth, he gave a stern warning. "A mob is coming to hang the other ninety-five of you damned scoundrels and I'm undecided whether to stick here with you or go out and lead them."

During the twelve months he had been in the Senate, Huey had become increasingly aggressive. He treated his fellow senators as if they were a "shoeless rabble at a lynching"; his attacks became bitterly personal. He told his colleagues they were "among the unemployed and do not know it." He mimicked the speech and walk of senators he didn't like, attacked one senator for not paying his bills, and dredged up an incident from 1924 when Joe Robinson lost a fistfight with a fellow golfer at the Chevy Chase Country Club. An argument on the Senate floor with Senator Pat Harrison provoked a particularly savage attack. "The Senator from Mississippi has another way of standing by his friends," Huey declared. "Catch your friend in trouble, stab him in the back and drink his blood." When his opponents struck back, he counterattacked even more viciously. "Never touch a porcupine unless you expect to get some quills in you," he threatened one colleague. Even Alben Barkley of Kentucky, one of the Senate's most caustic wits, respected Huey's talent for razor-sharp debate. To Barkley, he resembled a horsefly. "He lights on one part of you, stings you, and then, when you slap at him, flies away to land elsewhere and sting again."

Huey defied senatorial decorum when he attacked one of the more respected members, Senator Carter Glass. A diminutive, white-haired seventy-five-year-old Virginian, Glass had held public office since 1899, serving as a congressman for sixteen years, treasury secretary under Woodrow Wilson, and senator since 1920. One of the Senate's experts on banking and finance, Glass marched proudly in line with other conservative Democrats. During the lame-duck session in January 1933 and while the Depression worsened, Glass led an effort to stem the epidemic of bank closings across the nation. He introduced a bill calling for major bank reform, including giving the Federal Reserve Board greater authority and placing national banks on a parity with state banks. Glass's bill had broad conservative support and Senate leaders expected the legislation to pass easily.

Huey Long and Carter Glass, as dissimilar as two men could be, had a running feud that went back to 1928 when Glass fought the seating of Long delegates at the Houston Democratic convention, and again in 1932 during the Chicago convention. Glass also infuriated Huey, calling him a "demagogic screech owl from the swamps of Louisiana," when he opposed the Kingfish's cotton reduction plan in 1931. On the floor of the Senate, Huey sarcastically referred to Glass as "our financial prophet." Now, in January 1933, Huey fought the Glass emergency banking bill, arguing that the legislation favored national banks over state institutions. With the bill sure to pass, his only weapon was the filibuster. When the bill reached the Senate floor on January 10, Huey opened his harangue with a four-hour sermon, quoting from the two Bibles sitting on his desk. "Go to now, ye rich men," he preached to his colleagues, "weep and howl for your miseries that shall come upon you." Huey, who hadn't attended church in years, proselytized his colleagues on the necessity of following the Lord's command to redistribute the wealth, referring to the Glass bill only in passing.

Day after day, Huey kept going, alternating the floor with a few other senators opposing the bill. Nine days into the filibuster, Joe Robinson moved to invoke cloture and throttle Huey. The Senate defeated the motion, 58–30, two votes short of the necessary two-thirds. Republicans, delighted whenever Huey embarrassed the conservative Democrats, voted to let him and other oppositionists continue to speak. The filibuster ran for nearly three weeks. When it appeared that a cloture vote to stop the filibuster finally would pass, Huey yielded and agreed to a watered-down banking bill. The Senate passed the revised Glass bill on January 26, 54–9, but it arrived in the House too late for passage and was buried in committee when the session ended. "A piece of legislation that was assumed to move through Congress with ease had fallen victim," the *New York Times* lamented, "to a man with a front of brass and lungs of leather."

Carter Glass fumed. He labeled Huey's performance "rhetorical rubbish" and privately referred to the Kingfish as "the creature who seems to have bought and stolen his way into the United States Senate." Glass's fellow senator from Virginia, Harry Byrd, asked to be assigned a different seat on the floor so he did not have to sit next to Huey, "even if I have to sit on the Republican side." Byrd warned Huey, "You'd better leave the old man alone. If you don't, he's going to shoot you." A few weeks later, Glass, still upset, was leaving the Senate with Joe Robinson. As they passed Huey at the back of the chamber, Glass stopped. "I'm tired of having him try to make a personal issue of this discussion," Glass told Robinson. Whirling about, he turned on Huey. "You damned sonofabitch," the old man spumed. Huey, calling Glass the same name, leaped at the old senator. Robinson separated the two and ushered Glass quickly from the chamber. "I couldn't hit you," Huey yelled at the departing Glass. "You are too old a man."

"HUEY LONG HAD rooms twenty-six-forty-three, twenty-six-forty-four, twenty-six-forty-five, and twenty-six-forty-six at the Hotel New Yorker when he was here last week," James Thurber wrote in the summer of 1933. "He needs a lot of space."

Thurber found the Kingfish sprawled on a bed in his shirtsleeves when he visited Huey in his hotel room one sultry afternoon in late August. Huey told Thurber that he was a bit tuckered from his two-mile walk through the city's streets. He said that it was not his legs that were tired, it was his eyes. "Not enough green grass and trees to look at along Broadway," he complained.

Even when Huey rested he was in constant motion. "The phone rang every minute or so while we talked," Thurber remembered, "and he would get up and walk through a couple of rooms to answer it and come back and fling himself heavily on the bed again so that his shoulders and feet hit it at the same moment. He didn't relax quietly. He kept tapping the headboard with his fingers and twisting from side to side."

Thurber tried to steer the conversation away from politics but Huey leaped out of his bed and into one of his typical political tirades. With eyes blazing, jabbing and flailing his arms at imaginary enemies, he attacked "the rats and blankety-blanks" back in Louisiana. "I'd like to have an election down there every month," he stated loudly. Back on the bed, he rolled around and gestured wildly. "I've saved the lives of little children, I've sent men through college, I've lifted communities from the mud, I've cured insane people with therapy, I've . . ." Even in bed, Huey never stopped stumping.

A half hour later, with Huey still going strong, Thurber backed out of the room. Walking down the hall, the writer could still hear his voice raised again about some horrible condition brought about by the "rats." As Thurber stepped onto the elevator, he remembered hearing "one last purple word" booming from the far end of the corridor.

HUEY LONG CREATED his own Mardi Gras celebration when he arrived in New Orleans during the first week in February 1933. As usual, about a thousand of his followers waited at the Louisville & Nashville Station to see him jump from the *Crescent City Limited,* which arrived at seven-thirty in the morning. Dressed in a neatly tailored brown business suit, matching fedora, and spit-polished wing tips, he gathered the crowd behind and, with a jazz combo blaring away, led an impromptu parade down bustling Canal Street past fur dealers, clothing stores, and newspaper stands.

Huey had rushed back to New Orleans before the Senate session ended to fight another battle. At the beginning of the session, lame-duck senator Ed Broussard convinced a majority of his colleagues to reopen the investigation into his election loss to John Overton. Broussard argued that "fraud and corruption had been practiced on a large scale" during the recent Senate race and Overton had been elected illegally. The Senate voted for a formal investigation to finish the preliminary inquiry begun by Senator Connally the previous October. Huey fought the probe but was outvoted.

On February 3, the Overton hearings began on the third floor of the Customs House overlooking the Mississippi River. Off in the distance, workers could be seen constructing the first towers of the Huey P. Long Bridge, which would cross the river. Senator Robert Howell, a distinguished Nebraska Republican, chaired the twelve days of hearings. Senator John Carey of Wyoming also sat on the panel, and Samuel Ansell served as committee counsel. Ansell was a tall, gray-haired West Pointer who served as judge advocate general of the army during World War I and now defended some of the country's most noted clients, including William Randolph Hearst. A dominating courtroom presence and one of the country's sharpest legal minds, Ansell had come to New Orleans to win a war of words and epithets with Huey Long.

The Overton hearings provided an entertaining show for the crowd of more than three hundred spectators that each day jammed the chamber from wall to wall. According to a reporter, the hearing room was so stuffed that "when one person moved, they all moved." The crowd over-flowed into the hall, down the wide marble stairs, and along the streets. Whenever the hearings were in session, passersby heard loud applause, laughter, and prolonged booing from the open windows of the Customs House.

After the committee reviewed the October investigation by Senators Connolly and Bratton, Ansell called his first witness, Allen Ellender, to testify. When questioned about rampant patronage appointments made by the Long machine, Ellender replied with the excuse that "to the victor belong the spoils." Huey's speaker of the house added that he saw noth-ing improper with accepting campaign funds from state employees, and that dummy candidates were appropriate if also used by the opponents. Ellender admitted that dummy candidates were perjurers and "offensive to my moral sense, but they are legally right." When Ellender finished, Ansell called several of Huey's candidates to the stand, who gave absurd testimony as to their qualifications for running for Congress. One "dummy" cut grass for the Dock Board and another was a house painter.

It was clear from Ansell's questions that he was more interested in exposing crookedness in Huey's political machine than investigating the Overton election. Ansell questioned Dr. Joseph O'Hara, head of the state Board of Health and also president of Huey's political organization, re-cently named the Louisiana Democratic Association. When Ansell asked whether employees of the Board of Health were forced to contribute 10 percent of their salary to the Long machine, O'Hara, whom a reporter described as a somber man with "gray hair, gray face, and gray hands," did not hesitate. "Oh, no," he answered, "they had to pay it voluntarily." Seymour Weiss testified for three days and provided a stubborn, uncom-municative performance similar to his appearance during the impeach-ment trial in 1929. In answer to many of Ansell's questions about campaign finances, Weiss snapped back, "That's none of your business." Ansell threatened to jail Weiss for contempt but Seymour did not budge. By this time, Huey had arrived from Washington. When Ansell kept pressing for an answer, Huey interrupted loudly, telling Weiss, "Don't answer that question, on my instructions."

"On what ground?" Ansell asked.

"Because I said not to do so," snapped back Huey.

"Is that sufficient?"

"That is plenty. Kingfish of the lodge."

Ansell called a number of Huey's opponents to the stand. Harley Bozeman, boyhood friend and now bitter enemy, gave a scathing description of Huey's brutal methods. Julius and Earl Long ganged up on their brother with more damaging testimony. Julius claimed that Huey extorted between $500 and $1,000 from every road contractor working for the state in order to finance his 1930 Senate race. Earl, still sore at Huey for not supporting his bid for lieutenant governor, sat next to Ansell and frequently leaned over to whisper questions to ask. On February 14, Earl testified that during the 1928 election he saw a representative of the New Orleans public utility company place a $10,000 bribe in Huey's bathrobe pocket. "I saw it," Earl declared. "It was a hundred brand new hundred dollar bills that looked like they had been run off the same press." Huey leaped from his seat and raged at his brother, "That is a goddamn lie!"

Earl testified that Sheriff Mereaux of St. Bernard Parish came to the Roosevelt Hotel with a blank election tally sheet the day after "Bathtub Joe" Fernandez upset incumbent Congressman O'Connor in 1930. Mereaux asked Huey how to fill in the sheets because, according to Earl, Mereaux worried that the total vote was larger than the registration. Huey told the sheriff not to worry, as it "will be fixed all right." Earl told Huey not to get involved with the crooked St. Bernard vote but he ignored his brother. "I had just got him out of one mess when he kidnaped the two men," Earl said, "and I didn't want him to get into another." Huey interrupted his brother and turned to the committee. "Say the word, and I'll telephone the Sheriff of St. Bernard Parish to bring those ballot boxes right down," he told the chairman. "Have 'em here in half an hour and count the ballots right here in front of you gentlemen."

From the start of the hearings, Huey and Ansell constantly sniped at each other. At one point Huey tilted back insolently in his chair and asked Ansell, "Are you trying to get funny? If so the Dauphine Theater burlesque has an ad for a second-rate comedian." Ansell, dressed in a dapper gray three-piece suit, remained unfazed. "You should be there to take the job immediately," he replied curtly. Later Ansell challenged Huey to step outside. "I will walk out with you and whip hell out of you," Huey snarled. "Would you walk alone or with a lot of armed guards?" Ansell sneered back. Ansell lashed out at Huey's organization as "damnable, corrupt, cheap, the work of a set of blood sucking leeches." The hearings adjourned on February 17, and that night someone set Huey's New Orleans house afire. Firemen arrived quickly and little damage occurred.

When Huey returned to Washington later that month, he took the floor of the Senate and delivered over a hundred telegrams from Louisianans demanding that the Overton investigations be terminated. He then began a two-hour tirade against Ansell, attacking his military record and calling him a "liar, crook, scoundrel, forger, dog-faced son of the wolf." On March 1, Ansell sued Huey for libel in the District of Columbia Supreme Court and filed for a half-million dollars in damages.

In October, the Senate investigation reconvened. Senator Tom Connally returned to New Orleans to chair the probe, replacing Senator Howell, who had died in March. The latest round of hearings, more crowded and rowdier than before, had to be held at the Scottish Rite Cathedral because of the overflow. On the second day the crowd was so thick around the entrance to the building that Connally had to climb a fire escape and scramble through a ladies' restroom window. To the senator's chagrin, a newspaper photographer, probably tipped off by Huey's men, waited on the other side of the window to record his embarrassing entrance. Inside the crowded hearing room, the spectators disrupted the testimony with loud whoops and hollers. Connally tried to control the crowd, and at one point pounded his wooden gavel so hard that the head flew off, splashed into his pitcher of water, and drenched the angry Texan.

The hearings themselves were less explosive, however, as the combative Sam Ansell resigned earlier as committee counsel, leaving Huey with no formidable antagonist to trade insults. Connally and his colleagues listened to much of the same testimony as before revealing election fraud and political tomfoolery, but finally concluded that even if a completely honest election had been held, Overton still would have won. In January 1934, Connally reported back to the Senate that election practices in Louisiana were a "fraud upon the rights of citizens . . . and vicious and abhorrent practices," but recommended seating Overton. "There probably is no great difference in the methods of operation so far as the Old Regulars of the city of New Orleans and [Huey's] Louisiana Democratic Association are concerned." On June 16, 1934, three days before Congress adjourned and nearly two years since the contested election, the Senate voted Huey a clean bill of health and dismissed all charges against him and Senator Overton, ruling that the latter had not been elected fraudulently. Brushing aside the Overton investigation as little more than a nuisance, Huey denied the charges that corruption ran rampant in his state. "Politics in Louisiana is as clean as an angel's ghost," he bragged to a reporter.

CHAPTER 11

1933
A BLACK EYE FOR
THE KINGFISH

It was only a matter of time before Huey Long and Franklin Roosevelt parted ways. The redneck Louisianan and the patrician, blueblood New Yorker could never become friends or even loyal political allies, and both men knew it. Neither man trusted the other, both were ambitious and egotistic and refused to share the spotlight with another, and by the beginning of 1933 no longer needed each other. Roosevelt had the presidency and Huey could not use the presidential campaign to gain national exposure. Roosevelt deplored Huey's crude radicalism. "When anyone eats with Huey, it'd better be with a long spoon," the president told an aide.

Huey was no less critical of the president. "[Roosevelt's] a phony," he told a close friend. "I can out promise him and he knows it. People will believe me and they won't believe him. His mother's watching him and she won't let him go too far. . . . He's living on inherited income." Over time, Huey developed an almost pathological hatred of the disabled Roosevelt. "[Huey believed] that anyone with a physical infirmity was bad or affected in other ways," a supporter recalled. "He would quote the Bible to the effect God had put his mark on such people."

Signs of a split between the two men began to emerge before Roosevelt took office. On January 20, 1933, they met in Washington's Mayflower

Hotel. Huey, who arrived thirty minutes late, found the president-elect cordial but noncommittal and showing no interest in his advice. At the same time, Huey made no effort to befriend Roosevelt's close advisers. A day or two before the inauguration, he barged into a meeting of Roosevelt's associates in Raymond Moley's room in the Mayflower. Chewing viciously on an apple, Huey neglected any friendly greeting and immediately went on the attack. "I don't like you or your goddamned banker friends," he announced belligerently to the stunned group and departed the room as abruptly as he had entered.

By the middle of March 1933 and shortly after the inauguration, Huey began to distance himself from the president. He vainly opposed the nomination of Henry Morgenthau as Roosevelt's treasury secretary. Outwardly, Huey feigned support of the president. Quoting the Bible, Theodore Roosevelt, Daniel Webster, and William Jennings Bryan, he delivered a lengthy speech on NBC radio that implied Roosevelt supported his bills to share the wealth. In the Senate, Huey introduced three wealth-sharing bills. One imposed a capital levy on fortunes, beginning at one percent on $1 million of income and doubling on each additional million, a second bill limited yearly incomes to $1 million, and a third restricted individual inheritances to $5 million. He knew that if the president really supported his bills to redistribute wealth, then Roosevelt would prompt loyal Democratic senators to back him. Huey got no backing. One of his bills to appropriate $1 billion for the college education of needy students failed in the Senate, 75–5.

The split widened over patronage. Huey wanted control of the thousands of federal jobs in Louisiana and so did the New Orleans Ring. Federal patronage was a rich plum, including sought-after jobs such as marshals, court clerks, postmasters, and judges. In addition, the New Deal had created a new army of bureaucrats that administered unemployment relief, industrial recovery, agricultural adjustment, and other federal programs. These programs created a vast new patronage arsenal. Traditionally, the awarding of federal jobs occurred only after consulting a state's senior senator. Soon after the inauguration, however, the president began to ignore Huey. Roosevelt knew the political value of federal jobs in Depression-riddled Louisiana and dealt out the spoils of victory with shrewd precision. His political strategist, now Postmaster General

Jim Farley, at first gave federal patronage jobs in Louisiana on a nonpartisan basis through the state director of the Federal Emergency Relief Administration, Harry Early. Soon though, Roosevelt administrators consulted only with anti-Long leaders like John Parker, Edward Rightor, or John Sullivan when awarding federal jobs. As expected, the jobs went exclusively to anti-Longs, including Huey's estranged brother Earl, whose enmity earned him a federal job at the Home Owner's Loan Corporation.

The federal presence in Louisiana grew quickly under the New Deal. By the end of 1933, about 326,000 Louisianans received welfare checks or had federal jobs. By 1935, FERA employed 70,000 in New Orleans alone and the Civilian Conservation Corps employed 42,000 men in the state. Huey bristled as the increasing federal influence lessened his own political power. On April 11, 1933, he lost his patience on the Senate floor, attacked the Roosevelt administration, and refused federal patronage. "So far as I am concerned," he grumbled, "they can take all my patronage and go to—well, they can keep all my patronage." Later, while in New Orleans, Huey suggested that Louisiana secede from the union so that the state would no longer be under the control of the Roosevelt administration. He claimed that a bunch of Washington "crats" were ruining the state. "We've got bureaucrats, autocrats, hobocrats, and fifty-seven other varieties of 'crats that are trying not only to run the United States government, but sticking their noses into the affairs of individual states."

In early 1933, Huey had supported some of Roosevelt's New Deal legislation, including creation of the Tennessee Valley Authority, the repeal of Prohibition, and several significant tax and tariff proposals. Despite his progressive rhetoric, he joined his conservative colleagues from the South when he voted against the Costigan-Wagner anti-lynching bill. Overall, he voted for about half of Roosevelt's early bills. "Whenever this administration has gone to the left I have voted with it," he stated later, "and whenever it has gone to the right I have voted against it."

However, that spring Huey openly broke with Roosevelt and insisted that legislation be passed to redistribute the nation's wealth. On May 12, he failed to amend Senate revenue legislation by adding a tax on large amounts of capital. "Where is the corner groceryman?" Huey asked his colleagues from the Senate floor. "He is gone or going. The little independent business operated by middle class people has been fading

out . . . as the concentration of wealth grows like a snowball." Now opposing even the most progressive of Roosevelt's proposals, he voted against
all farm, banking, and economic recovery efforts of the New Deal, including the Emergency Banking Act, Economy Act, Civilian Conservation
Corps, National Industrial Recovery Act, and Agricultural Adjustment
Act.

In early June, Roosevelt introduced his National Recovery Act, which
proposed bold and unprecedented measures to cope with the Depression.
The controversial act suspended the antitrust laws and allowed industries
to collaborate with the federal government in setting prices, production
quotas, wages, and hours of labor. Huey and other rural progressives opposed the act as a sellout to big business, an encouragement for monopoly, and a grant of too much power to the federal government in
regulating the economy. "Every fault of socialism is found in this bill,
without one of its virtues," he argued on the Senate floor. "Every crime of
a monarchy is in here." His opposition made little difference and the act
passed.

Huey made other futile attacks on the Roosevelt administration.
Throughout the session he favored giving a bonus and other benefits to
veterans, while Roosevelt opposed the proposal as being too costly. Near
the end of the session, Huey and other pro-bonus senators tacked an
amendment limiting cuts in veterans benefits onto an appropriation bill.
When the bill appeared likely to pass, Roosevelt sent word to the Senate
that he would veto the legislation if the veterans measure remained. Huey
tried to get enough votes to override a veto but failed to overcome the
president's demand.

Roosevelt watched Huey's resistance closely and in June 1933 decided
to confront the Kingfish. Just before Congress adjourned, the president
had Farley bring him to the White House for a morning meeting. Wearing a brilliant white-linen summer suit and a straw hat with a brightly colored band, he urged Roosevelt to yield control over federal patronage.
While they met, Huey took a seat near the president's desk and removed
his hat only to punctuate his points by rapping Roosevelt's paralyzed knee
with it. Roosevelt, leaning back in his chair, perfectly relaxed and a smile
on his face, appeared outwardly cordial, but inside had lost his patience

with Huey's insolence. "It did get on Franklin's nerves," remembered an aide to the president. Roosevelt listened passively but did not yield.

Exasperated, Huey tried to be upbeat to the press as he left the White House. "The President and I are never going to fall out," he told one reporter. "I'll be satisfied whichever way matters go." But Huey knew he made little progress. "What the hell is the use of coming down to see this fellow?" he muttered to Farley. "I can't win any decision over him." Later, he was more candid. "I'm never going over there again." He then told the story of his grandfather who once had a man working for him who picked twice as much cotton as anyone else on the farm. Naturally grandfather fired him, saying, "You're so smart that if you stayed around here, first thing I know I'd be working for you."

"That's the way I feel about Roosevelt," Huey said. "He's so goddamn smart that first thing I know I'll be working for him—and I ain't going to."

Congress adjourned a week later. Many of Roosevelt's supporters were in good humor because of the unprecedented amount of New Deal legislation passed. Huey, still upset over Roosevelt's recalcitrance and his defeats over the National Recovery Act and veterans bonuses, rose on the floor during the final session. "No, I will not participate in the Democratic victory tonight," he told his fellow senators. "I do not care for my share in a victory that means that the poor and the downtrodden, the blind, the helpless, the orphaned, the bleeding, the wounded, the hungry and the distressed, will be the victims."

DURING THE SENATE investigation of John Overton's election held in the New Orleans Customs House during the fall of 1933, a small dark-haired woman wearing a neat frock dress and a flapper hat sat on the back row of the chamber quietly listening to the proceedings. The mother of two small children, Hilda Phelps Hammond was a harmless-looking little lady who lived in the fashionable Garden District. The *New Orleans Times-Picayune* paid Hilda $10 a week to write a cooking column where she described her favorite Creole dishes like Daube Glace, Trout Marguery, and Crawfish Bisque. Her father had founded that newspaper at the turn of the century and her brother, Esmond Phelps, was a powerful attorney who set policy for the paper and a diehard foe of Huey Long. At first, Mrs. Hammond attended the hearings out of curiosity but soon was appalled at the proceedings. Thereafter, she sat through almost every session. Intensely watching Huey's legal antics, she concluded that he "represents pure evil" and quickly became one of his fiercest and most indefatigable enemies. She also had personal reasons to despise Huey. In 1930 he fired her husband, Arthur Hammond, from his position as attorney for two separate state boards, each drawing $400 per month. After the February 1933 round of hearings ended, Hilda packed a small suitcase, tucked a brown fur coat under her arm, and boarded the *Crescent City Limited* for Washington. Arriving in the capital two days later, she began the first of many trips to convince the Senate to refuse to seat Overton and to censure Huey. Her first trip was fruitless, getting little support from senators who believed that the corrupt Overton election was a problem for the voters of Louisiana to solve, not the United States Senate. Hilda was undaunted, however, in her crusade against Huey and would soon return.

On Sunday afternoon, March 5, 1933, the day after Franklin Roosevelt became president and John Overton was escorted into the Senate by Huey, Hilda was back in New Orleans, where she invited twenty-nine of the city's more elite women to her home. That day, they formed the Women's Committee of Louisiana with the sole purpose of fighting Huey. To raise funds, the women auctioned off family heirlooms, including antique furniture, Oriental rugs, and expensive pieces of china. Some of the money they raised helped pay for a law firm to build the case against Huey. One of the partners of the firm Hilda hired was Sam Ansell, the former congressional counsel who had clashed with Huey a few months before. Hilda set up a small office on Royal Street. Huey dubbed her "Hilda, the antique queen, the Picayune damsel" and claimed that the *Times-Picayune* paid her $100 a month to attack him.

In April, Hilda returned to Washington. She delivered a stack of petitions to Vice President Garner calling for Huey's ouster from the Senate. The petitions listed eleven articles of charges and were signed by ex-governor Parker and scores of others. Two days later, five more petitions arrived, signed by nearly three hundred New Orleans citizens. For the next two years Hilda shuttled back and forth between Washington and

New Orleans, pressuring legislators and delivering petitions questioning Huey's fitness to be senator and trying to convince anyone who would listen to her that Louisiana had become a "ballot-less state in the hands of political racketeers, who, like all political racketeers on the route to dictatorship, have convinced simple people that everything they do is in the interest of the public."

Hilda was not alone, as former governors Parker and Sanders, as well as Mrs. Ruffin Pleasant, also took the train to the nation's capital to fight Huey. "Psychiatrists have stated in my presence [Huey] is a dangerous paranoiac," Parker told Vice President Garner. "The Senate should have him examined by experts and, to save certain trouble and probable future killing, have him permanently incarcerated in the criminal insane hospital in Washington." Sanders wrote Carter Glass that "insolence, arrogance, unscrupulousness, mental bravery, and physical cowardice go to the makeup of this remarkable creature with every vice and not a redeeming virtue." When Mrs. Pleasant testified before a Senate committee that he should be removed from office, Huey, who was in the audience grinning, interrupted her and asked if she had been treated for a mental disorder. The unstable ex-governor's wife, admitting that she once had a nervous breakdown, began to "weep hysterically."

DOTTED WITH THE MANSIONS of Wall Street millionaires, mob bosses, and movie stars, the village of Sands Point sat on a picturesque crop of land jutting from Long Island's north shore, about an hour's train ride from New York city. On August 26, 1933, Huey traveled to the village, where he attended a ball and dinner given by composer Gene Buck at the Sands Point Bath and Country Club. Six hundred wealthy guests attended Buck's charity event, and the party lasted into the early hours of the morning. Huey got rip-roaring drunk, flirting with women and insulting other guests. He called a black musician "coon" and "shine" and seized a dinner plate from a plump woman, declaring, "I'll eat this for you. You're too fat already." Near midnight, Huey staggered into the men's room, remained there for a half hour, and stumbled out with a handkerchief over a bleeding and swelling left eye that soon shined purple. "Gene, let's get out of here," he told his host. "I'm on the spot."

Accounts of the embarrassing bathroom altercation varied. One version said that Huey insulted a lady at the club and her escort knocked him down in the men's room. Other versions described his attacker as a "forty-year-old architect, a police chief, a young Navy pilot," and even one of crime boss Frank Costello's mobsters. Huey tried to explain the incident and gave several different versions of what happened. At one point he said five Wall Street agents cut him with a knife, and later claimed "a member of the house of Morgan slipped up behind me and hit me with a blackjack." He probably provoked a punch in the eye when he urinated on another person. "He was always kind of sloppy, and that night he had been drinking," Murphy Roden, one of his more reliable bodyguards, remembered. "He went to the rest room and to the urinal. That aviator, [Al] Williams, was standing next to him. It was an accident. He just swung it too far and hit the fellow's shoe and he socked him."

Roden and the other bodyguards threw Huey into a taxi and whisked him back to the Hotel New Yorker. The next day, he caught the first train for Milwaukee to give a speech to the Veterans of Foreign Wars. On August 30, he returned to New Orleans, stepping from the train in bad humor and still sporting his Sands Point shiner. A large group of reporters and photographers confronted him at the railroad station but he was in no mood for interviews. As he pushed his way through the crowd, he turned to his burly bodyguards and shouted, "Bust 'em up, boys! Hit 'em! Don't let them take my picture." The burliest bodyguard, Joe Messina, pulled out a blackjack, flattened an Associated Press photographer, and smashed his camera to pieces on the concrete floor of the railroad shed.

The anti-Long newspapers pounced on the Sands Point fracas with scathing satire. Several writers referred to him as "Huey Pee Long." The *Hammond Daily Courier,* for example, lambasted Huey for "establishing an unprecedented record for dancing, twisting, and wool-pulling in his intoxicating whirl for a toe hold on the winning band wagon in the magnificent march of progress." More damaging, however, was the public relations nightmare caused by the incident. The Louisiana people, especially those of the rural parishes, up until now enjoyed Huey's shenanigans when he flouted authority, whether it be insulting a German ship captain or filibustering the United States Senate. Sands Point, however, was different, and even his most loyal followers disapproved of his unchivalrous, crude, and cowardly conduct. In October, two months after the incident, he still faced upset followers. While on a tour of the state to rouse popular support for new taxes, he attended the South Louisiana State Fair in Donaldsonville, a town normally friendly to the Kingfish. He expected twenty thousand spectators to hear his speech, but only eight thousand showed up and many of them hissed, booed, and heckled him over Sands Point. "What about the Long Island affair?" a spectator taunted from the stands. "Come down from that grandstand," Huey screamed back, "and I'll man-to-man it with you." With Huey surrounded by his bodyguards and a half-dozen state policemen, the heckler refused the challenge.

Hecklers also attacked Huey at the Washington Parish Fair in Franklinton and again during a speech in Minden. The crowds not only showed their displeasure over Sands Point, they questioned his call for new taxes and disapproved of his attacks on the president. By now, Roosevelt had become a popular figure in the South and his efforts to end the Depression appeared to be working. Many Louisianans were aware that Huey's bitter attacks on the New Deal caused the Roosevelt administration to halt federal aid to their state. In Alexandria, an angry crowd forced Huey from the stage on the City Hall steps when they pelted him with rotten eggs and overripe vegetables. On October 20, he traveled to Shreveport in Harvey Couch's private railroad car to dedicate the new Long-Allen Bridge over the Red River and to watch LSU play Arkansas in the city's stadium. Spectators heckled and booed him for Sands Point at every event. By November, he had enough criticism and canceled all of his remaining speeches. Huey never had faced such unpopularity and, according to one newspaperman, "can't get to first on his own diamond."

IN OCTOBER 1933, two months after Sands Point, Huey Long published his autobiography, titled *Every Man a King*. He dictated the book to a secretary a year before, shortly after he took his Senate seat, and completed the manuscript during the summer of 1933. He hired a New York journalist to edit it. After publishers rejected the manuscript, he incorporated his own publishing house in New Orleans and ordered that only union labor be used to set the book into type. He insisted that the book be wrapped in a gold jacket and have his picture on the cover. While self-serving, he was surprisingly candid in the book and made no excuses for his harsh methods to crush his political enemies. He priced his book deliberately at a dollar to increase sales among the less wealthy. More interested in publicity than money, Huey printed 100,000 copies and sold about 20,000. Once, when his friend Will Rogers complained that his own books were not selling, Huey laughed. "Why don't you do what I did," he told Rogers, "give them away."

In New Orleans, Hilda Hammond and her Women's Committee of Louisiana tried to stop Huey's book from being sold. The ladies telephoned bookstores throughout the city and demanded that the book be taken from the shelves. If the stores continued to carry the book, they would cancel their charge accounts. Huey was delighted when the stores ignored the women's threats and continued to sell *Every Man a King*.

ALMOST THREE YEARS to the day, the political truce between Huey Long and Semmes Walmsley collapsed. On September 13, 1933, the *Baton Rouge State-Times* suggested a break between the two men. The paper also confirmed that Roosevelt would give no patronage to the Long machine. The Old Regulars depended on patronage, but for the last three years Huey had taken thousands of state jobs from the Choctaws and the loss of federal jobs had been the final straw. During this time, Huey bristled after Walmsley began voicing approval of Roosevelt. Huey's dissatisfaction with the alliance appeared that fall when he printed a circular that accused Walmsley and the Old Regulars, those "lice and rats who have mulcted our people," of betrayal.

By the time winter set in, the Choctaws had lost patience with Huey's demands for more patronage and control over city finances. They also sensed that he was more politically vulnerable and that his popularity had waned due to Sands Point, new taxes, and other notorious acts. Before breaking completely, the Choctaws decided to try to negotiate a better deal. Beginning on December 19, Huey and Walmsley met for several days at the Roosevelt Hotel. Instead of relinquishing any control, Huey demanded even more of the patronage in New Orleans. He also demanded at least half of the candidates for the upcoming January election, a requirement that Walmsley found impossible. "He wants everything," the mayor complained. Walmsley also insisted that Huey back his reelection as mayor, or at least remain neutral and not enter another candidate, but Huey offered no commitment of support.

Each man probably had decided before the meeting that their alliance was over, as each no longer needed the other and each made demands that he knew the other would not accept. Huey had never been comfortable with his pact with the Choctaws and desired his own powerful and independent political machine that required no alliance with any other political faction, especially Walmsley and the Old Regulars. When Huey refused to make any concessions, Walmsley walked out. Strolling into the brisk December air with a dark hat protecting his balding head, the mayor headed directly to the Choctaw Club, where the powerful seventeen ward leaders of the Old Regulars voted 12–5 to break all political ties. Within hours, New Orleans police chief George Reyer withdrew the police officers who had been guarding Huey's home since suspicious fires broke out.

Huey fought another major political battle that winter. The previous June, Sixth District congressman Bolivar Kemp died with eighteen months remaining on his term. Kemp, who represented the twelve parishes surrounding the Baton Rouge area, had stayed neutral in the brawls between Huey and the anti-Longs. Louisiana law required the Democratic Executive Committee to call a primary election to select the party's nominee to replace Kemp. Huey feared that if a primary was held in the anti-Long district, one of his opponents would win the seat. He ordered a delay, claiming that an election would be too expensive. Five months after Kemp's death, on November 28, 1933, Huey ordered Governor Allen to declare that there was too little time to hold a Democratic primary and scheduled a general election for December 5. Huey announced from New Orleans that Lallie Kemp, the congressman's widow, would be the only nominee on the ballot.

The anti-Longs were furious, as Huey's delay tactic prevented them from entering their own candidate to qualify for the election. His opponents announced they would boycott the general election. A young anti-Long judge, Nat Tycer, outlawed the election in his own judicial district, which covered four of the twelve parishes. Tycer declared, "It's a poor judge who can't enforce his own rulings," and swore in a hundred special deputies to keep the election from being carried out. Tycer ordered his deputies, including the anti-Long editor of the *Hammond Daily Courier*, Hodding Carter, to burn the election boxes and ballots. Three hundred anti-Longs broke into the Amite courthouse and destroyed 11,000 ballots. Another group of Huey's opponents met in the offices of the *Hammond Daily Courier*, where they stuffed a black-eyed effigy of the Kingfish, dragged it to the corner of Cherry and Thomas Streets, and burned it under a banner reading, "Long Island Huey."

Tension built as both sides armed themselves. "If ever there was a need for shotgun government, that time is now," wrote Carter in his *Courier*. He spent the night of December 4 "scared witless" in a ditch with a .38 revolver and sawed-off shotgun loaned by J. Y. Sanders, guarding a bridge with other anti-Longs. Firing shots in the night, Carter and his fellow deputies forced Huey's state policemen, bringing new ballots to the parish, to retreat back to Baton Rouge. When the polls closed the next evening, only 4,800 of 45,000 registered voters had cast ballots.

Meanwhile, Huey's opponents held a mass meeting in Baton Rouge, nominated J. Y. Sanders, Jr., for Kemp's vacant seat, and called for "the rope" for Huey. The meeting ended with a little girl singing a song written for the occasion titled "Huey Doesn't Live Here Anymore." Three weeks later, on December 27, the anti-Longs held their own election in Baton Rouge. This time 19,500 voters unanimously elected the only candidate on their ballot, J.Y. Jr. When Congress convened after the new year, both Mrs. Kemp and Sanders showed up in Washington and presented their credentials to Congress. The House leaders, appalled at events in Louisiana, declared both elections illegal and refused to seat either candidate. The House ordered another election for the following spring.

In April 1934, a more legitimate election finally was held. As expected, J. Y. Sanders, Jr., defeated Huey's candidate for the Sixth Congressional seat, Agriculture Commissioner Harry D. Wilson, by 2,376 votes. After the election, Sanders staged Huey's political funeral through the streets of Baton Rouge. Sanders marched at the head of a crowd of Huey's opponents, who pulled an antique hearse with a large sign hanging on the side saying "The Crawfish Is Hunting for His Hole."

"I WANT TO TELL YOU that [Huey Long] belongs to the hog family," former lieutenant governor Paul Cyr roared in a speech, "and the piney

woods razorback type at that." Most observers agreed with Dr. Cyr that
Huey behaved despicably at the dinner table. His horribly bad manners
had become legendary in Baton Rouge and Washington. In some of the
fanciest and most expensive restaurants, diners observed the Kingfish
crudely tearing broiled chicken apart with grease-covered fingers or leaning over his bowl and loudly scooping huge gulps of soup into his mouth.
On one occasion he threw his plate full of oysters onto the floor of the
Heidelberg Hotel's restaurant because they were not fried to his liking.
"In some ways he didn't act like a normal human being," a friend recalled, adding that eating with Huey was an ordeal. "He would reach over
and take your meal and eat it."

Huey took pride in his bad manners. His crude behavior was neither
an accident nor oversight, for everything the Kingfish did had a well-
designed purpose. Whether it be by foul language, green pajamas, or
scratching his backside while giving a speech in the United States Senate,
he made it clear to all around him that he would not bend to stuffy mannerisms. No one controlled Huey Long. He made his own rules and if he
so desired, he could act the polished gentleman. When he dined with Seymour Weiss in a swank New Orleans restaurant such as Galatoire's or
Antoine's, he used all the proper forks and folded his linen napkin neatly
across his lap, no longer tied around his neck like a redneck peckerwood

Huey rarely attended Washington social functions, as he received few
invitations and desired fewer. He had only a couple of friends among his
Senate colleagues and of those, he visited only the apartment of Burton
Wheeler, the Montana progressive, until Wheeler, too, tired of his loud
and uncouth outbursts. After he quit drinking, Huey spent most evenings
contentedly in his three-room suite in the Broadmoor Hotel, eating Italian food cooked by one of his bodyguards and listening to the phono-
graph blare his favorite dance band tunes.

Just before Christmas 1933, Huey showed that he had the same dis-
gust for Washington society as he had for Baton Rouge. From the Roosevelt Hotel in New Orleans, he wrote the editor of the *Washington Social
Register* and demanded that his name be stricken from the list of Washington's rich, famous, and powerful. In the outlandish letter, he complained that Washingtonians were not sufficiently cultured. "When I first
ventured toward this nation's capital, I imagined that I might find that

field of social practices that would grasp some of the finer mannerisms of which I had devoted years of my life and study," Huey wrote. "I set to work to train some of Washington's social elites on the art of eating potlikker, to no avail, however. . . . My! My! How far behind in manners [is Washington]." He ended the letter by noting that the removal of his name from the *Register* might save those who were responsible for the list from embarrassment. Huey printed the letter in his newly resurrected *Progress* newspaper to amuse his supporters, while a Baton Rouge newspaper printed the letter to amuse his enemies.

CHAPTER 12

1934
CUT THEIR NAILS AND
FILE THEIR TEETH

"I am going to choke those words down Huey Long's cowardly throat the next time we meet," roared Mayor Semmes Walmsley. Speaking to the Young Businessmen's Association at the Roosevelt Hotel's Tip Top Inn on January 7, 1934, Walmsley had lost his temper at Huey's latest insult upon New Orleans. The mayor, normally a reserved and soft spoken man, trembled with anger as he clenched his fist, shook it in the air, and threw aside his written speech. He ended his talk stammering uncontrollably

Huey gave Walmsley good reason to lose his temper. For months Huey had avoided the race for mayor of New Orleans, leaving Walmsley and the Choctaws to fight it out with his longtime enemy Francis Williams. But at the last minute, Huey ignored the advice of Seymour Weiss to stay clear of internal New Orleans politics and decided to oppose both Walmsley and Williams. A few weeks before the January election, he entered his own candidate for mayor, John Klorer, a well-regarded New Orleans flood prevention engineer and the father of the *Progress*'s editor. White-haired and dignified in his round spectacles, Klorer was a colorless and uninspiring candidate. His performance made little difference, however, because the election focused on only one question, whether you were for Huey Long or against him.

On January 10, Huey returned to New Orleans from Washington to take charge of the mayoralty race. He gave his first speech for Klorer in the chilly night air at McCarthy Park in the middle of a working-class neighborhood. He seldom mentioned Klorer and instead spent the next two hours attacking the mayor, whom he now called "Turkey Head," a reference to the mayor's small head, which perched upon his long neck. For a week Huey repeated his blistering personal assaults in radio addresses during the day and public speeches at night. He charged Walmsley and the Choctaws with looting municipal funds and shaking down whores and gamblers. He denounced the mayor for allowing gambling and corruption to operate wantonly in the city and printed a story in the *Progress* stating that Walmsley once sat at the same luncheon table with Oscar De Priest, the black congressman from Chicago. Huey forecast the mayor's demise. "You know the turkey head usually goes on the block," the Kingfish shouted in a speech, "and we're fixing to have a little execution here."

A week later, Huey gave Walmsley another reason to lose his temper. The New Orleans District Court issued a restraining order that prohibited any tampering with the voter registration books before the mayoral election. Huey ignored the order and, late in the evening on January 16, a week before the election, sent C. S. Barnes to doctor the books. A spectacled, donnish-looking little man, Barnes was the state-appointed registrar of voters. Along with several of Huey's men carrying revolvers, Barnes entered the darkened Gallier Hall and began poring through huge volumes of voter records and crossing out names with a red pen. By Barnes's own estimate, over forty thousand fraudulent names were on the books in New Orleans. While Barnes was busy, a passerby noticed the lights in the registrar's office and called the police. When Walmsley's policemen arrived, they arrested Barnes, seized the voting register books, and locked the records in a city jail cell normally reserved for prisoners condemned to death. A few hours later, an angry Walmsley fumed at Huey's attempt. "They stealthily entered in the middle of the night," the mayor declared, "and without one whit of legality began their reckless misconduct."

The failed attack on the voting records revealed Huey's crude and illegal tactics and alienated even more voters in New Orleans. The incident probably did not affect the outcome, however, as Walmsley had the unbeatable support of both the uptown elite and the Choctaws. He also had aligned himself with Franklin Roosevelt, more popular than ever in New

Orleans, where the president had won 93 percent of the vote in 1932. In all of his campaign speeches, Walmsley criticized Huey for having "broke with President Roosevelt, opposed and betrayed him."

On January 23, Walmsley won handily with 45 percent of the vote. Klorer received 29 percent and Williams, 26 percent. Seeing Walmsley's strength, Huey ordered Klorer not to demand a second primary and concede the election to the mayor. The defeat was Huey's first on a major front since becoming governor. The *New York Herald Tribune* declared that the Long machine was "crumbling." The Old Regulars also sensed he was losing control. Soon after the election, Ulic Burke, a Choctaw ward leader, visited Huey in the Roosevelt Hotel. When he shook Huey's hand, Burke pressed a steel-cased pistol cartridge in his palm. The bullet was a special calling card, Burke's way of challenging Huey to a duel under New Orleans's historic dueling oaks in City Park. The duel never took place.

Burke was not the only one still angry at Huey. Despite his election victory, Semmes Walmsley did not calm down. Instead, the mayor became more obsessed with thrashing Huey. At the end of January, after Huey returned to the Senate, Walmsley and his wife, Julia, took the *Crescent City Limited* north to Washington and checked into the Mayflower Hotel where Huey was staying. For the next week, Walmsley stalked Huey. "If I see Long I'm going to beat him up," Walmsley told reporters. The mayor prowled the city looking for that "yellow coward" and camped out for hours in the Mayflower lobby. Dozens of photographers and reporters, including sports reporters, followed him around town, hoping to observe the mayor and the senator go toe-to-toe. Bookies placed odds on the bout, with Walmsley, who lettered in five sports at Tulane, including boxing, and still stayed in fighting shape, heavily favored over the pudgy Kingfish. While Walmsley waited for Huey, a *Washington News* reporter, Ray Moulden, a slight 120-pounder, wrote a story telling how he tried to interview Huey, only to have the enraged senator attack him with a heavy cane and shove him in the snow as his bodyguards stood by. After Huey used the hotel's back stairs to avoid Walmsley for a week, the mayor gave up and returned to New Orleans.

HUEY LONG'S WEALTH-SHARING proposal to provide every American "a home, an automobile, a radio, and the ordinary conveniences" received little support in either the United States Senate or the Roosevelt White House. He introduced wealth-sharing legislation several times in the Senate but never got more than fourteen votes from among the ninety-six senators. According to columnist Drew Pearson, his colleagues avoided him "like a small pox epidemic." Undaunted, Huey pressed ahead and entered his Share Our Wealth plan into the *Congressional Record* on February 5, 1934. He blamed the Depression on a failure to redistribute the wealth. "So, in 1929," he argued, "when the fortune holders of America grew powerful enough that one percent of the people owned nearly everything, ninety-nine percent of the people owned practically nothing, not even enough to pay their debts, a collapse was at hand." Huey attacked the millionaires of the country, arguing that "one percent of the people could not eat any more than any other one percent. They could not wear much more than any other one percent. They could not live in any more houses than any other one percent."

Although Washington insiders discarded Huey's plan, a vast and growing number of poor Americans looked upon his promise to redistribute wealth as a workable answer to the economic ravages caused by the Depression. He appealed to large numbers of poor Americans with his plan to limit fortunes, provide a $30 pension for needy persons over sixty, cut work hours to thirty a week, launch a war on disease, insanity, and drug addiction, eliminate agricultural overproduction, and give a free college education to deserving students. He rested his case on rhetoric and the Scriptures while disregarding fiscal realities. "I never read a line of Marx or Henry George or any of them economists," he admitted. "It's all in the law of God."

When pressed on how he would execute Share Our Wealth, Huey gave vague responses. To people who did not understand how he would make Share Our Wealth work, he fired back tersely, "Well, you don't have to [understand]. Just shut your damned eyes and believe it!" On the day before Easter 1934, Rose Lee of *The New Republic* interviewed Huey in his twelfth-floor suite of the Roosevelt Hotel. Escorted to his bedroom, the reporter found him "talking with that magnetic gentleness" and curled up on his bed like a small boy. When he saw the female writer, he got up, took off his coat and vest, lathered his face and began shaving. When she asked how he would redistribute the nation's wealth, he answered through the foamy lather that he would attack Wall Street millionaires and confiscate most of their riches. "I'd cut their nails and file their teeth and let them live," he swore loudly into his shaving mirror.

Huey didn't worry about either the feasibility or accuracy of his statements and continued to use the same questionable statistics in 1935 that he first used in 1918. He overestimated the number of millionaires in the United States and underestimated the number of families who needed their income increased to the $5,000 threshold. Economists across the country ridiculed Huey's plan as an impossible panacea and agreed that his numbers did not add up. According to one estimate using 1933 economic statistics, Huey would have needed to confiscate all incomes over $4,000 to assure a scant $1,400 to the needy. He also offered no workable method for dividing capital assets such as railroads or factories and disregarded the dilemma that, once industries were taken from their owners, there would be no expertise to run them. He offered no incentives for industrialists to continue production and appeared unconcerned that enforcement of any mechanisms to redistribute wealth would require a police state.

Critics dismissed the Share Our Wealth plan as "a monstrous and tragic joke" or just another passing fad and one of many utopian ideas that "come and go like the waves of the sea, pounding loudly for a little while on the beach of public attention and then receding to the silent depths of history." Conservatives condemned Huey's plan as recklessly confiscatory, labeling it communism dressed in populist garb and calling it his "Share Our Swag" program. Liberals condemned it as irrelevant since it did not touch the real source of power, namely ownership and the means of production. "This is not bread for the hungry, but a stone," Walter Lippmann wrote in the *New York Herald Tribune*. "This is not water for the thirsty, but a mirage. This is not rest for the weary, but disappointment. . . . [Share Our Wealth] is no less a fraud and a fake."

On February 23, Huey incorporated the Share Our Wealth Society and copyrighted the slogan "Every Man a King." Launching Share Our Wealth in a nationwide radio speech, he declared that his drastic economic program was intended "to hit the roof with the axe." He implored millions of listeners to "enroll with us . . . Share Our Wealth Societies are now being organized and people have it within their power to relieve themselves from this terrible situation." He ordered that the Share Our Wealth clubs collect no dues from members. This allowed the poor to join and kept the clubs without funds because, according to Huey, "most organizations are broken up by the treasurer running away with the money."

Huey's national popularity soared. By the middle of 1934, he received more mail than all other senators combined, more even than the president, and expanded his suite in the old Senate Office Building near Union Station to five rooms and employed twenty-five female clerks to handle the mail, including a night shift of another fourteen workers. Soon after launching his Share Our Wealth clubs, he received sixty thousand letters a week in his Washington office and later, when he attacked Roosevelt in a series of radio broadcasts, more than thirty thousand letters poured in daily for twenty-four straight days. Using his senatorial franking privilege, Huey mailed hundreds of thousands of copies of his Senate speeches to club members. Membership rose quickly. A month after he incorporated Share Our Wealth, he claimed 200,000 members. By the end of 1934, three million had joined, and in April 1935, he announced that eight million people belonged to 27,000 local clubs. Huey acted as happy as a newborn father when he bragged about Share Our Wealth. "It stood alone in one day, talked in two days, and began to run in three days," he told a newspaperman on its anniversary. "And now it is crying all over the length and breadth of the United States in one year."

HUEY LONG WAS always in motion, shuttling by train from Baton Rouge to Washington to attend Senate sessions and racing back home to ensure he kept tight control over his political machine in Louisiana. Even the seemingly tireless Huey, however, knew that he could not be everywhere at the same time and knew that he needed help in running his Share Our Wealth Society. He recognized the political value of his share the wealth crusade and needed a sophisticated, well-oiled operation. To manage his Share Our Wealth clubs across the country, he hired a fire-breathing clergyman, the Reverend Gerald L. K. Smith.

Gerald Smith, according to H. L. Mencken, was the most gifted speaker in the nation, the "gustiest and goriest, the deadliest and damnedest orator ever heard on this or any other earth—the champion boob-bumper of all epochs." Smith had preached at churches in Wisconsin, Illinois, and Indiana, and, a few months before the stock market crash of 1929, moved to Shreveport and became minister of the large and fashionable First Christian Church. Smith met Huey and asked him to save the homes of his congregants foreclosed during the Depression. Huey sponsored state legislation "blocking the realty sharks" and saved the homes. Smith never forgot it and became one of his most devoted followers. When Huey gave him his old suits to wear, Smith bragged to everyone where his clothes came from.

In 1933, the thirty-year-old Smith, after being forced from his Shreveport pulpit by his anti-Long congregation, became Huey's full-time national organizer of the Share Our Wealth Society. While "as meek as Moses when Huey was around," Smith also nourished a dark desire for power. Tall, muscular, with wavy auburn hair and an aquiline nose, he displayed a winning smile, but his cool, clear blue eyes revealed hardness, cunning, and bull-like ambition. He was a virulent anti-Semite who became one of the most famous hate mongers of the 1930s. He hated Roosevelt intensely, vowing, "We're going to get that cripple out of the White House."

Smith was an efficient campaigner who understood how to win people's hearts. "In order to succeed, a mass movement must be superficial for quick appeal, fundamental for permanence, dogmatic for certainty, and practical for workability," Smith wrote. "It must demonstrate its practical virtue by political success. A steam locomotive is not a pretty object. It puffs, it belches soot and cinders, it curses, it blows off steam, and it lacks the gracious attributes of refinement. But the beautiful and refined parlor car is quite helpless without it. Huey Long, whose thinking is a correct representation of the mass mind, is the locomotive whose power moves the entire Share the Wealth train, and his ego is the fire that generates the motive force of steam pressure in the boiler."

After becoming the Share Our Wealth Society organizer, Smith toured Louisiana. His energy matched Huey's, his speeches were even more stirring, and, according to Mencken, he was "a rhetorician who was even greater than [William Jennings] Bryan." Smith mesmerized his audiences with a mixture of profanity and scripture. He painted dramatic images of the poverty and hardship of the South during the Depression.

"Pull down those huge piles of gold until there should be a real job," he exhorted his audience, Bible in hand, "not a little old sow-belly, black-eyed pea job but a real spending money, beefsteak and gravy, Chevrolet, Ford in the garage, new suit, Thomas Jefferson, Jesus Christ, red, white, and blue job for every man."

Smith spoke to over a million people in the state during 1934 and expanded Huey's crusade into other Southern states during the following year. Share Our Wealth spread like wildfire. While his message was secular, Smith always ended his speeches in a prayer. "Lift us out of this wretchedness, O Lord, out of this poverty, lift us who stand here in slavery tonight," he preached. "Rally us under this young man who came out of the woods of north Louisiana, who leads us like a Moses out of the land of bondage into the land of milk and honey where every man is a king but no one wears a crown. Amen."

ON MAY 13, 1934, the day before the regular session of the Louisiana legislature convened, five hundred handpicked, tough-looking men from across the state arrived in Baton Rouge. They were all fierce enemies of Huey Long and most of them came to the capital city heavily armed. Several weeks before, anti-Long politicians plotted to dismantle Huey's political machine and they summoned the armed men in case the coming days turned violent. Huey's enemies sensed weakness in his political power after he broke with Walmsley, the Old Regulars, and the Roosevelt administration, and lost the New Orleans election. They planned an attack during the May legislative session that would begin while Huey was in Washington. The anti-Longs first planned to unseat Allen Ellender as speaker and replace him with George Perreault, a Dynamite Squad member and a reliable, rotund friend of the Old Regulars. Next, they would remove Lieutenant Governor John Fournet by a two-thirds vote of both houses, and finally they would impeach O. K. Allen and make Perrault governor. The anti-Longs were confident they had gathered enough votes to eject Huey's men from office.

As usual, Huey learned of the plot through his network of informers. Few secrets were ever safe in Baton Rouge and his spies uncovered most of them. "The Kingfish can see a few things better with one eye," Heywood Broun wrote after Sands Point, "than some of our politicians can see with two." Hurrying from Washington to quell the revolt, Huey strong-armed legislators and offered them the customary enticements such as patronage, favors for their parishes, even money, to change their votes and support his machine. Several fence-sitters from rural parishes stuck with Huey because they knew he still had the support of the people, especially the poor country folk who worshipped "Jesus, Joseph, Mary, and Huey Long." Legislators had not forgotten that if they opposed him they would be committing political suicide back home.

During this hectic period, Huey displayed his tremendous capacity for leadership, especially in the thick of political battle, when decisiveness, quick thinking, and cool judgment counted most. Caucusing late each night in the Heidelberg Hotel with his floor leaders, he gave specific orders for his men to carry out the following day. He knew the makeup of every legislative district in the state, how many votes were cast and who got them, and the political strengths and weaknesses of every legislator. He knew exactly which ones to target, and his efforts paid off. The vote to unseat Ellender never came to the floor when the anti-Longs realized they were three votes short. Huey's opponents gave up and the five hundred armed men they summoned to the capital returned home. Huey emerged from the fight more powerful than ever and his enemies once again were left sapped and bewildered.

AFTER CRUSHING THE ATTEMPTED overthrow at the beginning of the session, an angry Huey struck back with increased vengeance. He ordered the legislature to pass a number of unprecedented bills, many of them punishing New Orleans and Walmsley, whom he removed as chairman of the state Democratic Committee. One bill denied $700,000 that the state earlier appropriated to New Orleans for road repair. Another stripped the city of its power to grant liquor licenses to thousands of bars and restaurants, removing a source of revenue of tens of thousands of dollars each year. Henceforth, the state supervisor of public accounts, Alice Lee Grosjean, issued all liquor permits.

Huey placed the New Orleans police department, a rich source of patronage for the Old Regulars, under the direct control of a state-appointed board of police commissioners. He raised taxes on the New Orleans Cotton Exchange, "a den of linen-suited blue bloods" whose members detested Huey. He pushed through a constitutional amendment that raised homestead exemptions to $2,000, but in a blow to New Orleans, omitted large cities. He lowered license fees for cheap cars and trucks, thereby depriving New Orleans of thousands of dollars more in revenue. He boasted at the time that he had "taken over every board and commission in New Orleans except the Community Chest and the Red Cross."

Huey tightened his control over the state's election machinery. He stripped parish sheriffs of the custody of ballot boxes and gave it to his own state election supervisors. He no longer needed to resort to dummy candidates, as he created his own state-appointed election commissioners to replace commissioners selected by candidates. He also ordered a bill forbidding local courts from interfering with state commissioners who removed voter lists from registrar's offices, thereby legalizing C. S. Barnes's nighttime raid on the New Orleans voter registration office. Representative Rupert Payton, an anti-Long who watched helplessly as Huey seized control of elections, offered his own facetious amendment. Payton's election bill empowered election officers to "shoot and kill any person known or suspected of having cast his or her ballot against the present administration or against the desires of Senator Long." Payton's amendment received lots of laughs but no support.

Huey angered many legislators when he proposed a constitutional amendment to repeal the one-dollar poll tax. Many conservative, white Louisianans looked upon the poll tax, adopted thirty-six years before, as a way of denying the vote to blacks and poor whites. Huey's enemies fought his proposal and at first appeared successful in denying the two-thirds vote he needed for a constitutional amendment. Huey, needing one more vote, persuaded Representative Gilbert Fortier, a New Orleans Old Regular and staunch anti-Long, to change his vote at the last minute and support the repeal of the poll tax. Later, Governor Allen appointed Fortier as curator of the Louisiana State Museum at a salary of $5,000 a year.

In November 1934, voters overwhelmingly approved the amendment repealing the poll tax and enfranchising 300,000 poor whites who never had voted. Blacks were still without the right to vote, as the all-white Democratic primary denied them the vote in Louisiana. Huey knew that when poorer white voters went to the polls, he had them firmly in his grasp. During the final days of the debate on the poll tax, he marched

Representative Jesse Lucas, a railway engineer, through the chamber in greasy dungarees and carrying an oil can. "I'm here in the uniform of the people," Lucas announced to his colleagues.

Still needing more revenue to fund his political machine, Huey added new taxes on liquor and personal property, and increased the personal income tax to a maximum of 6 percent on incomes over $50,000. He placed a tax on the huge deposits of sulfur being mined beneath the swamps of Plaquemines Parish, the marshy isthmus at the extreme southeastern part of the state that stuck out into the Gulf of Mexico. In a reward to Leander Perez and his Plaquemines allies, he levied the tax but then allowed the parish to take back one third of the revenue.

Huey returned to Washington confident that his huge legislative package would pass easily. The anti-Longs, feeble when he was in town, found new courage when he left. On June 6, 1934, they held an anti-tax mass meeting in Baton Rouge, with five Illinois Central trains carrying more than seventy coaches filled with Old Regular loyalists from New Orleans. On the next day they took their demonstration back to New Orleans, where they held a rally in the Municipal Auditorium. More than a thousand attended and listened to Mayor Walmsley attack Huey and his new taxes. The rallies bolstered the courage of Huey's opponents and, with the Kingfish absent, anti-Long legislators stalled most of the tax legislation in committees.

On June 21, Huey rushed back to Baton Rouge to salvage his tax program and other legislation. Clearly, he had to be present to exert his power, for it could not be delegated to his weak-kneed supporters. When he left the state, his machine faltered and his enemies gained new footholds. After arriving in the capital, he took charge of every bill that was in question and, seemingly within minutes, regained complete mastery over the statehouse. Huey was as dominant as ever. Displeased with the handling of his tax legislation, he ordered the speaker to remove his House floor leader and replace him with Isom Guillory, a loyal but ineffective supporter from St. Landry Parish. Guillory, a comical little Frenchman, spent much of his time prancing around the floor demanding, "De Governor wants dis bill, de Governor wants dis bill."

On Monday, July 2, Huey held a meeting of the Ways and Means Committee on the tenth floor of the capitol and ordered passage of the three major bills containing the income tax increase, the tax on the New Orleans cotton exchange, and a 2 percent tax on the receipts from newspaper advertising. He was impatient to see his tax bills passed and pushed the legislature hard. When a clerk reading the bills did not read fast enough to suit him, he snapped at one of his leaders. "Tell him to hurry up. They don't have to hear a damn thing. All they've got to do is vote." During the early hours of the morning on Sunday, July 8, some senators complained of working on the Sabbath. "The Bible says if the ox gets stuck in the ditch to work Sunday to get him out," Huey answered, ordering the senators "to follow the Bible's teachings and when the legislature is stuck in the ditch it's up to you to work Sunday to get it out."

During the House debate on the tax on newspapers, anti-Long Representative Joe Hamiter of Caddo Parish argued that the tax ultimately would be passed on to the public. Huey's new floor leader, Isom Guillory, asked Hamiter, "Isn't it true that every tax is passed on to the consumer?" "Yes," Hamiter replied. "That's exactly what I've been preaching in this legislature for the past six years." Seeing Guillory's question as a concession to the opponents, Huey jumped up and shouted across the House floor, "Sit down, Isom!" Guillory immediately sat down and asked no further questions. With Huey standing inside the rail of the House floor and shouting, "Vote yes, vote yes," the House passed the newspaper tax, 56–36.

During the session, Huey used a favorite ploy of attaching controversial and power-grabbing amendments onto routine legislation during the last minutes of a session. As a bill went smoothly through the House or Senate, with legislators anxious to adjourn, a Long leader would rush in and propose an amendment, sometimes hundreds of pages in length. After the clerk mumbled a few sentences, the amended bill went to a vote. In one of his spite moves, Huey used this last-minute ruse to remove the entire city government of Alexandria, including the mayor and commissioner of finance, because Huey was pelted with eggs during a speech there. Huey used another legislative ploy after opponents introduced a bill prohibiting the removal of voting records from a registrar's office except by court order. More specifically, the bill would keep Huey's henchmen from doctoring the registration lists, as attempted earlier by C. S. Barnes. On the night before the bill went to the floor for a vote, Huey upended the legislation, amending it to *prohibit* any court from ordering the removal of records from the state-appointed registrar's office. When Huey's irate opponents saw the change, they tried to withdraw the bill. Huey ordered floor leaders to refuse to allow them to withdraw, the first time such a request had been denied, and the revised bill passed. Anti-Long legislators were powerless, their angry protests dying away "like the feeble bleats of shorn sheep in a raging tempest."

Having directed the votes in the House, Huey marched across the capitol to the Senate and grabbed his floor leader, Senator Coleman Lindsey. "Why don't you bring those three [tax] bills up and pass 'em?" he ordered. "That's all we want to pass." The Senate passed the three taxes within twenty minutes. Huey stood on the Senate secretary's desk and carefully watched as the lights on the voting machine indicated how each senator voted.

On the final day of the session, July 12, Governor Allen signed bills authorizing the newspaper advertising tax, an income tax increase, a tax on the New Orleans cotton exchange, taxes on liquor, chain stores, sulfur, and utilities, and repeal of the poll tax. By the end of the session, Huey had regained firm control of the legislature, including one third of the Old Regular bloc from New Orleans. Again, he staggered his opponents. Instead of leading a revolt and overthrowing his speaker, they found themselves more completely under his domination. He had run roughshod over the legislature, treating it with such contempt and domination that several of his most embittered opponents gave up and abandoned any serious effort to thwart him.

Huey trounced his opponents but did not destroy their sense of humor. On the Fourth of July, legislators celebrated by throwing firecrackers under each other's feet. One of Hugo Dore's well-aimed firecrackers landed on Huey's foot. Busy on the floor lobbying legislators, Huey "jumped a yard" into the air when the firecracker exploded and, after calming down, laughed off the prank. On the last day of the session, anti-Long leader Rupert Payton marched into the House chamber wearing a gilt paper crown, a lavender bathrobe with simulated ermine collar, and a stubby putty nose that bore an unmistakable resemblance to the Kingfish. As the tall, gangly Payton strutted up and down the aisles, legislators blew horns and shot cap pistols and squirt guns. Mounting the rostrum and mimicking Huey, Payton declared, "Newspapers, consider yourselves glared at. I'm here a-fightin' for the common people. I'm for the redistribution of pot likker, now controlled by J. P. Morgan and Standard Oil. I'm for the Share the Swag Society." When Representative Isom Guillory rose to speak to another member, Payton shouted, "Sit down, Isom." He then proposed a bill that conferred the title of "Your Majesty" on every man and woman in the state and gave every man a pair of green pajamas, a castle, a hotel suite, a queen, and an income of $90,000 yearly. To Huey's amusement, the House immediately approved the farce.

CHAPTER 13

1934
A TAX ON LYING

On July 30, 1934, a convoy of olive-drab trucks rumbled through the streets of New Orleans and kicked up a choking dust cloud that hung in the suffocating summer swelter. The trucks carried twelve companies of the Louisiana National Guard. Later that night, dozens of the young soldiers, "clad in khaki, with helmets strapped beneath smooth chins, with rifles on their shoulders," marched across tree-lined Lafayette Square and busted through the double wooden doors of the Soule Building, where the registrar of voters' office was located. The troopers belonged to Huey Long, who recently had passed legislation giving him control over local elections, and he had sent them to commandeer the voting lists and finish the job that C. S. Barnes started.

About two hours later, Mayor Walmsley, dressed in a light seersucker suit on this oppressively warm night, drove up in his Pierce-Arrow followed by carloads of other city officials. The Soule Building sat directly across the street from the mayor's office in white-marbled Gallier Hall and just up the block from the Choctaw Club. Seeing Huey's troopers standing guard across the street, Walmsley ordered several hundred of his own policemen to defend Gallier Hall. A stifling tenseness permeated the night as soldiers and policemen, rifles and machine guns cocked and loaded, took aim at each other across the thirty-foot street. A few yards away, derelicts still slept peacefully on park benches, unaware that a firefight might erupt at any time. "I warn you, Huey Long, you cringing coward," Walmsley shouted to newspapermen gathered around, "that if a life is spent in the defense of this city and its right of self-government, you shall pay the penalty as other carpetbaggers have done before you."

Huey had declared open war on New Orleans, the Old Regulars, and the city's mayor. As his national guardsmen surrounded City Hall, he ordered Governor Allen to declare martial law throughout the city. Soon after, he had the state's remaining 2,500 national guardsmen brought by train from garrisons across the state. The soldiers camped at the Jackson Barracks, at the Toulouse Street warehouses owned by the Dock Board, and in tents on the Robin Street Wharf. A few of them bivouacked at Huey's home on Audubon Boulevard, where, according to his son Russell, "they camped right out there in our garage." Meanwhile, Walmsley deputized four hundred special policemen and armed some of them with machine guns and tear gas. With dozens of rifle barrels sticking out of its windows, the white-marbled City Hall looked like a fortress under siege.

One of Huey's motives for invading New Orleans was to embarrass Mayor Walmsley on the eve of the Democratic primary scheduled for September 11. He hoped that his invasion would make Walmsley appear weak and unable to control his own city and, if necessary, he could station guardsmen at the voting precincts to ensure the election went his way. His attempt to embarrass Walmsley backfired somewhat, as the press widely covered the invasion of the national guardsmen and, with few exceptions, condemned the military action. "By order of the twenty-seven laws passed by the legislature in special session last month," the *New York Times* reported in a front-page article, "Senator Huey P. Long became de facto dictator of this state at noon today and immediately began acting the part." In theaters across the country, newsreels showed music-scored scenes of a confidently smiling Huey standing in front of his Audubon Boulevard home, Walmsley sitting sternly at his desk, and guardsmen wearing gas masks and manning machine gun nests in government buildings.

A week before, Huey had ordered the legislature to create a special committee from both houses to investigate charges of corruption in New Orleans and had himself appointed as counsel to the committee. "Law and order is needed in New Orleans," he declared before the special session. "The good people of the city must be protected." On September 1, just after his forty-first birthday, he arrived in New Orleans to begin the investigation, roaring through the streets at the head of a cavalcade of huge sedans, their sirens wailing. Wearing a striped straw hat, a tan silk suit over a lavender shirt, and white spats over his sporty shoes, he was in a combative mood as he strutted into the Roosevelt. With him were the seven legislators of his new committee, none of them from New Orleans, that would investigate gambling and vice in the city. After he arrived, he set up a radio studio in his Roosevelt suite and spoke several times a day on a regular schedule. "Ladies and gentlemen," he began each broadcast, "it's Huey P. Long again, telling you how we're going to clean out this rotten bunch of grafters." He promised that he would stamp out prostitution in the city. "The red light district has expanded to the point of national disgrace," he declared.

Soon after dark on September 2, Huey and his investigating committee crowded into a bare, paper-littered room of the State Insurance Commission's suite on the eighteenth floor of the Canal Bank Building, one block from the Roosevelt Hotel. Fifty of his national guardsmen filled the lobby and refused admission to newspapermen, photographers, and visitors, including Earl Long, while a crowd of several hundred stood outside. For the next two weeks, Huey interrogated dozens of people as he sat at a wooden table in front of two microphones broadcasting across the state by radio. His aides hustled friendly witnesses, many never identified, secretly in and out of the hearings by freight elevators. They described rampant vice and corruption in the city, named gambling dens and brothels, and swore that payoffs went to police and even to the mayor. Huey claimed that Walmsley and his Ring cronies collected $13 million a year in graft. After calling several people who testified they had bribed New Orleans policemen, he ordered Police Chief George Reyer to appear. Huey grilled the chief about his lavish lifestyle and how he managed to deposit $31,900 into the policemen's credit union on a salary of $400 a month. The aggressive questioning made Reyer sweat. "Take off your coat, Chief," he told Reyer at one point of the interrogation. "You look like it's getting hot in here." Soon after Reyer testified, Huey felt satisfied that he had embarrassed Walmsley and the Old Regulars and closed the hearings.

While Huey was holding his hearings, the tension in the city rose on September 6 when Colonel Guy Molony arrived in New Orleans on board the SS *Sixada*. Powerful, square-jawed, with wavy dark hair, Molony served as New Orleans police chief from 1920 to 1925 but was forced to resign because of his strong-arm tactics. Since then he spent most of his time as a soldier of fortune, traveling around Central and South America and fighting in insurrections. He had returned from Honduras after Walmsley and the Ring telegraphed him to come to the city. Once settled into the St. Charles Hotel, the hotbed of anti-Long sentiment, Molony met with Walmsley at Gallier Hall to devise a plan to combat Huey's forces. Walmsley agreed to hire several thousand special policemen and Molony, a skilled and ruthless mercenary, would lead them. Molony soon realized that the New Orleans police force was no match for the young, well-trained, heavily armed national guardsmen. If a firefight erupted, the police would be destroyed. "They didn't dare look at us twice," remembered one of Huey's guardsmen. "We were young, we were crazy, and we would do what we were told. They had big fat bellies and weren't about to start a fight with us."

Two nights after Molony arrived, the Old Regulars held an anti-Long rally at the corner of Claiborne and Canal Streets. Six thousand spectators, mostly city workers, showed up for the entertainment, including fireworks, jazz bands, bonfires, and a rousing speech by Walmsley attacking the "Mad Hatter of Louisiana." Blocks away at the river's edge, more than three thousand cheered the Long ticket and jeered the Old Regulars. Throughout the night, the potential for violence ran high.

Rain began to pour down early on September 11, but the stormy weather did not stop New Orleaneans from turning out to vote in the Democratic primary. The *New York Times* reported that the election was "as peaceful as a Quaker village on a Sunday morning," for at the last minute Police Chief Reyer and the National Guard's General Fleming agreed to keep the police and the guardsmen away from the polls. "Without that agreement who knows what might have happened," a newsman remembered. "Everyone had a gun. These guardsmen were all over the streets, and the election was just a couple of days away. It could have been a disaster." On the day after the election, Huey's three thousand national guardsmen began boarding trains to leave the city.

Huey's candidates did well. His slate totaled more than 141,000 votes compared to roughly 100,000 for the Old Regulars. In New Orleans, all four of his major candidates won, including incumbent congressmen Paul Maloney and Bathtub Joe Fernandez, and his candidate for Louisiana Supreme Court, Judge Archie Higgins. James O'Connor, Huey's candidate for the Public Service Commission, defeated his bitter enemy Francis Williams. By winning all the important New Orleans races, Huey handed Walmsley and the Choctaws a devastating defeat and captured a political stronghold that had eluded him for years. His only defeats were in congressional races outside the New Orleans area, where five anti-Long congressmen, led by J. Y. Sanders, Jr., were victorious. All of them had declared their allegiance for Roosevelt.

During the campaign, Huey supported John Overton's brother, incumbent Supreme Court Justice Winston Overton, who was opposed by Thomas Porter. Overton was the likely winner, but he died two days before the election. State law required that if a candidate died within seven days of an election, then the office went to the other candidate. Porter, however, was not acceptable to Huey. "If I owned a whorehouse," he remarked, "I wouldn't let [Porter] pimp for me." Ignoring state law, Huey called the Democratic district committee to a meeting in Crowley and ordered them to reject Porter and call a new election on October 9. By then, he selected Lieutenant Governor John Fournet to run for the Supreme Court vacancy.

Huey was rough on Fournet. Before the election, he grabbed the lieutenant governor and told him to buy some good clothes, to get himself fixed up. "Goddamnit, at least try to look like a judge," he growled as he straightened Fournet's tie. Later, Huey chewed out Fournet for his poor speaking ability. "John, if you don't get better by tomorrow morning you're a beat potato. You're going to stay up all night practicing your speech." Huey, along with his brother Earl, who had rejoined the Long forces, campaigned hard for Fournet. In a special election, Fournet won by more than four thousand votes, defeating Porter, an able jurist with years of experience on the bench, despite the fact that Fournet had never held any judicial position, never tried an important law case, and never practiced beyond the immediate neighborhood of the small country town of Jennings.

"FREEDOM OF SPEECH is one thing and freedom of taxation is another," Huey declared during the summer of 1934. "I believe in freedom of speech, but it's got to be truthful speech, and lying newspapers should have to pay for their lying. I'm going to help these newspapers by hitting them in the pocketbooks. Maybe then they'll try to clean up." From the beginning of his political career, Huey fought a stubborn battle against the large newspapers. While he wantonly spewed epithets and personal attacks on his enemies, he himself was extremely thin-skinned when attacked by the papers. Even the slightest newspaper snippet sent him into a rage, which now happened daily.

Most politicians would never have been so rash as to attack the large newspapers. Huey was different. Although one of the state's shrewder attorneys, he saw no conflict between his efforts to throttle newspaper coverage and the Constitutional guarantee of freedom of the press. He vowed to "always hit the big man first" and to him the press was just another big man. His battle with the newspapers became intensely personal. If he did not like what the press printed about him, he did not hesitate in taking whatever action necessary to throttle coverage. Soon after becoming governor, he ordered the chairman of the Tax Commission to raise the property assessments on the three New Orleans newspapers that opposed him. When the communist newspaper the *Daily Worker* criticized the Kingfish near the end of 1934, he pressured the New Orleans post office to halt delivery of the paper.

In February 1933, Huey lost his temper at New Orleans's largest paper. The Depression was causing banks across the nation to fail and runs on banks were common. At the time, the Hibernia Bank of New Orleans experienced a run that exhausted a million dollars of its cash reserve. Huey learned that the *Times-Picayune* published an extra in the afternoon that leaked the proceedings of a secret meeting he held to stave off the bank crisis. Huey, who had not eaten but was drunk in his Roosevelt Hotel suite, exploded. With his eyes popped out and face crimson, he told Seymour Weiss to call General Fleming and order the National Guard to march downtown, take over the *Times-Picayune,* and wreck its presses. Weiss, who feared the public outcry of destroying the presses as well as the legal aftermath, went to another room to make the call and told Fleming to drag his feet and delay getting to the Roosevelt. By the time Fleming arrived a couple of hours later, Weiss had sobered Huey enough to call off the raid.

Huey had failed in his early attempts to strangle the press. During the 1930 regular legislative session, he proposed a 15 percent tax on all gross revenues received by Louisiana newspapers from advertising sales. Another bill would have allowed the state to halt the printing of any newspaper that was "malicious, scandalous, or defamatory." His opponents killed both the newspaper tax and the gag bill in committee. Undaunted, he again attacked the press by publishing a second, more ambitious newspaper.

On August 24, 1933, Huey released the first issue of *American Progress*. He had discontinued his original *Louisiana Progress* when the *New Orleans Item* began supporting him in 1930, but three years later the *Item* joined the anti-Long forces after he broke with Walmsley and the Old Regulars. With no New Orleans daily supporting him, Huey created another newspaper. At first he published *American Progress*, similar in style and pugnacity to its predecessor, as a weekly but in April 1934 converted the paper to a monthly with 150,000 subscribers. He printed *American Progress* in Meridian, Mississippi, to avoid Louisiana libel laws.

Huey never abandoned his obsession to tax the state's large city newspapers out of business. In November 1933, he warned the daily newspapers in a speech in Marksville. "Take those lying *Times-Picayune*, *Shreveport Times*, and *Alexandria Town Talk*. We are going to sock a tax on those damned rascals. Let them scoundrels pay for the privilege." At the same time, his *American Progress* listed a newspaper tax among legislation to be sought at the next session. "The people must again fight their own battle," reported the *Progress*. "Watch out for the lying newspapers!"

During the regular session of the summer of 1934, Huey proposed a 2 percent tax on the gross advertising sales by newspapers with circulations over twenty thousand. The tax affected only the dailies in New Orleans and other urban centers, and of those papers, only the *Lake Charles American Press* was not rabidly anti-Long. "It's a tax on lying," he declared. Later, anti-Long representative Rupert Payton of Caddo Parish pointed out that if the newspaper tax was a tax on lying, then Huey himself would be affected because he published his own propaganda vehicle, and if "every lie published in the *American Progress* is taxed, money will flood the state's treasury." On Monday, July 2, with little discussion from legislators, the House Ways and Means Committee reported the newspaper tax bill favorably by a vote of 10–3.

The bill reached the House floor three days later. Huey paced up and down the aisles giving orders to his supporters on how to vote. Representative Payton protested his presence on the floor. "We are treated to the rotten spectacle of his piscatorial majesty, the Crawfish, giving orders in this house, interrupting debate and otherwise disporting himself as anything but a gentleman," Payton declared. "I am sick and tired of this and I think every other member is disgusted too." Representative Norman Bauer attacked the newspaper tax as "a spite bill pure and simple. It is a punitive measure and should receive no consideration at all!" Huey, standing nearby, responded with "a Bronx cheer and a satisfied smile" and Speaker Ellender rapped for order. A Long supporter asked Bauer what effect the tax on advertising would have on freedom of the press. Bauer responded that "the only purpose of this tax is to warn every paper in the state, large and small, to line up and stop criticizing the administration or they will suffer a similar fate. . . . I hope the members of the House will not bow to the will of the dictator." When one of Huey's supporters, Representative Lorris Wimberley, seemed uncertain what motion to offer, Bauer sarcastically observed, "I wish [Senator Long] would make up his mind so Mr. Wimberley will know what to do." On July 10, with Huey standing inside the rail, the House passed the tax "like it was greased," 56–38. Huey personally cast the vote for an absentee legislator. No one objected.

On the next day the Senate Finance Committee considered the newspaper tax bill. Huey arrived early and supervised the proceedings. With little discussion, the committee approved the bill, 9–2. When the bill reached the Senate floor, Huey paced back and forth impatiently. Soon he rushed up to his floor leader, Senator Coleman Lindsey of Webster Parish, and ordered a vote taken. While he stood menacingly in the front of the chamber carefully watching the lights on the voting machine signal how each senator voted, the Senate passed the newspaper tax within twenty minutes and without further discussion.

The large state newspapers angrily attacked the tax. "Freedom of the press will survive this assault in Louisiana just as surely as representative government, now chloroformed by the usurper, will be restored," the *Times-Picayune* reported. "But the rape of representative government, and the assault upon the free press just driven to success by the openly wielded lash of a dictator without principle, honest conviction, or scruple, constitute the blackest chapter in Louisiana's history." On the same day, the *Monroe News-Star* angrily reported that "Louisiana becomes the first state in the Union to throw a halter around the press in an effort to stifle criticism of legislative authority." The *New Orleans Item* warned that the tax, if carried to its logical conclusion, "will mean the end in practice not only of freedom of the American press, but virtually to freedom of speech as well."

Eight months later, on March 22, 1935, a three-judge federal court ruled Huey's 2 percent gross revenue tax on newspapers discriminatory because it taxed only large newspapers. The court did not rule on the constitutionality of the tax and its infringement upon freedom of the press. A year later, however, the U.S. Supreme Court, usually split during New Deal fights, made an unusual unanimous decision invalidating Huey's newspaper advertising tax as a violation of free press.

ON A FALL AFTERNOON in November 1934, student leaders at Louisiana State University called a mass rally at the outdoor Greek Theater, which sat on a pastoral hillside on the edge of campus. When the students arrived they did not know why the rally was called, but saw Huey sitting on the stage with one of his bodyguards. After the students took their seats, one of Huey's student leaders stepped to the rostrum and announced that the rally was now a political mass meeting. As the Kingfish sat smiling with approval, the student declared that the purpose of the rally was to elect a replacement for the state Senate seat that had become vacant after J. Y. Sanders, Jr., had been elected to Congress. The students promptly nominated LSU's most prominent student, Abe Mickal, as the new senator from Baton Rouge. Mickal was neither old enough to be a senator nor was he a Louisiana resident, but he was the president of the student body, colonel of the cadet corps, star halfback of the football team, and most importantly, Huey's favorite.

Huey's sham nomination of Mickal was obviously a gag designed to entertain the students and embarrass Sanders, but it backfired and turned quickly into another political embarrassment for the Kingfish. Several national newspapers reported Mickal's election as a serious appointment. The mistake by the press was understandable, given Huey's previous appointment of Alice Lee Grosjean as secretary of state. Mickal, who was away with the football team at the time, refused to participate in the farce but his appointment soon was a national sensation. "Huey Long is trying to make senators out of football players," Will Rogers wrote. "He better be trying to make something out of senators. I don't blame the boy for not wanting to be demoted."

During a special legislative session a week later, Huey was on the Senate floor when he was handed an advance copy of the LSU student newspaper, the *Reveille*. The paper planned to print a letter condemning his appointment of Mickal as senator. The rally at the Greek Theater had been "a mockery of constitutional government and democracy," an agricultural student wrote. Reading the letter, Huey turned purple. He knew that the editor of the *Reveille* was Jesse Cutrer, the nephew of old preacher Bill Cutrer, a representative who voted against him during impeachment. Huey sent a dozen state policemen to the *Reveille*'s print shop where they stopped the presses and destroyed four thousand copies of the paper. Just before Thanksgiving, he ordered President Smith to restrain the *Reveille*'s staff. "I'll fire any student that dares to say a word against me," Huey warned. "I'll fire a thousand. We've got ten thousand to take their places. That's my university. I built it, and I'm not going to stand for any students criticizing Huey Long." When President Smith hired Helen Gilkison, a newspaperwoman friendly to Huey, to censor the student paper, the staff resigned. On December 4, Smith suspended seven student staff members. When the students appealed the decision to him, Smith just shook his head and admitted, "We're living under a dictatorship and the best thing to do is to submit to those in authority." The university president added that he would "dismiss the entire faculty and 4,000 students before offending the Louisiana Senator." The students later enrolled at the University of Missouri, with their expenses paid by unnamed New Orleans donors.

By this time, Huey held a tight grip on the university. President Smith obeyed his every command and loyal Longites packed the LSU Board of Supervisors, including O. K. Allen, Senator Harvey Peltier, Senator Hugo Dore, and Representative Smith Hoffpauir. Huey ordered the board to grant a special law degree to Kemble K. Kennedy, one of his supporters employed by the Louisiana Tax Commission in New Orleans.

Kennedy was the law student who earlier published the *Whangdoodle* in 1930 that led to a libel suit by *Cane Juice* author John Uhler. Now, Huey ordered his board not only to grant Kennedy a special degree but force the retirement of the crusty dean of the law school, Robert Tullis, who earlier refused to allow Kennedy to graduate. Seeing the law school dean and other professors fired, faculty members felt the pressure of teaching in Huey's university and worried about their comments angering pro-Long students. "If you get a man scared enough you won't have to shut him up," a professor recalled. "He is already shut up."

ON AUGUST 15, 1934, the Kingfish strode into a meeting of the House Ways and Means Committee and plopped his straw hat down on the long wooden table. He had just called the legislature back to Baton Rouge for a special session and the hat was filled with thirty bills that he wanted the legislature to pass immediately. A few nights before, he had personally dictated many of the bills off the top of his head, rattling off complex legislation and wearing out the state's most efficient stenographers.

In three short days, the legislature passed all thirty of his bills, each one expanding the power of Governor Allen, who of course was completely subservient to Huey. The legislature granted the governor authority to use the state militia any way he saw fit, overrule any ruling by a local district attorney, and grant reprieves for any reason. A few minutes before the session ended, Huey had a bill passed that prohibited any special policemen appointed by the New Orleans mayor from carrying weapons.

In August, the FBI's J. Edgar Hoover instructed his senior FBI agent in New Orleans "that every day hereafter we want a telegraph report on any developments" regarding Huey and his sidekicks. Hoover ordered the agent to "give it all to us," including political information, because the daily reports were required by a "confidential source." All the reports went directly to the White House. Soon after the legislative session ended, Hoover reported that Huey had ordered all newspaper writers excluded from the legislature and that "there was a fight on the floor of the House of Representatives between several of the legislators . . . and that a newspaper photographer was assaulted by Administration officials." Hoover concluded that the state legislature "has given the Senator [Long] through the state administration dictatorial powers, including complete dominance of election machinery and officials." To his enemies, Huey's legislative mastery was frightening, but it only foreshadowed more repressive lawmaking in the very near future.

On November 6, Louisiana voters overwhelmingly endorsed Huey's fourteen constitutional amendments, including establishing a homestead exemption, an income tax and other new taxes, and abolishment of the poll tax. In ordinary times, creation of an income tax and abolishment of the poll tax would have been extremely unpopular proposals in conservative Louisiana. Huey's popularity, however, was never stronger and the amendments passed by majorities averaging seven to one.

On November 12, Huey called the legislature back to Baton Rouge for another six-day session. He gave his floor leaders forty-four bills that he drafted. All were adopted as fast as they could be read by the clerk. As the bills rolled through the legislature, one of his opponents asked Huey, "When will we know what these bills are all about?" Smiling, the Kingfish answered back, "Tuesday, when they are passed." One bill created a Civil Service Commission, composed of the governor and other high-ranking officials, and empowered the commission with authority over the hiring and firing of all municipal policemen and firemen. Police and fire departments, traditionally rich sources of patronage for city and parish officials, now fell within his control.

One of Huey's spite bills stripped the Louisiana Bar Association of all supervisory power over admissions to the bar. He had turned against the Bar Association the previous June when the association expelled the pro-Long attorney general, Gaston Porterie, after several controversial decisions, including blocking an election fraud investigation by the New Orleans district attorney and interfering with grand jury proceedings. After the legislature created his new State Bar Association, Huey selected his own loyalists as board members and required all attorneys to join it. In 1935 Porterie became its first president. During the session Huey also limited the salary of the district attorney of Baton Rouge to $4,000 per year. Soon after the session adjourned, he admitted that the forty-four bills were full of surprises that increased his power. "There's lots of things in these bills they don't know about yet," Huey bragged to a reporter.

A month later, on Sunday, December 16, Huey called a five-day special session of the legislature to run until Christmas Eve. He was in a foul mood. On the day before the session convened, he attended the Sugar Bowl game between LSU and Oregon State in New Orleans, where coach Biff Jones refused to let Huey enter the locker room and resigned after the game. Huey still fumed. The special session was the most provocative since impeachment. He aimed many of his thirty-three bills at New Orleans. Previously, a seven-man local board of assessors set property values in the city, but he now ordered legislation giving the state Tax Commission absolute authority over assessments, and the powers became retroactive for three years. Huey's commission now could lower the assessment of a friend while raising an enemy's with no recourse, and his state assessors could go to a business and say they needed a thousand-dollar campaign contribution and if they didn't get it they'd raise the assessment. Soon after the special session, state assessors cut the appraised value of Seymour Weiss's Roosevelt Hotel and trimmed $300,000 off the value of the New Orleans Fairgrounds after some of his friends bought the property. The assessors also retroactively reduced the value of the Louisiana & Arkansas Railway, owned by Huey's millionaire friend and Louisiana Quarry Company partner Harvey Couch, by 41 percent.

Among the thirty-three bills, one stripped local school boards of the power to hire, fire, and pay teachers. Huey's bill created a state Budget Committee, consisting of the governor, superintendent of education, and state treasurer, which held absolute authority over the jobs of every teacher, school bus driver, and school janitor in the state. At the first meeting of the Budget Committee, dozens of teachers from the anti-Long parishes failed to be rehired, including twenty from Baton Rouge. Huey took from the sheriffs the power to name more than five deputies. He took from district attorneys in the big-city parishes the right to name more than three assistants, required all police and firemen to obtain commissions from the state, and required employers dismissing employees to pay them a pro rata share of pension benefits, a measure aimed at Standard Oil. In a thrust at Tulane University, governed by his enemies, he established the LSU School of Dentistry and Pharmacy at New Orleans, raising the corporate capital tax by 50 percent to pay for it.

On Huey's orders, the legislature passed a law that allowed the Fisher family, Leander Perez, and Morris Steinberg to create a monopoly over the fur-rich swamps around Barataria Bay. Previously, 150,000 people, mostly Cajuns, depended upon the fur industry for their livelihood. The new law forced thousands of the independent trappers out of business, and the few that remained became economic slaves to the new monopoly. The state Conservation Commission, run by Robert Maestri, ensured that the trapping leases covering the seven million acres of state-owned swamps went to the Fishers and their cronies.

During the session, Huey ordered the Public Service Commission to appoint him as its special attorney and to pay him fat legal fees. He also directed the Tax Commission to hire him as a roving prosecutor and tax investigator, a lucrative job where he kept one third of the sums he recovered from delinquencies. Huey saw no conflict of interest in his appointments and, in fact, bragged about them. "I admit that I'm the best lawyer in Louisiana, and I don't see why this state should not have a good lawyer." In 1935, Huey received over $150,000 in fees from the two commissions.

Huey continued his vendetta against Baton Rouge for voting against him and for its society shunning of him. He told his aides that he would make Baton Rouge another District of Columbia and no longer empowered to govern itself. Of Baton Rouge's thirteen police jurors, only two were friendly to Huey. He ordered the legislature to double the number of jurors from thirteen to twenty-six. Soon, he appointed the thirteen new jurors and gained control of the capital city government. At their first meeting the new Longite majority elected one of their own, Dr. Cecil Lorio, as commission president and promptly dismissed all 225 city employees. Another bill allowed Huey's state police to choose all deputies for Baton Rouge. He aimed similar legislation at Alexandria, where eggs splattered him in 1933, and he sacked the city's chief of police for allowing the anti-Long demonstration. He also found time to fire a motorcycle policeman who had arrested his teenage son, Russell, for speeding. According to Huey, his son was "only doing twenty."

AT SIX IN THE MORNING on the last day of the special session, Huey asked Chick Frampton to play golf at the LSU course. Frampton did not play but showed up anyway. After Huey teed off, halfway down the first fairway, he stopped. "You wondered why I brought you out here?" he said to Frampton. "I have something to tell you where there wasn't a chance in the world of anybody overhearing it. You know in 1929 they tried to impeach me for putting that gas tax on the refining of oil. Well, today I'm going to put it on."

"That's impossible, Huey," Frampton replied. "This is the last day of the session and you don't even have a bill in there."

"There are many ways to do things, just watch," Huey said. "I'm going to do it . . . there's a bill in there on oil and I'm going to put an amendment on it. It has already passed the House and it's already over in the Senate and when it comes up in the Senate I'm going to have this amendment tacked on it."

That afternoon, a routine bill calling for the codification of existing licensing laws passed the House and Senate committees and quickly was approved by the entire House. Shortly before the Senate floor vote, a pro-Long senator offered an amendment one hundred pages long, which passed almost immediately with scarcely a ripple of protest, then was sent back to the House and approved with no debate. Just before the amended bill was passed, anti-Long Norman Bauer glanced at the wording and rose on the floor. "Is not this the same bill which led to the impeachment of Governor Long in 1929?" The House ignored Bauer's question and moved on. The enactment of the oil processing tax, which in 1929 took twenty days to go down in defeat, took less than twenty minutes to pass in 1934. Only afterward did most legislators realize that they had enacted the same notorious bill levying a 5-cents-per-barrel tax on refined oil. Within a month, Standard Oil began laying off employees at its Baton Rouge refinery.

SOMETIME AROUND 1934, Huey met the New York mob boss Frank Costello in a Long Island nightclub where the politician and the gangster made a lucrative deal. Costello needed a new market for his gambling racket, as Mayor Fiorello La Guardia had been cracking down on his operations in New York City. Huey and the mobster agreed that Costello's organization would move slot machines into the New Orleans area. James "Diamond Jim" Moran, a former bootlegger, prizefighter, and underworld associate of Costello and Lucky Luciano, installed the machines. Moran also once served as one of Huey's bodyguards. Carlos Marcello, another underworld boss and owner of the Jefferson Music Company, operated the slots. Soon the one-armed bandits sprouted in bars, pharmacies, grocery stores, and gas stations across wide-open Jefferson Parish, where the Sicilian Mafia had operated since the 1880s and which remained under the tight political grip of Senator Jules Fisher, a trusted member of Huey's inner circle.

Despite ordering the National Guard to raid gambling houses early in his administration, Huey never seriously cracked down on gambling around New Orleans. "Ninety-five percent of the people in this grand and glorious city and its environs love to gamble," he told reporters in May 1935, as he called off what little enforcement remained. On the next day, the gambling halls of Jefferson and St. Bernard Parishes reopened after being closed for five months. Huey now controlled the New Orleans police, who obeyed his order to turn a blind eye to gambling and other vice activities. By late 1935, over a thousand of the slot machines, known as "chiefs" because of the elaborate bronze head of an Indian chief mounted above the dial, operated in New Orleans and the surrounding parishes. They raked in "a million and a quarter" each year. Huey's machine got 10 percent of the take for providing protection.

IN JANUARY 1934, just as Prohibition ended, President Roosevelt ordered federal investigators to increase their probe of Huey Long. Treasury Secretary Henry Morgenthau instructed Elmer Irey to intensify the income tax investigation of Huey and his closest associates. Irey's agents spent the next year checking Huey's income and expenditures, poring through bank statements, canceled checks, and sales records from hundreds of Louisiana businesses. The agents enlisted Pat O'Rourke, an informant used to trap Al Capone, to come to New Orleans and pose as a radio executive. Moving into the Roosevelt Hotel, O'Rourke became a frequent player at the nighttime poker games held in Huey's suite. From a pay phone up the street, O'Rourke reported daily to Irey's agents.

Irey's investigation of the Long machine was well known. According to the *New Orleans Item*, "the country's most skilled and daring detectives are weaving a web of evidence to entrap some of the state's most prominent characters." By October 1934, Irey won federal indictments for tax evasion against the Jefferson Parish boss, state Senator Jules Fisher, accused of making $348,000 over four years and paying only $41.18 in taxes, and his nephew Representative Joe Fisher, accused of paying no taxes on an income of $122,000 over four years. The Fishers' loyalty to Huey had made their family wealthy. In 1930, the Fishers made a huge profit on $117,000 worth of shells sold to the state Highway Department for road construction, and since then they had soaked the state treasury with no-bid contracts. A federal jury later found Joe Fisher guilty of tax evasion and sentenced him to eighteen months in the federal prison in Atlanta.

Irey's agents also indicted Huey's wealthy friend Abe Shushan. Shushan was owner of a New Orleans dry goods company that consistently bid lower than its competitors on orders from state institutions. He was nicknamed "the collector" because of his ability to raise large sums of cash for last-minute emergencies. The federal agents accused Shushan of receiving a half-million dollars in bribes over five years and reporting only a fraction of his income. On December 13, 1934, Irey's investigators got much closer to Huey when they won an indictment against Seymour Weiss. They accused Weiss, president of the Dock Board, soon to be president of the New Orleans Fire Department Board and still holder of the purse strings of Huey's political machine, with making $232,000 in income over five years and reporting only $55,000.

Irey was making progress and believed he soon would have sufficient evidence against Huey to present to a grand jury. On March 7, 1935, Attorney General Homer Cummings announced that former Texas governor Dan Moody would prosecute the Louisiana income tax cases. Much of Irey's evidence against Huey related to the shady finances of the Win or Lose Oil Company. Huey's close friend Senator James Noe was president of Win or Lose with thirty-one of the one hundred shares, and Weiss was vice president with twenty-four shares. Huey held thirty-one shares, and the remaining shares were split among other aides, including Alice Lee Grosjean. No shareholder invested any cash. Their oil company drilled no wells but leased mineral rights on state property that sat above rich petroleum resources. Win or Lose's first transaction took place when Governor Allen transferred an oil lease near New Orleans to Noe, who sold it to a wealthy oil operator for $29,937. The proceeds, reaped from the sale of state property, went into the Win or Lose coffers. Win or Lose then leased twenty oil patches in gas fields near Monroe in north Louisiana. The company had bought the leases from Noe, who a month earlier acquired them from Allen for free, and then sold the mineral rights to all twenty locations for $16,000 each. Win or Lose could not lose and cleared about $350,000 in 1935. Huey's share, costing nothing and soon valued at thousands of dollars, eventually would be worth millions.

Over the next few years, Huey's followers duplicated the Win or Lose process and established a number of dummy holding corporations to exploit mineral leases. Their monopoly over leases helped convert the small Texas Oil Company, which sent its drilling rigs into millions of acres of Louisiana swampland, into a huge commercial empire. Leander Perez, Huey's shrewd impeachment attorney, became a master at turning state leases into private income, and would amass almost $100 million over the next four decades.

On Saturday, September 7, 1935, Irey and his Treasury agents flew to Dallas where they presented hundreds of pages of evidence to Moody. Sitting in the ex-governor's office, Irey soon convinced Moody that the case against Huey was so overwhelming that he easily could convict the Kingfish of income tax evasion. After listening to Irey for several hours, Moody agreed to present the evidence to a grand jury early the next month. When Irey and his agents left the meeting later that afternoon, they were confident that, after years of investigation, they finally could convict Huey Long and topple him from power.

CHAPTER 14

1935
TEAR-DIMMED EYES
AND HUNGRY SOULS

While thousands of citizens across Louisiana worshipped Huey Long, thousands of others detested him. Some of his enemies even talked of ways to have him killed and, although most of them probably would not have committed the murderous act if given the chance, there were some who despised him enough to pull the trigger. Many of those who hated Huey were middle- and upper-class and some were otherwise refined women like Hilda Hammond and the unstable Mrs. Pleasant. Kathleen Gibbons, Mayor Walmsley's niece, recalled that the table talk always seemed to be about killing him. "Huey Long was just hated," she told an interviewer years later.

Betty Carter was one of those refined ladies who despised the Kingfish. Born into New Orleans's elite society, Mrs. Carter represented the archetypal Southern gentlewoman, the kind who wore a string of pearls and white lace gloves to afternoon teas where black waiters in starched white coats served little cucumber sandwiches with the crust cut off. Cultured, well bred, and perfectly coiffed, she was an unlikely candidate to plot a murder. "We used to try to think of ways to kill [Huey]," Mrs. Carter admitted. "He would come and speak in the bandstand in the park and listeners would sit on folding chairs. I thought we should take a sharp nail with the point made even sharper and dip it in tetanus and stick it up in one of those chairs, where he'd sit on it. He wouldn't know it, and he'd die the death he deserved, the death of a mad dog."

The hotbed of Huey hatred was Baton Rouge. On New Year's Day 1935, Standard Oil fired thirty-eight hundred workers from its Baton Rouge refinery to offset the cost of his latest 5-cents-per-barrel tax. When Huey learned that Standard Oil threatened to move its refinery from Louisiana, he showed no concern. "If they got to leave," he declared, "they can go to hell and stay there." Three weeks later, the Baton Rouge police jury met and thirteen new Long-appointed council members fired 225 city workers. To Baton Rougeans, the combined firing of city employees and Standard Oil workers was the tragic final scene of a six-year melodrama of repressive attacks by Huey upon the capital city. Tempers flared and there was a wildness in the air.

That week, several dozen of Huey's more angry enemies met in Baton Rouge and formed the Square Deal Association. Led by Ernest Bourgeois, a twenty-nine-year-old unemployed Standard Oil engineer, the Square Dealers at first demanded the repeal of "all dictatorial laws," especially the 5-cent oil processing tax, but soon they turned more hostile and threatened armed violence to topple Huey. Several hundred members joined in Baton Rouge and chapters sprung up in a dozen parishes. Members included Mayor Walmsley and former governor Parker, while Hilda Hammond and Mrs. Pleasant joined the Square Dealers' women's auxiliary. The more belligerent chapters organized themselves into militialike companies, began gathering weapons, and drew up plans to march on the capitol.

Huey returned from Washington on January 19 after he learned of the Square Dealer threat. When he talked to reporters he appeared unworried. "The fellows won't march unless you give them a buggy or a rickshaw," he remarked. "They're too lazy to march." But Huey knew that they were determined to challenge his power. On Friday, January 25, the day after the firing of the parish workers, about three hundred of Bourgeois's men, all armed and wearing buttons pinned on their lapels saying "Direct Action," marched on the Baton Rouge courthouse and barricaded themselves behind locked doors. Huey ordered National Guard troops sent to Baton Rouge, and later that day the first truck rolled into town with an infantry company from Crowley. Soon, eight hundred troops encamped around the capitol, and when the Square Dealers learned of the force mustered against them, they abandoned the courthouse. That afternoon, Huey told O. K. Allen to declare martial law in Baton Rouge. Allen outlawed the carrying of firearms, forbade newspapers from criticizing state government, and prohibited "crowds of two or more people." The martial law order lasted six months.

On the following day, a cool Saturday afternoon, about 350 Square Dealers, many armed with hunting rifles, gathered at the Baton Rouge airport located three miles east of the city at the end of Government Street. Huey learned of the meeting beforehand and ordered two companies of his national guardsmen to the scene. The ragtag group of Square Dealers was no match for his five hundred dragoons armed with military rifles and machine guns. When the soldiers deployed in battle line and hurled tear gas bombs, half of the Square Dealers surrendered and the other half retreated into the woods behind the airport. "We seized a truckload of guns," one of Huey's bodyguards remembered. The only Square Dealer injured was George Alessi, a Tangipahoa Parish police juror who received an accidental shotgun wound in the arm from one of his retreating compatriots.

On Sunday night, Huey returned to Washington after learning that Bourgeois and other Square Deal leaders had fled the state. A week later, Governor O. K. Allen responded to a newspaper reporter's question about the battle of the airport with the terse comment "I don't wish to discuss anything except fishing."

"OUR MEN OF AFFAIRS and the powers that be are in a maze of confusion," Huey Long bellowed loudly on the floor of the United States Senate in late January 1935. "The hand of death has gripped the souls of our leaders, it has calloused their hearts and cankered their minds." Now fighting almost every measure put forth by the Roosevelt administration, he rose to attack a resolution supported by the president to abide by the rulings of the World Court. The Los Angeles Times reported that Huey, "with the fury of a fire-breathing monster," thundered for three straight hours, providing his colleagues and a packed gallery of amused spectators with a masterful example of his infamous oratory—loud, long, and scathing. Swinging his long arms like an angry gorilla, Huey wove in and out of the aisles and desks and tore into every adversary. His voice rising to camp-meeting pitch, he attacked the Roosevelt administration, Standard Oil Company, United Fruit Company, the Department of Justice and its "Mother Hubbard" opinions, the League of Nations, and Postmaster General Jim Farley. He labeled Presidents Hoover and Roosevelt "Tweedledum and Tweedledee" and rhetorically answered his own question, "To get rid of the devil, did we get a witch?"

Just when Huey's harangue began to become tiresome and trite and no longer humorous, he returned to his fight against the World Court. Emphasizing the few facts he possessed, he gave a reasoned argument to vote against a resolution that otherwise would have passed quickly and with little debate. Senator William Borah of Idaho claimed that Huey was the only man he knew who could defend a wrong premise and reach the right conclusion. Huey argued that the nation should never again become entangled in European disputes. "We wound up with all of Europe under dictatorship, and we are trying to set up one in this United States at the same time," he declared. "I do not intend to have these gentlemen whose names I cannot even pronounce let alone spell, passing upon the rights of the American people. I do not intend to vote for this infernal thing." When he finished, the Senate defeated the World Court resolution, fifty-two senators for it, thirty-six against, seven votes short of the needed two-thirds majority.

Huey no longer obliquely criticized the Roosevelt administration. His attacks now were head-on, barefaced, brutish, and disrespectful, as when he snidely lingered over each syllable of the president's name, "Franklin Dee-lah-no Rosy-felt." With the galleries packed and a hundred congressmen lining the walls of the Senate chamber, he charged that Roosevelt's men in New Orleans controlled a red-light district "eighteen squares long and sixteen squares wide" and packed with houses of ill fame and gambling dens. In another speech, he accused Roosevelt of going back on his word to redistribute the nation's wealth. "He's a liar and a faker!" Huey roared. "No heart has ever been so saddened, no person's ambition was ever so blighted as was mine when I came to the realization that the President of the United States was not going to undertake what he said he would do, and what I knew to be necessary if the people of America were ever to be saved from calamity and misery." No longer hiding his personal enmity for the president, Huey fought the second New Deal legislation intensely and made thinly veiled suggestions that he might himself run for the presidency.

Huey argued that both Hoover and Roosevelt had let the common man down. "Don't you remember when Mr. Hoover proposed to plow up every fourth row of cotton?" he asked the Senate. "Roosevelt's plan was to plow up every third row of cotton . . . while millions have starved and gone naked . . . while babies have cried and died for milk. So it has been that while people have begged for meat and bread, Mr. Roosevelt's administration has sailed merrily along, plowing under and destroying the things to eat and wear, with tear-dimmed eyes and hungry souls made to chant for this New Deal. . . . Is this government? It looks more like St. Vitus dance." During the first three months of 1935, he attacked the president dozens of times on the Senate floor and made six anti-Roosevelt radio broadcasts on NBC, including major addresses titled "Our Growing Calamity" on January 23 and "Our Plundering Government" on February 10.

On February 11, Huey strutted around the Senate with his hands stuck in his pockets and his coat unbuttoned to reveal bright red suspenders. He launched a bitter attack upon Roosevelt's former campaign manager, Postmaster General Jim Farley. Titling his speech "Farley, a Menace to Clean Politics," he branded the postmaster general as "a demon political ringmaster and political tyrant" and accused him of personally profiting from post office construction in New York City, being implicated in wire services to gambling houses, and giving $80,000 worth of new commemorative stamps to friends. When he accused Farley of forcing federal employees to make campaign contributions to the Democratic Party, another senator chided Huey that this was also the practice in Louisiana. Without breaking stride, he answered that donations were "voluntary" in Louisiana and besides, there was no *state* law against soliciting political contributions.

On Sunday night, March 3, Huey attacked Roosevelt and Farley on New Orleans radio. Still bitter over not being given federal patronage, he again lost his temper. "If I must kneel to such crooks as may be employed by men like Jim Farley," Huey shouted, "God send me to hell before I bring myself to go through that kind of thing to get patronage."

Later that month, Huey delivered several blistering tirades against Farley on the Senate floor. "Jim can take the corns off your feet without removing your shoes," he charged, as he motioned for a formal Senate investigation of the postmaster general. The Senate soon tired of the attacks on Farley, declared the accusations "frivolous and without merit," and rejected his motion for an investigation, 62–20, with the vote falling along party lines. After the Senate defeated his motion, a reporter asked Huey why he went after Farley. "Jim was the biggest rooster in the yard," he admitted, "and I thought that if I could break his legs, the rest would be easy."

Roosevelt lost his patience with Huey and struck back. In February the president ordered the Federal Emergency Relief Administration to provide him with a list of federal employees working in Louisiana and told his aides to fire any worker who was a Long supporter. In April, Roosevelt increased the pressure on Huey by withholding huge amounts of federal aid. The president suspended $2.5 million earmarked for New Orleans sewerage and water projects that would have employed at least two thousand workers. Later that month, Interior Secretary Harold Ickes stopped $10 million of Public Works Administration projects for Louisiana because the "Longislature" would use the projects and their associated jobs to further strengthen the Kingfish's machine. Huey curtly replied that Ickes could "go slap damn to hell!"

Roosevelt recruited General Hugh Johnson, the sharp-tongued former head of the National Recovery Administration, to lead a counterattack. On Monday night, March 4, Johnson assailed Huey in a speech at New York's Waldorf-Astoria. In the speech, broadcast on national radio, Johnson called Huey one of the "pied pipers of the lunatic fringe" and compared him to the führer. "Hitler couldn't hold a candle to Huey in the art of the old Barnum ballyhoo," Johnson bellowed into the microphone.

On the following Thursday night, NBC gave Huey forty-five minutes of airtime to respond to Johnson. Twenty-five million Americans listened in, expecting to be entertained with another of his colorful harangues. Huey, however, surprised his audience. He didn't swap insults with Johnson but used the time to give a steady, calculated twenty-minute critique of Roosevelt's New Deal, saying it differed little from Hoover's plan. "Back in the kitchen," he declared, "the same set of cooks are fixing up the vittles." Speaking earnestly into the radio microphone with finely chosen words, he then set forth his Share Our Wealth plan. He painted an idyllic picture of a national utopia created by his program to distribute the nation's wealth. Appearing calm and logical, he transformed himself, as one reporter described, "from a clown into a real political menace." By the time he finished, Johnson looked heavy-handed and probably had done more harm than good by attacking the Kingfish. Huey, on the other hand, used his radio time to convince millions of Americans that Share Our Wealth was a realistic solution to the Depression and that Huey Long, despite what his critics said, was not so crazy after all.

HUEY DELIVERED at least one of his anti-Roosevelt speeches while dead drunk. "He was so tight he could hardly walk," one of his workers remembered. "We had to hold him up there when he first started, but after he got into a speech, why you would never know he had had a drink. And he made some of his best speeches [drunk]." According to Chick Frampton, he needed only a half pint of whiskey to put him on a rip-roaring bender. "I've been under the influence [of liquor] more nights of my adult life than I've been sober," Huey told a bodyguard, "and out of this have come some of the most brilliant ideas of my career." Foreign embassies delivered whiskey by the case to his Washington hotel room. By the middle of 1934, however, he realized that he must curtail his night-owl lifestyle of noisy clubs and smoke-filled bars. He was not so much worried about his health, which had deteriorated from years of liquor and fried food and little sleep, but realized that his frequent carousing interfered with his one and only goal of amassing political power. Helen Clifford's hula dance and, most notorious of all, the Sands Point brouhaha provided embarrassing reminders that his social life could bring disaster upon his political well-being. He knew that he must be more careful if he was to survive in the fishbowl of Washington politics. From June 1934 through July 1935, he avoided the capital's racy nightspots, no longer drank, and gave up cigarettes and, for a while, his cherished cigars. "Liquor makes me soft," he admitted. "I used to have a fight and then meet a man and forgive him and get all over it. But then I began to find as I got older that I couldn't drink without fighting with people."

Several days a week, just after dawn, Huey played a round of golf at

Washington's Congressional Country Club. He went on a diet and reduced his weight from 200 pounds to about 175. Although still in generally poor health when he celebrated his forty-second birthday on August 30, 1935, Huey amazed his enemies in Washington with his unrelenting energy. His gumptious oratory never had been so masterful and mesmerizing and his in-your-face demeanor never so pugnacious.

When his opponents in the U.S. Senate attacked him, Huey charged back at them with, according to a Roosevelt aide, "the savageness of a mad bull." Some younger senators made the mistake of trying to cuss him out, but nobody could cuss better than the Kingfish. They found that he was impervious to sarcasm, that indeed their barbs incited him further, and no man could silence him. "It's like challenging a buzz saw," one of Huey's Senate foes admitted. His enemies soon feared Huey's quick wit and explosive temper and refrained from attacking him, for they knew that his retaliation would be twice as vengeful and his scathing words would show up the next morning on the front page of the *Washington Post*. "None of them has a stomach for a fight," a newsman observed. Even Alben Barkley, the Kentucky senator known to shrink an adversary with sharp-tongued satire, humor, and serious argument, could not fluster him. In one encounter on the Senate floor, Barkley raked the Kingfish with all his guns, called Huey "the smartest lunatic I ever saw in my whole life," and sat back down satisfied that he had put him in his place. Unperturbed, Huey rose. "Maybe that is the smartest description I've ever had applied to me," he replied. After facetiously apologizing for displeasing the senior senator from Kentucky, he then sallied into one of his homespun stories about a pious farmer he knew back in Louisiana. One day, this God-fearing man was plowing the back forty and later his wife heard loud groans coming from the field. When she ran out to investigate, she found her husband lying in a fence corner, bleeding from several ghastly wounds. The farmer explained that while he was plowing, the venerable farm billygoat, attracted by his posture, gored him deeply from the rear.

"Don't take on so, honey," said the wife. "You have lived the good life and you know you are going straight to heaven and will be received in full grace by God Almighty."

"Yes, wife, I know that," the dying man replied, "but I sure hate to be served up to God Almighty on the horns of a vicious old goat." Winking at Barkley, Huey sat down. Barkley, whose gallant manner toward the ladies was well known among his colleagues, stood up to reply, opened his mouth to snap back at the Kingfish, but realized he had nothing to say and sat down.

Huey met his match on one occasion, but not from another senator. As he rose to speak for an amendment to give free college education to needy students, a small, black-haired girl in a green dress watched Huey from the gallery above. The little girl became fascinated by his wildly jerking motions and flailing of his arms. She stood up and began to mimic the Kingfish, matching each gesture jerk by jerk. Spectators began to laugh and Huey looked up to see what was causing the commotion. When he saw the little girl imitating him, he faltered and, for a few moments, was speechless. After the youngster's mother ended her performance and placed her back in her seat, Huey continued his own performance.

In a Senate speech on March 5, Huey captivated the packed gallery with a virtuoso performance. "Mr. President, I am not undertaking to answer the charge that I am ignorant. It is true. I am an ignorant man," he declared in measured tones. "I have had no college education. I have not even had a high-school education. But the thing that takes me far in politics is that I do not have to color what comes into my mind and into my heart. I say it unvarnished. I say it without veneer. I know the hearts of the people because I have not colored my own. I know when I am right in my own conscience. I do not talk one way in the cloakroom and another way out here. I do not talk one way back there in the hills of Louisiana and another way here in the Senate. I have one language. Ignorant as it is, it is the universal language of the sphere in which I operate." Huey's unexpected humility and calm demeanor riveted his listeners. Even his Senate colleagues, sick of his inexorable polemics and filibusters, sat back in awe and marveled at the Kingfish at his best. "Nonetheless, my voice will be the same as it has been," he continued. "Patronage will not change it. Fear will not change it. Persecution will not change it. It cannot be changed while people suffer. The only way it can be changed is to make the lives of these people decent and respectable. No one will ever hear political opposition out of me when that is done."

—

SPECIAL SESSIONS OF the Louisiana legislature, like the one Huey called on February 26, 1935, now seemed like another festive event of the Mardi Gras season. The sessions no longer resembled the ordinary workings of democratic government but now had a surreal, carnival-like air. One observer described the spectacle as "Professor Long's Puppet Show in which the legislators danced, bobbed, pirouetted, and stood at attention in mechanical, blank obedience to every yank of the strings." Few legislators seemed to care. One representative, Pat McGrath of New Orleans, attended the session while "cock-eyed drunk" and was so besotted that he could not stand at his desk.

When the legislators arrived in Baton Rouge, Huey immediately handed them another eighty bills he had drafted. His ability to concoct new legislation continued to astound those around him. The House Ways and Means Committee approved twenty-two of the bills in an hour. The proceedings were brief because only one witness appeared to testify— Huey Long. One bill ousted Powers Higginbotham, the park and street commissioner of Baton Rouge, for his involvement in the Square Deal demonstrations. Another motion removed Senator Frank Peterman from his position as president pro tem of the Senate. Peterman, the short, bald former Long supporter, had defected to the New Deal crowd when Huey "started to go wild." Huey exploded when he learned that Roosevelt appointed Peterman, who had refused to sign the Round Robin, to replace Harry Early as the Federal Emergency Relief administrator in New Orleans. The Senate obeyed Huey's command and elected one of his cousins, Senator Thomas Wingate, as president pro tem by a vote of 26–7. In a slap at the "Roosevelt Boodle Brigade in Louisiana," Huey ordered the legislature to pass a bill making it a criminal offense to use federal funds for a political purpose.

Huey continued to punish New Orleans. One bill finished the job of taking complete control of the New Orleans police and fire departments. He ordered the legislature to give him control of the New Orleans private markets, and required New Orleans to pay $50,000 a year for upkeep of the state-owned courthouse. Mayor Walmsley soon had to place six thousand of his employees on half pay as city funds began to disappear. New

Orleans's plight worsened later that spring when the city's garbage collectors went on strike because of no pay.

Huey again needed to create new revenues to match his spending on highways and new state employees. He doubled the inspection fee paid by public utilities and raised the rates on several other taxes. When Huey took office in 1928, Louisiana was known as a state with few taxes, mainly a local property tax, inheritance tax, occupational license tax, and a severance tax on oil and minerals. By 1935, some forty-five separate taxes reaped $38 million in state revenues, a 75 percent increase over 1927. According to one of Huey's workers, his theory on taxation was to "cover everything in sight . . . and to throw out a network of taxes with low rates to cover everything." The increase in revenues was still not enough, however, as Huey continued to outspend the state's income. By this time, bonds had overtaken taxes as the primary source for financing his projects. In 1935, Louisiana had the second highest per capita state debt in the nation, with the debt increasing from $11 million to $150 million during his reign.

Near the end of the session, Huey surprised the citizens of Baton Rouge, who still could not gather in crowds because troops patrolled the streets under martial law. Only a couple of months before, the residents of the capital city fought the Kingfish bitterly over the new oil processing tax, but he now reversed direction and announced a compromise with Standard Oil. He agreed to rebate 4 of the 5 cents of the processing tax back to the oil company, while the president of Standard Oil, J. C. Hilton, agreed that the Baton Rouge refinery would get 80 percent of its crude oil from Louisiana wells and would take back the discharged workers. While Huey had been bitterly attacking Standard Oil in the press, he was negotiating behind the scenes with the oil giant to cut a deal. On January 22, a week before the session convened, Huey and Hilton had met secretly and made the agreement. Several of Huey's close supporters were independent oil drillers who would profit if Standard Oil agreed to use more Louisiana crude. Over a five-year period, Huey's tax assessors lowered the property value of Standard's Baton Rouge refinery from $44 million to $34 million.

On the Senate floor, Scott Heywood, a former Long ally who broke over the New Orleans fight the previous August, objected to Huey colluding with the oil trusts. While Heywood spoke, Huey strolled down the aisle to within twenty feet of the senator and stopped, staring at him with cold eyes and a half smile. Heywood saw him and sat down. Taking the floor, Huey began to speak, telling a short story about a boy who picked up a wounded snake, cared for it, and brought it back to health by warming it against his breast. Then the snake bit him. Finished with his story, he still glared at Heywood, now speechless, as the mostly Longite Senate broke into applause. Following his orders, the legislature ignored Heywood and quickly ratified the compromise tax rebate for Standard Oil.

On April 17, Huey called yet another special session. He drafted thirty-four bills and the legislature passed thirty-two of them in thirty minutes. One created a new state agency, the Bond and Tax Board, with authority to approve or disapprove any loan, grant, or bond issue that any parish or city government wanted to incur. The bill was aimed to keep New Orleans from borrowing. For its 1935 budget, New Orleans had to make $2.3 million in revenues meet $4.1 million in expenditures and was balanced on the brink of receivership. Huey's bill also prohibited cities from receiving federal public works loans and other funding. "This bill is harmless," anti-Long Rupert Payton declared in vain. "All it does is declare war on the United States."

At one point during the House session, Mrs. J. S. Roussell, a member of the anti-Long Square Deal Association, interrupted the proceedings. Before the sergeant-at-arms ejected the lady from the chamber, she marched defiantly back and forth waving a small American flag and singing "My Country 'Tis of Thee." "I'll be back," Mrs. Roussell shouted over her shoulder as she was ushered from the chamber.

HUEY NEVER GAVE UP trying to throttle the newspapers of Louisiana. During the April 1935 special session, he created the State Printing Board, which decided which newspapers could act as the official journal of a parish. Acting as an official journal to publish public notices, ordinances, and other official proceedings was an essential source of revenue for most papers and a matter of survival for many small weeklies. One of the first acts of Huey's new board was to prohibit the *Hammond Daily Courier* from acting as an official parish journal. A year before, Tangipahoa Parish chose the *Daily Courier* as its official journal and added several thousand dollars in revenue to the paper. The State Printing Board gave no reason for the cancellation, but the editor of the *Daily Courier* was Hodding Carter, the bitterly anti-Long newsman who earlier called for "shotgun government" to oppose the Kingfish. Huey also attacked the movie industry after seeing a *March of Time* newsreel criticizing his control over Louisiana. He created a state board of censors with the power to approve motion pictures and newsreels being shown in the state.

One of Huey's bills created in each parish a Board of Supervisors of Elections with two of its three poll commissioners appointed by the governor, abolishing their selection by lot, and eliminating local control of elections. The boards, in turn, selected all election commissioners and poll watchers at all precincts. During the debate over the bill, Representative Mason Spencer, one of Huey's few remaining foes left standing in the legislature, could not keep silent. "When this ugly thing is boiled down in its own juices, it disenfranchises the white people of Louisiana," Spencer declared on the House floor. He then offered an ominous premonition. "I am not gifted with second sight, nor did I see a spot of blood on the moon last night, but I can see blood on the polished marble of this capitol, for if you ride this thing through you will travel with the white horse of Death."

Spencer continued to argue against the election bill. "I maintain that the right to vote means the right to count the vote. To deprive the people of this right is putting too much power in the hands of one man who is mortal." The huge legislator ended his oration with another warning. "We have soldiers here with guns and we have armed men in this capitol," he concluded. "The great leader walks among us and there are shouts of 'Hail, Caesar.' I am not one who shouts 'Hail Caesar' because I have read history and know what happened to Caesar." Spencer's eloquence made little difference. The bill giving Huey lock-tight control over elections passed, 61–27.

On the Fourth of July, Huey flew from Washington to Louisiana in time for yet another special session. When the legislators arrived in Baton Rouge that holiday afternoon, a day traditionally spent at home celebrating national independence, he thrust at them another twenty-six bills. For the next five days, he rammed through more repressive legislation, aiming even more of his legislative salvos at Walmsley and New Orleans. One bill stripped the city of its ability to collect real estate, personal property, or liquor taxes and thus deprived the city of nearly $2 million in annual revenue and roughly two-thirds of its income. Another bill increased the power of his new state Civil Service Commission, which now could approve every state, parish, and municipal employee, meaning everyone in New Orleans except the mayor and the four councilmen. Walmsley could not even hire his own secretary. With all city employees now state employees, New Orleans District Attorney Eugene Stanley, a bitter anti-Long, discovered that he no longer had the ability to hire or fire his workers. A week later, Stanley resigned from office, saying the legislation "strips me of every power previously possessed."

Huey intended to put so much pressure on the Old Regulars that they would abandon Walmsley and force him from office. The mayor did not yield and fired back, "I will never let a draft dodger like Long run me out of office." Soon after the special session ended, Huey announced that he would stop his attack on New Orleans only if a majority of the city's citizens signed a petition calling for the mayor's removal. On July 10, 1935, Walmsley's political world began to crumble when two powerful city commission members, Choctaws Joseph Skelly and R. Miles Pratt, declared they were deserting the mayor and going over to Huey. The Choctaws were shrewd politicians and knew that Huey had become just too powerful. They liked Walmsley personally but he had become a political liability to their own survival. Soon, thirteen more Old Regular ward leaders followed and a week later, only one city commissioner, Fred Earhart, remained loyal to the mayor. "Walmsley is a political corpse and don't know it," Huey boasted.

Two days later, a sizzling New Orleans summer day, several powerful leaders of the Old Regulars lumbered downtown to the Roosevelt Hotel, where they surrendered to Huey. The group of Choctaws included Captain William Bisso, James Comiskey, and Ulic Burke, the man who earlier challenged Huey to a duel. Now a Long supporter, Burke received a thousand-dollar salary increase in his job as attorney for the Long-controlled city Board of Health. Walmsley's chief of police, George Reyer, also abandoned the mayor. Huey demanded that the Choctaw leaders carry out a block-by-block petition by the end of the next day recalling Walmsley, but abandoned the order when several precinct captains in the uptown Garden District refused to desert the mayor. The final blow hit Walmsley a few days later when the Old Regulars prevented him from attending their meetings. The once proud mayor became a pitiful figurehead, virtually stripped of his political power.

HUEY LONG WAS NOT alone in calling for drastic reform of the national economy. The Great Depression spawned a number of reformers who offered a range of panaceas to bring the prostrate nation to its feet. Senator Robert LaFollette and his brother, Governor Philip LaFollette, rebuilders of the Progressive Party in Wisconsin, hoped to expand into a national third party. Milo Reno, head of the Farm Holiday Association, campaigned for higher prices for crops and by 1935 championed his own third party. Upton Sinclair, author of *The Jungle,* offered the End Poverty in California program and gained support for a new socialist party. In 1933, the cadaverous Dr. Francis Townsend proposed that the federal government provide every person over sixty with a monthly pension of $200. The pensioners would immediately spend the money and create new jobs, ending the Depression. Townsend Clubs enlisted two million members by the end of 1935. In 1934, the Detroit priest Father Charles Coughlin organized the National Union for Social Justice, which denounced President Roosevelt's New Deal and advocated silver inflation and the nationalization of banks, utilities, and natural resources. Coughlin made weekly radio broadcasts over CBS to between thirty and forty-five million listeners.

Each of these reformers, by himself, did not constitute a major, nationwide political force. Only by combining the strength of two or more could a third party movement become a political threat to the Democrats and Republicans. Of the firebrand reformers, only Huey Long, with his steadily growing Share Our Wealth following, possessed a solid political base, and only Huey held a senatorial office to use as a springboard to gather about him millions of voters. During the spring of 1935, after Coughlin visited Huey several times in Washington's Broadmoor Hotel, speculation built that the two men would unite. Franklin Roosevelt, who would run for reelection in a year, feared that an ultraliberal third party candidate would not necessarily win the election, but would siphon off enough Democratic votes to enable a Republican victory. Roosevelt also knew that Huey was the man most capable of accomplishing this feat. A secret poll commissioned by Jim Farley predicted that Huey could garner as many as three million votes across the nation and could capture the swing vote in critical states such as New York, Ohio, and Pennsylvania.

Huey knew it too. On February 4, 1935, he donned his favorite red suspenders in honor of Georgia governor Eugene Talmadge and gave a rousing stump speech to the Georgia legislature in Atlanta. A month later, he appeared in Philadelphia, where 16,000 spectators packed the city's Convention Hall to listen to him attack Roosevelt for an hour and a half. "With Hoover it was stupidity. With Roosevelt it is betrayal," he roared. From Philadelphia, he took the train to Columbia, South Carolina, and gave more rousing speeches to large, mostly enthusiastic audiences. When University of South Carolina students jeered him and waved a banner reading "Too Much Hooey," Huey scolded the audience. "Your mothers ought to have taught you better manners."

Every time Huey spoke he drummed up more supporters and more national publicity. "He seems to have the integrity and insight of a Jefferson, the sturdy uncompromising and aggressive spontaneity of a Jackson and the combination of wit and humanitarianism that has made Lincoln a popular idol," one journalist wrote after being enthralled by one of his performances. As his popularity grew, Huey began to draw support from across the country and from the more affluent, not just from the poor living in the rural South. Of his many followers, probably his most unlikely admirer was a talented, wealthy young architect named Philip Johnson.

Strikingly handsome and exquisitely dressed, Johnson was a twenty-eight-year-old Harvard graduate with a cleft chin and a rebellious expression. In December 1934 he had just quit his job as head of the Museum of Modern Art's architecture department to pursue his passion for right-wing politics. The year before, Johnson had traveled across Europe, where he became captivated with Adolf Hitler after he heard the dictator speak at a Potsdam rally. He was impressed by Hitler's manipulation of power and populism and shared his racist contempt for Jews. "I became what was later called fascist," Johnson recalled years later.

After he returned to the United States, Johnson formed his own gray-shirted Nationalist Party. He was looking for a strong-willed political boss to whip weak America into shape. "Things were bad in the '30s. We've got plenty of wheat and grain and trees, and why is there hunger?" he asked himself. Admiring spellbinding orators, he turned to Huey Long. To him, Huey "was going to fix everything," and was the only man who could save America. "I am leaving in three weeks to be Huey Long's Minister of Fine Arts," Johnson wrote his boss at the Museum of Modern Art.

Just after Christmas in 1934, Johnson piled his clothes into his big Packard convertible and, accompanied by a Harvard classmate and several volumes of Nietzsche, Machiavelli, and Shakespeare, left New York City and drove south toward Louisiana. Johnson arrived in Baton Rouge after the new year and went immediately to the state capitol, where he must have gasped at its design. The architect, soon to be famous for his modernistic glass-box designs, despised the type of Art Deco decorating the capitol. Standing in the capitol's huge lobby among drably dressed politicians, Johnson looked out of place with his Manhattan socialite mannerisms and his foppish, Ivy League clothes. He asked to meet with Huey, ready to volunteer to become part of his political movement, write speeches, or help in any way he could. Huey, however, cared little about people like Philip Johnson and refused to see him. "One of his people said to me, 'How many votes do you control?' I was only asking if I could even work with the man," he recalled. The high-minded Johnson abruptly realized that Huey and his men were not interested in right-wing or populist ideology, but focused simply on winning more votes and grabbing more political power.

Johnson hung about Baton Rouge until he learned that Huey was returning to Washington. He jumped aboard Huey's train and continued to pressure his aides. Finally, Johnson was ushered into a stateroom where the Kingfish received him dressed in silk pajamas. Huey rejected the speeches he had drafted in polished English and sent him off to Ohio with orders to organize that state for his upcoming presidential bid.

Huey's popularity continued to soar during the following spring. On April 1, 1935, his smiling face appeared on the cover of *Time* magazine, and three weeks later he spoke at Milo Reno's Farm Holiday Association in Des Moines, Iowa. A crowd of 18,000 jammed into the state fairgrounds grandstand and loudly applauded his attacks on the New Deal. "I can take this Roosevelt," he boasted to a *New York Times* reporter after the rally. "He's scared of me. . . . I can out-promise him and he knows it." Wearing a blue double-breasted suit with red pinstripes, a dark bluish purple shirt, and a purple and white tie, he looked slimmer and healthier than a year before. He bubbled with confidence. "I could take this state like a whirlwind," he bragged to his workers. Three days later, on Labor Day, he gave a speech for Share Our Wealth in Oklahoma City before six thousand people. To no one's surprise, he announced that he was running for president.

Later that summer, Huey boasted to a *New York Times* writer that if the 1936 presidential election pitted the Democrat Roosevelt against the Republican Hoover, then "your next President will be Huey Long." Huey knew, however, that such a third-party victory was unlikely. Instead, he revealed to his close supporters a more realistic, simple, and rather sinister plan. According to Huey, either he or another third-party candidate would take enough left-wing votes from Roosevelt in the 1936 election to allow a Republican, probably Hoover, to win. With the economy still in shambles, the Republican president then would be an easy target for Huey as the 1940 Democratic nominee. He saw nothing wrong with letting the nation suffer for four miserable years in order to demonstrate that the country needed him as president. He planned to destroy both the Democratic and Republican parties and would be president for four terms. "I'm going to abolish the Electoral College," he told one writer, "have universal suffrage, and I defy any sonofabitch to get me out under four terms."

From Oklahoma City, Huey took the train to Dallas, drove by car to Shreveport, and arrived in Baton Rouge on September 3. He promptly ordered Governor Allen to call yet another special session of the legislature. While crisscrossing the country, he stopped in Harrisburg, Pennsylvania, where he signed a contract for a second book that he had recently finished, called *My First Days in the White House.* For six weeks while attending the last Senate session, Huey stayed up late each night in his hotel room dictating chapters to a secretary. Ray Daniel, a writer friendly to Huey, edited the 340-page manuscript. Partly satire and partly an expression of his grandiose economic reform proposals, it described a bizarre future, a utopia where Huey was now president, where Share Our Wealth had overcome the Depression, and where all Americans lived in comfort with a modest income, a car, and a radio. President Huey Long's cabinet included Herbert Hoover as commerce secretary, Al Smith as director of the budget, and Franklin Roosevelt as naval secretary.

CHAPTER 15

1935
NUTS RUNNING AMERICA

Standing under the drooping branches of a live oak in the square of a small north Louisiana town, Huey Long spoke to a crowd of farmers and their families. Many of his listeners, poor folks made poorer by the Depression, had come many miles to escape their dull isolation and hear him tell a few jokes and lift their spirits with words of hope and prosperity. "How many of you wear silk socks?" he asked loudly. No one raised a hand. "How many of you wear cotton socks?" he then asked. As hands shot up in the audience, Huey bent over and hitched up his pants leg to show that he too wore cotton socks. But he went a step further and asked, "How many of you have holes in your socks?" When a few farmers again raised their hands, he pulled off one of his shoes to show his big toe sticking through a large hole in his sock. For the rest of their lives, whenever the farmers in that crowd rose early in the morning and pulled on their socks, they chuckled and thought of Huey Long and his big toe. They also would give him their total loyalty, their votes in overwhelming numbers, and would have no problem with giving him complete mastery over their state.

Huey understood the will of the people and knew that their approval was the wellspring of his immense power. Money, allies, and patronage were critical, but useless if he did not first possess popular sanction. To keep the people firmly in his grasp, he knew that they had to look upon him as one of their own and not as some distant and overbearing politician. He bragged of growing up barefoot and impoverished, never admitting that in reality his family lived quite comfortably when compared to their poorer Winn Parish neighbors. To Huey, the truth was immaterial, such as when he suggested to one audience that he was Protestant and to another that he was Catholic. What mattered was that he identified with the masses and they identified right back. He never talked down to his country audiences, he talked *to* them and "just leveled down and talked his natural way." He spoke colloquially and concocted homespun images that they understood, like his big toe sticking through the hole in his sock, because once he captivated and charmed them, their unfading loyalty would follow and he could do the things he needed to do to increase his control of the state.

Knowing the powerful appeal of economics, Huey pledged to lift his people out of financial misery. Unlike typical Southern demagogues of the period, he did not resort to racism to build the support of poorer white voters, although he made no effort to promote racial equality or integration. While Governor Theodore Bilbo of Mississippi and Senator Tom Watson of Georgia used bitter attacks on African-Americans to strengthen their hold on newly enfranchised white sharecroppers, Huey refrained from racial rhetoric. He recognized that his uplifting economic message to take from the rich and give to the poor was much more appealing to Louisianans than bombastic racial diatribes, and besides, he was wise enough to know that someday in the distant future, the black population would become a potent voting force in the state.

Huey promised to do great things for the poor people of Louisiana, and for the first few years of his reign he kept his promise. The people, especially the rural, destitute, and illiterate, willingly ceded vast political power to him in return for schoolbooks, roads, and hopes of a better life. Whether or not Huey delivered did not seem important. "At least we got something," said a north Louisiana farmer. "Before him, we got nothing. That's the difference." But somewhere along the line, possibly after he came so very close to being impeached, something went wrong. Huey began to take power and then to do more good he seized still more and finally the means and ends became so twisted in his mind that he no longer could tell them apart. Even after he vanquished his opponents and victory was firmly in hand, he continued to use the same harsh methods. "He was like a racehorse with a bad strain," an opponent observed. "He couldn't change." Power became the end in itself and, indeed, his mastering god. Thus, he created his own paradox, that only through the democratic process could he build the absolute power that he hungered for, and in the end he undermined democracy itself.

Huey would do almost anything to acquire more power. "The end justifies the means," he admitted. "I would do it some other way if there was time or if it wasn't necessary to do it this way." He virtually destroyed the ability of any opposition to restrain his repressiveness or to remove him and his henchmen from office through traditional democratic means. As the "virus of success" took hold, he began to do dark and ruthless things, crushing anyone who tried to interfere, including his friends, and taking a savage delight not merely in defeating political enemies but in humiliating them.

Huey was able to gain unprecedented and immense power for several reasons. He was brilliant, talented, energetic, and unscrupulous. He benefited from disorganized opponents. His enemies were formidable, wealthy, and had the means to destroy him early in his political career, but over and over they underestimated his ruthless determination and he bounced back stronger each time they thought they had defeated him. On several occasions, the *New York Times* predicted that his reign was "rapidly coming to an end," only to see him rise again. His more powerful opponents, the Bourbon planters and New Orleans Ring, never before faced anyone of his energy, intelligence, and lust for power, and they were unable to put aside their own petty differences and build an organized effort to crush him. Before they realized it, it was Huey who did the crushing and by then it was too late.

Huey took advantage of the political strife that he created in Louisiana. By 1935, the state was divided down the middle between his followers and enemies. The struggle between the two warring factions was intense and the potential for armed conflict increased each day. Tempers flared and fistfights erupted with little provocation. There was no room for independence; everyone had to choose on which side to fight. One town in Acadiana was solidly behind Huey while the next town, only a couple of miles away, was bitterly anti-Long. Families were split and relatives on opposite sides of the political fence never spoke again. Huey shrewdly took advantage of the turmoil, wooing friendly factions and rewarding them with spoils and plunder while isolating his enemies and stripping them of political power, jobs, and sustenance.

The grinding poverty of the Depression that afflicted most Louisianans created a fertile environment for Huey's rise to power. An impoverished people wanted change and he offered lots of it. He kept attacking the rich. "The billionaires are becoming bigger billionaires, the millionaires are becoming bigger millionaires, the poor are becoming poorer, and the middle class is disappearing," he roared in a speech. While he attacked millionaires, there was not a single person earning a million dollars a year in Louisiana as late as 1930. The state's per capita income declined from $415 in 1929, to $344 in 1930, and $222 in 1933. The Depression provided the need for public works and deficit spending and he used his control over patronage to distribute thousands of precious state jobs. By 1932, his Highway Commission employed ten thousand construction workers building roads.

Louisiana's unique history contributed to Huey's rise. American political traditions never had gained a solid foothold in the state, where large-scale white illiteracy, poverty, and Negro disenfranchisement had deterred true democracy from thriving. Unlike states that began as British colonies with some representative government, democracy bypassed early Louisiana. Under the French and Spanish, Louisiana had no representative assembly and its royal governors were all the more powerful. In later years, few Louisianans were surprised when their elected leaders still ruled like sovereigns and abused power. While Huey's heavy-handed methods may have been more ruthless and increasingly demagogic, he nevertheless dominated the state much as the plantation aristocrats and New Orleans ward heelers had done for generations. Indeed, in 1935 the majority of the people of the state were happy to be dictated to by Huey and saw him as a much preferred alternative to the Bourbon oligarchy of the past.

IN JULY 1935, the vice president of the Louisiana Labor Federation wrote an open letter calling Huey Long the common enemy of state workers. "Wages in the state have declined," he wrote, "hours have been lengthened, and the condition of the workers has grown steadily worse." He pointed out that contractors paid construction workers far below the prevailing wage scale. "During [Long's] regime, not a single measure of a social character was passed." Two weeks after the union vice president wrote the letter, the Hotel Bentley in Alexandria fired him from his job as a barber. The hotel manager feared a boycott and other reprisals from Huey's henchmen.

Huey preached a pro-labor progressive platform but his actions contradicted his reform rhetoric. His enemy Lee Thomas earlier attacked his labor stance, saying Huey was "a laboring man's friend like a vulture is to a lamb, covering and devouring it." In recent years, Huey prevented passage of a state law giving labor the right to organize and bargain collectively, refused to allow Louisiana to adopt an old-age pension, minimum wage, or unemployment insurance, and defeated a prevailing wage law that he endorsed nationally. He rejected the federal child labor amendment, leaving thousands of children across the state to work for 7 cents an hour in strawberry and cotton fields and shrimp packing houses. He opposed child labor laws because, as he cracked, "picking cotton is fun for the kids, anyway." He threatened to use the National Guard to quell a streetcar worker strike in New Orleans. He killed an eight-hour work bill for women when his friend Jules Fisher, owner of a huge canning business and notorious sweatshop, objected to any restriction on work conditions. Despite his savage speeches condemning Standard Oil, the giant oil company stayed in Louisiana because the wages it paid were near the lowest in the country.

In 1935, Huey faced an attack from the far right. At a Ku Klux Klan convention in Atlanta, Imperial Wizard Dr. Hiram Evans declared that Huey was un-American. Evans vowed to go to Louisiana to campaign against the Kingfish. When Huey heard of the wizard's comments, he gathered newsmen in the press gallery of the state Senate and ordered them to "tell the toothpuller [Evans] he's a lying sonofabitch. That ain't secondhand information, and it ain't confidential." He warned Evans that if he came to Louisiana, he would leave the state "with his toes turned up." The wizard canceled his visit to Louisiana.

The humor surrounding Huey's antics had begun to turn sour. To those who fought him, his perversion of the legislative process had never been funny. Newspapers across the nation no longer described him as a comical buffoon but now expressed more sober fears. When some of them accused him of being a dictator, he refused to be catalogued or stereotyped, and bristled at the dictatorship label. After one critic called him another Hitler, he exploded. "Don't compare me with that so-and-so. Anybody that lets his public policies be mixed up with religious prejudices is a plain goddamn fool." When writers labeled him as a demagogue he twisted the definition to his own liking. "I would describe a demagogue as a politician who don't keep his promises," he explained. "On that basis I'm the first man to have power in Louisiana who ain't a demagogue because I kept every promise I ever made."

The *Mobile Register* reported that a "ruthless dictatorship" ruled Louisiana and doubted whether republican government functioned in the state, while an Arkansas paper declared, "It is impossible to conceive of any American state being governed permanently under such a dictatorship as that which Huey Long exercises in Louisiana." An Iowa newspaper characterized Louisiana as a "dictator's realm" and called for federal intervention to guarantee democratic government. "What's Washington going to do about it?" the newspaper pleaded. President Roosevelt watched events in Louisiana with rising concern. When Roosevelt read about Huey's roughshod legislative tactics and his invasion of New Orleans, he held a news conference to express his shock. The president admitted, however, there was little he could do. Roosevelt considered sending federal troops into the state but his advisers counseled him to avoid tangling with the Kingfish in his own backyard. "Roosevelt is no damned fool," Huey told a reporter. "He knows his place." The president did not abandon efforts to destroy Huey, however. To one senator, it was "perfectly obvious [Roosevelt] is doing everything he can with investigators and detectives in Louisiana to get something on Long, and even Long's friends." The *Memphis Commercial Appeal* reported that government agents in New Orleans had shadowed Huey's movements and tapped his phones since Roosevelt took office.

An intense anti-Long movement was mounting in the U.S. House of Representatives, where J. Y. Sanders, Jr., and five other Louisiana congressmen bitterly opposed Huey. On February 1, 1935, Sanders rose on the floor and attacked Huey's "profound contempt for democratic institutions." Sanders warned that the situation in Louisiana should be a warning to every state in the union and to every member of Congress. "There is being forged and constructed in Louisiana today a despotism, alien in every feature to American tradition . . . to stamp out the flames and watchfires of democracy."

As the August 1935 session of Congress ended, Speaker of the House Joseph Byrns appointed a seven-member committee "to investigate expenditures of candidates for the House of Representatives, and for other purposes." Using a last-minute maneuver, the speaker tacked his resolution for an investigation onto a routine piece of legislation that passed easily. On the next day the *Washington Post* revealed that "other purposes" meant a congressional probe of the Long regime to determine whether Louisiana had a representative form of government as guaranteed by Article IV of the Constitution. "I don't care," Huey snapped back when he learned of the speaker's action. "Let 'em investigate. We'll be glad of it." Huey knew, however, that if a House investigation requested intervention by the president, Roosevelt would gladly comply.

DURING HIS FIRST couple of years as governor, Huey Long made significant improvements to the lives of many Louisianans. He distributed more than a half-million free schoolbooks, increased school enrollment by 15,000, and provided free night schools to teach illiterate adults to read. He built nine thousand miles of new roads and over a hundred bridges, pulling Louisiana out of the horse-and-buggy days. He doubled the number of beds in the state charity hospital system and raised the state university to national stature in size and scholarship. While all of these sizable accomplishments took place in the first few years of Huey's reign, real improvements to the well-being of Louisianans did not continue. After his election to the U.S. Senate, he did little to foster the economic liberation of the people whose trust he captured. After 1931, true reform faltered, as he appeared to abandon his progressive crusade and devoted all of his energy to building, increasing, perpetuating, and centralizing his already enormous political power. Although deep in his heart he probably maintained genuine sympathy for the "wool hat boys," Huey gave the people only a few sops, such as repeal of the poll tax, a debt moratorium, and reduction in the cost of automobile license plates. Louisiana's spending on real improvements dropped drastically after 1931, when his road building program neared completion. While his speech making in the U.S. Senate and on nationwide radio called for sharing the nation's wealth, he put little of that philosophy into action in Louisiana, where, ironically, he could have ordered economic reforms with a nod of his head.

In 1930 Huey promised that an unabated wave of prosperity would sweep over Louisiana. "Growth will be almost magic," he vowed. "By the end of the year I expect to see the whole state thriving and booming in every line." Many of his bold promises, however, turned out to be hollow boasts. When new jobs, roads, books, and hospitals came to an end, he did little more to make prosperity happen. As poverty and backwardness actually increased, the only tangible changes the people of Louisiana saw coming from Baton Rouge were more and more taxes each year to finance his ever growing political machine. His increased taxation may indeed have worsened the maldistribution of wealth in his native state and caused conditions for the common people to grow worse, not better, during the latter years of his reign. While his power became more authoritative and absolute, the lives of his Depression-weary people ground on forlornly.

Sadly, Louisiana possessed the resources to lift itself out of poverty and become one of the richest, instead of poorest, states in the nation. Beginning with Huey's reign, oil companies and wildcatters discovered oil in most parts of the state. Over the next few years, their great black derricks cast long shadows across forty-two of the state's sixty-four parishes. Huey and a few of his closest associates leased valuable petroleum rights to dummy corporations, which then subleased the property to legitimate oil companies. Sometimes land was leased for as little as a few cents an acre, then subleased for thousands of dollars, plus royalties, which continued as long as the wells pumped oil. Royalties from oil leases could have filled the state's coffers but instead fattened the pockets of a few political insiders. The squandering of the state's natural riches by Huey and those who followed him remains a disgraceful episode of Louisiana history.

BY THE BEGINNING OF 1935, democratic rule held little sway in Louisiana. Huey now tightly controlled the executive, legislative, and judicial branches of government. Although he no longer retained any state office, he possessed vast political power and reigned over the state capitol. He treated his handpicked governor, O. K. Allen, as little more than his personal errand boy who carried out his orders without question, even moving out of his office while he was in town. He controlled state, city, and parish governments and their 24,000 workers. Most of these government employees, from clerk to constable, depended completely upon Huey for their jobs and in return gave him their vote and a portion of their salary. He commanded a legion of obsequious followers. Some he coerced, some feared him, some were freebooters, plunderbunds, and sycophants who joined him because they saw an opportunity for lucre. A few of his loyalists, such as Seymour Weiss, followed him because they agreed with his ideology and saw him as an energetic realist who sincerely tried to help the people of Louisiana. All of them, nevertheless, obeyed his orders unquestioningly.

Despite having no technical authority, Huey packed the membership of government boards, courts, and parish councils with his own majority, gerrymandered political divisions to remove enemies from office, stripped opposing public officials of their power to hire and fire and to make and spend money, and, without warning, revised the dates for elections and length of time in office to oust his enemies and open the door for his loyalists. When his cronies broke the law, he engineered their pardons.

Huey's rule over the legislature was near complete. Servile legislators rubber-stamped his bills in record numbers, in record time, and disregarded the repressiveness and immorality of the laws he forced them to enact. By now he had defeated most of his legislative foes at the polls, and the handful of anti-Long legislators who remained were powerless. A few diehards, like Cecil Morgan, eventually resigned when they recognized resistance was futile. Huey, who slept little, appeared to spend every waking moment contriving devious ways to increase his power. His shrewd genius was unbounded. Just when his enemies thought he had gone as far as he could go, he surprised everyone with yet another barrage of power-grabbing legislation. From August 1934 through September 1935, he called seven special sessions of the Louisiana legislature, in which his representatives blindly passed 463 bills, most of them unread and undebated, that created some of the most repressive legislation in American political history.

By 1935, Huey dominated the judiciary. Attorney General Gaston Porterie, as submissive to Huey as Governor Allen, provided legal justification for what Huey already decided he was going to do, including overriding the action of any district attorney in the state. Huey controlled almost every district judge, and of the few that he did not control, he ordered the state Supreme Court, now stacked with John Fournet and other loyalists, to overrule decisions he did not like. When he could not have recalcitrant judges or district attorneys voted out of office, he expanded the boundaries of bordering districts and eliminated their territories and their judgeships. After abolishing the state bar association and creating one of his own, he could make and break lawyers. "If a lawyer takes a case too obnoxious to Long," an attorney declared, "he will be walking the street in a week."

Huey dominated government commissions, departments, and agencies, the state treasury, the state universities, and the public hospitals. He controlled law enforcement throughout the state, including scores of state troopers, city policemen, parish sheriffs and their deputies, an undisclosed number of his secretive state Bureau of Criminal Identification operatives, and three thousand national guardsmen who served as his private janissaries, carrying out wanton martial law and warrantless civil action. All the pieces of a police state were now in place.

Huey had wrested control of the state election machinery, including the appointment of commissioners, the power to disqualify voters, and the privilege of padding voting lists wherever he deemed necessary. He now directed the counting of ballots and took from the courts any power to adjudicate election disputes or to oversee registrars.

Huey controlled the public school system and determined the hiring and firing of many teachers. Other than giving free schoolbooks, he did little to improve the state's woeful level of education and paid scant attention to elementary and secondary schools. In 1933, the U.S. Bureau of Education ranked Louisiana forty-fourth in general education and forty-seventh in attendance. Although his administration taught nearly 200,000 illiterates to read, Louisiana remained next to last in literacy level of its citizens. Teachers' salaries declined every year he was in power.

In 1932, white elementary teachers were paid $622 a year, black teachers, $219. While he piled funds upon LSU, he ignored the other state colleges and politicized higher education, even to the point of ensuring that only the children of his followers received scholarships. Academic freedom existed at his caprice and he crushed any university student or professor who disagreed with him.

Huey held an economic stranglehold over many Louisiana businesses. His public service commissioners, state tax commissioners, bank examiners, homestead agents, and property assessors dictated financial salvation or ruin. His bureaucrats prescribed licenses, permits, property assessments, and other commercial transactions not by necessity but often by political loyalty. They taxed misbehaving corporations into extinction and heaped contracts and largesse upon the businesses of their friends. Bank examiners stifled credit from opponents' businesses, and state dock inspectors banned fruit, vegetables, and other cargo belonging to anti-Long shippers from being stored on state-owned wharfs.

With few checks and balances to thwart his rule, Huey disregarded the state constitution. He far exceeded the ordinary bounds of democratic politics and the rest of the nation looked warily at the ominous political situation in Louisiana. "One man has become the power structure of an American commonwealth," one observer wrote. "Nothing quite like it has ever been witnessed in the nation's history." To Hodding Carter, the bitterly anti-Long newspaper editor, he had become, indeed, "the first true dictator out of the soil of America."

The poorer folk of Louisiana, however, worried little about Huey's roughshod political tactics and followed him blindly. The people voted overwhelmingly for his new taxes, unaware that they probably worsened the economy. "You have to convince them it's for them even if it isn't," Huey explained. The country people brushed aside the critics who claimed he was a dictator and firmly believed, with some good reason, that he was still the only politician who cared about their lot. Thousands of small dirt farmers and one-horse merchants saw only the free schoolbooks for their children, enjoyed driving along the new concrete highways, and listened raptly to his promises of a better life. From the piney woods of the north country to the swampy bayous in the south, his popularity remained widespread and rock solid.

A myth began to surround Huey. For years the country people of Louisiana repeated a story of the Kingfish speeding along one of the highways in his limousine. As the car passed a poor woman and her small daughter walking along the roadside, he yelled at his driver to slam on the brakes. Picking up the woman and her child, he learned that the woman had no money, was homeless, and was taking her daughter across the state to a relative's home. He took them to a train station, where he bought their tickets and gave the mother a handful of cash. When the woman later asked the driver who the man was who had given her the money, she was shocked to learn that it was Huey Long.

IN JUNE 1935, as Washington suffocated under an unusually early and beastly hot summer, thousands of Shriners invaded the nation's capital to attend their national convention. The fez-hatted conventioneers were a festive bunch and many of them took the streetcar to the Capitol, where they packed the galleries of the United States Senate in hopes of seeing the most entertaining show in town. On the afternoon of June 12, just before the end of the congressional session, dozens of Shriners showed up to watch the Kingfish perform. He did not disappoint them. At about three o'clock, Huey Long returned to the Senate chamber after a long lunch break. He wore a white flannel suit, pink shirt, and pink tie that contrasted sharply with his austerely dressed colleagues. He rose from his desk and began to speak. And speak he did.

For the next fifteen and a half hours Huey delivered a one-man filibuster against Roosevelt's National Recovery Act. He took the floor to oppose the president's legislation because he knew Roosevelt would use the NRA to give prized federal jobs to his political enemies in Louisiana. He lashed out at Roosevelt for flooding Louisiana with "prostitutes and scoundrels and scalawags and carpetbaggers," even attacking his old boyhood pal Harley Bozeman, now a federal worker, as a "pot-bellied character" who reminded him of a chicken snake. He had the Shriners chuckling when he suggested that NRA stood for "National Racketeers Association," "National Ruin Administration," "Nuts Running America," and "Never Roosevelt Again." As he spoke, his attack on the NRA became increasingly vicious. "I hope that if we give [the NRA] the sign of the Fasciti, known as the blue eagle, or the double eagle, or whatever they call it, we will at least let the eagle have a chance to live," he declared. "It is all right that the Germans have the Fascist sign in the form of a swastika. It is all right that the Mussolinites in Italy have their sign in the form of a black shirt, and it may have been all right that the Fasciti in America have their emblem in the form of the double eagle." People should dread Roosevelt's "blue buzzard," he continued, warning that the New Deal bird of prey was "stealing and eating children, taking them in its talons and carrying them to some far-away nest, stripping their flesh from their bones, and leaving them there, not to be discovered for ages."

Refusing to relinquish the floor, Huey continued his filibuster by discussing any topic that came into his head. He read and analyzed each section of the Constitution, gave a biographical sketch of Frederick the Great, quoted liberally from Victor Hugo, revealed his recipe for Roquefort salad dressing, and instructed his colleagues how to fry oysters "until they turn a gold-copper color and rise to the top." On and on he raved, sipping milk, nibbling at a sandwich, and popping chocolate caramels into his mouth. His filibuster filled eighty-nine pages of the *Congressional Record*. No man in the Senate had exceeded his feat of continuous and uninterrupted talking.

Throughout the night, an angry quorum of senators suffered through the Kingfish's brazen performance. The Shriners and other spectators had left hours earlier and many senators dozed at their desks. Huey suggested to Vice President Garner, who presided over the session, that every senator should be forced to stay awake and listen to him until excused. "That would be unusual cruelty under the Bill of Rights," Garner replied wearily. When some of the senators gulped down cups of coffee to keep awake, Huey pounced on them. "They have not drunk any real coffee," he roared. "That stuff is nothing but slop." He then gave detailed instructions on the proper way to brew strong Louisiana coffee.

The senators were miserable. A new cooling contraption had been installed in the Senate chamber but it did little to chill either the humid summer air or Huey's hot bluster. "We had a wretched exhibition here recently of the crazy man from Louisiana trying to run a one-man filibuster," Senator Hiram Johnson wrote in a letter to his son. "There neither was object, nor point, nor reason for the filibuster. Nobody knows what he was trying to do, and he does not know himself."

At five-thirty the next morning, with the first rays of daylight looming through the Capitol's windows, Huey began to stagger and stutter and his arms no longer threshed the air. Even the Kingfish had his limits. Unable to go on, he raced for the men's room. His opponents immediately took the floor and called the NRA bill to a vote. A half hour later, the Senate passed the bill, 41–13.

From January through August 1935, Huey staged five filibusters on the Senate floor opposing Roosevelt's second New Deal program. His colleagues regarded him as a pariah. "[Senator Long's] popularity is about as great as that of a cuckoo clock in a boys' dormitory at three o'clock in the morning," a senator proclaimed. For the first time in a century and a half, Senate leaders seriously discussed revising the rule that allowed unlimited debate so that they could throttle his interminable speeches. On August 26, the last day of the session, he gave his most vindictive filibuster to block a Social Security supplemental bill that would fund old-age pensions, railroad retirees, and crippled children. Huey, supposedly an advocate of old-age pensions and other welfare measures, rambled on until the session ended. "I have nothing to do," he told his angry colleagues. "I'm just having a high-heeled good time." When he said that he was in no hurry and had nowhere to go, Senator James Lewis, a gruff seventy-two-year-old Illinois Democrat, interrupted with a point of order. "Mr. President," Lewis asked, "would the able Senator from Louisiana like to have some senator tell him where they would like him to go?"

No vote took place and the supplemental for the nation's retirees died on the floor. Huey's filibuster delayed $100 million for Social Security programs and infuriated his colleagues. As the vice president's last gavel fell at midnight, killing the bill, Senator Lewis Schwellenbach of Washington turned angrily to Huey. "Because of your selfish desire to get publicity, you have defeated the aspirations and hopes of millions of people."

ON THE AFTERNOON OF July 17, 1935, as both the temperature and humidity approached one hundred, two dozen sweat-soaked Louisiana state policemen climbed the stairs to a third-floor apartment on St. Louis Street in New Orleans's French Quarter. With no warrant, Huey Long's heavily armed troopers smashed down the door of Oscar Whilden. A friend and backer of Mayor Walmsley, Whilden was a longtime horse and cattle breeder who led the New Orleans chapter of the Square Deal Association. He now belonged to a secretive and more violent anti-Long organization called the Minute Men who had organized in the Bunkie area and now claimed five thousand members statewide. At an earlier Minute Men rally, Whilden called for Huey to be tied to a stake and horsewhipped. The state troopers searched Whilden's armoire and confiscated a pistol found in a suitcase.

The ransacking of Oscar Whilden's apartment was not the only sign of conflict during the frightful summer of 1935, as the white-hot tension in New Orleans neared the boiling point. Angry city workers had been either laid off or, if still employed, unpaid, and nearly one thousand families fell off the welfare rolls as Huey refused to contribute state funds to Roosevelt's relief program. Garbage rotted in the streets. The July swelter ignited tempers across the city and the murder rate, already high, rose rapidly. Many New Orleaneans carried a gun, prepared to shoot someone, and agreed that if someone was to be shot, it should be Huey Long.

Four days after state policemen ransacked Whilden's apartment, about two hundred of Huey's most bitter opponents gathered in New Orleans and took over the entire fifth floor of the DeSoto Hotel. Located on Poydras Street in the center of the city, five blocks from the French Quarter, the DeSoto seemed an unlikely rendezvous for plotting murder. The old hotel reeked opulent formality, with many of its guest rooms draped in fine old damask and furnished with expensive antiques and nineteenth-century paintings.

Huey learned of the DeSoto meeting beforehand and sent his men to eavesdrop on the gathering. Johnny DeArmond, the former assistant manager of the Istrouma Hotel in Baton Rouge whom Huey used to check up on legislators and sober them up to vote, was now a member of the secretive Bureau of Criminal Identification. DeArmond set up a dummy room where Huey's men used fishing poles to hang microphones out the hotel's big bay window and listen to conversations in adjoining rooms. Herb Christenberry, an attorney and Long loyalist, listened to the microphone and took dictation, along with B. W. Cason, secretary of the state Senate.

The anti-Long attendees were a mixed lot. Some were Huey's diehard political foes, the same politicians, businessmen, and newspaper editors who had fought him for years. Mayor Walmsley attended, along with J. Y. Sanders, Jr., ex-governor Parker, and newspaper editor Hodding Carter. Others who showed up were lesser known but more prone to violence, men like Oscar Whilden who belonged to the Square Dealers or the Minute Men. The Minute Men called for a "free and independent people . . . to levy war" against the enemies of the state and began planning to march on Baton Rouge, take the capitol, and if necessary, kill Huey.

The advertised purpose of the conference was peaceful and political, a caucus that had to decide upon the candidates for the upcoming election in January, as well as to demonstrate to Roosevelt that a strong anti-Long political force remained in Louisiana. Five of the state's eight congressmen, including John Sandlin, Riley Wilson, J. Y. Sanders, Jr., Cleveland Dear, and Numa Montet, attended the conference, announcing they were "solidly behind President Roosevelt in his patriotic efforts to restore happiness and prosperity to the nation." The congressmen condemned Huey's attacks on the president as "malicious," "scurrilous," and "born wholly of unsatisfied ambition and inordinate vanity." The DeSoto conference selected Sandlin to run against Huey for the Senate and Cleveland Dear to run for governor.

The attendees later gave differing stories as to whether the DeSoto meeting was the scene of a murder plot. Frank Peterman, Huey's former president pro tem of the state Senate and now a New Dealer, said that the DeSoto meeting was purely political, its purpose being to persuade Dear to run for governor. "I don't think it was a murder plot," Johnny DeArmond remembered. "Just talk." Hodding Carter agreed, saying that the plotting was little more than hopeful comments such as "Good God, I wish somebody would kill the son of a bitch." Harry Gamble, an anti-Long attorney from Natchitoches, recalled, "A hundred said that the bastard ought to be killed, he ought to be shot, he ought to be boiled in oil, he ought to be skinned, and so on. But as for any plot to kill him being hatched there, that is ridiculous."

Others who were at the DeSoto remembered a much more sinister meeting, one that began in Room 506 at ten in the morning on the second day of the conference, spread to other parts of the hotel, and continued until the attendees departed. "There were three rooms," the hotheaded leader of the Minute Men, Dave Haas, recalled. "Five men at the meeting, four from Bunkie and Dr. Carl Weiss [a Baton Rouge physician unrelated to Seymour Weiss]. He drew the short straw. Weiss wanted it. . . . He would have killed Huey as he would a snake." Louie Jones and Elois Sahuc, two of Huey's bodyguards, remembered plots of murder. Jones was in the DeSoto room with Christenberry listening. "We heard about the gun," Jones recalled. "Judge Pavy was there. Didn't see Weiss." Another bodyguard and BCI member, Frank Manning, listened in and said that Oscar Whilden and Dave Haas plotted to murder Huey. Manning said that Carl Weiss made a telephone call from the DeSoto to his house in Baton Rouge.

Soon after the DeSoto meeting ended, one of Huey's men phoned the details to him in Washington, where he had returned a week before. On August 9, he took the Senate floor and waved the eavesdropped transcript high in the air. Red-faced and more animated than ever, he bared the plot to murder him. Senator Harry Truman, presiding over the Senate that day, was not convinced. Huey was "crooked as a ram's horn," Truman told colleagues, and "nothing but a damned demagogue." Ordering his comments printed in the *Congressional Record*, Huey quoted one of the conspirators as saying, "I would draw in a lottery to go out and kill Long. It would take only one man, one gun, one bullet." He suggested that Roosevelt may have been involved in the plot when he asked his Senate colleagues, "Does anyone doubt that President Roosevelt would pardon the man who rids the country of Huey Long?"

CHAPTER 16

1935
STRUCK LIKE A
RATTLESNAKE

On Saturday morning, September 7, 1935, a week after his forty-second birthday, Huey Long called another special session of the Louisiana legislature. Even though the legislators received only a few hours' notice of the five-day session, most of them were happy to travel to Baton Rouge. They received $10 a day and 10 cents a mile to attend each session, important income during the Depression, and the frequent special sessions offered the chance to come to the capital city and get drunk.

At ten that night, Senator Jimmy Noe called the Senate to order with thirty of thirty-nine senators present, while across the marble lobby Speaker Allen Ellender counted eighty-five of one hundred representatives at their desks. Huey already had forty-two bills drafted, printed, and ready for quick passage. He had composed most of these bills himself, dictating them off the top of his head to a secretary or, in the case of the more complicated legislation, giving detailed instructions to George Wallace, his legal assistant. A week before, he ordered Wallace to draft a bill prohibiting any federal official from disbursing federal funds in Louisiana if state officials determined the action violated the powers reserved to the state under the Tenth Amendment of the Constitution. Offenders would be sentenced to twelve months in jail. The *Washington Post* decried the bill, clearly aimed at Roosevelt's New Deal agents, as "the broadest and boldest defiance of federal authority since the Civil War." When Wallace advised Huey that the bill was unconstitutional, the Kingfish snapped back, "I don't give a damn."

Huey continued to tighten the noose around New Orleans, with several of his latest bills taking even more state money from the city. One bill revealed his fear of violent uprising and required the registration of rifles, sawed-off shotguns, and gas grenades with the BCI. All of the bills passed smoothly through the Ways and Means Committee. Years before, Huey removed legislative oversight from other House committees and ordered that all bills proceed only through Ways and Means, which he stacked with his more trustworthy followers.

Huey ordered several bills aimed to destroy his enemies in St. Landry Parish. Located about sixty miles west of Baton Rouge on the other side of the Atchafalaya Swamp, St. Landry produced rich bounties of cotton, rice, and sugarcane, and was the home of proud, hot-blooded Creole families. Two of these families, the Pavys and Garlands, had ruled parish politics since before the Civil War. The Pavys and the Garlands hated Huey, and the sheriff, Charlie Thibodaux, fought Huey's candidates in every election. St. Landry, one of the few parishes that Huey never controlled, was a thorn in his side. "I can run hell but I can't run St. Landry," he admitted to one of his workers.

One of Huey's bills gerrymandered the St. Landry district of Judge Benjamin Pavy to ensure the judge's defeat in the 1936 election. A large, jovial man with a gray mustache and full mane of silver hair, Judge Pavy wore a blue alpaca coat and white linen trousers reminiscent of antebellum years. A district judge for twenty-eight years, Pavy earlier angered Huey when he prohibited the use of dummy commissioners in St. Landry and tried to jail Huey's poll workers. Huey vowed to destroy Pavy and ordered Wallace to draft a bill that moved the St. Landry judicial district into one that also encompassed Acadia, Lafayette, and Vermilion Parishes, all Long strongholds. A similar bill gerrymandered St. Landry district attorney Lee Garland, who had held public office in the parish for forty-four years. When the gerrymander bills reached the Ways and Means Committee, the only anti-Long member of the fourteen members, twenty-three-year-old Jack Williamson from Lake Charles, objected to passing the bills without reading them. "I'm told this bill takes out some of the clockwork," Huey told Williamson with a smile, "and gives the hands a chance to move." The bills passed through committee, 13–1, and went to the floor for the next day's session.

At the same time, Huey ordered the printing of several thousand circulars to smear Pavy and Garland. According to a New Orleans printer, Huey prepared a circular on Judge Pavy that resurrected an old rumor that the Pavy family had "coffee blood" in its ancestry. Supposedly, he would distribute the circulars just before the vote on the legislation that gerrymandered the judge. "Huey struck like a rattlesnake but always warned first," a supporter recalled.

JUST AFTER SUNRISE on September 8, 1935, Huey's bodyguards drove him from his home in New Orleans to Baton Rouge, arriving in time to attend the session that convened at ten that morning. It was a Sunday but Huey ignored the Sabbath and kept the legislature hard at work passing his bills. September was still summer in Baton Rouge and the cloudy, windless day turned muggy, with the mercury soaring to ninety-five degrees by mid-afternoon. Like recent sessions, Baton Rouge seemed quiet but tense. Extra state troopers patrolled the streets and soldiers stood guard at strategic points around the capitol. For the first time, visitors could not observe the legislature from along the railings of the House and Senate chambers, but were confined to the upper gallery.

After the day session, Huey retired to his private apartment on the twenty-fourth floor of the capitol where he ate a dinner of cheese, crackers, and fruit. The apartment, furnished with a bed, icebox, and small stove, took up most of the top floor, where Huey felt the air was better for his chronic hay fever. At eight that night, he attended the full session of the House. Wearing a dark suit and sporty black-and-white shoes and surrounded by an unusually large number of bodyguards, he sat on the rostrum next to Speaker Allen Ellender to ensure that his legislators "voted right." About two hundred spectators watched the proceedings from the gallery until the House adjourned just before nine-thirty. Before Huey left the chamber, he spotted his old foe Mason Spencer standing alone by his desk. Usually he joked with the huge, amiable legislator but this evening he was in foul humor. "You remind me of an old nigger woman," snarled Huey as he passed Spencer. Huey then headed for the governor's office to give an interview to Chick Frampton. He marched quickly through the ornately marbled corridors accompanied by a large group of supporters, including John Fournet, now a justice of the state Supreme Court, James O'Connor of the Public Service Commission, the Reverend Gerald L. K. Smith, several legislators, and a half-dozen bodyguards trying to keep pace with the Kingfish.

As Huey approached the governor's office suite in the center of the capitol, just behind the main lobby, he passed the governor's secretary and asked, "Where is Bill Pegues?" The secretary replied that Pegues, a former anti-Long who now supported Huey, probably was home drunk. "Well, get him," Huey ordered. "We need his vote tomorrow. . . . We have to get all our men here tomorrow."

At that moment, a thin young man with black wavy hair and thick round spectacles and wearing a white linen suit stepped out from behind one of the huge marble pillars and approached Huey. "He flashed among us," remembered Fournet, "he brushed through." The man held a straw Panama hat in his left hand and, according to Fournet, who stood next to Huey, raised a small black automatic pistol in his right hand and fired one shot into Huey's chest from about four feet away. Huey yelped in pain, spun around, and ran down the hallway toward the stairwell. Murphy Roden, the bodyguard closest to Huey, lunged for the gunman, pulled his .38 Colt automatic from its holster, and shot the young man. Immediately, the other bodyguards began firing, pumping over thirty bullets into the man's lifeless body, now slumped in a corner of the corridor with his face resting on one arm, his white suit blood-soaked and ripped to shreds.

Meanwhile, as bullets ricocheted off the marble walls, Huey staggered from the scene alone, holding his hand against his side. Leaving a small trail of blood, he took the stairway down to the capitol basement. He encountered O'Connor, whom he had ordered a few minutes before to go down to the basement restaurant and buy him some cigars.

"Kingfish, what's the matter?" O'Connor asked when he saw Huey stagger into the basement lobby.

"Jimmie, my boy, I've been shot," Huey answered, blood trickling from his lips.

O'Connor helped Huey through the door and onto the driveway outside, where he flagged down a motorist in a small Ford two-seater convertible. Holding Huey, O'Connor ordered the driver to take them to Our Lady of the Lake Hospital a few blocks away. Still upstairs at the scene of the shooting, Chick Frampton, the newspaperman waiting to interview Huey, noticed that Huey disappeared during the shooting and followed his blood-specked trail to the basement. Learning that Huey had been driven off, Frampton took off running through the steamy Louisiana night toward the hospital.

THE SLENDER YOUNG man whose dead body lay on the marble floor grotesquely riddled by dozens of bullets from Huey's bodyguards was Carl Weiss. Retiring, scholarly, and quiet, he seemed an improbable assassin. Weiss was a thirty-year-old Baton Rouge doctor, a lover of music, painting, and mathematics, a devoted husband, and father of a newborn baby. After graduating from Tulane, he studied medicine in Paris and Vienna, then returned to Baton Rouge in 1932 to practice with his physician father as an ear, eye, nose, and throat specialist. A year later he married Yvonne Pavy, a beautiful young woman with raven hair and luminescent blue eyes, and in June 1935 their son was born.

Weiss had never met Huey. The only apparent connection between the two men was that Weiss's wife, Yvonne, was the daughter of Benjamin Pavy, the judge Huey was gerrymandering from office during the current session. Huey's accusation that Pavy's family contained "coffee blood" would have tainted the judge's daughter's reputation and, if aired, would have infuriated her proud young husband, Carl Weiss. Also, a few months before the shooting, Huey attacked the Pavy family when he fired Yvonne's uncle, Paul Pavy, from his job as principal of Opelousas High School, as well as her sister, Marie Pavy, from her position as a third-grade teacher in Eunice.

AT OUR LADY OF THE LAKE Hospital, a nun helped Jimmy O'Connor put Huey into a wheelchair and push him to the emergency room. Word spread quickly that Huey had been shot and hundreds of curious spectators arrived outside the hospital. "Third Street was just packed, you couldn't drive down it," an LSU student remembered. "It was just people all over the place." Inside, dozens of Huey's followers crowded into the small emergency room, jostling with the doctors and nurses trying to attend to him. Fournet, who arrived after Huey in the next car, pulled a small penknife from his pocket and cut off Huey's clothes. "What a scene, here was a man dying and the room was full of politicians," recalled one observer. "It was a vaudeville show," remembered another.

Huey had a small puncture wound in his abdomen just below his rib cage and another wound on his back near the spine where doctors assumed the bullet exited. He was bleeding from the mouth, his blood pressure dropped, and his pulse rate soared. The doctors agreed that Huey was hemorrhaging internally and concluded that an operation must be performed. Two skilled surgeons in New Orleans were called and they raced to Baton Rouge, but wrecked their car while en route and were delayed. Dr. Arthur Vidrine, the young country doctor whom Huey picked a few years earlier to head the state's charity hospital, was the ranking physician treating Huey and decided that if an operation was not performed immediately, he would die. Dr. Cecil Lorio, a Long supporter who helped overthrow the Baton Rouge police jury a year before, arrived to assist Vidrine.

In New Orleans, Huey's family was spending a typical Sunday evening, eating a light supper before settling down to listen to the Jack Benny show. Rose Long took the phone call from Baton Rouge informing her of Huey's shooting. She quickly called her three children together and they headed for Baton Rouge, with Huey's son Russell, now a freshman at LSU, driving the family's streamlined DeSoto at eighty miles an hour.

Huey's closest allies also headed for the capital. Seymour Weiss, in New Orleans supervising the installation of air-conditioning in the Roosevelt Hotel, also raced northward. Robert Maestri rode along with Weiss, who drove so fast that he burned up the engine in his huge Cadillac. Just after midnight, as Huey's family, Seymour Weiss, and carloads of other loyal supporters raced along the new four-lane Airline Highway paralleling the Mississippi River toward Baton Rouge, doctors placed the ether cone over Huey's face and began to operate.

Vidrine, talented but inexperienced, botched the operation. He opened the abdomen and sutured some internal bleeding but did not check the kidneys or bladder for internal injury, nor did he take X-rays. Vidrine sewed Huey up after the hour-long operation but his patient deteriorated. Still bleeding internally, probably from a damaged kidney, Huey lapsed into and out of a coma. When the surgeons finally arrived from New Orleans, they recognized that he needed another operation but decided he was too weak to undergo the trauma. Five blood transfusions helped little.

With no hope of Huey's survival, his family and a few close political allies gathered at his bedside. Just after four on Tuesday morning and thirty-one hours after being shot, Huey Long, worshipped by tens of thousands of Louisianans and despised by tens of thousands more, thrashed briefly in his oxygen tent, took one last labored breath, and died.

EPILOGUE

To many Louisianans, Huey Long was still alive. Some of his more loyal followers refused to believe he had been shot and killed. To the poor country folk, he was omnipotent and invincible and indeed, immortal. When sociologist Gunnar Myrdal traveled through impoverished north Louisiana during the autumn of 1938, he interviewed some white schoolchildren who believed that Huey not only was still living, but was the president of the United States. Even his enemies hesitated to believe he was dead. A few of his opponents joined the thousands of mourners standing in line at his funeral just to peer into his coffin and confirm that the body was Huey's and not some imposter. They would not have been surprised if he had played a macabre trick on them and suddenly jumped up, flailed his arms above his head, and launched into one of his tirades. Even in death, Huey's bigger-than-life personality continued to intimidate those around him.

The shooting of Huey Long ignited a controversy that continues today. Many anti-Longs believed Carl Weiss did not shoot Huey and argued that Weiss went to the capitol to rebuke him for firing his sister-in-law as a teacher in Opelousas. Weiss hit him on the mouth and when trigger-happy bodyguards began shooting Weiss, a bullet ricocheted off the marble wall and hit Huey. Others, like Fournet, Chick Frampton, and bodyguard Murphy Roden, swore they saw Weiss pull his small black pistol and fire the first shot, into Huey. Both supporters and enemies offered conspiracy plots suggesting that Weiss did not act alone. Several, including Reverend Gerald L. K. Smith, accused President Roosevelt of having a hand in Huey's murder. The number of bullets hitting Huey also created controversy. One nurse claimed three bullets, and a restaurant owner said Dr. Vidrine told him there were two bullets and one was a .38, the same caliber as the bodyguards' pistols. "There were three holes in him, all big from a big caliber gun," another claimed. "I'll never believe Carl did it." Dr. Cecil Lorio and a local politician, Fred Dent, who were in the operating room, both claimed to have seen only one bullet hole entering under the ribs and out the back, as did an undertaker preparing the body. No autopsy was performed.

For two days, Huey's body lay in state at the capitol as eighty thousand mourners filed by his casket. At four in the afternoon on Thursday, September 12, 1935, he was buried in the sunken garden directly in front of the capitol. The largest gathering in Louisiana history, roughly 200,000 people, attended the funeral. Cars waiting to cross the Mississippi River by ferry backed up for ten miles and hundreds of people passed out in the scorching heat. Floral tributes covered three acres. The LSU band, with drums muffled in black satin, played "Every Man a King" in a slow dirge. The pallbearers were those closest to Huey and included O. K. Allen, Seymour Weiss, John Fournet, Robert Maestri, Allen Ellender, and Jimmy Noe.

As spectators crowded toward the burial site, some climbing trees to get a better view, Reverend Gerald Smith stood behind the casket and gave the funeral oration. "The blood which dropped upon our soil shall seal our hearts," he thundered out to the masses. "This place marks not the resting place of Huey Long. It marks only the burial place for his body. His spirit shall never rest as long as hungry bodies cry for food, as long as human frames stand naked, as long as homeless wretches haunt this land of plenty." As he preached over Huey, old women cried and men wiped away tears.

HUEY'S DEATH CREATED a huge political vacuum. While in power he delegated little control to his underlings and left no one waiting in the wings to take over. At first, Reverend Gerald Smith tried to fill his shoes. An extraordinary orator and die-hard crusader for Share Our Wealth, Smith proved incapable of surviving the cutthroat battle that waged over control of the Long political machine. Huey's more powerful supporters, including Seymour Weiss, Allen Ellender, and Robert Maestri, later cut Smith's salary and pressured him to leave the state. The Longites also finished the job of taking complete control of New Orleans when they forced Mayor Walmsley to resign in June 1936 and replaced him with Maestri.

In 1936, one of Huey's lesser-known aides, Richard Leche, won the battle for control of the Long machine and became its candidate for governor, with Huey's brother Earl running on Leche's ticket as lieutenant governor. An easygoing, glad-handing chap who preferred roaming the canebrakes with his hunting dogs and shotgun, Leche was acceptable to the other Longites, who felt they could manipulate the young politician. Leche ran against anti-Long congressman Cleveland Dear in a bizarre election that dwelled on only one event—the murder of Huey. Leche, a huge man who described himself as "232 pounds of Huey P. Long candidate," branded his opponents as "the Assassination Ticket" and accused the entire anti-Long establishment of a huge murderous conspiracy. Cleveland Dear also waved the bloody shirt, arguing that one of the bodyguards, not Carl Weiss, killed Huey. The guard had been committed to an insane asylum, Dear claimed, and sat in his room mumbling, "I killed my best friend." Later that year Leche defeated Dear, 363,000 votes to 176,000, in one of the most lopsided victories in Louisiana history.

Before his death, Huey predicted that his cronies would get into trouble when he was no longer around to keep them in line. "If those fellows ever try to use the powers I've given them without me to hold them down," he told a reporter, "they'll all land in the penitentiary." He soon was proved right, as Louisiana quickly deteriorated into the nation's most notorious kleptocracy. After Leche made peace with the Roosevelt administration, the New Dealers showered public works projects upon the state in exchange for a guarantee of Louisiana's twenty electoral votes at the 1936 Democratic convention. Over $100 million poured into the state between 1936 and 1939, offering lucrative opportunities for graft, kickbacks, double billing, faked specifications, and outright theft. Corruption was awash across the state.

A federal investigation began in 1939 that eventually handed down 250 indictments against Louisiana state officials. The list of indicted covered the state's governing regime and included legislators, major department heads, university officials, contractors, architects, notaries public, and just about any official who could pocket a bribe or kickback. According to one observer at the time, Louisiana "has had more men who have been in jail, or who should have been, than any other American state."

When Huey died, the federal tax evasion case against the Kingfish also died, but Elmer Irey's Treasury agents continued their investigations of the remaining members of the Long machine. Federal prosecutors eventually tried Huey's former benefactor Abe Shushan for tax evasion. Attorneys claimed that the $400,000 Shushan had failed to report had been obtained illegally, and since the money was not legally his, then he was not obligated to report it. Incredibly, the jury acquitted Shushan. Later, federal prosecutors convicted Shushan of mail fraud. When he went to federal prison, the new Shushan Airport on Lake Pontchartrain was renamed New Orleans Airport. Treasury agents also won their tax case against Seymour Weiss, who served two years in Atlanta federal prison from 1940 to 1942. After being pardoned, Weiss became one of New Orleans's most influential businessmen, and when he died in 1969, he was worth more than $15 million.

The most prominent of former Long henchmen to be convicted was Governor Leche. He received ten years in federal prison for his involvement in an illegal scheme selling trucks to the Highway Department and committing mail fraud. He served five years, was pardoned by President Harry Truman, became a lobbyist, and resumed practicing law. Leche once bragged, "When I took the oath of office, I didn't take any vow of poverty."

The most embarrassing episode of corruption occurred at LSU. In June 1939, James Monroe Smith, the university president Huey had appointed, resigned and fled the state. Smith had embezzled a half-million dollars of the university's bonds and speculated LSU's money in the wheat market. When war in Europe became likely, wheat futures collapsed and Smith's investment was lost. Needing more bonds to cover his losses, he ordered the university print shop to run off fake ones. When law enforcement officers discovered his crime, Smith escaped to Canada

with his wife, Thelma. After he surrendered, he pled guilty to four em-
bezzlement charges and a Baton Rouge court sentenced him to a maximum of twenty-four years in Angola prison.

HUEY'S FAMILY AND RELATIVES carried on his political legacy after his
death. His wife, Rose, completed the remaining year of his term in the
U.S. Senate, where she sat on the back row next to Hattie Caraway. Allen
Ellender, one of the attorneys who defended Huey during the impeachment, was elected to the Senate seat in 1936 and served until his death in
1972.

Huey's brother George Long, the dentist whom Huey lived with
while studying briefly for the ministry in 1911, served in the Oklahoma
statehouse. After moving back to Louisiana, George was elected to Congress from the Eighth District, serving from 1953 until he died in 1958.
Huey's cousin Gillis Long was elected to the same Eighth District congressional seat, serving from 1963 to 1965 and again from 1973 until
1985. Gillis ran unsuccessfully for governor in 1963. Speedy Long, another of Huey's cousins, served as a state senator from 1956 until 1964,
when he too was elected to Congress from the Eighth District and served
until 1973.

Earl Long had a political career that was almost as colorful and controversial as his brother Huey's. In 1939 Earl, then lieutenant governor,
became governor after Richard Leche was indicted and forced to resign.
Defeated for reelection in 1940, Earl later ran successfully twice for governor, serving from 1948 to 1952 and from 1956 to 1960. Earl took over
the Long machine founded by his brother and ushered in his own brand
of populism. He championed a free lunch program for schoolchildren,
created a vocational school system, equalized the salaries of black and
white schoolteachers, and fought for highway construction and old-age
assistance. He paid for his improvements by increasing the tax burden on
New Orleans. Earl used his power, as Huey had, to punish enemies. He
tried to restrict the authority of New Orleans mayor Chep Morrison and
abolished the state civil service system to increase his own patronage.
Personal troubles, including alcoholism and philandery, dogged Earl's
last administration. After he made a rambling, incoherent speech to the
legislature defending the voting rights of blacks, who made up a large

segment of his political support, his wife, Blanche, committed him to an insane asylum. Still legally governor, Earl fired the asylum's administrator, who refused his release, and hired another administrator, who pronounced him sane and discharged him. Earl ran for Congress in 1960, won the primary, but died before the general election took place. Earl's death signaled the end of twenty-five years of sharp division in the state between the Longites and the anti-Longs.

In 1948, Huey's thirty-year-old son, Russell, was elected to the U.S. Senate to fill the vacancy caused by the death of John Overton. Serving for thirty-eight years until his retirement in 1986, Russell became one of Washington's most powerful and respected political figures, chairing the Senate Committee on Finance and becoming an expert on taxation and revenue policy. Russell died in 2003.

While Louisiana is no longer split between the Longites and anti-Longs, vestiges of Huey's domination still remain. Many Louisianans still respond to the populist rhetoric first popularized by Huey, later perpetuated by Earl, and continued into recent years by the charismatic but corruptive Governor Edwin Edwards. Compared to other states, Louisiana's governor possesses much of the unparalleled informal power amassed by Huey, including substantial political patronage. The state legislature still bows to most of the governor's wishes. Since Huey's reign, the governor traditionally has appointed the speaker of the House, the president of the Senate, and other important committee chairmanships, even when a different party has control of the legislature. Louisiana politics are still the most turbulent in the nation and, although the fisticuffs of Huey's time are a bygone distraction, corruption continues to occur from time to time.

ALTHOUGH A BULLET cut Huey Long's life short in 1935, his specter still plays the leading role in the melodramatic history of Louisiana politics. Many Louisianans, especially in the rural parts, revere him as a martyred champion of the common people, indeed a modern-day Robin Hood who took from the rich and gave to the poor. They remember Huey with awe and humor and dwell on the real improvements he brought to the state, such as roads and schoolbooks, while they ignore or minimize his brutal, dictatorial methods.

Each year, thousands of Louisianans travel to Baton Rouge to visit the towering state capitol that rises 450 feet above the nearby Mississippi River. Built in only a year during the worst years of the Depression, the tallest capitol in the nation could only have been created by a powerful politician of immense vision and iron-willed determination. "Build it big and build it quick," Huey once said. Today, visitors strolling about the beautifully landscaped capitol grounds cannot miss the huge bronze statue of Huey standing thirty-five feet above his grave, only a few yards in front of the steps that lead into the capitol where he held court and, in the end, was killed. The statue does not face away from the statehouse to welcome visitors, as would be the custom. Instead, Huey stares back eternally toward the capitol, a determined look on his face, still appearing like he is very much in charge of all that goes on there and just about to unleash a torrent of biblical phrases and foul-mouthed curses.

"More bunkum has been written about Huey Long and his place in history than any man in this region I know of," former Louisiana governor Sam Jones wrote a few years after Huey's death. Huey has fascinated writers and scholars for years and, fortunately, much of it has been excellent and not just bunkum. Three Pulitzer Prizes have emerged from scholarship on the Kingfish. T. Harry Williams's *Huey Long*, a landmark in oral history, won for biography in 1969; Robert Penn Warren captured the first of three Pulitzers in 1947 with his novel *All the King's Men*; and Hodding Carter established himself as a young journalist courageously fighting Long and later winning the Pulitzer in 1946 for his editorials on the racial, economic, and social problems of Mississippi. Some of America's most talented novelists vainly attempted to capture the essence of Huey's charisma and unparalleled dominance. In 1936, the year after Long's death, Sinclair Lewis unveiled a Huey-like protagonist, in the dark, Orwellian novel, *It Can't Happen Here*. Soon after, Hamilton Basso reincarnated Huey in *Sun in Capricorn;* John Dos Passos introduced "the most noisome, best-drawn demagogue in U.S. fiction" in *Number One;* and Adria Langley's *A Lion Is in the Streets,* the country's best-seller in 1945, created an evangelical ex-salesman who rises to the governorship and dictatorship of his state. It was Robert Penn Warren, however, who immortalized Southern political chicanery when he published *All the King's Men*. Warren's Willie Stark, like Huey Long, was a tragically flawed Southern demagogue whose personality was a chilling brew of good and evil, the Bible and blasphemy, sanctity and cynicism. Over the years, the persona of the fictitious Governor Stark has intertwined with the real-life Kingfish, yielding a tantalizing mix of historical fact and fanciful mythology.

In the research of this biography, numerous sources were consulted in order to make sense of Huey Long's complex and controversial life. The bedrock of research on Long is the Louisiana and Lower Mississippi Valley Collections housed in the Hill Library, Louisiana State University. The collection holds most of Long's surviving papers, including some personal letters, correspondence, and records from his early law practice, personal finance records, and political campaign material. Of particular value are fifty-seven scrapbooks compiled by various individuals who followed his career. A number of other personal papers are housed in the LSU collection, including those of Earl Long, Richard Leche, John Fournet, and Seymour Weiss. The New Orleans City Archives, housed in the New Orleans Public Library, holds Mayor Semmes Walmsley's papers and other documents and photographs pertaining to the Long period, and the Tulane Library holds the papers of Cecil Morgan. Northwestern State University holds the personal papers of several Long acquaintances, including Ernest Clements, William Dodd, and James Aswell. The Louisiana State Library holds an excellent picture collection of the Long era, several original scrapbooks, and other unique material. The State Archives of Louisiana has a valuable collection of newsreel films of Long speeches that have recently been digitized. During the research, all sixty-four parish libraries across Louisiana were contacted and several of them provided unique material on Long's life.

Several books were essential in studying Long's career. Huey's autobiography, *Every Man a King* (1933), is remarkable not so much for its portrayal of events during his times, which is self-serving and often inaccurate, but more so for its insight into Huey's candid, unabashed revelations of his unbounded political ambition and his brutal, unethical methods. In 1941 journalist Harnett Kane published *Louisiana Hayride: The American Rehearsal for Dictatorship,* a flamboyant account of the Long era and the corruption it spawned. Of the Huey Long biographies, T. Harry Williams's 884-page study stands alone in size and detail, although at times needlessly apologetic regarding Long's ruthless methods. Williams spent over ten years interviewing 295 individuals who personally knew Long. Most of the interviewees are now dead, and the transcripts of their reminiscences are priceless testimony to the turbulent times of Louisiana during the Long years.

In 1991, William Ivy Hair published *The Kingfish and His Realm: The Life and Times of Huey P. Long.* Hair places Huey in the Deep South setting and highlights the economics and racial tensions of the time. He provides a much more critical view than did Williams. In 1993, historian Glen Jeansonne published *Messiah of the Masses: Huey P. Long and the Great Depression.* Jeansonne's short but revealing study is also critical of Long. Gary Boulard's *Huey Long Invades New Orleans: The Siege of a City, 1934–36* (1998) is a lively, well-researched study of Huey's war with New Orleans and its mayor, Semmes Walmsley. Robert Mann's *Legacy to Power: Senator Russell Long of Louisiana* (1992) provides valuable insight into the family life of Huey Long, as seen through the eyes of his oldest son, Russell.

I owe deep gratitude to many people for their assistance in completing this project. Special thanks go to Judy Bolton and the entire staff of LSU's Hill Library; Carolyn Bennett and Kristin Coco of the Foundation for Historical Louisiana; Peggy Hunt of the Louisiana Old Governor's Mansion; Dr. Floren Hardy and Bill Stafford of the Louisiana State Archives; Judith Smith and Charlene Bonnette of the State Library of Louisiana; Dr. Donald Pavy of New Iberia; Lannie Keller of the *Baton Rouge Advocate;* Robert Mann of the Louisiana governor's office; Dr. Jim Richardson, Thomas Simpson, and Katie Ortega of LSU; Donald Richie of the U.S. Senate Historical Office; Adam Nossiter of the Associated Press; and Kay Long. My good friend and literary agent, David Madden, helped steer me through the publishing world. At Random House, a talented group of professionals made this biography a reality, including Dana Isaacson, Steve Messina, Cheryl Weinstein, and many others. I am especially grateful to Robert Loomis, Random House's incomparable vice president and executive editor, who personally guided this work to completion. An author can have no greater pleasure than to bask in the wisdom, enthusiasm, and friendship of Bob.

Finally, the love and support of Cindy, Mahalinda, Andrew, Elissa, and Chad are my inspiration.

NOTES

INTRODUCTION

ix *"Listen, there are smarter"* Davenport, "Yes, Your Excellency!" 23.

x *In the midst of* Snyder, "Huey Long and the Presidential Election of 1936," 121.

x *first-rate brains* Burns, *Huey Long* (video recording), interview with Robert Penn Warren.

x *"swarmed about his head"* Scaramouche, "Huey Long: Clown and Knave of the U.S. Senate," 35.

x *Ambitious, aggressive, uninhibited* For various descriptions, see: Huey Long Scrapbook #12, Mss. 1666, Louisiana and Lower Mississippi Valley Collections, Hill Memorial Library, Louisiana State University Libraries, Baton Rouge; hereafter HPL Scrapbook #12, LSU LLMVC; Davenport, "Yes, Your Excellency!" 23; Opotowsky, *The Longs of Louisiana*, 389; Harris, *The Kingfish*, 4.

x *To thousands of ill-housed* Snyder, "Huey Long and the Presidential Election of 1936," 121.

x *"They did not merely vote"* *St. Louis Post-Dispatch*, 3 Mar. 1935.

x *His enemies called him* Loria, "Senator Long's Assassination," 7; Moley, 27 Masters of Politics, 221.

xi *His Machiavellian lust for power* Rubin, "Versions of the Kingfish," 5, attributed to T. Harry Williams.

xi *He proposed that Congress* Bennett, *Demagogues in the Depression*, 125; Snyder, "Huey Long and the Presidential Election of 1936," 121.

xi *Although economists discarded* Snyder, "Huey Long and the Presidential Election of 1936," 120.

xi *Disregarding fiscal realities* Schlesinger, *The Age of Roosevelt*, 60; Graham, *Huey Long*, 157.

xii *"as an actor wipes off greasepaint"* Moley, *After Seven Years*, 305.

xii *"A perfect democracy"* *New York World Telegram*, 25 Mar. 1933.

xii *One observer coined* Deutsch, "Prelude to a Heterocrat," 5.

xii *"Just say I'm"* Kane, *Louisiana Hayride*, 140.

xii *"the heights were there"* Basso, "The Huey Long Legend," 121.

xii *According to novelist* Brinkley, "Robert Penn Warren, T. Harry Williams, and

Huey Long: Mass Politics in the Literary and Historical Imaginations," in Jean-sonne, ed., *Huey at 100*, 25

xii *"There are many things"* Swing, "The Menace of Huey Long," 100.

CHAPTER 1 · A WEDDED MAN WITH A STORM FOR A BRIDE

4 *"Am I therefore become"* HPL "Campaign Circular," Seymour Weiss Papers, Mss. 4165, LSU LLMVC; Scripture quote from Galatians 4:16.

4 *He branded his political* Kane, *The Bayous of Louisiana*, 55.

4 *Huey's crowd of farmers* Liebling, *The Earl of Louisiana*, 8.

4 *"like a saddling pony"* Mason Spencer, interviewed by T. Harry Williams, 20 Jan. 1960, Tallulah, LA, transcript in T. Harry Williams Papers (hereafter THW Papers), Mss. 2489, 2510, LSU LLMVC.

4 *As Huey dazzled* Schlesinger, *The Age of Roosevelt*, 42; Graham, *Huey Long*, 146, "overgrown small boy" attributed to John Dos Passos.

4 *"The only kind of band"* Deutsch, "Huey Long: The Last Phase," 27.

4 *"I can't remember back"* Davis, *Huey Long*, 33.

4 *"I don't care what they say"* Don Devol, interview, 7 Oct. 1982, Washington, DC, THW Papers, Mss. 2489, LSU LLMVC; Jeansonne, *Messiah of the Masses*, 56.

4 *for a known thief* Jeansonne, *Messiah of the Masses*, 56.

4 *"Drama was his natural art"* Typewritten notes of Gerald L. K. Smith, in Helen Gilkison Papers, Mss. 1901, 2175, LSU LLMVC.

4 *"energy of ten men"* Harry Gamble, interview, THW Papers, Mss. 2489, LSU LLMVC.

5 *"He never relaxed"* Davis, *Huey Long*, 33.

5 *"I left because I was afraid"* Robert D. Jones, interview, THW Papers, Mss. 2489, LSU LLMVC.

5 *Huey Long was born* Boulard, *Huey Long Invades New Orleans*, 46–47; W. Harry Talbot, interview, June 26, 1957, THW Papers, Mss. 2489, LSU LLMVC; Williams, "Presidential Address, Southern Historical Association," in Carleton, Howard, and Parker, *Readings in Louisiana Politics*, 367; Martin, *Dynasty*, 23; Jeansonne, *Messiah of the Masses*, 7; Sindler, *Huey Long's Louisiana*, 45; Boze-man, "Winn Parish as I Have Known It," *Winn Parish Enterprise*, 31 Jan. 1957, in Bozeman scrapbooks, State Library of Louisiana.

5 *A year before Huey* Long, *Every Man a King*, 2–4.

5 *After 1900, Winnfield became* Bozeman, "Winn Parish as I Have Known It," *Winn Parish Enterprise*, 21 Mar. 1957, in Bozeman scrapbooks, State Library of Louisiana.

5 *The railroad built* Davis, *Huey Long*, 52; Long, *Every Man a King*, 4; Mann, *Legacy to Power*, 1.

6 *Two big white oaks* Mrs. Stewart Hunt, interview, THW Papers, Mss. 2489, LSU LLMVC.

6 *Hugh Long turned forty* Mrs. Stewart Hunt, interview, THW Papers, Mss. 2489, LSU LLMVC; Harry Gamble, interview, THW Papers, Mss. 2489, LSU LLMVC.

6 *Hugh was eccentric* Basso, "The Huey Long Legend," 106.

6 *Huey's mother, Caledonia* Adams, "Huey the Great," 72.

6 *Always inquisitive* From handwritten notes by Russell Long about his father, Huey Long, undated, Louisiana State Archives, Baton Rouge.

6 *As a rebellious teenager* Davis, *Huey Long,* 53–54; Mrs. Lottie Davis, interview, THW Papers, Mss. 2489, LSU LLMVC.

6 *Known throughout the parish* Long, *Every Man a King,* 3.

6 *"none should be too poor and none too rich"* From handwritten notes by Russell Long about his father, Huey Long, undated, Louisiana State Archives.

6 *If one of the youngsters* Long, *Every Man a King,* 3; Mrs. Stewart Hunt, interview, THW Papers, Mss. 2489, LSU LLMVC; Mrs. Lottie Davis, interview, THW Papers, Mss. 2489, LSU LLMVC.

6 *At an early age* Mrs. W. M. Knott, interview, THW Papers, Mss. 2489, LSU LLMVC; Mrs. Lottie Davis, interview, THW Papers, Mss. 2489, LSU LLMVC; Harley Bozeman, interview, THW Papers, Mss. 2489, LSU LLMVC; Williams, *Huey Long,* 21, 34, 76.

7 *Huey was bright, outspoken* Martin, *Dynasty,* 24–25. The children were, in order, Charlotte (Lottie), Julius, George, Olive, Clara, Callie, Huey, Earl, and Lucille.

7 *Huey learned to set type* Hoteling, "Huey Pierce Long as Journalist and Propagandist," 21.

7 *"The boy was a perfect portrait"* Harris, *The Kingfish,* 125; LeVert, *Huey Long,* 21.

7 *When he turned seven* Jeansonne, *Messiah of the Masses,* 8.

7 *In 1908, fourteen-year-old Huey* Williams, *Huey Long,* 43; Clay, *Coozan Dudley LeBlanc,* 41; Brinkley, *Voices of Protest,* 12.

8 *Huey never had much patience* Graham, *Huey Long,* 15; Deutsch, "Prelude to a Heterocrat," 5–11.

8 *He left Winnfield in July* Long, *Every Man a King,* 8; Kane, *Louisiana Hayride,* 42; Hair, *The Kingfish and His Realm,* 42.

8 *"I used the Bible on them"* Opotowsky, *The Longs of Louisiana,* 34.

8 *"If I couldn't convince the woman"* Deutsch, "Prelude to a Heterocrat," 8.

9 *"after being given a few warnings"* Long, *Every Man a King,* 9–10.

9 *In late September 1911* Meigs O. Frost, "The Romantic Fighting Career of Huey Long," *New Orleans States,* 28 Aug. 1927; Bozeman, "Winn Parish as I Have Known It," *Winn Parish Enterprise,* 12 Sept. 1957, in Bozeman scrapbooks, State Library of Louisiana.

9 *"I didn't learn much law there"* Adams, "Huey the Great," 72; Jeansonne, *Messiah of the Masses,* 17.

10 *"He's the damnedest character"* Bozeman, "Winn Parish as I Have Known It," 19 Sept. 1957, in Bozeman scrapbooks, State Library of Louisiana.

10 *Frank Odom, a fellow salesman* Frank Odom, interview, 21 May 1958, Baton Rouge, THW Papers, Mss. 2489, LSU LLMVC.

10 *smooth-tongued hawker* Mann, *Legacy to Power,* 2.

10 *In October 1910* Rose McConnell Long, interview, 17 Mar. 1960, THW Papers, Mss. 2489, LSU LLMVC; Basso, "The Huey Long Legend," 107.

10 *"outshines these girls up here"* Letter from HPL to Rose Long's mother, dated 20 Apr. 1913, from the Gayoso Hotel, Memphis, Huey Long Collection, Louisiana State Archives; Mann, *Legacy to Power,* 3.

11 *During his Christmas vacation* Bozeman, "Winn Parish as I Have Known It,"

Winn Parish Enterprise, 26 Sept. 1957, in Bozeman scrapbooks, State Library of Louisiana; Long, *Every Man a King,* 14; Rose McConnell Long, interview, 17 Mar. 1960, THW Papers, Mss. 2489, LSU LLMVC.

11   *He sold patent medicines*   Hair, *The Kingfish and His Realm,* 51.

11   *Huey lost his job*   Clay, *Coozan Dudley LeBlanc,* 17.

11   *With a wife to support*   Jeansonne, *Messiah of the Masses,* 10.

11   *Huey and Rose moved*   Long, *Every Man a King,* 15.

11   *S. J. Harper*   An old-fashioned frontier American and irascible radical, state Senator S. J. Harper knew the Long family for years and was an early influence on Huey. Harper hated war, plutocracy, and the grinding down of the poor. In 1918, Harper ran for Congress from the Eighth District against Congressman James B. Aswell on a platform calling for conscription of wealth and abolishment of the draft. During the campaign, a grand jury indicted Harper for violating the Espionage Act and obstructing the draft. Huey and Julius Long became his counsel and Harper was acquitted. However, the trial ruined Harper's political career and he resigned from the state legislature. Harper was anti-Semitic, believing Jewish bankers incited war.

11   *"his nose to the grindstone"*   Mrs. Stewart Hunt, interview, THW Papers, Mss. 2489, LSU LLMVC; Martin, *Dynasty,* 28.

11   *"We had a typewriter"*   Deutsch, "Prelude to a Heterocrat," 5–11.

12   *By then he had completed*   Mrs. Stewart Hunt, interview, THW Papers, Mss. 2489, LSU LLMVC; Julius Long, interview, THW Papers, Mss. 2489, LSU LLMVC; Charles E. Dunbar, interview, THW Papers, Mss. 2489, LSU LLMVC; Bozeman, "Winn Parish as I Have Known It," *Winn Parish Enterprise,* 3 Oct. 1957, in Bozeman scrapbooks, State Library of Louisiana.

12   *"Whenever I saw one"*   Deutsch, "Prelude to a Heterocrat," 8.

12   *"When the bell rang"*   H. Lester Hughes, interview, THW Papers, Mss. 2489, LSU LLMVC.

12   *The bar exam was scheduled*   Long, *Every Man a King,* 16; Frost, "The Romantic Fighting Career of Huey Long," 1.

12   *"I was born into politics"*   Hair, *The Kingfish and His Realm,* ix.

13   *"It almost gave you the cold chills"*   Rose McConnell Long, interview, 17 Mar. 1960, THW Papers, Mss. 2489, LSU LLMVC; Hair, *The Kingfish and His Realm,* 44.

13   *seemed unable to make up its mind*   Kane, *Louisiana Hayride,* 3.

13   *He stopped at every crossroad village*   LeVert, *Huey Long,* 67.

13   *On Sundays, he put his circulars*   Mrs. Gaston Porterie, interview, 12 Oct. 1959, Alexandria, THW Papers, Mss. 2489, LSU LLMVC.; Williams, *Huey Long,* 124.

13   *"All over the neighborhoods"*   Long, *Every Man a King,* 41.

14   *"He would mention that one"*   Leon Gary, interview, THW Papers, Mss. 2489, LSU LLMVC.

14   *Rising early before breakfast*   Jeansonne, *Messiah of the Masses,* 43–44, 50.

14   *He passed through miles*   Keyes, *All This Is Louisiana,* 212.

14   *In October Huey raced*   Baimonte, *Immigrants in Rural America,* 61.

15   *"highway coppers are so numerous"*   Huey Pierce Long Papers (hereafter HPL Pa-

pers), Mss. 2005, LSU LLMVC, Scrapbook #4; *New Orleans Times-Picayune*, 6 Oct. 1927.

15 **Shunning the support**   Rupert Peyton, interview, 28 Jan. 1958, Baton Rouge, THW Papers, Mss. 2489, LSU LLMVC.

16 **"burglars code among politicians"**   HPL Papers, Mss. 2005, LSU LLMVC, Scrapbook #17.

16 **He also delivered**   Burns, *Huey Long* (video recording); Boulard, *Huey Long Invades New Orleans*, 157.

16 **On the road, he employed**   Jeansonne, *Messiah of the Masses*, 45.

16 **"coon chasin' possum watchin' brigade"**   Martin, *Dynasty*, 38.

16 **As he ground away**   Mixon, "Huey P. Long's 1927–1928 Gubernatorial Primary Campaign: A Case Study in the Rhetoric of Agitation," in Logue and Dorgan, eds., *The Oratory of Southern Demagogues*, 184.

17 **"I want every man"**   *New Orleans Item*, 23 Oct. 1927, HPL Papers, Mss. 2005, LSU LLMVC, Scrapbook #5.

17 **"Huey, you ought to remember"**   Confidential interview, THW Papers, Mss. 2489, LSU LLMVC; Williams, *Huey Long*, 3.

17 **Flanked by mounted policemen**   Sindler, *Huey Long's Louisiana*, 83; Bennett, *Demagogues in the Depression*, 124, from Bryan's famous "Cross of Gold Speech" of 1900.

17 **William Jennings Bryan (1860–1925)**   Gifted speaker, lawyer, three-time presidential candidate, and devout Protestant. Born in Salem, Illinois, he made his career in Nebraska politics, serving in the U.S. House of Representatives from 1891 to 1895, and as secretary of state from 1912 to 1915. His defense of the small farmer and laborer earned him the title "the Great Commoner." His advocacy of free silver brought him the Democratic presidential nomination in 1896 and again in 1900, he lost both times to William McKinley. Nominated for a third time in 1908, he lost to William Howard Taft. In 1925, Bryan served as prosecuting attorney in the trial of John Scopes, a Tennessee schoolteacher accused of teaching evolution. After a legendary courtroom debate with Clarence Darrow, Bryan won the case. He died less than a week later of a heart attack. Although the nation had consistently rejected him for the presidency, it eventually adopted many of his reforms, including the income tax, popular election of senators, woman suffrage, and Prohibition.

17 **Seven hundred of Huey's**   *Donaldsonville Chief*, 30 July 1927, HPL Papers, Mss. 2005, LSU LLMVC, Scrapbook #2.

18 **"we must bear in mind"**   "Huey P. Long's Platform," *Alexandria Daily Town Talk*, 4 Aug. 1927.

18 **"a man buying a plug"**   Field, "The Campaigns of Huey Long, 1918–1928," 91; *New Orleans Times-Picayune*, 6 Sept. 1927.

18 **He finished third**   Davis, *Huey Long*, 86.

18 **"His pants didn't meet his shoes"**   Henry Larcade, interview, 29 July 1958, Baton Rouge, THW Papers, Mss. 2489, LSU LLMVC.

18 **His campaign manager**   Various correspondence, HPL Papers, Mss. 2005, LSU LLMVC, Box 4; Long, *Every Man a King*, 82.

19 *Harvey Couch, a utilities* Pusateri, "The Stormy Career of a Radio Maverick, W. K. Henderson of KWKH," 395.

19 *Huey's cousin Swords Lee* Jess M. Nugent, interview, 25 Jan. 1957, THW Papers, Mss. 2489, LSU LLMVC.

19 *Robert Maestri (1889–1974)* Born in New Orleans of Italian ancestry. In 1896, his father and his two uncles formed the Maestri Furniture Company, with a store on Rampart Street at the corner of Iberville Street. By 1911, when he was twenty-two, Robert had saved $1,000 and made his first real estate investment. He served as mayor of New Orleans from 1936 until 1946.

20 *Unlike other contributors* Daniell, "Huey's Heirs," 5.

20 *Conner, a three-term legislator* Mary Helen Byrd, interview with author, 24 Aug. 2004, Baton Rouge.

20 *a French Catholic dentist* Hair, *The Kingfish and His Realm*, 221.

21 *The New Orleans political machine* *New Orleans Morning Tribune*, 8 July 1927, HPL Papers, Mss. 2005, LSU LLMVC, Scrapbook #3.

21 *"a coward with the conduct"* Jeansonne, *Messiah of the Masses*, 46–47.

21 *"quixotic and notionate"* Lee Thomas, typed text of speech, James B. Aswell Papers, Mss. 1408, LSU LLMVC.

21 *"A great many citizens"* *New Orleans Times-Picayune*, 11 June 1927, HPL Papers, Mss. 2005, LSU LLMVC, Scrapbook #4.

21 *Another who failed* *New Orleans Times-Picayune*, 6 July 1927, HPL Papers, Mss. 2005, LSU LLMVC, Scrapbook #4.

21 *Oramel Hinckley Simpson (1870–1932)* Born in Washington, Louisiana. Attended Centenary College and Tulane Law School. Clerk of the state House of Representatives for twenty years, then elected lieutenant governor. Governor of Louisiana, 1926–1928.

21 *"I love this place"* Simpson campaign speech, 24 Sept. 1927, James B. Aswell Papers, Mss. 1408, LSU LLMVC.

21 *A weak campaigner* Paul Habans, interview, THW Papers, Mss. 2489, LSU LLMVC.

22 *"stench in the nostrils"* *New Orleans Times-Picayune*, 9 July 1927, HPL Papers, Mss. 2005, LSU LLMVC, Scrapbook #4; Letter from HPL to Frank Odom, 11 July 1927, HPL Papers, Mss. 2005, LSU LLMVC.

22 *Riley Joseph Wilson (1871–1946)* Born in Winn Parish, Louisiana. Democrat. Attorney. State court judge in Louisiana. U.S. representative from Louisiana's Fifth District, 1915–1937.

22 *A rugged square-jawed man* Long, *Every Man a King*, 97.

22 *"embalmed in the House"* Kane, *The Bayous of Louisiana*, 54.

CHAPTER 2 · I WAS BORN BAREFOOT

23 *"One day you pick up the papers"* HPL campaign circular, Seymour Weiss Papers, Mss. 4165, LSU LLMVC.

23 *"pledging himself to cure"* *New Orleans Item*, 15 Oct. 1927, HPL Papers, Mss. 2005, LSU LLMVC, Scrapbook #5.

23 *"pentecostal fanfaronades"* Deutsch, "Prelude to a Heterocrat," 8.

23 *"There is as much honor"* LeVert, *Huey Long*, 68.

23 *he mockingly portrayed* Walker, *Reminiscences and Recollections of Huey P. Long*, 18.

24 *"I am tired of your lies"* New Orleans States, 10 Oct. 1921, HPL Papers, Mss. 2005, LSU LLMVC, Scrapbook #1.

24 *Sporting a bristling* Cortner, *The Kingfish and the Constitution*, 20; Long, *Every Man a King*, 270; Martin, *Dynasty*, 40.

24 *"cut out the rough stuff"* Various campaign correspondence, HPL Papers, Mss. 2005, LSU LLMVC, Box 3.

24 *"racing, gambling, and whiskey"* Shreveport Times, 12 June 1927, HPL Papers, Mss. 2005, LSU LLMVC, Scrapbook #2; Letter from Ellis to HPL, 21 Apr. 1927, HPL Papers, Mss. 2005, LSU LLMVC, Box 4.

24 *"I never saw or bet on a horse race"* Letter from HPL to Ellis, Ibid.; Beals, *The Story of Huey Long*, 74.

25 *Once Sullivan agreed* New Orleans States, 2 Dec. 1927, HPL Papers, Mss. 2005, LSU LLMVC, Scrapbook #2.

25 *The large New Orleans daily papers* Hammond, *Let Freedom Ring*, 41.

25 *Of the state's small* Donaldsonville Chief, 9 July 1927, HPL Papers, Mss. 2005, LSU LLMVC, Scrapbook #2; Field, "The Campaigns of Huey Long, 1918–1928," 78.

25 **Houma Courier** 3 Nov. 1927, HPL Papers, Mss. 2005, LSU LLMVC, Scrapbook #2.

25 **Shreveport Caucasian** 1 Oct. 1927, HPL Papers, Mss. 2005, LSU LLMVC, Scrapbook #2.

25 *Throughout the winter* Simpich, "The Great Mississippi Flood of 1927," 243–89; Hair, *The Kingfish and His Realm*, 147.

26 *On Good Friday* Barry, *Rising Tide*, 15, 228, 234, 255.

26 *On Friday afternoon* New York Times, 1–2 May 1927; Hair, *The Kingfish and His Realm*, 147.

27 *With theatrical coolness* Various clippings, HPL Papers, Mss. 2005, LSU LLMVC, Scrapbook #2.

27 *Louisiana paid $2* Mixon, "Huey P. Long's 1927–1928 Gubernatorial Primary Campaign: A Case Study in the Rhetoric of Agitation," Logue and Dorgan, eds., *The Oratory of Southern Demagogues*, 187.

27 *"Our present state government"* Long, *Every Man a King*, viii; Deutsch, "Prelude to a Heterocrat," 8.

27 *Huey had learned a lot* Mixon, "Huey P. Long's 1927–1928 Gubernatorial Primary Campaign," 201.

28 *On a Sunday night* Smith, *The Kingfish*, 23.

28 *John Holmes Overton (1875–1948)* Representative and senator from Louisiana. Born in Marksville, Avoyelles Parish. Graduated from the Louisiana State University and Tulane Law School. Practiced in Alexandria. Elected on May 12, 1931, to the Seventy-second Congress to fill the vacancy caused by the death of James B. Aswell and served from May 1931 to March 1933. Elected to the U.S. Senate in 1932, reelected in 1938 and 1944. When Overton died, his Senate seat was won by Huey's son, Russell B. Long.

28 *"sounded like a funeral dirge"* Alexandria Daily Town Talk, 4 Aug. 1927; Overton typewritten speech notes, HPL Papers, Mss. 2005, LSU LLMVC, Scrapbook #9.

28 *"right to be a candidate"* Mixon, "Huey P. Long's 1927–1928 Gubernatorial Primary Campaign," 188; *New Orleans Times-Picayune,* 22 Sept. 1927, HPL Papers, Mss. 2005, LSU LLMVC, Scrapbook #4.

28 *"they are hiring men"* Beals, *The Story of Huey Long,* 80; Jeansonne, *Messiah of the Masses,* 44.

28 **William Ernest Henley (1849–1903)** English poet, critic, and author whose "Invictus" remains his most famous and popular poem.

28 *"It matters not how strait"* Typewritten speech notes, HPL Papers, Mss. 2005, LSU LLMVC, Scrapbook #9.

28 **On one hot afternoon** Mixon, "Huey P. Long's 1927–1928 Gubernatorial Primary Campaign," 178.

29 *"Wilson is a candidate"* Davis, *Huey Long,* 91; Martin, *Dynasty,* 41.

29 *"jumped on the wagon"* Field, "The Campaigns of Huey Long, 1918–1928," 92; *New Orleans Times-Picayune,* 22 Sept. 1927.

29 **After Simpson claimed** *New Orleans States,* 23 Oct. 1927, HPL Papers, Mss. 2005, LSU LLMVC, Scrapbook #7; Coad, "I'm the Constitution in Louisiana," 419; Field, "The Campaigns of Huey Long, 1918–1928," 94; *New Orleans States,* 7 Oct. 1927.

29 **The Eunice Fair** *Shreveport Times,* 12 Nov. 1927; Mixon, "Huey P. Long's 1927–1928 Gubernatorial Primary Campaign," 188–89.

30 **A three-story Creole-style building** Beals, *The Story of Huey Long,* 75.

30 **On a scale that resembled** Boulard, *Huey Long Invades New Orleans,* 183.

30 **Through the ward leaders** Davis, *Huey Long,* 216; Williams, *Huey Long,* 188.

31 *"if they like you"* Mann, *Legacy to Power,* 9.

31 *"they were a bunch of bums"* Boulard, *Huey Long Invades New Orleans,* 138.

31 **Elections were preordained** Williams, *Huey Long,* 189.

31 **The city had 20 percent** Sindler, *Huey Long's Louisiana,* 23–24.

31 **It was lunchtime** Hair, *The Kingfish and His Realm,* 142.

32 *"Gravel Roads" Sanders* Dethloff, "The Longs: Revolution or Populist Retrenchment?," 401–2.

32 **Huey claimed he had opposed** Carleton, "The Longs and the Anti-Longs," in Jeansonne, ed., *Huey at 100,* 101.

32 *"when it comes to arousing prejudice"* "Campaign of 1926," *Tangipahoa Parish News,* 2 Dec. 1926; Snyder, "The Concept of Demagoguery: Huey Long and His Literary Critics," 66.

32 *"damned liar"* *New Orleans Item,* 16 Nov. 1927.

32 **The two men wrestled** *New Orleans States,* 15 Nov. 1927, HPL Papers, Mss. 2005, LSU LLMVC, Scrapbook #7; Fineran, *The Career of a Tinpot Napoleon,* 14; Field, "The Campaigns of Huey Long, 1918–1928," 95; *New Orleans Times-Picayune,* 16 Nov. 1927; Beals, *The Story of Huey Long,* 81–82.

33 **On a Thursday evening** *New Orleans States,* 5 Nov. 1927, HPL Papers, Mss. 2005, LSU LLMVC, Scrapbook #7.

33 **Evangeline** Published in 1847 and selling tens of thousands of copies, Henry Wadsworth Longfellow's *Evangeline* remains one of the most popular epic poems in American literary history. Its central character is torn away from her home and family and travels south and west across the American landscape on

a forlorn quest for her lover. She comes to accept her unhappiness as the will of a God to which she must submit.

33 *"Where are the schools"* Davis, *Huey Long*, 92; Long, *Every Man a King*, 99; *New Orleans States*, 5 Nov. 1927, HPL Papers, Mss. 2005, LSU LLMVC, Scrapbook #7; Hodding Carter, "Huey Long: American Dictator," in Isabel Leighton, ed., *The Aspirin Age: 1919–1941* (New York: Simon & Schuster, 1949), 349; Beals, *The Story of Huey Long*, 81.

33 *"I was born barefoot"* Haas, "Black Cat, Uncle Earl, Edwin and the Kingfish: The Wit of Modern Louisiana Politics," 218.

33 *He estimated that he had* *New Orleans States*, 15 Jan. 1928, HPL Papers, Mss. 2005, LSU LLMVC, Scrapbook #8; Jeansonne, *Messiah of the Masses*, 50.

34 *As the election returns began* *New Orleans Item*, 26 Nov. 1927.

34 *Indeed, the New Orleans tally* Mann, *Legacy to Power*, 13.

VOTE IN DEMOCRATIC GUBERNATORIAL PRIMARY, JANUARY 17, 1928

	Orleans Parish	Other Parishes	State	State Percent	Majority Parishes	Plurality Parishes
LONG	17,819	109,023	126,842	43.9	38	9
SIMPSON	22,324	58,002	80,326	27.8	6	3
WILSON	38,244	43,503	81,747	28.3	4	4
TOTAL	78,387	210,518	288,915	100.0	48	16

34 *"What did I tell you?"* Long, *Every Man a King*, 102.

35 *"We'll show 'em who's boss"* Brinkley, *Voices of Protest*, 22; Parent, *Inside the Carnival*, 70.

CHAPTER 3 · SCHOOLBOOKS, SCANDALS, AND SKULDUGGERY

36 *"the grass grow in Third Street"* *Baton Rouge State-Times*, 16 Aug. 1930, HPL Papers, Mss. 2005, LSU LLMVC, Scrapbook #12.

36 *Most of the crowd* Brinkley, *Voices of Protest*, 23; Davis, *Huey Long*, 96; Mann, *Legacy to Power*, 15; *Baton Rouge Advocate*, 18 May 1928.

37 *"It seemed as if over half"* W. C. Alford, interview, THW Papers, Mss. 2489, LSU LLMVC; Mrs. J. Polk Morris, Jr., interview, THW Papers, Mss. 2489, LSU LLMVC.

37 *After a seventeen-gun salute* *Alexandria Daily Town Talk*, 21 May 1928; Jeansonne, *Messiah of the Masses*, 58; HPL photo album, Mss. 4495, LSU LLMVC.

37 *"Our face is to the rising"* Beals, *The Story of Huey Long*, 86; *Lake Charles American Press*, 21 May 1928.

37 *To cool off the spectators* Brinkley, *Voices of Protest*, 23.

37 *At two that afternoon* *Luke Charles American Press*, 22 May 1928.

38 *The worst incident of the day* E. J. Oakes, interview, 25 June 1957, THW Papers, Mss. 2489, LSU LLMVC; *Baton Rouge State-Times*, 21 May 1928.

38 *When Russell was born* Russell Long, "Remembrances of Huey P. Long."

38 *"pretty and popular"* *Baton Rouge Advocate*, 21 May 1928.

38 *Alice Lee first appeared*   Murphy Roden, interview, THW Papers, Mss. 2489, LSU LLMVC; Hair, *The Kingfish and His Realm*, 126–27; Williams, *Huey Long*, 317.

39 *Pleasant threatened to beat up*   Beals, *The Story of Huey Long*, 60, 85.

39 *"They say that they were steam rolled"*   New Orleans Times-Picayune, 25 Feb. 1928; Wingo, "The 1928 Presidential Election in Louisiana," 409; Harris, *The Kingfish*, 36.

40 *Huey also accused Hoover*   Alexandria Daily Town Talk, 28 Oct. 1928.

40 *Only eighteen of one hundred*   Augusta Chronicle, 23 Apr. 1935, HPL Papers, Mss. 2005, LSU LLMVC, Scrapbook #28; "Knew how to trade" attributed to Gerald L. K. Smith; Jeansonne, *Gerald L. K. Smith*, 37.

40 *John Baptiste Fournet*   Schoolteacher and principal in St. Martin, Jefferson Davis, and Pointe Coupee Parishes, 1913–1917; practicing attorney in St. Martin, East Baton Rouge, and Jefferson Davis Parishes, 1925–1930; state representative from Jefferson Davis Parish and speaker of the Louisiana House of Representatives, 1928–1935; lieutenant governor, 1932–1935; associate justice of the Louisiana Supreme Court; chief justice (1949–1970). Died 1984.

40 *Despite the legislator's lack*   Lake Charles American Press, 22 May 1928; LeVert, *Huey Long*, 77.

41 *He ordered Old Regular*   New Orleans Times-Picayune, 20 May 1928; Williams, *Huey Long*, 290.

41 *Like Huey, New Orleans*   Hair, *The Kingfish and His Realm*, 110; Barry, *Rising Tide*, 215; Smith, *The Kingfish*, 12.

41 *Gambling was widespread*   Boulard, *Huey Long Invades New Orleans*, 54.

42 *"you can make it illegal"*   Kane, *Louisiana Hayride*, 33.

42 *Deeply etched by racial*   The WPA Guide to New Orleans, lxi; Rose and Souchon, *New Orleans Jazz—A Family Album*, 216; Boulard, *Huey Long Invades New Orleans*, 53–54; Barry, *Rising Tide*, 213.

42 *Perched atop his ornate float*   Boulard, *Huey Long Invades New Orleans*, 17.

42 *The New Orleans uptown elite*   New Orleans States, 14–16 Feb. 1928.

43 *Gathering in the Tip Top Inn*   New Orleans Times-Picayune, 16 Feb. 1928.

43 *Colonel Robert Ewing*   New Orleans Morning Tribune, 16 Feb. 1928; New Orleans Times-Picayune, 16 Feb. 1928; New Orleans Item, 15 Feb. 1928.

43 *When the dinner ended*   "Mourners, Heirs, Foes," 13; New Orleans Item, 15 Feb. 1928.

44 *"kick the rascals out"*   Davis, *Huey Long*, 97.

44 *With thousands of workers*   Adams, "Huey the Great," 73.

44 *He detested the president*   Davis, *Huey Long*, 97.

45 *To take control of the board*   LeVert, *Huey Long*, 77.

45 *"I'd rather violate every"*   Opotowsky, *The Longs of Louisiana*, 45.

45 *"Maybe you've heard of this book"*   Coad, "I'm the Constitution in Louisiana," 419; Smith, *The Kingfish*, ii.

45 *Although he did not hold*   Martin, *Dynasty*, 47; Long, *Every Man a King*, 109–10.

46 *One of the bills*   Louisiana Acts, Regular Session, 1928, No. 99.

46 *With paint peeling*   Long, *Every Man a King*, 223–25.

46 *"full of damn rats"*   Baton Rouge Advocate, 2 Nov. 1928; Long, *Every Man a King*, 223–24; Carleton, *River Capital*, 167.

47 *"the structure is in"*   Baton Rouge Advocate, 27 Oct. 1928.

47 *Huey asked his treasurer* Interview, Mary Helen Byrd, 24 Aug. 2004, Baton Rouge; *New Orleans Times-Picayune*, 26 Jan. 1929.

47 *"I can see where the criticism"* Long, *Every Man a King*, 224–25.

47 *The antique furniture* New Orleans Times-Picayune, 24 Apr. 1929.

48 *"I can beat that old man"* Mann, *Legacy to Power*, 6.

48 *Stumping tirelessly across* Davis, *Huey Long*, 75; Long, *Every Man a King*, 41.

48 *One of them, Francis Williams* Williams, *Huey Long*, 167.

48 *Dudley J. LeBlanc (1894–1971)* Born of humble French Acadian Catholic parents, father was a blacksmith. After graduating from college in Lafayette, became a traveling salesman selling Battleax shoes. June 1923 ran as a candidate for the House from Vermilion Parish, defeated J. Camille Broussard, 1,706–1,658. September 1926 defeated incumbent Shelby Taylor for public service commissioner, 27,569–12,107. Called himself the "Huey P. Long of southwest Louisiana," successful businessman, invented alcohol patent medicine called Hadacol and promoted it so successfully that it outsold Bayer aspirin in early 1950s. Became millionaire before FDA took Hadacol off market.

49 *From the first, Huey hated* Clay, *Coozan Dudley LeBlanc*, 1–40, 61.

49 *"No music ever sounded"* Hair, *The Kingfish and His Realm*, 166, 219.

49 *One of them, District Judge H. C. Drew* Long, *Every Man a King*, 187.

49 *At first, he failed* Martin, *Dynasty*, 50–51.

49 *Late that summer* O'Conner, "The Charity Hospital at New Orleans: An Administrative and Financial History," 87–88; *New Orleans States*, 4 Jan. 1931.

50 *A drawbridge tender* Harris, *The Kingfish*, 77; Beals, *The Story of Huey Long*, 168.

50 *"On election day the Governor"* Louisiana House of Representatives, 1929, *Impeachment Proceedings*, I; Smith, *The Kingfish*, 124–26.

50 *He appointed his brother Earl* Long, *Every Man a King*, 260.

50 *"New Lakefront TB Hospital"* Kane, *Louisiana Hayride*, 65

50 *Within months of taking office* Smith, *The Kingfish*, 183.

51 *"Look at old Jess"* W. A. Cooper, interview, THW Papers, Mss. 2489, LSU LLMVC.

51 *When newspapers published* Harris, *The Kingfish*, 79–80.

51 *Of all of Huey's* Boulard, *Huey Long Invades New Orleans*, 29.

51 *The new severance tax* Banta, "The Pine Island Situation: Petroleum, Politics, and Research Opportunities in Southern History," 589–610; Letter from Wallace to HPL, 25 July 1928, HPL Papers, Mss. 2005, LSU LLMVC, Box 5.

51 *Wallace, who shared Huey's* Sindler, *Huey Long's Louisiana*, 58–59; Martin, *Dynasty*, 55; Cortner, *The Kingfish and the Constitution*, 23.

51 *On Friday, May 25, 1928* Lake Charles American Press, 25 May 1928.

52 *"It ain't going to be paid"* Long, *Every Man a King*, 114; Martin, *Dynasty*, 49.

52 *"It's the greatest cesspool"* Hair, *The Kingfish and His Realm*, 281.

52 *The area that stretched* Clay, *Coozan Dudley LeBlanc*, 36.

53 *"We are not going to stand"* New Orleans Times-Picayune, 12 Aug. 1928.

53 *On August 18, he ordered raids* Martin, *Dynasty*, 53.

53 *"We found cases of dice"* E. P. Roy, interview, 20 Mar. 1961, THW Papers, Mss. 2489, LSU LLMVC; Bridges, *Bad Bet on the Bayou*, 32.

53 *"sagebrush green in color"* Baton Rouge Advocate, 12 Nov. 1928.

53 *Just before Mardi Gras* New Orleans States, 19 Feb. 1929.

53   *On February 13, just after midnight*   New Orleans States, 14 Feb. 1929; Martin, *Dynasty*, 54.

54   *Huey's attack on gambling*   Jeansonne, *Messiah of the Masses*, 69–70.

54   *"boon companion of indicted criminals"*   Smith, *The Kingfish*, 60.

55   *"I am a better lawyer"*   Harris, *The Memoirs of T. H. Harris*, 159.

55   *In the northwest corner*   Various clippings, HPL Papers, Mss. 2005, LSU LLMVC, Box 5.

55   *"This is a rich section"*   Long, *Every Man a King*, 115; Beals, *The Story of Huey Long*, 95.

55   *In December 1928*   Long, *Every Man a King*, 108, 115, 180; Jeansonne, *Messiah of the Masses*, 71. The validity of the free textbook law was upheld by the U.S. Supreme Court in 1930 (*Cochran v. Louisiana State Board of Education*, 281 U.S. 370, 1930).

56   *During the school year*   Adams, "Huey the Great," 73.

56   *With many families previously*   Graham, *Huey Long*, 96; Swing, *Forerunners of American Fascism*, 43.

56   *"Dear Governor Long"*   Letter from Helen Edwards to HPL, 12 Sept. 1928, HPL Papers, Mss. 2005, LSU LLMVC, Box 5.

56   *"I hope that natural gas"*   New Orleans Times-Picayune, 16 Mar. 1928.

56   *For several years before*   Williams, *Huey Long*, 283–85.

56   *"It is plain to me"*   New Orleans Item, 16 Mar. 1928.

57   *He ordered his lieutenants*   New Orleans Morning Tribune, 4 July 1928; New Orleans Times-Picayune, 8 July 1928; New Orleans States, 8 July 1928.

58   *On a steamy night*   Scaramouche, "Huey Long: Clown and Knave of the U.S. Senate," 35.

58   *"Never had a more conscienceless"*   Long, *Every Man a King*, 127.

58   *"mockery against decency"*   Baton Rouge Advocate, 16 Dec. 1928.

58   *The board's vote, however*   Long, *Every Man a King*, 126–32.

59   *"How long," roared Cyr*   Martin, *Dynasty*, 54.

CHAPTER 4 · ENOUGH MONEY TO BURN A WET MULE

60   *Above his head*   Carleton, *River Capital*, 156–57.

61   *"Do you think I can forget that?"*   Baton Rouge State-Times, 23 Sept. 1923; Smith, *The Kingfish*, 33.

61   *As public service commissioner*   Clay, *Coozan Dudley LeBlanc*, 42.

61   *"the Invisible Empire"*   Martin, *Dynasty*, 33; Beals, *The Story of Huey Long*, 44.

61   *Three months before*   Long, *Every Man a King*, 110–11.

62   *"like a deck of cards in my hands"*   "The Case of Governor Long"; Sindler, *Huey Long's Louisiana*, 102.

62   *"Jim Buie always had"*   C. Arthur Provost, interview, 6 May 1960, New Iberia, THW Papers, Mss. 2489, LSU LLMVC.

62   *The session started off*   New Orleans States, 20 Mar. 1929; Smith, *The Kingfish*, 66.

62   *Unlike the severance tax*   New Orleans States, 16 Mar. 1929; Jeansonne, *Messiah of the Masses*, 72.

63   *He calculated that the new tax*   Long, *Every Man a King*, 123.

63   *The oil companies estimated*   Baton Rouge Advocate, 17 Mar. 1929.

63   *"I am hoping that the oil trusts"*   New Orleans *Times-Picayune,* 16 Mar. 1929.

63   **Standard Oil president**   Martin, *Dynasty,* 55–56.

63   **Huey claimed that Weller**   Williams, *Readings in Louisiana Politics,* 372.

63   *"You could pick up fifteen"*   Confidential interviews, THW Papers, Mss. 2489, LSU LLMVC

63   *Its loss would devastate*   Davis, *Huey Long,* 19.

63   *So dominant was the oil company*   Harris, *The Kingfish,* 193.

64   *In a front-page article*   Cortner, *The Kingfish and the Constitution,* 24–25; *Baton Rouge Advocate,* 19–20 Mar. 1929.

64   *The first sign of serious trouble*   New Orleans *States,* 20 Mar. 1929.

64   *Rarely content to stay*   Martin, *Dynasty,* 47.

64   *"This House has stood"*   New Orleans *Item,* 21 Mar. 1929; Martin, *Dynasty,* 56; Sindler, *Huey Long's Louisiana,* 62.

65   *"feathering the family nest"*   New Orleans *States,* 21 Mar. 1929.

65   *Cyr also attacked Huey*   *Baton Rouge State-Times,* 19 Nov. 1931, HPL Papers, Mss. 2005, LSU LLMVC, Scrapbook #14.

65   *Cyr, besides being a dentist*   Gary Leon, interview, THW Papers, Mss. 2489, LSU LLMVC; Harris, *The Kingfish,* 53.

65   *Cyr revealed that several*   New Orleans *States,* 21 Mar. 1929.

65   *Bombarded by his enemies*   *Baton Rouge State-Times,* 21 Mar. 1929; *New York Times,* 28 Mar. 1929: Sindler, *Huey Long's Louisiana,* 62; Martin, *Dynasty,* 57; Cortner, *The Kingfish and the Constitution,* 25.

65   *"Always take the offensive"*   Jeansonne, *Messiah of the Masses,* 75.

65   *"They say I made a terrible offense"*   New Orleans *Times-Picayune,* 2 May 1929.

66   *"Did you ever hear of shell shock"*   New Orleans *Times-Picayune,* 12 May 1929; Cortner, *The Kingfish and the Constitution,* 30–31.

66   **Cecil Morgan (1898–1999)**   Graduate of LSU law school, member of Louisiana state legislature, 1927–1934. Dean of Tulane University School of Law. Last surviving legislator to have served in the old state capitol. Died in New Orleans.

66   *"I couldn't do it"*   Cecil Morgan, interview, THW Papers, Mss. 2489, LSU LLMVC.

66   *"This House is not a den of thieves"*   *Louisiana House Journal,* Fifth Extra Session, 1929, 376; Harris, *The Kingfish,* 49–52.

66   *"swift and determined action"*   *Shreveport Journal,* 22 Mar. 1929; Goldsmith, "A Study of the Objectivity of Treatment of Governor Huey P. Long by Six Louisiana Daily Newspapers During Long's First Eleven Months in Office," 124; Smith, *The Kingfish,* 74.

67   *"Governor Long's tyranny over Louisiana"*   *Baton Rouge Advocate,* 26 Mar. 1929; Goldsmith, "A Study of the Objectivity of Treatment of Governor Huey P. Long," 127–36.

67   *"The water is rising"*   Long, *Every Man a King,* 138.

67   *"My ground had begun to slip"*   Long, *Every Man a King,* 125; Martin, *Dynasty,* 58.

67   *On Monday evening*   Smith, *The Kingfish,* 78.

67   *An electric tenseness filled the air*   New Orleans *Times-Picayune,* 24 Apr. 1929.

68   *Like Morgan, Sanders was*   Martin, *Dynasty,* 58–59.

68   *"Put Mr. Morgan in his seat"*   Cecil Morgan, interview, THW Papers, Mss. 2489, LSU LLMVC.

68   *"This is a dastardly outrage!"*   Smith, *The Kingfish*, 79.

68   *Still banging his gavel loudly*   *New Orleans States*, 26 Mar. 1929.

68   *"You goddamn crook"*   *New Orleans Item*, 26–27 Mar. 1929.

68   *"Blood and fire shone"*   Long, *Every Man a King*, 134.

69   *Fights broke out*   Sidney Marchand, interview, 28 June 1962, Donaldsonville, THW Papers, Mss. 2489, LSU LLMVC.

69   *"The bald headed wild fellow"*   Lester Lautenschlaeger, interview, 9 July 1957, THW Papers, Mss. 2489, LSU LLMVC.

69   *As Lautenschlaeger and others*   Cecil Morgan, interview, 12 Mar. 1965, New Orleans, THW Papers, Mss. 2489, LSU LLMVC.

69   *Depending on the source*   *New Orleans States*, 26 Mar. 1929; Williams, *Huey Long*, 357.

69   *"Let us be sane"*   Mason Spencer, interview, 20 Jan. 1960, Tallulah, THW Papers, Mss. 2489, LSU LLMVC; Cecil Morgan, interview, 12 Mar. 1965, New Orleans, THW Papers, Mss. 2489, LSU LLMVC; Martin, *Dynasty*, 59.

69   *"as if a threshing machine"*   *New Orleans States*, 26 Mar. 1929.

69   *"a few hundred highly intelligent"*   Long, *Every Man a King*, 134.

70   *"against Long from now until"*   Various clippings, HPL Papers, Mss. 2005, LSU LLMVC, Scrapbook #10.

70   *"I'll bet there were five hundred pistols"*   William C. Boone, interview, THW Papers, Mss. 2489, LSU LLMVC.

70   *"Those boys were not amateurs"*   Richard Leche, interview, THW Papers, Mss. 2489, LSU LLMVC.

70   *"During the impeachment"*   Cecil Morgan, interview, 12 Mar. 1965, New Orleans, THW Papers, Mss. 2489, LSU LLMVC.

71   *"whereas, Huey P. Long"*   *Louisiana Impeachment Proceedings*, I, 27–28, 32–33.

71   *However, even Dynamite Squad*   J. Y. Sanders, Jr., interview, THW Papers, Mss. 2489, LSU LLMVC; *New Orleans States*, 26 Mar. 1929. Battling Bozeman was not related to Huey's boyhood friend Harley Bozeman.

71   *"No, I didn't believe"*   Mason Spencer, interview, 20 Jan. 1960, Tallulah, THW Papers, Mss. 2489, LSU LLMVC.

71   *Later, the House dropped*   *Louisiana House Journal*, Fifth Extra Session, 1929, 12–54.

72   *"incompetency, corruption"*   *Louisiana Senate Journal*, Fifth Extra Session, 1929, 186–87.

72   *"It was so bad during the impeachment"*   Joe Fisher, interview, THW Papers, Mss. 2489, LSU LLMVC.

72   *"sons of men through whose veins"*   *New Orleans States*, 26 Mar. 1929.

72   *That Tuesday afternoon, placards*   *Baton Rouge Advocate*, 26 Mar. 1929; *New Orleans States*, 26 Mar. 1929.

73   *On a balcony*   Long, *Every Man a King*, 141.

CHAPTER 5 · BOUGHT LIKE A SACK OF POTATOES

74   *His brother Julius*   Julius Long, interview, THW Papers, Mss. 2489, LSU LLMVC; Harry Gamble, interview, THW Papers, Mss. 2489, LSU LLMVC.

74 *"Huey was wild up in his rooms"*   Norman Bauer, interview, THW Papers, Mss. 2489, LSU LLMVC.

74 *"Don't use any of that"*   Joseph B. David, interview, THW Papers, Mss. 2489, LSU LLMVC. Between 1928 and 1933, Huey distributed approximately 26 million circulars across Louisiana.

75 *"the greatest of all friends"*   Long, *Every Man a King*, 151.

75 *"This is the fight of my life"*   Smith, *The Kingfish*, 98.

75 *"I would rather go down"*   Cortner, *The Kingfish and the Constitution*, 29.

75 *"Has it become a crime"*   Long, *Every Man a King*, 152.

75 *"Watch out for the lying newspapers"*   Political circular, Seymour Weiss Papers, Mss. 4165, LSU LLMVC, Box 1.

75 *"bring the boys to Baton Rouge"*   Rolo C. Lawrence, interview, 14 Oct. 1959, Alexandria, THW Papers, Mss. 2489, LSU LLMVC.

75 By sunset, *"the city was swamped"*   Long, *Every Man a King*, 148.

76 *"could have been a riot"*   Rolo C. Lawrence, interview, 14 Oct. 1959, Alexandria, THW Papers, Mss. 2489, LSU LLMVC.

76 *"As I see him there now"*   Long, *Every Man a King*, 149.

76 *"an unscrupulous Bryan and a political Barnum"*   *Time*, 1 Apr. 1935.

76 *"The buzzards have returned"*   Long, *Every Man a King*, 149–50.

76 *"I saw people in front"*   W. S. Foshee, interview, THW Papers, Mss. 2489, LSU LLMVC.

76 *"only in snatches"*   Deutsch, "Paradox in Pajamas," 14.

76 *Early in the week, Earl Long*   L. P. Bahan, interview, THW Papers, Mss. 2489, LSU LLMVC.

76 *To fund his defense and buy votes*   George Ginsberg, interview, THW Papers, Mss. 2489, LSU LLMVC.

76 *They offered a huge sum*   Leander Perez, interview, 28 May, 1961, THW Papers, Mss. 2489, LSU LLMVC; William C. Boone, interview, THW Papers, Mss. 2489, LSU LLMVC.

77 *The president pro tem of the Senate*   Harry Gilbert, interview, THW Papers, Mss. 2489, LSU LLMVC.

77 *The Long forces enticed Senator*   Mason Spencer, interview, 20 Jan. 1960, Tallulah, THW Papers, Mss. 2489, LSU LLMVC; Leander Perez, interview, 28 May 1961, THW Papers, Mss. 2489, LSU LLMVC.

77 *Huey's opponents were no less nasty*   Lester Lautenschlaeger, interview, THW Papers, Mss. 2489, LSU LLMVC.

77 *"If Henry Larcade votes to acquit"*   Henry Larcade, interview, 29 Jul. 1958, Baton Rouge, THW Papers, Mss. 2489, LSU LLMVC.

77 *"Until impeachment, I never knew"*   Confidential interview, THW Papers, Mss. 2489, LSU LLMVC.

77 *A few days before the impeachment*   Rose McConnell Long, interview, 17 Mar. 1960, THW Papers, Mss. 2489, LSU LLMVC.

77 *"packed with perspiring humanity"*   *New Orleans States*, 27 Mar. 1929.

77 *The twelve House members*   Smith, *The Kingfish*, 99.

78 *Joining Huey at his defense table*   Harvey Peltier, interview, 3 Mar. 1960, Thibodaux, THW Papers, Mss. 2489, LSU LLMVC; Jeansonne, *Leander Perez*, 11.

78 **Leander Perez**   White supremacist, lawyer, and district judge who presided over court wearing a pearl-handled revolver. Had come to power in Plaquemines Parish in 1919. Perez clamped down on all political opposition, restricted free elections, disenfranchised black citizens, and made millions from oil. In the 1950s and 1960s Perez became a national spokesman for racial segregation, bankrolling George Wallace, and leading the White Citizens Council against desegregation. Perez viewed integration as communist-inspired. His vehement opposition to the integration of Catholic schools led the pope to excommunicate him. Perez died in 1969.

78 **The first witness called**   Fineran, *The Career of a Tinpot Napoleon*, 67; clipping from *Official Journal* of the Louisiana House of Representatives, HPL Papers, Mss. 2005, LSU LLMVC, Scrapbook #10.

78 **"a fight to death between"**   Mencken, "The Glory of Louisiana," 507–8.

78 **"You talk about appropriating"**   Smith, *The Kingfish*, 115.

79 **"I wore a straw skirt"**   *Louisiana House Journal*, Fifth Extra Session, I, 1929, 782–86; *New Orleans Times-Picayune*, 25 Apr. 1929.

79 **Humorous testimony occurred**   *Louisiana House Journal*, Fifth Extra Session, I, 1929, 798.

79 **One of the few legislators**   *Louisiana House Journal*, Fifth Extra Session, I, 1929, 798; Jeansonne, *Messiah of the Masses*, 76, 79; Hair, *The Kingfish and His Realm*, 184–85.

80 **The close friendship between**   Boulard, *Huey Long Invades New Orleans*, 24–25.

80 **Weiss met Huey in 1927**   James Noe, interview, THW Papers, Mss. 2489, LSU LLMVC; James Angelle, interview, THW Papers, Mss. 2489, LSU LLMVC; Kane, *Louisiana Hayride*, 160.

81 **"Jesus Christ," Weiss moaned**   Seymour Weiss, interview, THW Papers, Mss. 2489, LSU LLMVC.

81 **Fourteen governors attended**   Various clippings, HPL Papers, Mss. 2005, LSU LLMVC, Scrapbook #10; *Proceedings of the House of Representatives*, 16 Apr. 1929; HPL Papers, Mss. 2005, LSU LLMVC, Box 4.

81 **"There is an insect here from New Orleans"**   *Louisiana House Journal*, Fifth Extra Session, I, 1929, 188.

81 **The impeachers pressed on**   Frank Odom, interview, 21 May 1958, Baton Rouge, THW Papers, Mss. 2489, LSU LLMVC.

81 **One of the Dynamiters**   Mason Spencer, interview, 20 Jan. 1960, Tallulah, THW Papers, Mss. 2489, LSU LLMVC.

82 **At Greensburg on April 12**   Smith, *The Kingfish*, 138.

82 **Delivering as many as seven**   Cortner, *The Kingfish and the Constitution*, 30–31; *New Orleans Times-Picayune*, 12 May 1929.

82 **"I can't begin to get over to you"**   Norman Bauer, interview, THW Papers, Mss. 2489, LSU LLMVC.

82 **"He rode into office on my coat tails"**   Smith, *The Kingfish*, 155.

83 **"What's the matter with all these old boys?"**   Various clippings, HPL Papers, Mss. 2005, LSU LLMVC, Scrapbook #10; Davenport, 1930, 23.

83 **Perrault called for the House**   *New Orleans States*, 26 Mar. 1929, 6 Apr. 1929; Pavy, *Accident and Deception*, 38.

83 *"By the graves of my ancestors"* Louisiana House Journal, Fifth Extra Session, I, 1929, 291–92.

84 *"[I am] ashamed of Louisiana"* Ibid.

84 *The legislators charged Huey* Ibid.

84 *The last charge passed* William C. Boone, interview, THW Papers, Mss. 2489, LSU LLMVC; New Orleans Times-Picayune, 27 Apr. 1929; Smith, The Kingfish, 159–62.

85 *Just after noon on April 27, 1929* Smith, The Kingfish, 160–61.

85 *"They can impeach you because"* Otho Long, interview, 10 Feb. 1961, Winnfield, THW Papers, Mss. 2489, LSU LLMVC; Long, Every Man a King, 145; Memphis Commercial Appeal, 27 Apr. 1929.

85 *On May 14, the Senate convened* Williams, Huey Long, 340, 383; Haas, "Black Cat, Uncle Earl, Edwin and the Kingfish: The Wit of Modern Louisiana Politics," 213–27, 220.

86 *"the legislature would stop being"* Jeansonne, Leander Perez, 67.

86 *Two days after the Senate convened* Long, Every Man a King, 169–71.

87 *Gilbert's petition, thence emblazoned* Harley Bozeman, interview, THW Papers, Mss. 2489, LSU LLMVC; Smith, The Kingfish, 169–71.

87 *During a speech at Alexandria's* George Ginsberg, interview, THW Papers, Mss. 2489, LSU LLMVC.

87 *The truce, arranged by his millionaire* New Orleans Times-Picayune, 19–21 July 1929; Harris, The Kingfish, 79.

87 *"vindictive beyond description"* George Ginsberg, interview, THW Papers, Mss. 2489, LSU LLMVC.

87 *"killed him as dead as a door nail"* J. Maxime Roy, interview, 5 May 1960, Lafayette, THW Papers, Mss. 2489, LSU LLMVC.

87 *"you couldn't be independent"* Donald Labbe, interview, 4 May 1960, Lafayette, THW Papers, Mss. 2489, LSU LLMVC.

88 *He appointed Lester Hughes* Lester Hughes, interview, THW Papers, Mss. 2489, LSU LLMVC; William Boone, interview, THW Papers, Mss. 2489, LSU LLMVC.

88 *"Preacher" Anderson, the senator* Davis, Huey Long, 214.

88 *Robineer T. A. McConnell* Harry Gilbert, interview, THW Papers, Mss. 2489, LSU LLMVC.

88 *Round Robin signers who did not receive* C. Arthur Provost, interview, 6 May, New Iberia, THW Papers, Mss. 2489, LSU LLMVC.

88 *Henry Larcade signed the Round Robin* Otho Long, interview, 10 Feb. 1961, Winnfield, THW Papers, Mss. 2489, LSU LLMVC; Henry Larcade, interview, 29 July 1958, Baton Rouge, THW Papers, Mss. 2489, LSU LLMVC.

88 *In February 1930, the state Supreme* Martin, Dynasty, 69–70; Smith, The Kingfish, 173.

88 *When Lester Hughes's nine-year-old son* H. Lester Hughes, interview, THW Papers, Mss. 2489, LSU LLMVC.

89 *The men piled into huge black Packards* Marc Picciola, interview, 23 Aug. 1961, Golden Meadow, LA, THW Papers, Mss. 2489, LSU LLMVC.

89 *"the mosquitoes were as big as grasshoppers"* Sidney Marchand, interview,

28 June 1962, Donaldsonville, THW Papers, Mss. 2489, LSU LLMVC; Otho Long, interview, 10 Feb. 1961, Winnfield, THW Papers, Mss. 2489, LSU LLMVC.

CHAPTER 6 · GREEN SILK PAJAMAS AND A KIDNAPPING

90 *"He didn't put his cards"*   Mrs. W. M. Knott, interview, 18 Apr. 1960, THW Papers, Mss. 2489, LSU LLMVC.

90 *During the spring after*   Liebling, *The Earl of Louisiana*, 8.

90 *"Very effective at close range"*   *St. Louis Post-Dispatch*, 10 Feb. 1935, attributed to George McQuiston.

90 *"Forgetting nothing and forgiving no one"*   Sokolsky, "Huey Long," 525.

90 *He summarily fired enemies*   Hammond, *Let Freedom Ring*, 102.

90 *"Everybody who ain't with us"*   Irey, *The Tax Dodgers*, 88.

90 *"I used to try to get things done"*   Davis, *Huey Long*, 118–19; Mann, *Legacy to Power*, 19.

91 *"I want power so that"*   Irvin F. Polmer, interview, 20 Nov. 1960, THW Papers, Mss. 2489, LSU LLMVC; Jeansonne, *Messiah of the Masses*, 64, 92; Mann, *Legacy to Power*, 10; Williams, *Huey Long*, 546.

91 *State employees paid 5 to 10 percent*   Garlin, *The Real Huey P. Long*, 29.

91 *If they refused to pay*   Michie and Ryhlick, *Dixie Demagogues*, 120; Long, *Every Man a King*, xx–xxi.

91 *Contractors doing business*   Harris, *The Kingfish*, 98; Kane, *Louisiana Hayride*, 206.

91 *At this time, Huey revived*   Sindler, *Huey Long's Louisiana*, 105; Graham, *Huey Long*, 167.

91 *As early as April 1929*   *New Orleans Times-Picayune*, 24 Apr. 1929.

91 *He ordered the prisoners back*   *Baton Rouge Advocate*, 14 Dec. 1928.

92 *"If I can't get him out any other way"*   Martin, *Dynasty*, 73; *New Orleans Morning Tribune*, 3 Dec. 1929; *New Orleans Times-Picayune*, 3 Dec. 1929; Ira Gleason, interview, THW Papers, Mss. 2489, LSU LLMVC.

92 *The German cruiser* Emden   LeVert, *Huey Long*, 99; Kane, *Louisiana Hayride*, 81; Long, *Every Man a King*, 192–95.

93 *To replace his ubiquitous straw boater*   *New Orleans Times-Picayune*, 10 Mar. 1930; Smith, *The Kingfish*, 188–89; Seymour Weiss, interview, THW Papers, Mss. 2489, LSU LLMVC; Long, *Every Man a King*, 193; "Undressed Governor," 19; Cortner, *The Kingfish and the Constitution*, 33.

93 *"I have too much Cajun blood"*   *New Orleans Times-Picayune*, 31 Aug. 1930.

93 *"Governor, hell's broke loose"*   Long, *Every Man a King*, 292; Beals, *The Story of Huey Long*, 26.

93 *Precipitated by hectic stock speculation*   LeVert, *Huey Long*, 92; Jeansonne, *Messiah of the Masses*, 92.

94 *"I've never been for you politically"*   Long, *Every Man a King*, 242.

94 *Late that night Huey and Seymour*   Ibid., 242–44; Deutsch, "Paradox in Pajamas," 14–18; Swing, *Forerunners of American Fascism*, 85.

94 *Blanketed in a painted ceiling*   *WPA Guide to New Orleans*, liv; *New Orleans Times-Picayune*, 3 Oct. 1934; Boulard, *Huey Long Invades New Orleans*, 18, 23, 131.

95 *Huey's uptown enemies*   Martin, *Dynasty,* 68–69; *New Orleans Times-Picayune,*
24 Apr. 1929.

95 *Wealthy cotton planter*   Beals, *The Story of Huey Long,* 44.

96 *Huey and Parker soon broke*   Long, *Every Man a King,* 59; Davis, *Huey Long,* 79.

96 *In the first fifteen minutes*   *New Orleans Times-Picayune,* 24 Apr. 1929; *New Orleans States,* 23 Mar. 1929; Beals, *The Story of Huey Long,* 166.

96 *The league filed a lawsuit*   Jeansonne, *Messiah of the Masses,* 83; LeVert, *Huey
Long,* 89; Williams, *Huey Long,* 423.

96 *"self seeking demagogue, a despot"*   Open letter from Shirley G. Wimberley to
members of the U.S. Congress, undated, contained in FBI Archives, "Huey P.
Long," File # 62-32509, section 1, page 12.

96 *"There is not a thief or safe-blower"*   Various papers and newspaper clippings,
HPL Papers, Mss. 2005, LSU LLMVC, Scrapbook #12, *The Story of Huey Long,*
181.

97 *The Hammond Daily Courier, for example*   Waldron, *Hodding Carter,* 51; Beals,
The Story of Huey Long, 182.

97 *Starting a newspaper was not a new idea*   Various clippings, HPL Papers, Mss.
2005, LSU LLMVC, Box 2.

97 *He had no difficulty getting readership*   Earle J. Christenberry, interview, THW
Papers, Mss. 2489, LSU LLMVC.

97 *Huey hired John Klorer*   *Louisiana Progress,* 26 Mar. 1930.

97 *"a weekly newspaper which proposes"*   Clay, *Coozan Dudley LeBlanc,* 73.

98 *"If the daily papers"*   *Louisiana Progress,* 26 Mar. 1930.

98 *"How long does it take you to read"*   Handwritten speech written during senatorial campaign by HPL on cardboard in green ink, HPL Papers, Mss. 2005, LSU
LLMVC, Box 6.

98 *The tabloid rhetoric of the Progress*   *Shreveport Times,* 9 June 1930, HPL Papers,
Mss. 2005, LSU LLMVC, Scrapbook #12.

98 *"four oracles of New Orleans"*   *Louisiana Progress,* 17 Apr. 1930.

98 *After the Times-Picayune lacerated*   *Louisiana Progress,* 3 Apr. 1930; *New Orleans
Item,* 3 June 1930.

99 *Huey's Progress personally attacked*   *Louisiana Progress,* 8 May 1930.

99 *During the regular legislative session*   Cortner, *The Kingfish and the Constitution,*
2, 41–42.

99 *Charles Manship, the publisher*   *Baton Rouge Advocate,* 22 June 1930; *Editor &
Publisher,* 13 Sept. 1930, 48.

99 *A year later, the U.S. Supreme Court*   *Near v. Minnesota* (283 U.S. 697, 1931).

100 *On May 11, 1930, the legislature*   Jeansonne, *Messiah of the Masses,* 85; *Shreveport
Journal,* 12 June 1930, HPL Papers, Mss. 2005, LSU LLMVC, Scrapbook #12.

100 *"the Governor's creature in the Speaker's chair"*   *New Orleans Times-Picayune,* 12
May 1930.

100 *Allen J. Ellender (1890–1972)*   Born in Montegut, Terrebonne Parish, graduated
from St. Aloysius College, New Orleans, and from Tulane University Law
School, admitted to the bar and practiced in Houma. District attorney of Terrebonne Parish 1915–1916. Served as a sergeant in the Army Artillery Corps during the First World War. Delegate to the constitutional convention of Louisiana
in 1921. Member, state House of Representatives 1924–1936, served as floor

leader 1928–1932 and speaker 1932–1936. Elected to the U.S. Senate in 1936, reelected in 1942, 1948, 1954, 1960, and 1966 and served from 1937 until his death on July 27, 1972.

100 *The removal of Dupre outraged*   New Orleans Times-Picayune, 23 July 1930.

101 *"blubbering two-year-old"*   Various newspaper clippings, HPL Papers, Mss. 2005, LSU LLMVC, Scrapbook #12; *New Orleans Times-Picayune* 6 June 1930, HPL Papers, Mss. 2005, LSU LLMVC, Scrapbook #11.

101 *He pressured senators to elect*   Long, *Every Man a King*, 203.

101 *Huey's strong-arm tactics worked*   New Orleans States, 8 Sept. 1927, HPL Papers, Mss. 2005, LSU LLMVC, Scrapbook #7.

102 *"The trip on the river road from New Orleans"*   Charles Frampton, interview, THW Papers, Mss. 2489, LSU LLMVC.

102 *In 1928, Huey had funded*   Jeansonne, *Messiah of the Masses*, 203; Sindler, *Huey Long's Louisiana*, 103; Graham, *Huey Long*, 85.

102 *"We had started on the road system"*   Long, *Every Man a King*, 201; Sindler, *Huey Long's Louisiana*, 40.

103 *"We got the roads in Louisiana, haven't we?"*   Jeansonne, *Messiah of the Masses*, 68–69; Sokolsky, "Huey Long," 526.

103 *To fund the completion of the roads*   Sindler, *Huey Long's Louisiana*, 40.

103 *The $68 million highway*   Davis, *Huey Long*, 128.

103 *On June 17, 1930, Huey's*   New Orleans Times-Picayune, 18 June 1930.

103 *Initially Huey counted on the New Orleans*   New Orleans Times-Picayune, 18, 19, 20, 26 May 1930; *Baton Rouge State-Times*, 19 May 1930.

103 *"God forbid," declared the* **Shreveport Times**   Shreveport Times, 22 June 1930.

104 *His enemies feared that he would use*   Smith, *The Kingfish*, 193.

104 *The Senate refused to go along*   Long, *Every Man a King*, 205–6.

104 *Years before, when Mark Twain*   Davis, *Huey Long*, 19.

104 *"eclectic hodge-podge of Norman"*   Jensen, *Historic Baton Rouge*, 7.

104 *He asked the legislature for $5 million*   Shreveport Journal, 21 May 1930, HPL Papers, Mss. 2005, LSU LLMVC, Scrapbook #11; Carleton, "The Longs and the Anti-Longs," in Jeansonne, ed., *Huey at 100*, 101.

105 *"Turn it over to some collector of antiques"*   Shreveport Journal, 27 Jan. 1930.

105 *Huey was sure he had two-thirds*   New Orleans States, 12 July 1931, HPL Papers, Mss. 2005, LSU LLMVC, Scrapbook #13; Long, *Every Man a King*, 238–39.

105 *He slashed $6,400*   Long, *Every Man a King*, 210.

105 *About this time Huey charged*   New Orleans Times-Picayune, 15 Mar. 1931, HPL Papers, Mss. 2005, LSU LLMVC, Scrapbook #12.

105 *A few weeks later, as Huey walked*   Shreveport Journal, 10 June 1931, HPL Papers, Mss. 2005, LSU LLMVC, Scrapbook #13.

105 *On July 16, 1930, Highway Department trucks*   Louisiana Progress, 17 July 1930.

106 *His announcement puzzled many Louisianans*   Lake Charles American Press, 21 May 1928; *New Orleans Times-Picayune*, 16 Feb. 1928.

106 *"the fight for Huey Long's political life"*   Long, *Every Man a King*, 211–12; Beals, *The Story of Huey Long*, 185; *New York Times*, 31 Aug. 1930.

106 *Huey announced that, if elected senator*   Long, *Every Man a King*, 258.

106 *"I will have to stay out of the Senate"*   New Orleans Times-Picayune, 18 July 1930.

107 *He added that he would not collect*   Shreveport Journal, 14 Apr. 1930; *New Orleans Times-Picayune*, 5 May 1930.

107 *Joseph Eugene Ransdell (1858–1954)*   U.S. representative and senator from Louisiana. Born in Alexandria, Louisiana, graduated from Union College, Schenectady, New York, studied law, admitted to the bar in 1883 and practiced in Lake Providence, Louisiana, 1883–1889. District attorney for the Eighth Judicial District of Louisiana 1884–1896. Elected to the Fifty-sixth Congress to fill the vacancy caused by the death of Samuel Baird. Reelected to the Fifty-seventh and five succeeding Congresses, serving from August 29, 1899, to March 3, 1913. Elected to U.S. Senate in 1912, reelected in 1918 and 1924, and served until March 3, 1931. Returned to Lake Providence and engaged in the real estate business, cotton planting, and pecan growing.

107 *Tall and thin, his gaunt face*   Louisiana Progress, 24 July, 7 Aug. 1930; Davis, *Huey Long*, 132; *Lake Charles American Press*, 15 July 1930.

107 *All eighteen of Louisiana's daily newspapers*   Clay, *Coozan Dudley LeBlanc*, 75.

107 *"You are being asked to help send"*   Shreveport Times, 7 Sept. 1930.

107 *"[Huey Long] is the liar, crook, petty larceny thief"*   New Orleans States, 1 Aug. 1930.

108 *"merely a scrap of paper"*   Shreveport Journal, 9 Aug. 1930.

108 *To fight the New Orleans Ring*   Graham, *Huey Long*, 97; Swing, *Forerunners of American Fascism*, 36; Waldo Dugas, interview, THW Papers, Mss. 2489, LSU LLMVC.

108 *With plenty of campaign funds*   Campaign circular, "Landmarks of Senator Ransdell's Progress," Seymour Weiss Papers, Mss. 4165, LSU LLMVC, Box 1.

108 *"If the good roads plan were passed"*   HPL campaign broadside, HPL Papers, Mss. 2005, LSU LLMVC.

109 *"that gang of ballot-box stuffers"*   Fineran, *The Career of a Tinpot Napoleon*, 133; HPL campaign broadside, HPL Papers, Mss. 2005, LSU LLMVC; Beals, *The Story of Huey Long*, 189.

109 *"If you don't think you can vote for both"*   Robert Angelle, interview, THW Papers, Mss. 2489, LSU LLMVC.

109 *"Is that what you want, for the big businesses"*   John T. Hood, interview, THW Papers, Mss. 2489, LSU LLMVC.

109 *"Is there a single person in this audience"*   John Doles, interview, THW Papers, Mss. 2489, LSU LLMVC; *Louisiana Progress*, 7 Aug. 1930.

109 *"as amusing as it was depressing"*   New York Times, 31 Aug. 1930.

109 *In August, Huey's opponents accused*   New Orleans Times-Picayune, 15 Aug. 1930, HPL Papers, Mss. 2005, LSU LLMVC, Scrapbook #12.

109 *In its many outrageous cartoons*   Martin, *Dynasty*, 77.

110 *"a stench in the nostrils"*   Shreveport Journal, 12 Aug. 1930, HPL Papers, Mss. 2005, LSU LLMVC, Scrapbook #12.

110 *"common beyond words"*   Shreveport Journal, 26 Aug. 1930.

110 *When he sent his state police*   Beals, *The Story of Huey Long*, 189; Martin, *Dynasty*, 78–79.

110 *"If you believe that Louisiana is to be ruled"*   Louisiana Progress, 7 Aug. 1930.

110 *According to a reporter at the scene*   Paul Flowers, interview, THW Papers, Mss. 2489, LSU LLMVC.

110 *Six days before the Senate election* Dave McConnell, interview, THW Papers, Mss. 2489, LSU LLMVC; *Shreveport Journal*, 4 Sept. 1930.

111 *Irby and Terrell disappeared* Jules Fisher, interview, THW Papers, Mss. 2489, LSU LLMVC; various clippings, HPL Papers, Mss. 2005, LSU LLMVC, Scrapbook #12; Beals, *The Story of Huey Long*, 194–98; *Baton Rouge State-Times*, 8 Sept. 1930; Davenport, "Yes, Your Excellency!" 23; William Wiegand, interview, THW Papers, Mss. 2489, LSU LLMVC.

112 *"Let's take the son of a bitch"* Louie Jones, interview, 2 Mar. 1962, Baton Rouge, THW Papers, Mss. 2489, LSU LLMVC.

112 *Huey sent Abe Shushan, one of his wealthy* E. J. Oakes, interview, 25 June 1957, THW Papers, Mss. 2489, LSU LLMVC.

112 *They steamed south through the bayous* Joe Fisher, interview, THW Papers, Mss. 2489, LSU LLMVC.

112 *In the midst of these far-fetched events* *Baton Rouge State-Times*, 1 Apr. 1930; Williams, *Huey Long*, 460.

112 *Walking through the plush lobby* Opotowsky, *The Longs of Louisiana*, 56.

112 *In a radio broadcast from his Roosevelt Hotel* Joe Fisher, interview, THW Papers, Mss. 2489, LSU LLMVC; Charles Frampton, interview, THW Papers, Mss. 2489, LSU LLMVC; Abe Shushan, interview, THW Papers, Mss. 2489, LSU LLMVC.

113 *On Tuesday, September 9, 1930, Huey Long won* Clay, *Coozan Dudley LeBlanc*, 75; Boulard, *Huey Long Invades New Orleans*, 52.

113 *While Huey lost New Orleans* Sindler, *Huey Long's Louisiana*, 71.

114 *"extremely bad odor about them"* *Baton Rouge State-Times*, 16 Sept. 1930, HPL Papers, Mss. 2005, LSU LLMVC, Scrapbook #12; Jeansonne, ed., *Huey at 100*, 383.

114 *"They had trees registered down there"* Theophile Landry, interview, 10 July 1957, New Orleans, THW Papers, Mss. 2489, LSU LLMVC.

CHAPTER 7 · SELL THEM PLUGS

115 *"I can't lead a normal life"* Burns, *Huey Long* (video recording).

115 *During a stay in New Orleans* Mann, *Legacy to Power*, 39.

115 *To attack his "bay window"* *Baton Rouge Advocate*, 8 Feb. 1931, HPL Papers, Mss. 2005, LSU LLMVC, Scrapbook #12.

116 *Tuxedoed Seymour Weiss* Robert Hunter Pierson, interview, 12–14 Oct. 1959, Alexandria, THW Papers, Mss. 2489, LSU LLMVC.

116 *Guests listened to serenades* *Baton Rouge Advocate*, 28 May 1930, HPL Papers, Mss. 2005, LSU LLMVC, Scrapbook #12.

116 *One of the few occurred the following winter* *Shreveport Journal*, 26 Feb. 1931, HPL Papers, Mss. 2005, LSU LLMVC, Scrapbook #12.

116 *"She had the Indian sign on him"* Cleveland Fruge, interview, THW Papers, Mss. 2489, LSU LLMVC.

117 *"Mrs. Long was very much the boss"* W. E. Butler, interview, THW Papers, Mss. 2489, LSU LLMVC; Mrs. Clarence Pierson, interview, 13 Oct. 1959, Alexandria, THW Papers, Mss. 2489, LSU LLMVC.

117   *Like Huey, Rose avoided*   Don Devol, interview, 7 Oct. 1962, Washington, D.C., THW Papers, Mss. 2489, LSU LLMVC.

117   *"many a gossipy tongue to wagging"*   *New Orleans Tribune*, 8 Oct. 1930, HPL Papers, Mss. 2005, LSU LLMVC, Scrapbook #12; *Time*, 20 Oct. 1930, 18–19.

117   *A year later, Huey planned a dance*   *Shreveport Journal*, 1 Oct. 1931, HPL Papers, Mss. 2005, LSU LLMVC, Scrapbook #13.

117   *While Huey hailed from the impoverished*   Williams, *Huey Long*, 427; Boulard, *Huey Long Invades New Orleans*, 34–37, 43–44.

118   *During the first of many disputes*   Open letter from Shirley G. Wimberley to members of the U.S. Congress, undated, contained in FBI, "Huey P. Long," File Number 62-32509, section 1, page 12; *Shreveport Times*, 9 June 1930, HPL Papers, Mss. 2005, LSU LLMVC, Scrapbook #12; Williams, *Huey Long*, 481.

118   *On Thursday, September 11*   Sindler, *Huey Long's Louisiana*, 71.

118   *"He is always trying to trade"*   *New Orleans Times-Picayune*, 10 Mar. 1931.

118   *"We've accepted your proposition"*   Long, *Every Man a King*, 225.

119   *With a twist of vengeance, Huey ordered*   Assorted clippings, HPL Papers, Mss. 2005, LSU LLMVC, Scrapbook #12; Martin, *Dynasty*, 85.

119   *"By joining forces they hope"*   *New Orleans Times-Picayune*, 9 Mar. 1931; Smith, *The Kingfish*, 229.

119   *"prevent Governor Huey P. Long"*   Long, *Every Man a King*, 225; Martin, *Dynasty*, 68–69.

119   *Starting at eight in the evening*   *Bogalusa News*, 19 Sept. 1930; Davis, *Huey Long*, 139; Sindler, *Huey Long's Louisiana*, 75; Harris, *The Kingfish*, 91.

120   *Although elderly and deaf, Dupre could read*   Pavy, *Accident and Deception*, 19; Long, *Every Man a King*, 239.

120   *"slept in his clothes and shaved"*   Norman Bauer, interview, THW Papers, Mss. 2489, LSU LLMVC.

120   *"We'll order pistols and coffee for two"*   Frank Odom, interview, 21 May 1958, Baton Rouge, THW Papers, Mss. 2489, LSU LLMVC.

120   *"He turned and put his finger"*   Lester Lautenschlaeger, interview, 9 July 1957, THW Papers, Mss. 2489, LSU LLMVC.

120   *"Are you going to vote for the new Capitol?"*   E. J. Oakes, interview, 25 June 1957, THW Papers, Mss. 2489, LSU LLMVC.

120   *Every time it rained*   Interview, Leon Gary, Louisiana State Archives; Long, *Every Man a King*, 239; *New Orleans Times-Picayune*, 4 June 1930.

121   *In the midst of the special session*   *New Orleans States*, 18 Sept. 1930; *New Orleans Item*, 18 Sept. 1930.

121   *Taking the rostrum after the glowing*   *New Orleans Morning Tribune*, 17 Sept. 1930, HPL Papers, Mss. 2005, LSU LLMVC, Scrapbook #12.

121   *He then told them the story of a man*   Long, *Every Man a King*, 227–35; Beals, *The Story of Huey Long*, 201.

121   *He began calling himself the Kingfish*   Davis, *Huey Long*, 28; Harley Bozeman, interview, THW Papers, Mss. 2489, LSU LLMVC.

121   *"It has served to substitute gaiety"*   Long, *Every Man a King*, 278.

122   **Vanity Fair, for example**   *Vanity Fair*, June 1933, 42.

122   *During the following summer*   *New Orleans Times-Picayune*, 3 July 1931.

122 *On the day after the people passed* Ibid., 5 Nov. 1930.

122 *In a full-page Sunday spread* *Kansas City Star*, 12 Oct. 1930.

122 *"the worst sort of Fascist demagogue"* Givner, *Katherine Anne Porter*, 355–56; Boulard, *Huey Long Invades New Orleans*, 115.

122 *"backwoods demagogue of the oldest"* Mencken, "The Glory of Louisiana," 507.

123 *Years before as a teenager* Long, *Every Man a King*, 8.

123 *"I remember to this day how"* "Speech and Platform of Huey P. Long," HPL Papers, Mss. 2005, LSU LLMVC, Scrapbook #1.

123 *The LSU board had selected* *New Orleans States*, 23 Mar. 1929; Martin, *Dynasty*, 68–69.

123 *"any other damned department"* Jeansonne, *Messiah of the Masses*, 93.

123 *"This is a hell of a note"* Fred C. Frey, oral history interview, Mss. 4700.0019, LSU LLMVC.

123 *After President Atkinson* Long, *Every Man a King*, 247.

124 *"There's not a straight bone in Jim Smith's body"* Jeansonne, *Messiah of the Masses*, 93; Martin, *Dynasty*, 89.

124 *"go out and buy yourself some clothes"* Louie Jones, interview, 2 Mar. 1962, Baton Rouge, THW Papers, Mss. 2489, LSU LLMVC.

124 *When Huey first visited LSU after becoming* "Louisiana State University," 33–38.

124 *Pumping thousands of state dollars* Davis, *Huey Long*, 20.

124 *Over the next few years, the university enjoyed* McSween, "Huey Long at His Centenary," 519.

124 *By 1937, when most of Huey's innovations* "The Man Who Understood Huey," 22; Long, *Every Man a King*, 249; Jeansonne, *Messiah of the Masses*, 95.

124 *In the center of campus he constructed* *New Orleans Morning Tribune*, 29 Mar. 1932, HPL Papers, Mss. 2005, LSU LLMVC, Scrapbook #15; *Baton Rouge State-Times*, 29 Mar. 1932; Troy Middleton, interview, THW Papers, Mss. 2489, LSU LLMVC.

125 *Second best never satisfied Huey* Castro Carazo, interview, THW Papers, Mss. 2489, LSU LLMVC; Gene Austin, interview, THW Papers, Mss. 2489, LSU LLMVC.

125 *In 1931, LSU spent $14,345* LSU Receipts and Disbursements, 1 July–31 Dec. 1931, THW Papers, Mss. 2489, LSU LLMVC, Box 2, File 47; Jeansonne, ed., *Huey at 100*, 8; Jeansonne, *Messiah of the Masses*, 95–96; Troy Middleton, interview, 28 Sept. 1961, Baton Rouge, THW Papers, Mss. 2489, LSU LLMVC; *New Orleans Morning Tribune*, 29 Mar. 1932, HPL Papers, Mss. 2005, LSU LLMVC, Scrapbook #15; *Baton Rouge State-Times*, 29 Mar. 1932.

126 *When he ordered several of the finest pianos* Carlos Rabby, interview, 28 Oct. 1959, Baton Rouge, THW Papers, Mss. 2489, LSU LLMVC.

126 *By 1933 more than half the student body* Kane, *Louisiana Hayride*, 235.

126 *"Hell, I've got a university down in Louisiana"* Clay, *Coozan Dudley LeBlanc*, 76.

126 *"I just Longized it"* *New Orleans Morning Tribune*, 4 Dec. 1931, HPL Papers, Mss. 2005, LSU LLMVC, Scrapbook #14.

126 *"We were all so scared we couldn't say anything"* Paul C. Young, oral history interview, 1980, Baton Rouge, Mss. 4700.0066, LSU LLMVC.

126 *When LSU students delivered a copy* Alton E. Broussard, interview, THW Papers, Mss. 2489, LSU LLMVC.

126 *"Sell them plugs"* "The Man Who Understood Huey," 22; Kane, *Louisiana Hayride*, 226.

126 *Cotton was the lifeblood of rural Louisiana* Keyes, *All This Is Louisiana*, 212.

127 *On August 8, 1931, the U.S. Department of Agriculture* Martin, *Dynasty*, 94; *New Orleans Times-Picayune*, 17 Aug. 1931; Snyder, "Huey Long and the Cotton-Holiday Plan of 1931," 137–38.

127 *Of the governors, only Huey Long* Brinkley, *Voices of Protest*, 37.

127 *"Hold your cotton"* Martin, *Dynasty*, 94; *New Orleans Times-Picayune*, 17 Aug. 1931; Snyder, "Huey Long and the Cotton-Holiday Plan of 1931," 137–38.

128 *"It's Governor Long's baby"* *New Orleans Times-Picayune*, 24 Aug. 1931; *Baton Rouge State-Times*, 24 Aug. 1931.

128 *"Hell, if the government can tell a man"* Smith, *The Kingfish*, 235.

128 *"Now I can take this damned thing off"* *Time*, 3 Oct. 1932, 10–11.

128 *Huey used the radio to sell* Malone, *Hattie and Huey*, 36.

128 *"[Long] may be able to demand that his legislature"* Beals, *The Story of Huey Long*, 212; Sindler, *Huey Long's Louisiana*, 117; Davis, *Huey Long*, 147.

129 *"paid off like a slot machine"* LeVert, *Huey Long*, 100.

129 *Huey's proposal was popular across the South* Snyder, "Huey Long and the Cotton-Holiday Plan of 1931," 133–60; *New Orleans Times-Picayune*, 9 Aug.–17 Sept. 1931; various correspondence, Cotton Holiday files, HPL Papers, Mss. 2005, LSU LLMVC; Davis, *Huey Long*, 146.

129 *On January 9, 1931, one of the few* *Bogalusa News*, 9 Jan. 1931.

129 *"cats go for miles for a place to scratch"* Handwritten notes by Russell Long about his father, Huey Long, undated, Louisiana State Archives.

129 *At noon on Thursday, February 12* *New Orleans States*, 12 Feb. 1931, HPL Papers, Mss. 2005, LSU LLMVC, Scrapbook #12.

130 *His attire changed abruptly* *New Orleans States*, 26 Mar. 1931, HPL Papers, Mss. 2005, LSU LLMVC, Scrapbook #12.

130 *Earlier, one of his bitter political enemies* Various correspondence, James Aswell Papers, Mss. 1408, LSU LLMVC; various undated clippings, HPL Papers, Mss. 2005, LSU LLMVC, Scrapbook #12.

130 *James B. Aswell (1869–1931)* Politician and educator from Natchitoches, state superintendent of education (1904–1908), president of Louisiana State Normal College (1910–1911), candidate for governor (1911), U.S. Representative (1913–1931).

130 *On April 14, Overton* Mrs. John H. Overton, interview, 12 Oct. 1959, Alexandria, THW Papers, Mss. 2489, LSU LLMVC; assorted undated clippings, HPL Papers, Mss. 2005, LSU LLMVC, Scrapbook #12.

130 *Another death provided more political* *Baton Rouge State-Times*, 3 July 1931; Martin, *Dynasty*, 92.

130 *One of Huey's passions was football* Davis, *Huey Long*, 20.

130 *"I don't fool around with losers"* Oliver P. Carriere, interview, THW Papers, Mss. 2489, LSU LLMVC.

130 *In December 1930 he called LSU coach* *New Orleans Morning Tribune*, 2 Dec. 1930, HPL Papers, Mss. 2005, LSU LLMVC, Scrapbook #12.

130 *"There was no training table then"* Sidney Bowman, interview, THW Papers,

Mss. 2489, LSU LLMVC; W. E. Butler, interview, THW Papers, Mss. 2489, LSU LLMVC.

131 *Before a game with Vanderbilt*   Davis, *Huey Long*, 226.

131 *When the circus owners refused to move*   Harry Rabenhorst, interview, THW Papers, Mss. 2489, LSU LLMVC; Beals, *The Story of Huey Long*, 204; Jeansonne, *Messiah of the Masses*, 8, 98; Martin, *Dynasty*, 90–91.

131 *"from now on the coach is going to be my assistant"*   Beals, *The Story of Huey Long*, 204; Jeansonne, ed., *Huey at 100*, 8.

131 *"Next time one of those Tigers tries"*   Lawrence M. Jones, interview, 28 Dec. 1961, Washington, D.C., THW Papers, Mss. 2489, LSU LLMVC.

132 *When the game turned against LSU*   *New Orleans States*, 28 Nov. 1930, HPL Papers, Mss. 2005, LSU LLMVC, Scrapbook #12.

132 *During the Sugar Bowl game against Oregon State*   Dr. Abe Mickal, interview, 18 July 1957, THW Papers, Mss. 2489, LSU LLMVC; Lawrence M. Jones, interview, THW Papers, Mss. 2489, LSU LLMVC; Fred Digby, interview, THW Papers, Mss. 2489, LSU LLMVC; Troy Middleton, interview, THW Papers, Mss. 2489, LSU LLMVC; Davis, *Huey Long*, 229; *New Orleans Item*, 17 Dec. 1934.

132 *called him a "liar and a poltroon"*   *New Orleans Times-Picayune*, 12 Feb. 1931, HPL Papers, Mss. 2005, LSU LLMVC, Scrapbook #12.

132 *"Governor, Senator-Elect, and a Prisoner in His Own State"*   *St. Louis Post-Dispatch*, 22 Mar. 1931.

133 *"I want Huey Long to get out of office"*   *Baton Rouge State-Times*, 14 Oct. 1931, HPL Papers, Mss. 2005, LSU LLMVC, Scrapbook #13.

133 *"Huey was deathly opposed to guns"*   Charles Frampton, interview, THW Papers, Mss. 2489, LSU LLMVC.

133 *"It was an armed camp"*   Leon Gary, interview, THW Papers, Mss. 2489, LSU LLMVC.

134 *"throw Cyr out on North Street"*   Sidney Bowman, interview, THW Papers, Mss. 2489, LSU LLMVC; *New York Times*, 14 Oct. 1931.

134 *He argued that Cyr*   Leon Gary, interview, 12 July 1995, Louisiana State Archives, Tape OH 0021.

134 *"Taking the oath of office as governor ends Dr. Cyr"*   Jeansonne, *Messiah of the Masses*, 91; Sindler, *Huey Long's Louisiana*, 76.

134 *On November 3, Huey traveled to Shreveport*   Long, *Every Man a King*, 258.

134 *He was persuasive*   *Baton Rouge State-Times*, 18 Nov. 1931, HPL Papers, Mss. 2005, LSU LLMVC, Scrapbook #14.

134 *"had about as much chance being installed"*   *Bienville Democrat*, 29 Sept. 1931, HPL Papers, Mss. 2005, LSU LLMVC, Scrapbook #14.

CHAPTER 8 · WITCHES BOUND AT THE STAKE

135 *Oscar Kelly Allen (1882–1936)*   Country schoolteacher at fifteen, sawmill laborer, and businessman. Assessor of Winn Parish 1916, elected to state Senate in 1928, chairman of Highway Commission. Governor of Louisiana, 1932–1936. Elected to the U.S. Senate but died on January 25, 1936, of a cerebral hemorrhage before taking office.

135 *In late 1931, Huey neared the end*   Shreveport Journal, 22 June 1931, HPL Papers, Mss. 2005, LSU LLMVC, Scrapbook #13.

135 *Allen, eleven years older than Huey*   Long, *Every Man a King*, 19, 40.

135 *"Between Huey and his wife"*   Richard Leche, interview, THW Papers, Mss. 2489, LSU LLMVC.

136 *Because several of the offices*   Smith, *The Kingfish*, 243.

136 *"Huey was fond of Earl"*   Fred Dent, interview, THW Papers, Mss. 2489, LSU LLMVC; Martin, *Dynasty*, 97.

137 *"Why if I had a cow as stupid and dumb looking"*   Baton Rouge State-Times, 29 Dec. 1931.

137 *"this state of Long and all of his blood-sucking"*   Clay, *Coozan Dudley LeBlanc*, 89; Michie and Ryhlick, *Dixie Demagogues*, 125; Jeansonne, *Messiah of the Masses*, 104.

137 *Dudley branded Huey as a "cowardly slacker"*   Beals, *The Story of Huey Long*, 221; Clay, *Coozan Dudley LeBlanc*, 1–40.

137 *"yellowest physical coward that God had ever let live"*   Shreveport Journal, 8 Jan. 1932; Sid Copeland, interview, THW Papers, Mss. 2489, LSU LLMVC; Beals, *The Story of Huey Long*, 218.

137 *"operates a nigger burial lodge and shroud"*   New Orleans Times-Picayune, 6 Dec. 1931.

137 *"LeBlanc is going to pay pensions to Negroes"*   Baton Rouge Advocate, 29 Nov. 1931, HPL Papers, Mss. 2005, LSU LLMVC, Scrapbook #14; Jeansonne, *Messiah of the Masses*, 103–4.

138 *"You pronounce LeBlanc's name"*   New Orleans Times-Picayune, 11 Dec. 1932; Beals, *The Story of Huey Long*, 221.

138 *Near the end of 1931, the* New Orleans Item   Hair, *The Kingfish and His Realm*, 239; Cortner, *The Kingfish and the Constitution*, 56.

138 *First published from Lafayette*   Clay, *Coozan Dudley LeBlanc*, 109.

138 *On New Year's eve, Huey raced across*   Campaign flyer, HPL Papers, Mss. 2005, LSU LLMVC, Box 6.

138 *O.K. received 214,699 votes*   *Report of the Louisiana Secretary of State*, 1933.

139 *"ignorant and meaningless a campaign as was ever"*   Beals, *The Story of Huey Long*, 223.

139 *An eighteen-year-old voter in New Orleans*   A. O. Rappelet, interview, 5 Mar. 1963, THW Papers, Mss. 2489, LSU LLMVC; Haas, "Black Cat, Uncle Earl, Edwin and the Kingfish: The Wit of Modern Louisiana Politics," 226.

139 *"What the hell happened to those two fellows?"*   Theophile Landry, interview, 10 July 1957, New Orleans, THW Papers, Mss. 2489, LSU LLMVC; Richard W. Leche, interview, 30 June 1957, New Orleans, THW Papers, Mss. 2489, LSU LLMVC.

139 *Dupre decided to abandon the House seat*   New Orleans Item, 11 Oct. 1931, HPL Papers, Mss. 2005, LSU LLMVC, Scrapbook #13.

140 *His columns stooped to antebellum racism*   American Progress, 7 Aug. 1934.

140 *On Thanksgiving Day 1931*   Baton Rouge State-Times, 27 Nov. 1931, HPL Papers, Mss. 2005, LSU LLMVC, Scrapbook #14.

140 *Huey felt sympathy for Dupre*   Pavy, *Accident and Deception*, 19; New York Times, 27 Nov. 1931.

140 *"Jim, I want to get acquainted with you!"* Schlesinger, *The Age of Roosevelt*, 45; Graham, *Huey Long*, 149.

141 **Just before nine in the evening on January 23** *New Orleans Times-Picayune*, 24 Jan. 1932; *Baton Rouge State-Times*, 23 Jan. 1932, HPL Papers, Mss. 2005, LSU LLMVC, Scrapbook #14; Long, *Every Man a King*, 284.

141 *"I'm going to get an education in Washington"* *New York Times*, 25 Jan. 1932.

141 **At four in the morning on January 25** Seymour Weiss, interview, THW Papers, Mss. 2489, LSU LLMVC.

141 **On his first day, he sauntered onto the floor** *New Orleans States*, 26 Jan. 1932.

141 **On that day, he snubbed another old enemy** *Baton Rouge State-Times*, 25 Jan. 1932, HPL Papers, Mss. 2005, LSU LLMVC, Scrapbook #14; Davis, *Huey Long*, 170; HPL Photo Album, HPL Papers, Mss. 4495, LSU LLMVC.

142 *"farthest spot from the United States I've seen"* Unlabeled newspaper clipping, 6 Feb. 1932, HPL Papers, Mss. 2005, LSU LLMVC, Scrapbook #18.

142 **Paul Cyr, the ousted lieutenant governor** *Baton Rouge State-Times*, 28 Jan. 1932, HPL Papers, Mss. 2005, LSU LLMVC, Scrapbook #14.

142 **A week before, the Louisiana Supreme Court** Davis, *Huey Long*, 153.

142 **Later, when Huey was back in Washington** Raymond Fleming, interview, THW Papers, Mss. 2489, LSU LLMVC.

142 **Their new home was a pink stucco** *Baton Rouge State-Times*, 8 Nov. 1932; HPL Papers, Mss. 2005, LSU LLMVC, Scrapbook #16.

143 *"Stand back," he roared* *Baton Rouge State-Times*, 9 Feb. 1932, HPL Papers, Mss. 2005, LSU LLMVC, Scrapbook #14.

143 *"a handkerchief regrettably on the pink side"* Adams, "Huey the Great," 74–75.

143 *"galloped about the Senate floor"* Smith, *The Kingfish*, 248.

143 **If he was interested in the debate he moved** *New York Times*, 26 Jan. 1932.

143 **Over the next five months, he enraged his colleagues** Brinkley, *Voices of Protest*, 42; Opotowsky, *The Longs of Louisiana*, 61; Jeansonne, *Messiah of the Masses*, 105.

144 **On April 4, 1932, he took the Senate floor** Davis, *Huey Long*, 154; Long, *Every Man a King*, 293.

144 **Titled "The Doom of America's Dream"** Long, *Every Man a King*, 293; Graham, *Huey Long*, 53.

144 *"There is no rule so sure as that one"* Long, *Every Man a King*, 291–92.

144 **A week later Huey introduced** Davis, *Huey Long*, 174.

144 *"I don't believe he could get"* Burdette, *Filibustering in the Senate*, 181; Martin, *Dynasty*, 137–38; Opotowsky, *The Longs of Louisiana*, 70, attributed to Senator Kenneth McKellar of Tennessee.

144 *"cooler than a fresh cucumber"* Kincaid, *Silent Hattie Speaks*, 130, from journal entry of Senator Hattie Caraway dated 19 May 1932.

144 *"always hit the big man first"* Rupert Peyton, interview, 28 Jan. 1958, Baton Rouge, THW Papers, Mss. 2489, LSU LLMVC.

145 *"Robinson and Hoover work together for the same things"* *Memphis Commercial Appeal*, 1 May 1932, HPL Papers, Mss. 2005, LSU LLMVC, Scrapbook #15.

145 **He blamed the Depression on a conspiracy** Davis, *Huey Long*, 157.

145 *"every nefarious interest on the living face of the globe"* Jeansonne, *Messiah of the Masses,* 106.

145 *"Joe doesn't look really as well with his hair dyed"* Kincaid, *Silent Hattie Speaks,* 119, from journal entry of Senator Hattie Caraway dated 3 May 1932.

145 *During Huey's tirade, Senator Reed* Davis, *Huey Long,* 158.

145 *"It was an epitome of bad taste"* Kincaid, *Silent Hattie Speaks,* 125, from journal entry of Senator Hattie Caraway dated 12 May 1932.

145 *"I send to the desk, Mr. President"* *Congressional Record,* 72nd Cong., 1st Sess., 9202, 9213–14.

145 *"makes one think of the schoolboy"* *Lafayette Tribune,* 19 May 1932, HPL Papers, Mss. 2005, LSU LLMVC, Scrapbook #15.

145 *"comic opera performance unworthy"* Jeansonne, *Messiah of the Masses,* 106.

145 *The* Washington Post *called for Huey to resign* *Washington Post,* 1 May 1932, HPL Papers, Mss. 2005, LSU LLMVC, Scrapbook #15; Davis, *Huey Long,* 156–57.

146 *On May 16, he delivered a three-hour filibuster* *Congressional Record,* 72nd Cong., 1st Sess., May 16, 1932; Kincaid, *Silent Hattie Speaks,* 125.

146 *"I am beginning to be convinced"* *Baton Rouge State Times,* 17 May 1932, HPL Papers, Mss. 2005, LSU LLMVC, Scrapbook #15; *Congressional Record,* 72nd Cong., 1st Sess., 10294–309.

146 *As he gave his filibuster, he ignored the rule* Davis, *Huey Long,* 160.

146 *"When the people go to the circus"* Barkley, *That Reminds Me,* 161.

146 *"For leading the masses and illustrating your point"* Boulard, *Huey Long Invades New Orleans,* 69; Goodwin, *Lyndon Johnson and the American Dream,* 92.

146 *At a meeting of the LSU Board of Supervisors* *Baltimore Sun,* 12 Oct. 1931, John Earle Uhler papers, Mss. 1902, LSU LLMVC; *Time,* 26 Oct. 1931, 28.

147 *"These Cajun boys and girls climbed up"* Uhler, *Cane Juice,* 4.

147 *The tepid prose of* Cane Juice, *however* *Time,* 26 Oct. 1931, 28; letter from Glasser to Uhler, John Earle Uhler Papers, Mss. 1902, LSU LLMVC.

147 *"I realize that behind my dismissal"* *Baltimore Sun,* 12 Oct. 1931, John Earle Uhler papers, Mss. 1902, LSU LLMVC.

147 *"servitude in such a hole"* Letter, Mencken to Uhler, John Earle Uhler papers, Mss. 1902, LSU LLMVC.

148 *"LSU professor dope fiend [Uhler]"* Unofficial LSU *Whangdoodle* scandal sheet, undated, LSU LLMVC, microfilm 1714.

148 *The crusty dean of the law school* Joe Cawthorn, interview, THW Papers, Mss. 2489, LSU LLMVC; Dave McGuire, interview, 14 Mar. 1960, THW Papers, Mss. 2489, LSU LLMVC; *Newsweek,* 5 Jan. 1935, 34; *Baton Rouge State-Times,* 2 June 1930; *Baton Rouge Advocate,* 18 Nov. 1930.

148 *"Huey just made them and broke them"* Paul C. Young, oral history interview, 1980, Mss. 4700.0066, LSU LLMVC.

148 *On April 5, 1932, six months after the dismissal* Letter from Smith to Uhler, 5 Apr. 1932, John Earle Uhler Papers, Mss. 1902, LSU LLMVC; Paul C. Young, oral history interview, 1980, Mss. 4700.0066, LSU LLMVC.

148 Cane Juice, *a mediocre novel at best* Various newspaper clippings, John Earle Uhler Papers, Mss. 1902, LSU LLMVC; *Time,* 26 Oct. 1931, 28. John Earle

Uhler (1876–1962) took the *Cane Juice* episode in stride, remaining at LSU for the rest of his academic career, becoming a noted scholar of English Renaissance literature, and raising his family in Baton Rouge.

CHAPTER 9 · HATTIE AND HUEY

149 *When the storm passed, O.K. stepped*   *Baton Rouge Advocate*, 17 May 1932; Hair, *The Kingfish and His Realm*, 238.

149 *"That's some building," Huey boasted*   Carleton, *River Capital*, 134; Graham, *Huey Long*, 91; Davis, *Huey Long*, 14–15, 26.

150 *"Only an otiose soul, struck"*   Davis, *Huey Long*, 13.

150 *Huey no longer served as governor*   Haas, "Huey Long and the Communists," 32; *Columbus* (Ohio) *State-Journal*, 2 Feb. 1935, HPL Papers, Mss. 2005, LSU LLMVC, Scrapbook #18.

150 *To keep an eye on Allen*   Richard Leche, interview, THW Papers, Mss. 2489, LSU LLMVC.

150 *A modern highway system, a hundred new bridges*   "Democrats: Incredible Kingfish," 11; Jeansonne, *Messiah of the Masses*, 66.

151 *"You'll never get a job in the state"*   Mary Helen Byrd, interview, 24 Aug. 2004, Baton Rouge. After Huey's death, Conner returned to Baton Rouge as a state bank examiner.

151 *Now needing new sources of revenue*   Martin, *Dynasty*, 104.

151 *When the legislature convened on May 12, 1932*   Various clippings, HPL Papers, Mss. 2005, LSU LLMVC, Scrapbook #15.

151 *As legislators worked through the bills*   Gene Quaw, interview, 27 June 1961, Baton Rouge, THW Papers, Mss. 2489, LSU LLMVC.

151 *Huey's new taxes, normally inflammatory*   Long, *Every Man a King*, 299; Harris, *The Kingfish*, 109.

152 *Huey's opposition, depleted by the recent election*   *New Orleans Times-Picayune*, 26 May 1932, HPL Papers, Mss. 2005, LSU LLMVC, Scrapbook #15.

152 *"I'll never invest another cent in Louisiana"*   "Democrats: Incredible Kingfish," 11, attributed to Henry Hardtner.

152 *On June 13, Mrs. Ruffin Pleasant*   Scaramouche, "Huey Long: Clown and Knave of the U.S. Senate," 38.

152 *"If this tax bill passes, it will mean nothing"*   *Baton Rouge State-Times*, 7 June 1932, HPL Papers, Mss. 2005, LSU LLMVC, Scrapbook #15.

153 *"She carried a pistol in her bag"*   Louie Jones, interview, 2 Mar. 1962, Baton Rouge, THW Papers, Mss. 2489, LSU LLMVC.

153 *Huey's opponents held an anti-tax rally*   Martin, *Dynasty*, 105–6.

153 *Before the session ended, Huey appointed*   *Time*, 20 Oct. 1930, 18–19.

153 *"twenty-six-year-old girl who doesn't know"*   Martin, *Dynasty*, 105–6.

153 *Mrs. Pleasant failed to mention that Alice Lee*   Various clippings, HPL Papers, Mss. 2005, LSU LLMVC, Scrapbook #15.

154 *On June 7, 1932, Huey introduced*   *Louisiana House Journal*, Sixth Regular Session, 1932, 7–8, 9–22.

154 *"crookedest scheme in Louisiana"*   *Baton Rouge Advocate*, 29 Nov. 1931, HPL Papers, Mss. 2005, LSU LLMVC, Scrapbook #14.

154 *Ironically, the Association's records*   Various clippings, HPL Papers, Mss. 2005, LSU LLMVC, Scrapbook #1.

154 *"as nothing more than an attempt to crucify LeBlanc"*   *Lake Charles American Press,* 24 June 1932.

154 *"I am going to be first of all a man"*   *New Orleans Item,* 8 June 1932, HPL Papers, Mss. 2005, LSU LLMVC, Scrapbook #15.

154 *"because a man is defeated politically"*   *New Orleans Times-Picayune,* 23 June 1932, HPL Papers, Mss. 2005, LSU LLMVC, Scrapbook #15.

155 *Meanwhile, one of Huey's bodyguards*   Louie Jones, interview, THW Papers, Mss. 2489, LSU LLMVC; Beals, *The Story of Huey Long,* 233–35.

155 *The House voted to postpone the LeBlanc bill*   *Lake Charles American Press,* 25 June 1932.

155 *Now back in town, an iron-willed Huey*   Various newspaper clippings, Helen Gilkison Papers, Mss. 1901, LSU LLMVC, Box 2.

155 *That afternoon, Governor Allen signed the bill*   *Lafayette Daily Advertiser,* 7 July 1932; Clay, *Coozan Dudley LeBlanc,* 105–7, 119.

155 *"Sitting there quiet as a mouse in her little black dress"*   Adams, "Huey the Great," 74.

156 *Hattie was "this brave little woman"*   Kincaid, *Silent Hattie Speaks,* 24, 48.

156 *Hattie and Huey first met*   Deutsch, "Hattie and Huey," 6–7, 88–90, 92; Malone, *Hattie and Huey,* 1–2; Kincaid, *Silent Hattie Speaks,* 127.

156 *On May 21, Huey met Hattie on the Senate floor*   Brinkley, *Voices of Protest,* 47–48; Mann, *Legacy to Power,* 25; Kincaid, *Silent Hattie Speaks,* 24; Malone, *Hattie and Huey,* xii.

156 *While she agreed with his populism*   Kincaid, *Silent Hattie Speaks,* 24, 48, 97, 109, 130.

157 *First, the Arkansas campaign offered the opportunity*   Harvey Peltier, interview, THW Papers, Mss. 2489, LSU LLMVC; Seymour Weiss, interview, THW Papers, Mss. 2489, LSU LLMVC.

157 *He kept his promise to Hattie*   Snyder, "Huey Long and the Presidential Election of 1936," 128–29.

157 *"how his pardner was and whether she was true"*   Kincaid, *Silent Hattie Speaks,* 22–24.

157 *The first day in August 1932 was already a scorcher*   *New York Times,* 2 Aug. 1932; Malone, *Hattie and Huey,* xii.

157 *"I'm here to get a bunch of pot-bellied politicians"*   *Time,* 3 Oct. 1932, 10; *New Orleans Item,* 1–2 Aug. 1932; Deutsch, "Hattie and Huey," 6–7, 88–90, 92.

157 *In Magnolia, the Kingfish wore a neatly tailored*   *New Orleans Times-Picayune,* 11 Aug. 1932; Malone, *Hattie and Huey,* 54; Brinkley, *Voices of Protest,* 51; Snyder, "Huey Long and the Presidential Election of 1936," 128–29.

158 *As word of Huey and Hattie's "circus hitched to a tornado"*   Fields, *A True History of the Life, Works, Assassination, and Death of Huey Pierce Long,* 12.

158 *In Pine Bluff, they drew more than twenty thousand*   Harley Bozeman, "Winn Parish as I Have Known It," *Winn Parish Enterprise,* 29 Aug. 1957, in Bozeman scrapbooks, State Library of Louisiana.

158 *Now, the waiters delivered his food*   Smith, *The Kingfish,* 269; Malone, *Hattie and Huey,* 60.

158 *"The gravel roads were hell on cars"* Brinkley, *Voices of Protest*, 51; Snyder, "Huey Long and the Presidential Election of 1936," 128–29; Malone, *Hattie and Huey*, 66, 350; Hair, *The Kingfish and His Realm*, 248; Mann, *Legacy to Power*, 25; Murphy Roden, interview, 25 Sept. 1961, Baton Rouge, THW Papers, Mss. 2489, LSU LLMVC.

158 *Huey and Hattie maintained a grueling schedule* Deutsch, "Hattie and Huey," 6–7, 88–90, 92; Malone, *Hattie and Huey*, 25, 50, 63; Snyder, "Huey Long and the Presidential Election of 1936," 128–29; Martin, *Dynasty*, 108–9.

159 *Edwin Sidney Broussard (1874–1834)* Born near Loreauville, in Iberia Parish, Louisiana, graduated from LSU in 1896. Taught in the public schools of Iberia and St. Martin Parishes, 1896–1898. During the Spanish-American War served as a captain in Cuba 1898–1899. Accompanied the Taft Commission to the Philippines in 1899. Graduated from Tulane Law School in 1901 and practiced in New Iberia. Prosecuting attorney for the Nineteenth District 1903–1908. Unsuccessful candidate for lieutenant governor in 1916. Elected to the United States Senate in 1920, reelected in 1926, and served until March 3, 1933. Resumed law practice in New Iberia, where he died in 1934.

159 *In 1926 Huey campaigned across the state* Long, *Every Man a King*, 82, 253; Beals, *The Story of Huey Long*, 248.

159 *Huey also targeted a minor local election* Clay, *Coozan Dudley LeBlanc*, 109–11; "Mourners, Heirs, Foes," 13.

160 *Meanwhile, LeBlanc took a monkey on a string* Clay, *Coozan Dudley LeBlanc*, 111.

160 *"I'm always afraid of an election"* Harry Gilbert, interview, THW Papers, Mss. 2489, LSU LLMVC.

160 *In one New Orleans precinct, votes were tallied* Jeansonne, *Messiah of the Masses*, 131–32.

160 *"Paying the poll taxes kept all of the politicians broke"* Cleveland Fruge, interview, THW Papers, Mss. 2489, LSU LLMVC.

160 *"I paid some poll taxes, twenty-five or thirty"* C. C. Barham, interview, THW Papers, Mss. 2489, LSU LLMVC.

160 *The purpose of the dummy candidates* Hammond, *Let Freedom Ring*, 58.

161 *A few days before the election, Judge Benjamin Pavy* Jeansonne, *Messiah of the Masses*, 130–31.

161 *"They'll tell you what you've got to do is tear up Longism"* Martin, *Dynasty*, 111.

161 *Huey won and so did his candidates* Clay, *Coozan Dudley LeBlanc*, 114.

162 *"I advise anyone who thinks he knows something about politics"* *Congressional Record*, 73rd Cong., 2nd Sess., 1552–64; *Time*, 30 Jan. 1934, HPL Papers, Mss. 2005, LSU LLMVC, Scrapbook #19.

162 *"wallowing in the mud"* Connally, *My Name Is Tom Connally*, 273.

162 *"Cain has cried for the blood of Abel"* U.S. Senate, *Overton Hearing Report*, 1932, I, 1–3, 7–14, 54; Williams, *Huey Long*, 604–6.

162 *By the end of 1932, the Federal Bureau of Investigation's chief* Federal Bureau of Investigation, "Huey P. Long," File # 62-32509, 14 sections.

163 *Elmer Irey, the intelligence chief* Davis, *Huey Long*, 182.

163 *Irey successfully developed the tax evasion case* Fried, *FDR and His Enemies*, 87.

163 *"When are you going to do something about Long?"* Hair, *The Kingfish and His Realm*, 285–86; Jeansonne, *Messiah of the Masses*, 159.

163   *"let the chips fall where they may"*   Irey, *The Tax Dodgers*, 88–91.

163   *"my skirts are clear"*   Drew Pearson, column, *New York Daily Mirror*, 12 Dec. 1934.

CHAPTER 10 · WHO IS THAT *AWFUL* MAN?

164   *"Don't spoil my chances of putting you in the White House"*   Finan, *Alfred E. Smith*, 297–98.

165   *The previous February, he called a meeting*   Davis, *Huey Long*, 153.

165   *"just a bunch of exes"*   *Shreveport Times*, 15 June 1932.

165   *"Huey Long ain't vice to anybody or anything"*   Beals, *The Story of Huey Long*, 238–39.

165   *He was also the most combative*   Heinemann, *Harry Byrd of Virginia*, 150.

165   *On Tuesday night, June 27, 1932*   Long, *Every Man a King*, 312; Hair, *The Kingfish and His Realm*, 242.

166   *"I am the Democratic Party in Louisiana"*   Davis, *Huey Long*, 167–68.

166   *Once having won his case before the credentials committee*   *New York Times*, 27–28 June 1932; Williams, *Huey Long*, 573–76; Boulard, *Huey Long Invades New Orleans*, 65–66.

166   *"The eyes of the nation were turned his way"*   Farley, *Behind the Ballots*, 125.

166   *Soon, though, the crowd began to quiet*   *New York Times*, 29 June 1932; Boulard, *Huey Long Invades New Orleans*, 66.

166   *"He sensed the fact that it was time to cut out"*   Farley, *Behind the Ballots*, 125.

166   *"Who is our delegation?"*   Davis, *Huey Long*, 167–68.

167   *He grabbed the huge wooden sign of the Louisiana delegation*   *Time*, 3 Oct. 1932, 10–11; *New York Times*, 28–29 June 1932.

167   *"perpetually erupting volcano"*   Tugwell, *The Brains Trust*, 230–31.

167   *"Wherever Huey appeared the temperature shot up"*   Farley, *Behind the Ballots*, 125.

167   *"If you break the unit rule you sonofabitch"*   Brinkley, *Voices of Protest*, 46.

168   *"men and women, forgotten in the political philosophy"*   Graham, *Huey Long*, 70.

168   *"When I was talking to Governor Roosevelt"*   LeVert, *Huey Long*, 106–7.

168   *The president-elect worried that if the Depression*   Snyder, "Huey Long and the Cotton-Holiday Plan of 1931," 117–18; Tugwell, *The Democratic Roosevelt*, 349; Schlesinger, *The Crisis of the Old Order, 1919–1933*, 417–18; Moley, *27 Masters of Politics*, 229.

168   *Henry L. Stimson (1867–1950)*   Born in New York City. Attended Yale University and Harvard Law School. Law partner with Elihu Root. Republican. Candidate for governor of New York, 1910; secretary of war, 1911–13; secretary of state, 1929–33. Appointed secretary of war by Franklin Roosevelt in 1940 and urged President Truman to use the atomic bomb in 1945.

168   *"I'm leaving state politics for good"*   Davis, *Huey Long*, 172.

168   *Confident that he now held a firm grip*   Russell Long, "Remembrances," typescript dated 1985, HPL Papers, Mss. 2005, LSU LLMVC.

168   *Only a few months before, the populistic Farmer-Labor Party*   *New York Times*, 18 June 1932; Beals, *The Story of Huey Long*, 238.

169   *Huey intended to spearhead the Roosevelt campaign*   Farley, *Behind the Ballots*, 170–71.

169   *"the greatest heart for mankind I have ever seen"*   Davis, *Huey Long*, 172.

169 *"You know, there's a striking resemblance"* Washington Star, 10 Oct. 1932, HPL Papers, Mss. 2005, LSU LLMVC, Scrapbook #16.

169 *"Who is that awful man?"* Brinkley, Voices of Protest, 58; Tully, FDR, 323–24; Schlesinger, The Crisis of the Old Order, 1919–1933, 418.

169 *During the last week of October, he took his fleet* Williams, Huey Long, 603; Louie Jones, interview, 2 Mar. 1962, Baton Rouge, THW Papers, Mss. 2489, LSU LLMVC.

170 *Farley and other Roosevelt aides considered* Farley, Behind the Ballots, 171; Boulard, Huey Long Invades New Orleans, 66; Jeansonne, Messiah of the Masses, 110–11.

170 *"about a postmastership in Winship, Louisiana"* Baton Rouge State-Times, 30 Nov. 1932, HPL Papers, Mss. 2005, LSU LLMVC, Scrapbook #16.

170 *"When I talk to him he says, 'Fine, Fine, Fine!' "* Brinkley, Voices of Protest, 58; Schlesinger, The Crisis of the Old Order, 1919–1933, 452.

171 *"Imagine ninety-five Senators trying to outtalk Huey Long"* Will Rogers, column, New York Times, 14 Jan. 1993.

171 *"A mob is coming to hang the other ninety-five"* Birmingham News-Age-Herald, 19 Feb. 1933.

171 *"shoeless rabble at a lynching"* Moley, 27 Masters of Politics, 221.

171 *"among the unemployed and do not know it"* Congressional Record, 74th Cong., 1st Sess., 9098.

171 *He mimicked the speech and walk* Kane, Louisiana Hayride, 100.

171 *"The Senator from Mississippi has another way"* Congressional Record, 73rd Cong., 2nd Sess., 6081, 6093, 6105; Hammond, Let Freedom Ring, 199.

171 *"He lights on one part of you, stings you"* Barkley, That Reminds Me, 159; Schlesinger, The Age of Roosevelt, 42; Graham, Huey Long, 147–48.

171 *Huey defied senatorial decorum when he attacked* Congressional Record, 72nd Cong., 2nd Sess., 1330–35; Williams, Huey Long, 620–21.

172 *Huey Long and Carter Glass* New Orleans Times-Picayune, 13 Mar. 1933, HPL Papers, Mss. 2005, LSU LLMVC, Scrapbook #16.

172 *"demagogic screech owl"* Smith and Beasley, Carter Glass, 365–66, 346.

172 *filibuster* The term derives from the mid-nineteenth century and describes an armed adventurer who wages unauthorized and irregular warfare against foreign states for plunder or power.

172 *"Go to now, ye rich men"* Congressional Record, 73rd Cong., 2nd Sess., 1451–64; Baton Rouge Advocate, 11 Jan. 1933; Burdette, Filibustering in the Senate, 172.

172 *"A piece of legislation that was assumed"* Brinkley, Voices of Protest, 56.

172 *He labeled Huey's performance "rhetorical rubbish"* Jeansonne, Messiah of the Masses, 112; Davis, Huey Long, 176.

173 *"You'd better leave the old man alone"* Allen Ellender, interview, THW Papers, Mss. 2489, LSU LLMVC.

173 *"I'm tired of having him try to make a personal issue"* New Orleans Times-Picayune, 12 Mar. 1933; Williams, Huey Long, 628.

173 *"I couldn't hit you"* Mann, Legacy to Power, 26.

173 *"Huey Long had rooms"* Thurber, "Talk of the Town: Rough on Rats," 8–9.

173 *James Thurber (1894–1961)* The greatest American humorist since Mark

Twain. At the time of the interview, Thurber wrote articles and penned cartoons for *The New Yorker*. He is best known for his Walter Mitty character.

174 **Huey Long created his own Mardi Gras** *WPA Guide to New Orleans*, 290; Boulard, *Huey Long Invades New Orleans*, 17.

174 **At the beginning of the session, lame-duck senator** Davis, *Huey Long*, 182; Adams, "Huey the Great," 71.

174 **On February 3, the Overton hearings began** Hammond, *Let Freedom Ring*, 64.

174 **Senator Robert Howell, a distinguished Nebraska Republican** *Baton Rouge State-Times*, 3 Feb. 1933.

175 **"when one person moved, they all moved"** *New Orleans States*, 11 Feb. 1933; *New Orleans Times-Picayune*, 3 Feb. 1933.

175 **"to the victor belong the spoils"** U.S. Senate, *Overton Hearings*, I, 630–38.

175 **It was clear from Ansell's questions** Sindler, *Huey Long's Louisiana*, 70.

175 **"gray hair, gray face, and gray hands"** U.S. Senate, *Overton Hearings*, I, 419–28; Hammond, *Let Freedom Ring*, 64–65, 71–75; Jeansonne, *Messiah of the Masses*, 133.

176 **Harley Bozeman, a boyhood friend** Various newspaper clippings, Seymour Weiss Papers, Mss. 4165, LSU LLMVC, Box 6; Davis, *Huey Long*, 186.

176 **Earl, still sore at Huey for not supporting his bid** U.S. Senate, *Overton Hearings*, I, 953–54; *New York Times*, 15 Feb. 1933.

176 **Earl testified that Sheriff Mereaux of St. Bernard Parish** *New Orleans Item*, 14 Feb. 1933, HPL Papers, Mss. 2005, LSU LLMVC, Scrapbook #16.

176 **"Say the word, and I'll telephone the Sheriff"** Adams, "Huey the Great," 71.

177 **"Are you trying to get funny?"** U.S. Senate, *Overton Hearings*, I, 472; Williams, *Huey Long*, 613–14.

177 **"damnable, corrupt, cheap"** *New Orleans States*, 7 Feb. 1933, HPL Papers, Mss. 2005, LSU LLMVC, Scrapbook #16.

177 **that night someone set Huey's New Orleans house afire** Seymour Weiss Papers, Mss. 4165, LSU LLMVC, Box 6.

177 **When Huey returned to Washington later that month** *Baton Rouge State-Times*, 23 Feb. 1933, HPL Papers, Mss. 2005, LSU LLMVC, Scrapbook #16; *New Orleans Times-Picayune*, 2 Mar. 1933.

177 **"liar, crook, scoundrel, forger, dog-faced son of the wolf"** Beals, *The Story of Huey Long*, 254.

177 **On March 1, Ansell sued** After Ansell won his libel suit in the Washington, D.C., courts, Huey appealed the case to the U.S. Supreme Court. In *Long v. Ansell*, 293 U.S. 76 (1934), the Court upheld the lower courts' decision in Ansell's favor. The settlement was pending when Huey died.

177 **Senator Tom Connally returned to New Orleans** Davis, *Huey Long*, 203; Hammond, *Let Freedom Ring*, 135.

177 **On the second day the crowd was so thick** *Newsweek*, 25 Nov. 1933, 9.

177 **Connally tried to control the crowd** Connally, *My Name Is Tom Connally*, 168.

178 **"fraud upon the rights of citizens"** Davis, *Huey Long*, 203, 215; *Time*, 30 Jan. 1934, HPL Papers, Mss. 2005, LSU LLMVC, Scrapbook #19.

178 **"Politics in Louisiana is as clean as an angel's ghost"** Jeansonne, *Messiah of the Masses*, 134.

CHAPTER 11 · A BLACK EYE FOR THE KINGFISH

179 *"When anyone eats with Huey"* Tugwell, *The Brains Trust*, 433.

179 *"[Roosevelt's] a phony"* Leslie Gardiner, interview, THW Papers, Mss. 2489, LSU LLMVC; Jeansonne, *Messiah of the Masses*, 149.

179 *Signs of a split between the two men* Schlesinger, "Messiah of the Rednecks," in Dethloff, ed., *Huey P. Long: Southern Demagogue or American Democrat?* 84.

180 *He vainly opposed the nomination of Henry Morgenthau* Martin, *Dynasty*, 137–38.

180 *Quoting the Bible, Theodore Roosevelt, Daniel Webster* Ibid.

180 *In addition, the New Deal had created* Fried, *FDR and His Enemies*, 69.

180 *Traditionally, the awarding of federal jobs* New Orleans Times-Picayune, 20 Oct. 1933.

181 *By the end of 1933, about 326,000* Jeansonne, *Messiah of the Masses*, 151–52.

181 *"So far as I am concerned"* New Orleans Morning Tribune, 12 Apr. 1933, HPL Papers, Mss. 2005, LSU LLMVC, Scrapbook #16.

181 *"We've got bureaucrats, autocrats, hobocrats"* New York Times, 18 Nov. 1934, HPL Papers, Mss. 2005, LSU LLMVC, Scrapbook #18.

181 *In early 1933, Huey had supported* Beals, *The Story of Huey Long*, 356.

181 *"Whenever this administration has gone to the left"* Congressional Record, 73rd Cong., 2nd Sess., 11451–52, Senate speech, 14 June 1934.

181 *"Where is the corner groceryman?"* Brinkley, *Voices of Protest*, 146; Congressional Record, 73rd Cong., 1st Sess., 3321.

182 *Now opposing even the most progressive of Roosevelt's proposals* Sindler, *Huey Long's Louisiana*, 86.

182 *"Every fault of socialism is found in this bill"* Congressional Record, 73rd Cong., 1st Sess., 5238–5308.

182 *Near the end of the session* Ibid., 6106–10.

182 *Just before Congress adjourned* Jeansonne, *Messiah of the Masses*, 150; Tugwell, *The Democratic Roosevelt*, 351.

183 *"The President and I are never going to fall out"* Fried, *FDR and His Enemies*, 68; Farley, *Behind the Ballots*, 240–42.

183 *"No, I will not participate in the Democratic victory tonight"* Congressional Record, 73rd Cong., 1st Sess., 13 June 1933, 6130.

183 *The mother of two small children, Hilda Phelps Hammond* Cortner, *The Kingfish and the Constitution*, 144; Hammond, *Let Freedom Ring*, 45–46, 89.

184 *On Sunday afternoon, March 5, 1933* Chicago Tribune, 14 June 1934; Tyler, "Silk Stockings and Ballot Boxes: Women of the Upper Class and New Orleans Politics, 1930–1955."

184 *"Hilda, the antique queen, the Picayune damsel"* American Progress, 7 Aug. 1934, 4; 4 Jan. 1935.

184 *She delivered a stack of petitions* Hair, *The Kingfish and His Realm*, 283; Boulard, *Huey Long Invades New Orleans*, 68; Hammond, *Let Freedom Ring*, 33.

185 *"Psychiatrists have stated in my presence"* Letter, Parker to Nance, 12 Apr. 1933, John M. Parker Papers, University of North Carolina, Chapel Hill; Snyder, "The Concept of Demagoguery: Huey Long and His Literary Critics," 65.

185 *"insolence, arrogance, unscrupulousness, mental bravery"* Letter, Sanders to Glass,

Carter Glass Papers, University of Virginia; Snyder, "The Concept of Demagoguery: Huey Long and His Literary Critics," 66.

185 **When Mrs. Pleasant testified before a Senate committee**   Chicago Daily Tribune, 30 May 1934.

185 **Dotted with the mansions of Wall Street millionaires**   Davis, Huey Long, 195.

185 **Gene Buck**   Nationally famous composer of popular songs such as "Mother Is Her Name" and "Tulip Time," was president of the American Society of Composers, Authors, and Publishers. Buck and Huey met during one of Huey's frequent trips to New York.

185 **Six hundred wealthy guests attended**   George Maines, interview, THW Papers, Mss. 2489, LSU LLMVC.

185 **One version said that Huey insulted a lady**   Baton Rouge State-Times, 31 Aug. 1933, HPL Papers, Mss. 2005, LSU LLMVC, Scrapbook #16; Reed, Requiem for a Kingfish, 108–9.

186 **At one point he said five Wall Street agents**   New Orleans Times-Picayune, 29 Aug. 1933; Murphy Roden, interview, 25 Sept. 1961, Baton Rouge, THW Papers, Mss. 2489, LSU LLMVC.

186 **"Bust 'em up boys! Hit 'em!"**   San Francisco Chronicle, 2 Feb. 1935; Zinman, The Day Huey Long Was Shot, September 8, 1935, 105; Cortner, The Kingfish and the Constitution, 60.

186 **Several writers referred to him as "Huey Pee Long"**   Kurtz, "Longism and Organized Crime," in Jeansonne, ed., Huey at 100, 112.

186 **"establishing an unprecedented record for dancing, twisting"**   Waldron, Hodding Carter, 53.

187 **"What about the Long Island affair?"**   Davis, Huey Long, 201; New Orleans Times-Picayune, 10 Oct. 1933.

187 **Hecklers also attacked Huey at the Washington Parish Fair**   Harris, The Kingfish, 143–46.

187 **Many Louisianans were aware that Huey's bitter attacks**   New York Times, 10–11 Nov. 1933; Davis, Huey Long, 202; Carter, "Kingfish to Crawfish," 302.

187 **In October 1933, two months after Sands Point**   Earle J. Christenberry, interview, THW Papers, Mss. 2489, LSU LLMVC.

188 **"Why don't you do what I did"**   Long, Every Man a King, ix, xxvi.

188 **The ladies telephoned bookstores throughout the city**   Baton Rouge State-Times, 23 Oct. 1933.

188 **Almost three years to the day, the political truce**   Baton Rouge State-Times, 13 Sept. 1933; New York Times, 14 Sept. 1933; New Orleans Times-Picayune, 20–21 Dec. 1933; Boulard, Huey Long Invades New Orleans, 71.

189 **Strolling into the brisk December air**   Baton Rouge State-Times, 20 Dec. 1933.

189 **The previous June, Sixth District congressman**   Sindler, Huey Long's Louisiana, 87.

189 **"It's a poor judge who can't enforce his own rulings"**   Davis, Huey Long, 204; Carter, "Huey Long: American Dictator," in Leighton, ed., The Aspirin Age, 339–41.

190 **"If ever there was a need for shotgun government"**   Waldron, Hodding Carter, 54–56. Hodding Carter won the Pulitzer Prize in 1946 for courageous editorials calling for racial moderation in the Greenville, Mississippi, Delta Democrat-Times.

190 *When the polls closed the next evening*   New Orleans Times-Picayune, 5 Dec. 1933.

190 *"Huey Doesn't Live Here Anymore"*   New Orleans Times-Picayune, 27 Dec. 1933.

190 *Three weeks later, on December 27*   Baton Rouge State-Times, 28 Nov. 1933.

190 *In April 1934, a more legitimate election finally was held*   Hair, The Kingfish and His Realm, 264; Davis, Huey Long, 211.

190 *"I want to tell you that [Huey Long] belongs to the hog family"*   Williams, Huey Long, 536; Carter, "Huey Long: American Dictator," 339.

190 *"In some ways he didn't act"*   W. A. Cooper interview, THW Papers, Mss. 2489, LSU LLMVC.

191 *Huey rarely attended Washington social functions*   Time, 1 Apr. 1935, 16.

191 *From the Roosevelt Hotel in New Orleans*   Baton Rouge Advocate, 16 Dec. 1933; American Progress, 21 Dec. 1933.

CHAPTER 12 · CUT THEIR NAILS AND FILE THEIR TEETH

193 *"I am going to choke those words"*   New Orleans States, 7 Jan. 1934.

193 *But at the last minute, Huey ignored the advice*   Seymour Weiss, interview, THW Papers, Mss. 2489, LSU LLMVC.

194 *He gave his first speech for Klorer*   New Orleans Times-Picayune, 14 Jan. 1934.

194 *He charged Walmsley and the Choctaws*   American Progress, 1 Feb. 1934.

194 *"You know the turkey head usually goes on the block"*   New Orleans Times-Picayune, 18 Jan. 1934.

194 *Huey ignored the order*   New York Times, 8 Aug. 1934.

194 *"They stealthily entered in the middle of the night"*   New Orleans Item, 16 Jan. 1934.

194 *He also had aligned himself with Franklin Roosevelt*   New Orleans Item, 3 Jan. 1934.

195 *On January 23, Walmsley won handily*   New York Times, 28 Jan. 1934.

195 *"If I see Long I'm going to beat him up"*   New Orleans Item, 14 Feb. 1934; Hair, The Kingfish and His Realm, 265–66; Boulard, Huey Long Invades New Orleans, 95.

195 *The mayor prowled the city looking for that "yellow coward"*   Martin, Dynasty, 122; Carter, "Huey Long: American Dictator," in Leighton, ed., The Aspirin Age, 353.

195 *"a home, an automobile, a radio, and the ordinary conveniences"*   Haas, "Huey Long and the Communists," 29; Congressional Record, 73rd Cong., 2nd Sess., 3450–53.

196 *"like a small pox epidemic"*   Drew Pearson, column, New York Daily Mirror, 23 Apr. 1934; clipping from FBI File, "Huey P. Long," File #62-32509, section 1, page 20.

196 *"So, in 1929," he argued*   Long, Every Man a King, 290.

196 *"I never read a line of Marx"*   Snyder, "Huey Long and the Presidential Election of 1936," 120.

196 *"Well, you don't have to [understand]"*   Jeansonne, Messiah of the Masses, 165.

196 *On the day before Easter 1934, Rose Lee*   Lee, "Senator Long at Home," 68.

197 *Huey didn't worry*   Huey used much of the same statistics and wealth-sharing rhetoric written in a 1918 campaign brochure by his radical friend, state senator S. J. Harper. The brochure, Issues of the Day, Free Speech, Economic Slavery, led to the antiwar Harper being indicted under the Espionage Act.

197 *He overestimated the number of millionaires* Schlesinger, *The Age of Roosevelt,* 60; Graham, *Huey Long,* 157; Jeansonne, "Challenge to the New Deal: Huey P. Long and the Redistribution of National Wealth," 383; Bennett, *Demagogues in the Depression,* 121; Beals, *The Story of Huey Long,* 311–12.

197 *"a monstrous and tragic joke"* *Time,* 1 Apr. 1935, 15; Beals, *The Story of Huey Long,* 312.

197 *Conservatives condemned Huey's plan* Waldron, *Hodding Carter,* 51. "Share Our Swag" attributed to Hodding Carter.

197 *Liberals condemned it as irrelevant* Fried, *FDR and His Enemies,* 73.

197 *"This is not bread for the hungry, but a stone"* Unlabeled Lippmann clipping, HPL Papers, Mss. 2005, LSU LLMVC, Scrapbook #18.

197 *On February 23, Huey incorporated the Share Our Wealth Society* *Congressional Record,* 73rd Cong., 2nd Sess., 3450–53; Brinkley, *Voices of Protest,* 79; Snyder, "Huey Long and the Presidential Election of 1936," 119.

198 *"most organizations are broken up by the treasurer"* Bennett, *Demagogues in the Depression,* 126.

198 *By the middle of 1934, he received more mail* Don Devol, interview, 7 Oct. 1960, Washington, D.C., THW Papers, Mss. 2489, LSU LLMVC.

198 *Soon after launching his Share Our Wealth clubs* Hoteling, "Huey Pierce Long as Journalist and Propagandist," 26.

198 *"It stood alone in one day"* Bennett, *Demagogues in the Depression,* 125–26; Snyder, "Huey Long and the Presidential Election of 1936," 123; Kane, *Louisiana Hayride,* 6, 119–20; *New Orleans Item,* 10 Sept. 1935.

198 *Gerald L. K. Smith (1898–1976)* Born in Pardeeville, Wisconsin, Gerald L. K. Smith worked his way through Valparaiso University by sweeping floors and mowing lawns. Following Huey's assassination, Smith along with Dr. Francis Townsend and Father Coughlin formed the Union Party to contest the 1936 presidential election. The ticket won 800,000 votes. From about 1940 Smith opposed organized labor and promoted isolation. Following the outbreak of the Second World War, he concentrated on keeping America out of the war. Smith preached a gospel of hatred of Jews and blacks, of sinister conspiracies that threatened the American way of life. He was such an effective fund-raiser that by the 1960s he was a millionaire.

198 *"gustiest and goriest, the deadliest and damnedest"* Mencken, "Why Not Gerald?"; Bennett, *Demagogues in the Depression,* 125; Huie, "Gerald Smith's Bid for Power," 224.

199 *Smith met Huey and asked him to save* Bennett, *Demagogues in the Depression,* 116; Jeansonne, *Gerald L. K. Smith,* 27.

199 *When Huey gave him his old suits to wear* Charles Frampton, interview, THW Papers, Mss. 2489, LSU LLMVC.

199 *In 1933, the thirty-year-old Smith* Martin, *Dynasty,* 139; Simon, *As We Saw the Thirties,* 46; Bennett, *Demagogues in the Depression,* 116, 124–25; Kane, *Louisiana Hayride,* 150–51; Beals, *The Story of Huey Long,* 291.

199 *"In order to succeed, a mass movement"* Deutsch, "Huey Long: The Last Phase," 27–31.

199 *"a rhetorician who was even greater than [William Jennings] Bryan"* Schlesinger, *The Age of Roosevelt,* 64; Jeansonne, *Gerald L. K. Smith,* 37.

200 *Smith spoke to over a million people in the state*   F. Raymond Daniell, *New York Times*, 7 Feb. 1935; *Time*, 1 Apr. 1935; *American Progress*, 7 Aug. 1934.

200 *On May 13, 1934, the day before the regular session*   *New Orleans Times-Picayune*, 14 May 1934; Harris, *The Kingfish*, 160–62; Allen Ellender, interview, THW Papers, Mss. 2489, LSU LLMVC.

200 *"The Kingfish can see a few things better with one eye"*   Various clippings, HPL Papers, Mss. 2005, LSU LLMVC, Scrapbook #17.

201 *During this hectic period*   Fried, *FDR and His Enemies*, 45; Harris, *The Kingfish*, 160–62.

201 *He ordered the legislature to pass a number of unprecedented bills*   Davis, *Huey Long*, 213, 227; Beals, *The Story of Huey Long*, 270; *New Orleans Times-Picayune*, 8–12 July 1934.

201 *Huey placed the New Orleans police department*   Davis, *Huey Long*, 213; Harris, *The Kingfish*, 168–69.

202 *He stripped parish sheriffs of the custody of ballot boxes*   Martin, *Dynasty*, 123–24.

202 *"shoot and kill any person known or suspected"*   Associated Press newspaper clipping, 13 Aug. 1934, HPL Papers, Mss. 2005, LSU LLMVC, Scrapbook #18.

202 *Huey angered many legislators*   Harris, *The Kingfish*, 170–71.

202 *In November 1934, voters overwhelmingly approved*   Jeansonne, *Messiah of the Masses*, 138.

203 *"I'm here in the uniform of the people"*   Davis, *Huey Long*, 213.

203 *Still needing more revenue to fund his political machine*   Various newspaper clippings, HPL Papers, Mss. 2005, LSU LLMVC, Scrapbook #18; Jeansonne, *Messiah of the Masses*, 140; Martin, *Dynasty*, 123–24; Sindler, *Huey Long's Louisiana*, 89–90.

203 *Huey returned to Washington confident*   *New Orleans Tribune*, 13 June 1934.

203 *On June 21, Huey rushed back to Baton Rouge*   *Baton Rouge State-Times*, 21 June 1934.

203 *When he left the state, his machine faltered*   Graham, *Huey Long*, 98; Swing, *Forerunners of American Fascism*, 81.

203 *After arriving in the capital, he took charge of every bill*   Cortner, *The Kingfish and the Constitution*, 76; *New Orleans Times-Picayune*, 4 July 1934, HPL Papers, Mss. 2005, LSU LLMVC, Scrapbook #21; Harrison Jordan, interview, THW Papers, Mss. 2489, LSU LLMVC.

203 *On Monday, July 2, Huey held a meeting*   *Shreveport Times*, 3 July 1934; Beals, *The Story of Huey Long*, 275; Cortner, *The Kingfish and the Constitution*, 79.

204 *"Tell him to hurry up"*   *New York Times*, 17 Aug. 1934; Williams, *Huey Long*, 727.

204 *"The Bible says if the ox gets stuck in the ditch"*   *New Orleans Times-Picayune*, 8 July 1934; Cortner, *The Kingfish and the Constitution*, 86.

204 *"Isn't it true that every tax is passed on to the consumer?"*   *New Orleans Times-Picayune*, 10 July 1934; Robert Angelle, interview, THW Papers, Mss. 2489, LSU LLMVC; Cortner, *The Kingfish and the Constitution*, 88. In 1936, the U.S. Supreme Court declared the newspaper tax unconstitutional in *Grosjean v. American Press Company*, 297 U.S. 233 (1936).

204 *As a bill went smoothly through the House or Senate*   Harris, *The Kingfish*, 167.

205 *"Why don't you bring those three [tax] bills up"*   *New Orleans Times-Picayune*, 8 July 1934.

205 *On the final day of the session, July 12*   Cortner, *The Kingfish and the Constitution*, 76.

205 *He had run roughshod over the legislature*   Brinkley, *Voices of Protest*, 69.

205 *On the Fourth of July, legislators celebrated*   *Chicago Tribune*, 5 July 1934; Waldo Dugas, interview, THW Papers, Mss. 2489, LSU LLMVC.

205 *On the last day of the session*   *Time*, 23 July 1934; *Baton Rouge Advocate*, 12 July 1934.

CHAPTER 13 · A TAX ON LYING

207 *"clad in khaki, with helmets strapped beneath smooth chins"*   Hammond, *Let Freedom Ring*, 218–20.

207 *About two hours later, Mayor Walmsley*   *New Orleans Times-Picayune*, 31 July 1934.

208 *"I warn you, Huey Long, you cringing coward"*   Various newspaper clippings, HPL Papers, Mss. 2005, LSU LLMVC, Scrapbook #18; Sindler, *Huey Long's Louisiana*, 91; Martin, *Dynasty*, 125.

208 *"they camped right out there in our garage"*   Boulard, *Huey Long Invades New Orleans*, 151.

208 *One of Huey's motives for invading New Orleans*   Davis, *Huey Long*, 205.

208 *"By order of the twenty-seven laws passed by the legislature"*   *New York Times*, 8 Sept. 1934.

209 *A week before, Huey had ordered the legislature*   Davis, *Huey Long*, 221; *New Orleans Item*, 6 Sept. 1939.

209 *Wearing a striped straw hat*   *New Orleans Times-Picayune*, 1 Sept. 1934; *New Orleans Tribune*, 1 Sept. 1934.

209 *Soon after dark on September 2*   *New York Sun*, 10 Sept. 1934, HPL Papers, Mss. 2005, LSU LLMVC, Scrapbook #17; *New Orleans Times-Picayune*, 31 July 1934.

209 *Fifty of his national guardsmen filled the lobby*   Davis, *Huey Long*, 222.

209 *George Reyer (1895–1979)*   At thirty-six, named police superintendent of New Orleans and one of the youngest police chiefs in the nation. Reyer was a competent, fair man with a long memory and an iron nerve. He joined the police force in 1916 after being a streetcar conductor. By 1925 he was detective captain; 1928, night supervisor; 1930 chief of detectives; and the next year police superintendent. He was forced into retirement by political pressure in 1946 when de Lesseps "Chep" Morrison succeeded Robert Maestri as mayor.

209 *Huey grilled the chief about his lavish lifestyle*   *Washington Herald*, 15 Sept. 1934.

209 *"Take off your coat, Chief"*   *New Orleans Times-Picayune*, 11 Sept. 1934; George Reyer, interview, THW Papers, Mss. 2489, LSU LLMVC.

209 *While Huey was holding his hearings*   *New Orleans States*, 2 Aug. 1934.

210 *Two nights after Molony arrived*   Boulard, *Huey Long Invades New Orleans*, 123.

210 *"as peaceful as a Quaker village on a Sunday morning"*   *New York Times*, 12 Sept. 1934.

210 *"Without that agreement who knows what might"*   Boulard, *Huey Long Invades New Orleans*, 154, 170, 173, 162, attributed to James Gillis.

211 *During the campaign, Huey supported John Overton's brother*   Fried, *FDR and His Enemies*, 75.

211 *Ignoring state law* Harris, *The Kingfish*, 178.

211 *"Goddamnit, at least try to look like a judge"* Robert Angelle, interview, THW Papers, Mss. 2489, LSU LLMVC.

211 *"John, if you don't get better by tomorrow morning"* E. P. Roy, interview, 20 Mar. 1961, THW Papers, Mss. 2489, LSU LLMVC.

211 *Huey, along with his brother Earl* Martin, *Dynasty*, 129; Hermann Deutsch, "Huey Long for President," newspaper clipping dated 16 Oct. 1934, HPL Papers, Mss. 2005, LSU LLMVC, Scrapbook #17.

211 *"Freedom of speech is one thing"* Hair, *The Kingfish and His Realm*, 279.

212 *"always hit the big man first"* Rupert Peyton, interview, 28 Jan. 1958, Baton Rouge, THW Papers, Mss. 2489, LSU LLMVC.

212 *Soon after becoming governor, he ordered* *New York Times*, 16 Feb. 1933.

212 *When the communist newspaper the* **Daily Worker** Haas, "Huey Long and the Communists," 37.

212 *In February 1933, Huey lost his temper* Charles Frampton, interview, THW Papers, Mss. 2489, LSU LLMVC; Heleniak, "Local Reaction to the Great Depression in New Orleans," 305; *New Orleans Item*, 5 Feb. 1933.

212 *During the 1930 regular legislative session* Cortner, *The Kingfish and the Constitution*, 4; *Editor & Publisher*, 13 Sept. 1930, 48; *Near v. Minnesota* (283 U.S. 697, 1931).

212 *On August 24, 1933, Huey released the first issue* Sindler, *Huey Long's Louisiana*, 85.

213 *"Take those lying* **Times-Picayune, Shreveport Times**" Various newspaper clippings, HPL Papers, Mss. 2005, LSU LLMVC, Scrapbook #24; Cortner, *The Kingfish and the Constitution*, 73.

213 *"It's a tax on lying"* Davis, *Huey Long*, 213; *Shreveport Times*, 3 July 1934; Cortner, *The Kingfish and the Constitution*, 79. In 1936, the U.S. Supreme Court declared the newspaper tax unconstitutional in *Grosjean v. American Press Company*, 297 U.S. 233 (1936).

214 *"We are treated to the rotten spectacle of his piscatorial majesty"* *New Orleans Item*, 6 July 1934.

214 *"a spite bill pure and simple"* *New Orleans Times-Picayune*, 10 July 1934; *Baton Rouge Advocate*, 10 July 1934.

214 *"the only purpose of this tax is to warn every paper in the state"* *New Orleans Times-Picayune*, 6 July 1934.

214 *Huey personally cast the vote* Cortner, *The Kingfish and the Constitution*, 88; *New Orleans Times-Picayune*, 10 July 1934; *Grosjean v. American Press Company*, 297 U.S. 233 (1936); Jeansonne, *Messiah of the Masses*, 138.

214 *When the bill reached the Senate floor* *New Orleans Times-Picayune*, 7–8 July 1934; Cortner, *The Kingfish and the Constitution*, 85–86.

214 *"Freedom of the press will survive this assault"* *Monroe News-Star*, 10 July 1934; *New Orleans Item*, 10 July 1934. A three-judge federal court heard the *Grosjean* case on Huey's newspaper advertising tax and rendered a decision 22 Mar. 1935 that partially favored the newspapers.

215 *Eight months later, on March 22, 1935* Cortner, *The Kingfish and the Constitution*, 142, 168.

215 *On a fall afternoon in November 1934* Abe Mickal, interview, THW Papers, Mss.

2489, LSU LLMVC; Williams, *Huey Long*, 775; *New Orleans Times-Picayune*, 11 Nov. 1934.

216 *During a special legislative session a week later* Davis, *Huey Long*, 226.

216 *"a mockery of constitutional government and democracy"* *New Orleans Item*, 16 Nov. 1934.

216 *"I'll fire any student that dares to say a word against me"* *New York Times*, 5 Dec. 1934.

216 *When President Smith hired Helen Gilkison* Cortner, *The Kingfish and the Constitution*, 96–97; Beals, *The Story of Huey Long*, 388.

216 *"We're living under a dictatorship and the best thing"* Jeansonne, *Messiah of the Masses*, 99.

216 *The students later enrolled at the University of Missouri* Carl Corbin, interview, THW Papers, Mss. 2489, LSU LLMVC. Corbin was a member of the *Reveille* staff.

216 *By this time, Huey held a tight grip* Joe Cawthorn, interview, THW Papers, Mss. 2489, LSU LLMVC; Dave McGuire, interview, 14 Mar. 1960, THW Papers, Mss. 2489, LSU LLMVC.

217 *Kennedy was the law student who earlier published* *Newsweek*, 5 Jan. 1935, 34; *Baton Rouge State-Times*, 2 June 1930; *Baton Rouge Advocate*, 18 Nov. 1930.

217 *"If you get a man scared enough"* Paul C. Young, oral history interview, 1980, Baton Rouge, Mss. 4700.0066, LSU LLMVC.

217 *On August 15, 1934, the Kingfish strode into a meeting* *Baton Rouge Advocate*, 15–16 Aug. 1934.

217 *In three short days, the legislature passed all thirty* *Baton Rouge Advocate*, 18 Aug. 1934.

217 *"that every day hereafter we want a telegraph report"* Letter from E. A. Tamm to J. Edgar Hoover, 17 Aug. 1934, Federal Bureau of Investigation, "Huey P. Long," File #62-32509.

217 *"there was a fight on the floor of the House"* Letter from J. Edgar Hoover to Marvin McIntyre, assistant secretary to the president, 19 Aug. 1934, Federal Bureau of Investigation, "Huey P. Long," File #62-32509.

218 *On November 6, Louisiana voters overwhelmingly* Williams, *Huey Long*, 738.

218 *On November 12, Huey called the legislature back* Davis, *Huey Long*, 225.

218 *"When will we know what these bills are all about?"* Various newspaper clippings, HPL Papers, Mss. 2005, LSU LLMVC, Scrapbook #23.

218 *One of Huey's spite bills* *New Orleans Times-Picayune*, 25 June 1933.

218 *After the legislature created his new State Bar Association* In September 1936, after Huey's death, the American Bar Association disavowed Huey's bar association members and reseated members of the old Louisiana State Bar Association.

218 *During the session Huey also limited the salary* Davis, *Huey Long*, 229.

218 *"There's lots of things in these bills"* *Boston Globe*, 17 Nov. 1934, HPL Papers, Mss. 2005, LSU LLMVC, Scrapbook #18; *New Orleans Times-Picayune*, 16 Nov. 1934.

218 *A month later, on Sunday, December 16* Harry Rabenhorst, interview, 3 July 1963, Baton Rouge, THW Papers, Mss. 2489, LSU LLMVC; Lawrence M. Jones, inter-

view, 28 Dec. 1961, Washington, D.C., THW Papers, Mss. 2489, LSU LLMVC; Davis, *Huey Long*, 229; Swing, *Forerunners of American Fascism*, 63.

219 *He aimed many of his thirty-three bills*   Richard Leche, interview, THW Papers, Mss. 2489, LSU LLMVC.

219 *Soon after the special session*   Swing, *Forerunners of American Fascism*, 34; Beals, *The Story of Huey Long*, 220, 266; Harris, *The Kingfish*, 276.

219 *Among the thirty-three bills*   Martin, *Dynasty*, 126–28.

219 *At the first meeting of the Budget Committee*   Williams, *Huey Long*, 855.

219 *On Huey's orders, the legislature passed a law*   Beals, *The Story of Huey Long*, 336, 343.

220 *During the session, Huey ordered the Public Service Commission*   Davis, *Huey Long*, 238; Martin, *Dynasty*, 131.

220 *"I admit that I'm the best lawyer in Louisiana"*   Williams, *Huey Long*, 822–23.

220 *He told his aides that he would make Baton Rouge*   Martin, *Dynasty*, 131.

220 *At their first meeting the new Longite majority*   Bonnie V. Baker, interview, THW Papers, Mss. 2489, LSU LLMVC.

220 *Another bill allowed Huey's state police*   Davis, *Huey Long*, 227.

220 *He also found time to fire a motorcycle policeman*   George Bernard Rice, *True Story of Huey P. Long*, 1935, rare pamphlet in Louisiana and Lower Mississippi Valley Collections, Louisiana State University.

220 *At six in the morning on the last day of the special session*   Charles Frampton, interview, THW Papers, Mss. 2489, LSU LLMVC.

221 *That afternoon, a routine bill calling for the codification*   Harris, *The Kingfish*, 195–96.

221 *The enactment of the oil processing tax*   Martin, *Dynasty*, 131–32; George Wallace, interview, THW Papers, Mss. 2489, LSU LLMVC.

221 *Within a month, Standard Oil began laying off*   Davis, *Huey Long*, 231.

221 *Sometime around 1934*   According to at least one source, Huey and Costello may have met at the Sands Point Club on the night Huey received his black eye.

221 *Costello needed a new market for his gambling racket*   Kurtz, "Crime in Louisiana History: Myth and Reality," 370–71; Bridges, *Bad Bet on the Bayou*, 29–31.

222 *"Ninety-five percent of the people in this grand"*   Bridges, *Bad Bet on the Bayou*, 16.

222 *By late 1935, over a thousand of the slot machines*   Key, *Southern Politics in State and Nation*, 163; Davis, *Huey Long*, 31–35; Fox, *Blood and Power: Organized Crime in Twentieth-Century America*, 138, 373.

222 *Treasury Secretary Henry Morgenthau instructed Elmer Irey*   Irey, *The Tax Dodgers*, 91, 94; Hair, *The Kingfish and His Realm*, 286.

222 *"the country's most skilled and daring detectives"*   *New Orleans Item*, 19 Aug. 1934.

222 *By October 1934, Irey won federal indictments*   Irey, *The Tax Dodgers*, 95; Renwick, "The Longs' Legislative Lieutenants," 236.

223 *A federal jury later found Joe Fisher guilty*   Boulard, *Huey Long Invades New Orleans*, 178; Fried, *FDR and His Enemies*, 102; Irey, *The Tax Dodgers*, 95; Hair, *The Kingfish and His Realm*, 286.

223 *Abe Shushan*   Short, stout, and steadfastly loyal to Huey, Abe Shushan contributed generously to Huey's campaigns. Huey appointed Shushan president of the Orleans Parish Levee Board and named the New Orleans airport for him.

After Shushan went to prison for mail fraud, the airport was renamed New Orleans Airport.

223   *They accused Weiss, president of the Dock Board*   New Haven Journal Courier, 15 Dec. 1934, LSU LLMVC, Scrapbook #18; Davis, *Huey Long*, 229; Graham, *Huey Long*, 90; Swing, *Forerunners of American Fascism*, 75.

223   *On March 7, 1935, Attorney General Homer Cummings*   Davis, *Huey Long*, 263.

223   *Much of Irey's evidence against Huey*   Irey, *The Tax Dodgers*, 95–96.

224   *Huey's share, costing nothing*   Mann, *Legacy to Power*, 43; Davis, *Huey Long*, 228. After his election in 1940, reform governor Sam Jones ordered an investigation into the sale of state mineral rights during Huey's tenure. The Louisiana attorney general concluded that "there was no evidence of fraud involved in the issuance of the leases." Governor Jones overrode the attorney general's opinion and instituted litigation against Independent Oil and Gas Company, Inc., the successor of Win or Lose. After ten years of legal maneuvering, a compromise stipulated that over one million acres of mineral leases originally funneled through Win or Lose would be surrendered back to the state. Other lawsuits ensued. In 1979, the Louisiana Sixteenth Judicial District Court concluded that during the period that the leases were made, there was "no evidence of either fraud or conspiracy" and that there was no state law that prohibited the disposition of the leases by Win or Lose.

224   *Their monopoly over leases helped convert the small Texas Oil Company*   Jeansonne, *Messiah of the Masses*, 161; Jeansonne, "Huey P. Long, Robin Hood or Tyrant? A Critique of Huey Long," 2; Keyes, *All This Is Louisiana*, 21.

224   *On Saturday, September 7, 1935*   Irey, *The Tax Dodgers*, 96.

CHAPTER 14 · TEAR-DIMMED EYES AND HUNGRY SOULS

225   *Kathleen Gibbons, Mayor Walmsley's niece*   Boulard, *Huey Long Invades New Orleans*, 190, interview with Kathleen Gibbons.

225   *"We used to try to think of ways to kill [Huey]"*   Waldron, *Hodding Carter*, 52. Betty Carter was the wife of Hodding Carter, the anti-Long editor of the *Hammond Daily Courier*.

226   *"If they got to leave"*   Baton Rouge State-Times, 5 Jan. 1935.

226   *there was a wildness in the air*   Burns, *Huey Long* (video recording).

226   *That week, several dozen of Huey's more angry enemies*   New Orleans Times-Picayune, 19 Jan. 1935; Harris, *The Kingfish*, 197–202.

226   *"The fellows won't march"*   New Orleans Times-Picayune, 27 Jan. 1935.

226   *Huey ordered National Guard troops sent to Baton Rouge*   Davis, *Huey Long*, 233–34; Carleton, *River Capital*, 166.

227   *That afternoon, Huey told O. K. Allen to declare martial law*   New Orleans Item, 27 Jan. 1935; New York Times, 27 Jan. 1935; Raymond Fleming, interview, THW Papers, Mss. 2489, LSU LLMVC; Louis Guerre, interview, THW Papers, Mss. 2489, LSU LLMVC.

227   *On the following day, a cool Saturday afternoon*   Louie Jones, interview, THW Papers, Mss. 2489, LSU LLMVC; New York Times, 26 Jan. 1935; Kane, *Louisiana Hayride*, 113–14.

227   *"I don't wish to discuss anything except fishing"*   Newsweek, 9 Feb. 1935, 11.

227 *"Our men of affairs and the powers that be"* *Washington Post*, 17 Jan. 1935, HPL Papers, Mss. 2005, LSU LLMVC, Scrapbook #17.

227 *"with the fury of a fire-breathing monster"* *Congressional Record*, 74th Cong., 1st Sess., 2943; *Los Angeles Times*, 18 Jan. 1935, HPL Papers, Mss. 2005, LSU LLMVC, Scrapbook #17.

228 *Emphasizing the few facts he possessed* Williams, *Huey Long*, 681.

228 *"We wound up with all of Europe under dictatorship"* *Congressional Record*, 74th Cong., 1st Sess., 1114–1133; Gillette, "Huey Long and the Chaco War," 309–11.

228 *His attacks were now head-on, barefaced, brutish* Kane, *Louisiana Hayride*, 118; *New Orleans Item*, 14 Apr. 1935.

228 *"eighteen squares long and sixteen squares wide"* *New York Evening Journal*, 8 Jan. 1935; *New York Daily News*, 8 Jan. 1935, HPL Papers, Mss. 2005, LSU LLMVC, Scrapbook #17.

228 *"He's a liar and a faker!"* Long, *Vital Speeches of the Day*, 25 Mar. 1931, 393.

229 *"Don't you remember when Mr. Hoover proposed"* Martin, *Dynasty*, 136; *Newsweek*, 16 Mar. 1935, 5–7.

229 *During the first three months of 1935* Christman, *Kingfish to America, Share Our Wealth*, 103.

229 *Titling his speech "Farley, a Menace to Clean Politics"* *Congressional Record*, 74th Cong., 1st Sess., 1894–96.

229 *When he accused Farley of forcing federal employees* Harris, *The Kingfish*, 182.

229 *On Sunday night, March 3* Davis, *Huey Long*, 248–50; Jones, "An Administration Under Fire: The Long-Farley Affair of 1935," 6–7; Kane, *Louisiana Hayride*, 118.

229 *"If I must kneel to such crooks"* Brinkley, *Voices of Protest*, 75.

230 *"Jim can take the corns off your feet"* Kane, *Louisiana Hayride*, 118.

230 *The Senate soon tired of the attacks* Watkins, *Righteous Pilgrim*, 435; Beals, *The Story of Huey Long*, 399.

230 *"Jim was the biggest rooster in the yard"* Jones, "An Administration Under Fire: The Long-Farley Affair of 1935," 16.

230 *In February the president ordered the Federal Emergency* Snyder, "Huey Long and the Presidential Election of 1936," 139.

230 *The president suspended $2.5 million* Jones, "An Administration Under Fire: The Long-Farley Affair of 1935," 15; Davis, *Huey Long*, 245.

230 *Roosevelt recruited General Hugh Johnson* *New York Times*, 5 Mar. 1935; *Newsweek*, 16 Mar. 1935, 5–7.

230 *"Back in the kitchen," he declared* Jones, "An Administration Under Fire: The Long-Farley Affair of 1935," 14.

231 *By the time he finished, Johnson looked heavy-handed* *New York Times*, 8 Mar. 1935; Bennett, *Demagogues in the Depression*, 81.

231 *"He was so tight he could hardly walk"* Murphy Roden, interview, THW Papers, Mss. 2489, LSU LLMVC.

231 *Foreign embassies delivered whiskey by the case* Charles Frampton, interview, THW Papers, Mss. 2489, LSU LLMVC; Don Devol, interview, 7 Oct. 1982, Washington, D.C., THW Papers, Mss. 2489, LSU LLMVC.

231 *"Liquor makes me soft"* *New York Times*, 10 Feb. 1935.

231 *Several days a week, just after dawn* Various newspaper clippings, HPL Papers, Mss. 2005, LSU LLMVC, Scrapbooks #17 and #29.

232 *"the savageness of a mad bull"* Moley, *27 Masters of Politics,* 221.

232 *"It's like challenging a buzz saw"* Boston Post, 10 Mar. 1935.

232 *"None of them has a stomach for a fight"* New York Daily News, 8 Jan. 1935, HPL Papers, Mss. 2005, LSU LLMVC, Scrapbooks #17.

232 *"the smartest lunatic I ever saw in my whole life"* Schlesinger, *The Age of Roosevelt,* 42; Graham, *Huey Long,* 147; Krock, *Memoirs,* 175–76.

233 *As he rose to speak for an amendment* New York Times, 14 Mar. 1935.

233 *"Mr. President, I am not undertaking to answer the charge"* Sindler, *Huey Long's Louisiana,* 101; Graham, *Huey Long,* 144; Newsweek, 19 Jan. 1935, 8.

234 *Special sessions of the Louisiana legislature* Haas, "Huey Long and the Communists," 32.

234 *"Professor Long's Puppet Show"* Clay, *Coozan Dudley LeBlanc,* 101; Walter Davenport, "Too High and Too Mighty," 7.

234 *Few legislators seemed to care* Garlin, *The Real Huey P. Long,* 12.

234 *The House Ways and Means Committee approved* Davis, *Huey Long,* 214, 269; Frank Peterman, interview, 13 Oct. 1959, Alexandria, THW Papers, Mss. 2489, LSU LLMVC.

234 *Mayor Walmsley soon had to place six thousand* New York Times, 23 June 1935.

235 *He doubled the inspection fee paid by public utilities* Harris, *The Kingfish,* 275.

235 *According to one of Huey's workers* W. A. Cooper, THW Papers, Mss. 2489, LSU LLMVC.

235 *By this time, bonds had overtaken taxes* Graham, *Huey Long,* 95, 167–68; Swing, *Forerunners of American Fascism;* Sindler, *Huey Long's Louisiana,* 106; Opotowsky, *The Longs of Louisiana,* 86.

235 *He agreed to rebate 4 of the 5 cents* Davis, *Huey Long,* 231; Baton Rouge State-Times, 8 Jan. 1935; Harris, *The Kingfish,* 200–202; Beals, *The Story of Huey Long,* 335.

235 *On the Senate floor, Scott Heywood* John T. Hood, interview, THW Papers, Mss. 2489, LSU LLMVC.

236 *On April 17, Huey called* Sindler, *Huey Long's Louisiana,* 92; Beals, *The Story of Huey Long,* 324.

236 *At one point during the House session* Beals, *The Story of Huey Long,* 327.

236 *During the April 1935 special session* Carter, "Huey Long: American Dictator," in Leighton, ed., *The Aspirin Age,* 436.

237 *"When this this ugly thing is boiled down in its own juices"* Louisiana House Calendar, 17 Apr. 1935, 9; New Orleans Times-Picayune, 18 Apr. 1935; Kane, *Louisiana Hayride,* 131.

237 *When the legislators arrived in Baton Rouge* Baton Rouge State-Times, 5–6 July 1935; New Orleans Times-Picayune, 6 July 1935; Campbell, "Huey Long Chokes New Orleans," 94–95.

238 *Walmsley could not even hire his own secretary* New Orleans Tribune, 5–6 July 1935; New York Times, 5–6 July 1935; Jeansonne, *Messiah of the Masses,* 140, 153.

238 *"I will never let a draft dodger like Long"* Williams, *Huey Long,* 852. Walmsley referred to the fact that Huey did not join the armed forces during World War I,

obtaining a Class IV draft deferment for supporting a wife and child. "I wasn't mad at anybody over there," Huey declared later.

238 *"Walmsley is a political corpse and don't know it"* New Orleans Times-Picayune, 13, 14, 30 July 1935; *New York Times,* 25 July 1935. Earhart abandoned Walmsley later in the year. The mayor resisted pressure from the Old Regulars to quit until the summer of 1936 when he resigned, allowing Robert Maestri to become mayor.

238 *Two days later, a sizzling New Orleans summer day* New Orleans Tribune, 13 July 1935; *New Orleans Times-Picayune,* 30 July 1935; Harris, *The Kingfish,* 172.

239 *The Great Depression spawned a number of reformers* Watkins, *Righteous Pilgrim,* 414; Bennett, *Demagogues in the Depression,* 4–5.

239 *Of the firebrand reformers, only Huey Long* Kane, *Louisiana Hayride,* 126; Bennett, *Demagogues in the Depression,* 144; Watkins, *Righteous Pilgrim,* 415.

240 *"With Hoover it was stupidity"* Various newspaper clippings, HPL Papers, Mss. 2005, LSU LLMVC, Scrapbook #18.

240 *When University of South Carolina students jeered him* New York Times, 24 Mar. 1935.

240 *"He seems to have the integrity"* Ellis O. Jones, "The Truth About Huey Long," 2.

240 *Philip Johnson (1906–2005)* Born in Cleveland, Ohio. Educated at Harvard. Considered the dean of American architects and the man who set the tone in American corporate architecture for the latter twentieth century. Devotee of architectural modernism in his many soaring skyscrapers. Died age ninety-eight at his famous Glass House, in New Canaan, Connecticut. Johnson later renounced his Nazi sympathies.

240 *"I became what was later called fascist"* Adam Nossiter, "Onetime Fascist, Modernist Once Huey Long Fan"; Schulze, *Philip Johnson,* 114–19; Welch, *Philip Johnson and Texas,* 17.

241 *On April 1, 1935, his smiling face appeared on the cover* "Share the Wealth Wave," *Time,* 1 Apr. 1935, 15–17; *New York Herald Tribune,* 27 Apr. 1935, HPL Papers, Mss. 2005, LSU LLMVC, Scrapbook #17.

241 *"I can take this Roosevelt," he boasted* Bennett, *Demagogues in the Depression,* 128.

242 *"I could take this state like a whirlwind"* Brinkley, *Voices of Protest,* 237.

242 *Three days later, on Labor Day* New Orleans Tribune, 1 Sept. 1935; *Los Angeles Evening Herald & Express,* 13 Aug. 1935. By August 1935 Huey had admitted to several Senate colleagues and newspapermen that he would enter the 1936 presidential race.

242 *"your next President will be Huey Long"* New York Times, 28 Aug. 1935.

242 *Instead, he revealed to his close supporters* Jeansonne, "Challenge to the New Deal: Huey P. Long and the Redistribution of National Wealth," 334.

242 *"I'm going to abolish the Electoral College"* Davis, *Huey Long,* 22–24.

242 *From Oklahoma City, Huey took the train to Dallas* Cortner, *The Kingfish and the Constitution,* 154.

242 *Ray Daniel, a writer friendly to Huey* Charles Frampton, interview, THW Papers, Mss. 2489, LSU LLMVC.

242 *Partly satire and partly an expression* Bennett, *Demagogues in the Depression,* 121.

CHAPTER 15 · NUTS RUNNING AMERICA

244 *To Huey, the truth was immaterial*   Parent, *Inside the Carnival*, 69.

244 *"just leveled down and talked his natural way"*   Bozeman, "Winn Parish as I Have Known It," *Winn Parish Enterprise*, 25 Apr. 1957, vol. 1, #30, Bozeman scrapbooks, State Library of Louisiana.

244 *Theodore Bilbo (1877–1947)*   Studied at Vanderbilt University and the University of Michigan. Schoolteacher in Mississippi for five years; attorney. Mississippi state senator, 1908–1912; lieutenant governor, 1912–1916; governor, 1916–1920 and 1928–1932. Elected to U.S. Senate and served from 1934 until his death in 1947.

244 *Thomas Watson (1856–1922)*   Taught school in Georgia, studied law, practiced in Thomson, Georgia. Later was magazine publicist and novelist. Served as Georgia state representative, 1882–1883; elected to U.S. Congress as Populist and served 1891–1893. Unsuccessful for reelection. Elected as Democrat to U.S. Senate in 1921 and served until his death in 1922. In his early years Watson was characterized as a liberal but later emerged as a force for white supremacy.

244 *He recognized that his uplifting economic message*   Parent, *Inside the Carnival*, 25.

244 *"At least we got something"*   Kane, *Louisiana Hayride*, 137.

245 *"He was like a racehorse with a bad strain"*   Oliver P. Carriere, interview, THW Papers, Mss. 2489, LSU LLMVC.

245 *Power became the end in itself*   Carter, "Huey Long: American Dictator," in Leighton, ed., *The Aspirin Age*, 263; Leslie, "Louisiana Hayride Revisited," 286.

245 *"The end justifies the means"*   Jeansonne, *Messiah of the Masses*, 142.

245 *He virtually destroyed the ability of any opposition*   Moley, *After Seven Years*, 304–05.

245 *On several occasions, the* New York Times *predicted*   *New York Times*, 28 Mar. 1929, 6 July 1930, 15 July 1930, 31 Aug. 1930.

246 *"The billionaires are becoming bigger billionaires"*   Harris, *The Kingfish*, 181–82; Jeansonne, *Messiah of the Masses*, 5, 68–69, 92; Mann, *Legacy to Power*, 10.

246 *American political traditions never had gained*   Beals, *The Story of Huey Long*, 15.

246 *Under the French and Spanish*   Carter, "Huey Long: American Dictator," in Leighton, ed., *The Aspirin Age*, 343–44.

246 *In later years, few Louisianans were surprised*   Michie, "Huey Long's Heritage," 108.

246 *Indeed, in 1935 the majority of the people*   Harris, *The Kingfish*, 208.

246 *"Wages in the state have declined"*   "Labor Notes, Huey Long and Labor," 192.

247 *"a laboring man's friend like a vulture is to a lamb"*   Speech by Lee Thomas, 24 Sept. 1927, in Washington, Louisiana, James Aswell Papers, Mss. 1408, LSU LLMVC.

247 *In recent years, Huey prevented passage*   Kane, *Louisiana Hayride*, 142; Garlin, *The Real Huey P. Long*, 22.

247 *"picking cotton is fun for the kids, anyway"*   Jeansonne, "Challenge to the New Deal: Huey P. Long and the Redistribution of National Wealth," 337.

247 *He threatened to use the National Guard*   Haas, "Huey Long and the Communists," 33; Beals, *The Story of Huey Long*, 21, 347.

247 *At a Ku Klux Klan convention in Atlanta* Kane, *Louisiana Hayride,* 119; Associated Press clipping, 17 Aug. 1934, HPL Papers, Mss. 2005, LSU LLMVC, Scrapbook #28.

248 *"Don't compare me with that so-and-so"* King, "Huey Long: The Louisiana Kingfish," 160.

248 *"I would describe a demagogue as a politician"* Bennett, *Demagogues in the Depression,* 122; Kane, *Louisiana Hayride,* 140; Swing, *Forerunners of American Fascism,* 73.

248 **The Mobile Register** *reported that a "ruthless dictatorship"* *Mobile Register,* 31 Jan. 1935, HPL Papers, Mss. 2005, LSU LLMVC, Scrapbook #18; *Little Rock Gazette,* 15 Nov. 1934, HPL Papers, Mss. 2005, LSU LLMVC, Scrapbook #18.

248 *An Iowa newspaper characterized Louisiana* Brinkley, *Voices of Protest,* 79–80; Jeansonne, *Messiah of the Masses,* 139; Boulard, *Huey Long Invades New Orleans,* 146–47.

248 *The president did not abandon efforts* Beals, *The Story of Huey Long,* 260; *Memphis Commercial Appeal,* 23 Jan. 1933.

248 *An intense anti-Long movement was mounting* Harris, *The Kingfish,* 207.

249 *"to investigate expenditures of candidates for the House"* *Washington Post,* 28 Aug. 1935.

249 *While all of these sizable accomplishments took place* Beals, *The Story of Huey Long,* 21; Howard, *Political Tendencies in Louisiana,* 130.

249 *After 1931, true reform faltered* Cash, *The Mind of the South,* 284; Jeansonne, *Messiah of the Masses,* 137; Williams, *Huey Long,* 552, note 5.

250 *"Growth will be almost magic"* Beals, *The Story of Huey Long,* 340.

250 *Many of his bold promises, however, turned out* Jeansonne, "Challenge to the New Deal: Huey P. Long and the Redistribution of National Wealth," 336–37. In 1929, per capita wealth in Louisiana was $1,449; in 1934 it had fallen to $1,127.

250 *Sadly, Louisiana possessed the resources to lift* Jeansonne, "Huey P. Long, Robin Hood or Tyrant? A Critique of Huey Long," 29; Keyes, *All This Is Louisiana,* 21.

251 *Although he no longer retained any state office* Campbell, "Huey Long Chokes New Orleans," 93; Harris, *The Kingfish,* 107.

251 *Huey packed the membership of government boards* King, "Huey Long: The Louisiana Kingfish," 158.

251 *Servile legislators rubber-stamped his bills* Snyder, "The Concept of Demagoguery: Huey Long and His Literary Critics," 81.

251 *By now he had defeated most of his legislative foes* Hair, *The Kingfish and His Realm,* 289; Jeansonne, ed., *Huey at 100,* 39.

252 *By 1935, Huey dominated the judiciary* Garlin, *The Real Huey P. Long,* 15.

252 *"If a lawyer takes a case too obnoxious to Long"* Beals, *The Story of Huey Long,* 372.

252 *Huey had wrested control of the state election machinery* Leslie, "Louisiana Hayride Revisited," 282.

252 *Huey controlled the public school system* Beals, *The Story of Huey Long,* 358–60; Jeansonne, ed., *Huey at 100,* 9.

253 *Huey held an economic stranglehold* Kane, *Louisiana Hayride,* 129.

253 *Bank examiners stifled credit from opponents' businesses* Daniell, "The Gentleman from Louisiana," 174.

253 *He far exceeded the ordinary bounds of democratic politics* Brinkley, *Voices of Protest*, 118.

253 *"One man has become the power structure of an American commonwealth"* Long, *Every Man a King*, xxii, attributed to T. Harry Williams.

253 *"the first true dictator out of the soil of America"* Carter, "Huey Long: American Dictator," 343, 363.

253 *"You have to convince them it's for them even if it isn't"* Jeansonne, *Messiah of the Masses*, 50.

254 *In June 1935, as Washington suffocated* *Detroit News*, 12 June 1935, HPL Papers, Mss. 2005, LSU LLMVC, Scrapbook #18.

254 *For the next fifteen and a half hours* *Congressional Record*, 74th Cong., 1st Sess., 9098; Davis, *Huey Long*, 270.

255 *Refusing to relinquish the floor, Huey continued* *Congressional Record*, 74th Cong., 1st Sess., 9093; Williams, *Huey Long*, 376–78; Jeansonne, *Messiah of the Masses*, 156; Beals, *The Story of Huey Long*, 400. In 1908, Robert LaFollette occupied the Senate floor for eighteen straight hours but was relieved by twenty-nine quorum calls and three roll calls. Huey's opponents prevented any respite during his filibuster.

255 *"That would be unusual cruelty under the Bill of Rights"* Burdette, *Filibustering in the Senate*, 3.

255 *"They have not drunk any real coffee"* *Congressional Record*, 74th Cong., 1st Sess., 12 June 1935, 9175.

255 *"We had a wretched exhibition here recently"* Johnson, *The Diary Letters of Hiram Johnson*, letter dated 16 June 1935.

256 *At five-thirty the next morning* Davis, *Huey Long*, 270; "NRA: Huey Long's Filibuster Fails," *Newsweek*, 22 June 1935, 7 8.

256 *From January through August 1935, Huey staged five filibusters* Cortner, *The Kingfish and the Constitution*, 154.

256 *His colleagues regarded him as a pariah* Burdette, *Filibustering in the Senate*, 3, attributed to Senator Henry F. Ashurst of Arizona.

256 *"I have nothing to do"* *Congressional Record*, 74th Cong., 1st Sess., 26 Aug. 1935, 14689–752.

256 *When he said that he was in no hurry* *Congressional Record*, 74th Cong., 1st Sess., 14726.

256 *"Because of your selfish desire to get publicity"* Harris, *The Kingfish*, 263.

256 *On the afternoon of July 17, 1935* *New Orleans States*, 18 July 1935; *New Orleans Item*, 18 July 1935; Frank Manning, interview, New Orleans, THW Papers, Mss. 2489, LSU LLMVC.

257 *Angry city workers had been either laid off* *New Orleans Tribune*, 24 Aug. 1935.

257 *Huey learned of the DeSoto meeting beforehand* John DeArmond, interview, THW Papers, Mss. 2489, LSU LLMVC; Frank Manning, interview, THW Papers, Mss. 2489, LSU LLMVC; Louie Jones, interview, THW Papers, Mss. 2489, LSU LLMVC.

257 *The anti-Long attendees were a mixed lot* Dave Haas, interview, THW Papers, Mss. 2489, LSU LLMVC.

258 *The advertised purpose of the conference* Sindler, *Huey Long's Louisiana*, 96; Kane, *Louisiana Hayride*, 133.

258 *The congressmen condemned Huey's attacks*   Harris, *The Kingfish*, 221–22.

258 *Frank Peterman, Huey's former president pro tem*   Frank Peterman, interview, 13 Oct. 1959, Alexandria, LA, THW Papers, Mss. 2489, LSU LLMVC.

258 *"I don't think it was a murder plot"*   Johnny DeArmond, interview, THW Papers, Mss. 2489, LSU LLMVC.

258 *"Good God, I wish somebody would kill the son of a bitch"*   Carter, "Huey Long: American Dictator," 443; Harris, *The Kingfish*, 221–23.

258 *"A hundred said that the bastard ought to be killed"*   Harry Gamble, interview, THW Papers, Mss. 2489, LSU LLMVC.

258 *Others who were at the DeSoto*   Zinman, *The Day Huey Long Was Shot, September 8, 1935*, 231.

258 *"There were three rooms"*   Dave Haas, interview, THW Papers, Mss. 2489, LSU LLMVC; Sahuc, *The Policeman Who Knew Huey P. Long*. Weiss's family and other witnesses later refuted Haas's version, saying Weiss was in Opelousas and Baton Rouge during the period of the DeSoto meetings.

259 *"We heard about the gun"*   Frank Manning, interview, New Orleans, THW Papers, Mss. 2489, LSU LLMVC.

259 *On August 9, he took the Senate floor*   *Congressional Record*, 74th Cong., 1st Sess., 12786; *American Progress*, Aug. 1935.

259 *Senator Harry Truman, presiding over the Senate that day*   Harry Truman, interview, 24 Nov. 1959, Independence, Missouri, THW Papers, Mss. 2489, LSU LLMVC; Boulard, *Huey Long Invades New Orleans*, 69.

259 *"I would draw in a lottery to go out and kill Long"*   Pavy, *Accident and Deception*, 39; Kane, *Louisiana Hayride*, 132–33.

259 *"Does anyone doubt that President Roosevelt would pardon"*   *Congressional Record*, 74th Cong., 1st Sess., 12786–90.

CHAPTER 16 · STRUCK LIKE A RATTLESNAKE

260 *On Saturday morning, September 7, 1935*   Zinman, *The Day Huey Long Was Shot, September 8, 1935*, 13.

260 *Huey already had forty-two bills drafted*   *Washington Post* clipping, 9 Sept. 1935, Federal Bureau of Investigation, "Huey P. Long," File #62-32509.

261 *"I don't give a damn"*   Brinkley, *Voices of Protest*, 249.

261 *"I can run hell but I can't run St. Landry"*   D. J. Doucet, interview, THW Papers, Mss. 2489, LSU LLMVC.

261 *One of Huey's bills gerrymandered the St. Landry district*   Cortner, *The Kingfish and the Constitution*, 154–55.

261 *A large, jovial man with a gray mustache*   Zinman, *The Day Huey Long Was Shot, September 8, 1935*, 79, 18.

262 *According to a New Orleans printer*   Kane, *Louisiana Hayride*, 133; Joseph B. David, interview, THW Papers, Mss. 2489, LSU LLMVC.

262 *"Huey struck like a rattlesnake but always warned first"*   Joe Fisher, interview, THW Papers, Mss. 2489, LSU LLMVC; Kane, *Louisiana Hayride*, 134.

262 *Just after sunrise on September 8, 1935*   Martin, *Dynasty*, 142.

262 *After the day session, Huey retired*   Harry Gamble, interview, THW Papers, Mss. 2489, LSU LLMVC; James P. O'Connor, Jr., interview, THW Papers, Mss.

2489, LSU LLMVC; Charles Frampton, interview, THW Papers, Mss. 2489, LSU LLMVC; Allen Ellender, interview, THW Papers, Mss. 2489, LSU LLMVC.

262 *The apartment, furnished with a bed*   E. J. Bourg interview, THW Papers, Mss. 2489, LSU LLMVC.

262 *Wearing a dark suit and sporty black-and-white shoes*   Charles Frampton, interview, THW Papers, Mss. 2489, LSU LLMVC.

262 *"You remind me of an old nigger woman"*   Cortner, *The Kingfish and the Constitution*, 155; Zinman, *The Day Huey Long Was Shot, September 8, 1935*, 114–22.

262 *Huey then headed for the governor's office*   Martin, *Dynasty*, 144.

263 *As Huey approached the governor's office suite*   Charles Frampton, interview, THW Papers, Mss. 2489, LSU LLMVC; Williams, *Huey Long*, 864.

263 *"He flashed among us"*   John Fournet, interview, THW Papers, Mss. 2489, LSU LLMVC.

263 *The man held a straw Panama hat in his left hand*   Charles Frampton, interview, THW Papers, Mss. 2489, LSU LLMVC; Jeansonne, *Messiah of the Masses*, 172; Zinman, *The Day Huey Long Was Shot, September 8, 1935*, 32.

263 *"Kingfish, what's the matter?"*   James P. O'Connor, Jr., interview, 28 June 1957, New Orleans, THW Papers, Mss. 2489, LSU LLMVC; Zinman, *The Day Huey Long Was Shot, September 8, 1935*, 107.

263 *O'Connor helped Huey through the door*   John Fournet, interview, THW Papers, Mss. 2489, LSU LLMVC; Charles Frampton, interview, THW Papers, Mss. 2489, LSU LLMVC.

264 *The slender young man whose dead body lay*   Carleton, *River Capital*, 169.

264 *Weiss had never met Huey*   Zinman, *The Day Huey Long Was Shot, September 8, 1935*, 86; Kane, *Louisiana Hayride*, 134.

264 *"Third Street was just packed"*   Ruth Laney, LSU oral history interview, 24 June 1994, Baton Rouge, Mss. 4700.0476, LSU LLMVC.

265 *"What a scene, here was a man dying"*   John Fournet, interview, THW Papers, Mss. 2489, LSU LLMVC; Fred Dent, interview, THW Papers, Mss. 2489, LSU LLMVC; Jeansonne, *Messiah of the Masses*, 174.

265 *Huey had a small puncture wound in his abdomen*   James P. O'Connor, Jr., interview, THW Papers, Mss. 2489, LSU LLMVC; John Fournet, interview, THW Papers, Mss. 2489, LSU LLMVC.

265 *In New Orleans, Huey's family was spending*   Mann, *Legacy to Power*, x.

265 *Seymour Weiss, in New Orleans supervising*   Boulard, *Huey Long Invades New Orleans*, 195; Zinman, *The Day Huey Long Was Shot, September 8, 1935*, 141–42.

265 *Just after midnight, as Huey's family*   Mann, *Legacy to Power*, xi–xii; Kane, *Louisiana Hayride*, 134.

265 *Vidrine, talented but inexperienced*   Jeansonne, *Messiah of the Masses*, 175.

EPILOGUE

267 *When sociologist Gunnar Myrdal traveled*   Myrdal, *An American Dilemma*, 903, note b.

267 *Many anti-Longs believed Carl Weiss did not shoot Huey*   John G. Appel, interview, THW Papers, Mss. 2489, LSU LLMVC.

267 *Others, like Fournet, Chick Frampton*   George Beckom, interview, THW Papers, Mss. 2489, LSU LLMVC.

268 *"There were three holes in him"*   Perry Craddock, interview, THW Papers, Mss. 2489, LSU LLMVC.

268 *At four in the afternoon on Thursday*   Jeansonne, *Messiah of the Masses*, 176–77.

268 *"The blood which dropped upon our soil shall seal our hearts"*   Kane, *Louisiana Hayride*, 136.

268 *Huey's death created a huge political vacuum*   "The Man Who Understood Huey," 22.

269 *Before his death, Huey predicted that his cronies*   Jeansonne, *Messiah of the Masses*, 183.

270 *A federal investigation began in 1939*   Kane, *Louisiana Hayride*, 7.

270 *Federal prosecutors eventually tried Huey's former benefactor*   Jeansonne, *Messiah of the Masses*, 183.

270 *"When I took the oath of office"*   Kane, *Louisiana Hayride*, 145.

270 *In June 1939, James Monroe Smith*   Ibid. 385.

271 *In 1939 Earl, then lieutenant governor, became governor*   Parent, *Inside the Carnival*, 92; Mann, *Legacy to Power*, 81. By the time Earl left office, New Orleans contributed 25 percent of the state's tax income, yet received less than 10 percent of the revenue.

REFERENCES

BIOGRAPHIES/AUTOBIOGRAPHIES

Beals, Carleton. (1935). *The Story of Huey Long.* New York: Lippincott.

Burns, Ken. (1985). *Huey Long.* Baton Rouge: Louisiana Public Broadcasting (video recording).

Clay, Floyd Martin. (1973). *Coozan Dudley LeBlanc: From Huey Long to Hadacol.* Gretna, LA: Pelican.

Davis, Forrest. (1935). *Huey Long: A Candid Biography.* New York: Dodge.

Dethloff, Henry C., ed. (1976). *Huey P. Long: Southern Demagogue or American Democrat?* Lafayette: University of Southwestern Louisiana.

Deutsch, Herman. (1963). *The Huey Long Murder Case.* Garden City, NY: Doubleday.

Fields, Harvey G. (1945). *A True History of the Life, Works, Assassination, and Death of Huey Pierce Long.* New Orleans: Fields.

Fineran, John K. (1935). *The Career of a Tinpot Napoleon: A Political Biography of Huey P. Long.* New Orleans: John K. Fineran.

Garlin, Sender. (1935). *The Real Huey P. Long.* New York: Worker's Library.

Givner, Joan. (1982). *Katherine Anne Porter: A Life.* New York: Simon & Schuster.

Graham, Hugh Davis, ed. (1970). *Huey Long.* Englewood Cliffs, NJ: Prentice Hall.

Hair, William Ivy. (1991). *The Kingfish and His Realm: The Life and Times of Huey P. Long.* Baton Rouge: Louisiana State University Press.

Harris, T. O. (1938). *The Kingfish.* New Orleans: Pelican.

Heinemann, Ronald. (1996). *Harry Byrd of Virginia.* Charlottesville: University of Virginia Press.

Jeansonne, Glen. (1977). *Leander Perez: Boss of the Delta.* Lafayette: University of Southwestern Louisiana.

———. (1988). *Gerald L. K. Smith: Minister of Hate.* New Haven: Yale University Press.

———. (1993). *Messiah of the Masses: Huey P. Long and the Great Depression.* New York: Longman.

———, ed. (1995). *Huey at 100: Centennial Essays on Huey P. Long.* Ruston, LA: McGinty.

Kurtz, Michael, and Morgan D. Peoples. (1990). *Earl K. Long: The Saga of Uncle Earl and Louisiana Politics.* Baton Rouge: Louisiana State University Press.

LaBorde, Adras. (1951). *A National Southerner: Ransdell of Louisiana*. New York: Benziger.

LeVert, Suzanne. (1995). *Huey Long: The Kingfish of Louisiana*. New York: Facts on File.

Liebling, A. J. (1990). *The Earl of Louisiana*. Baton Rouge: Louisiana State University Press.

Long, Huey P. (1933). *Every Man a King*. New Orleans: National Book Company.

Mann, Robert. (1992). *Legacy to Power: Senator Russell Long of Louisiana*. New York: Paragon House.

Martin, Thomas. (1960). *Dynasty: The Longs of Louisiana*. New York: G. P. Putnam's Sons.

Opotowsky, Stan. (1960). *The Longs of Louisiana*. New York: E. P. Dutton.

Reed, Ed. (1986). *Requiem for a Kingfish*. Baton Rouge: Award.

Smith, Webster. (1933). *The Kingfish: A Biography of Huey P. Long*. New York: G. P. Putnam's Sons.

Waldron, Ann. (1993). *Hodding Carter: The Reconstruction of a Racist*. Chapel Hill, NC: Algonquin.

Walker, Calvit L. (1996). *Reminiscences and Recollections of Huey P. Long*. Woodville, TX: Dogwood.

Williams, T. Harry. (1969). *Huey Long*. New York: Vintage.

OTHER HISTORICAL WORKS

Baimonte, John V., Jr. (1990). *Immigrants in Rural America: A Study of the Italians of Tangipahoa Parish, Louisiana*. New York: Garland.

Barkley, Alben W. (1954). *That Reminds Me*. New York: Doubleday.

Barry, John M. (1997). *Rising Tide: The Great Mississippi Flood and How It Changed America*. New York: Simon & Schuster.

Basso, Hamilton. (1943). *Mainstream*. New York: Reynal & Hitchcock.

Bennett, David H. (1969). *Demagogues in the Depression: American Radicals and the Union Party, 1932–1936*. New Brunswick, NJ: Rutgers University Press.

Blain, Hugh M. (1937). *Favorite Huey Long Stories*. Baton Rouge: Otto Claitor.

Boulard, Garry. (1998). *Huey Long Invades New Orleans: The Siege of a City, 1934–36*. Gretna, LA: Pelican.

Bridges, Tyler. (2001). *Bad Bet on the Bayou*. New York: Farrar, Straus & Giroux.

Brinkley, Alan. (1982). *Voices of Protest: Huey Long, Father Coughlin and the Great Depression*. New York: Alfred A. Knopf.

———. (1995). "Robert Penn Warren, T. Harry Williams, and Huey Long: Mass Politics in the Literary and Historical Imaginations," in Glen Jeansonne, ed., *Huey at 100: Centennial Essays on Huey P. Long*. Ruston, LA: McGinty.

Burdette, Franklin L. (1940). *Filibustering in the Senate*. Princeton: Princeton University Press.

Carleton, Mark T. (1995). "The Longs and the Anti-Longs," in Glen Jeansonne, ed., *Huey at 100: Centennial Essays on Huey P. Long*. Ruston, LA: McGinty.

———. (1996). *River Capital: An Illustrated History of Baton Rouge*. Tarzana, CA: American Historical Press.

Carleton, Mark T., Perry H. Howard, and Joseph B. Parker, eds. (1975). *Readings in Louisiana Politics.* Baton Rouge: Claitor.

Carter, Hodding. (1949). "Huey Long: American Dictator," in Isabel Leighton, ed., *The Aspirin Age: 1919–1941.* New York: Simon & Schuster.

Cash, W. J. (1941). *The Mind of the South.* New York: Alfred A. Knopf.

Connally, Tom. (1954). *My Name Is Tom Connally.* New York: Crowell.

Conrad, Glenn R. (1995). "Huey Long and Two Louisiana Historians: An Editor's Critique of Two Biographies," in Glen Jeansonne, ed., *Huey at 100: Centennial Essays on Huey P. Long.* Ruston, LA: McGinty.

Cortner, Richard C. (1996). *The Kingfish and the Constitution: Huey Long, the First Amendment, and the Emergence of Modern Press Freedom in America.* Westport, CT: Greenwood.

Cummins, Light T., and Glen Jeansonne. (1982). *A Guide to the History of Louisiana.* Westport, CT: Greenwood.

Davis, John H. (1989). *Mafia Kingfish: Carlos Marcello and the Assassination of John F. Kennedy.* New York: McGraw-Hill.

Dethloff, Henry C. (1995). "Huey Long and Populism," in Glen Jeansonne, ed., *Huey at 100: Centennial Essays on Huey P. Long.* Ruston, LA: McGinty.

Dufour, Charles L. (1967). *Ten Flags in the Wind.* New York: Harper & Row.

Farley, James. (1938). *Behind the Ballots.* New York: Harcourt, Brace & World.

Finan, Christopher M. (2002). *Alfred E. Smith: The Happy Warrior.* New York: Hill & Wang.

Flynn, Edward J. (1947). *You're the Boss.* New York: Viking.

Fox, Stephen. (1989). *Blood and Power: Organized Crime in Twentieth-Century America.* New York: William Morrow.

Fried, Albert. (2001). *FDR and His Enemies.* New York: St. Martin's.

Gaske, Paul C. (1987). "Huey Pierce Long, Jr.," in Bernard K. Duffy and Halford R. Ryan, eds., *American Orators of the Twentieth Century: Critical Studies and Sources.* Westport, CT: Greenwood

Goodwin, Doris Kearns. (1976). *Lyndon Johnson and the American Dream.* New York: Harper & Row.

Haas, Edward F. (1995). "*My First Days in the White House:* The Presidential Fantasy of Huey P. Long," in Glen Jeansonne, ed., *Huey at 100: Centennial Essays on Huey P. Long.* Ruston, LA: McGinty.

Hammond, Hilda Phelps. (1936). *Let Freedom Ring.* New York: Farrar & Rinehart.

Howard, Perry H. (1971). *Political Tendencies in Louisiana.* Baton Rouge: Louisiana State University Press.

Howell, Roland B. (1969). *Louisiana Sugar Plantations, Mardi Gras, and Huey P. Long: Reminiscences of Roland Boatner Howell.* Baton Rouge: Claitor.

Ickes, Harold L. (1953). *The Secret Diary of Harold L. Ickes.* New York: Simon & Schuster.

Irby, Sam. (1932). *Kidnaped by the Kingfish.* New Orleans: Orleans Publishing Company.

Irey, Elmer L. (1948). *The Tax Dodgers.* New York: Fireside.

Jeansonne, Glen. (1975). "Leander Perez: Demagogue and Reformer," in Mark T. Carleton, Perry H. Howard, and Joseph B. Parker, eds., *Readings in Louisiana Politics.* Baton Rouge: Claitor.

Jensen, William Lee. (1975). *Historic Baton Rouge: A Revised Study of Historic Buildings and Sites*, Baton Rouge: City-Parish Planning Committee.

Johnson, Hiram W. (1983). *The Diary Letters of Hiram Johnson*. New York: Garland.

Kane, Harnett T. (1941). *Louisiana Hayride: The American Rehearsal for Dictatorship*. New York: William Morrow.

———. (1943). *The Bayous of Louisiana*. New York: William Morrow.

Key, V. O., Jr. (1950). *Southern Politics in State and Nation*. New York: Alfred A. Knopf.

Keyes, Frances Parkinson. (1950). *All This Is Louisiana*. New York: Harper & Brothers.

Kincaid, Diane D., ed. (1979). *Silent Hattie Speaks: The Personal Journal of Senator Hattie Caraway*. Westport, CT: Greenwood.

Klorer, John. (1936). *The New Louisiana: The Story of the Greatest State in the Nation*. Gretna, LA: Franklin.

Krock, Arthur. (1968). *Memoirs: Sixty Years on the Firing Line*. New York: Funk & Wagnalls.

Kurtz, Michael L. (1995). "Longism and Organized Crime," in Glen Jeansonne, ed., *Huey at 100: Centennial Essays on Huey P. Long*. Ruston, LA: McGinty.

———. (1998). *Louisiana Since the Longs: 1960 to Century's End*. Lafayette: University of Southwestern Louisiana.

Larson, Allan L. (1964). *Southern Demagogues: A Study in Charismatic Leadership*. Ann Arbor: University Microfilms.

Leighton, Isabel, ed. (1949). *The Aspirin Age: 1919–1941*. New York: Simon & Schuster.

Luthin, Reinhard H. (1959). "Huey P. Long: The Louisiana Kingfish," in Reinhard H. Luthin, ed., *American Demagogues: Twentieth Century*. Gloucester, MA: Peter Smith.

Malone, David. (1989). *Hattie and Huey: An Arkansas Tour*. Fayetteville: University of Arkansas Press.

McCoy, Donald R. (1976). "God's Angry Men," in Henry C. Dethloff, ed., *Huey P. Long: Southern Demagogue or American Democrat?* Lafayette: University of Southwestern Louisiana.

Michie, Allan A., and Frank Ryhlick. (1939). *Dixie Demagogues*. New York: Vanguard.

Mixon, Harold. (1981). "Huey P. Long's 1927–1928 Gubernatorial Primary Campaign: A Case Study in the Rhetoric of Agitation," in Cal M. Logue and Howard Dorgan, eds., *The Oratory of Southern Demagogues*. Baton Rouge: Louisiana State University Press.

Moley, Raymond. (1939). *After Seven Years*. New York: Harper Brothers.

———. (1949). *27 Masters of Politics*. New York: Funk & Wagnalls.

———. (1966). *The First New Deal*. New York: Harcourt, Brace & World.

Myrdal, Gunnar. (1944). *An American Dilemma: The Negro Problem and Modern Democracy*. New York: Harper & Row.

Parent, Wayne. (2004). *Inside the Carnival: Unmasking Louisiana Politics*. Baton Rouge: Louisiana State University Press.

Pavy, Donald A. (1999). *Accident and Deception: The Huey Long Shooting*. New Iberia, LA: Cajun.

Rose, Al, and Edmond Souchon. (1984). *New Orleans Jazz—A Family Album*. Baton Rouge: Louisiana State University Press.

Sahuc, Elois. (1977). *The Policeman Who Knew Huey P. Long*. New York: Carleton.

Schlesinger, Arthur. (1957). *The Crisis of the Old Order, 1919–1933.* Boston: Houghton Mifflin.

———. (1960). *The Age of Roosevelt: The Politics of Upheaval.* Boston: Houghton Mifflin.

———. (1976). "Messiah of the Rednecks," in Henry C. Dethloff, ed., *Huey P. Long: Southern Demagogue or American Democrat?* Lafayette: University of Southwestern Louisiana.

Schott, Matthew J. (1995). "Huey Long, The Biographer, and the Question of Character," in Glen Jeansonne, ed., *Huey at 100: Centennial Essays on Huey P. Long.* Ruston, LA: McGinty.

Schulze, Franz. (1994). *Philip Johnson: Life and Work.* New York: Alfred A. Knopf.

Simon, Rita. (1967). *As We Saw the Thirties: Essays on Social and Political Movements of a Decade.* Chicago: University of Illinois Press.

Sindler, Allan P. (1956). *Huey Long's Louisiana: State Politics, 1920–1952.* Baltimore: Johns Hopkins University Press.

Smith, Gerald L. K. (1967). "The Huey Long Movement," in Rita Simon, ed., *As We Saw the Thirties: Essays on Social and Political Movements of a Decade.* Chicago: University of Illinois Press.

Smith, Rixey, and Norman Beasley. (1939). *Carter Glass: A Biography.* New York: Longmans, Green.

Swing, Raymond. (1935). *Forerunners of American Fascism.* New York: J. Messner.

Tugwell, Rexford G. (1957). *The Democratic Roosevelt.* New York: Doubleday.

———. (1968). *The Brains Trust.* New York: Viking.

Tully, Grace. (1949). *FDR: My Boss.* New York: Scribner's.

Watkins, T. H. (1990). *Righteous Pilgrim: The Life and Times of Harold L. Ickes.* New York: Henry Holt.

Welch, Frank D. (2000). *Philip Johnson and Texas.* Austin: University of Texas Press.

Wilds, John, Charles F. Dufour, and Walter G. Cowan. (1996). *Louisiana: Yesterday and Today.* Baton Rouge: Louisiana State University Press.

Williams, T. Harry. (1959). "Presidential Address, Southern Historical Association." In Mark T. Carleton, Perry H. Howard, and Joseph B. Parker, eds. (1975). *Readings in Louisiana Politics.* Baton Rouge: Claitor.

———. (1961). *Romance and Realism in Southern Politics.* Athens: University of Georgia Press.

Woodward, C. Vann. (1951). *Origins of the New South: 1877–1913.* Baton Rouge: Louisiana State University Press.

WPA Guide to New Orleans. (rpt., 1983). New York: Pantheon.

Zinman, David H. (1993). *The Day Huey Long Was Shot, September 8, 1935.* Jackson: University Press of Mississippi.

JOURNAL AND PERIODICAL ARTICLES

Abernathy, Elton. (Winter 1955). "Huey Long: Oratorical 'Wealth Sharing.' " *Southern Speech Journal, 21,* 2, 87–102.

Adams, Mildred. (February 1933). "Huey the Great." *Forum, 89,* 70–75.

Banta, Brady M. (November 1986). "The Pine Island Situation: Petroleum, Politics, and Research Opportunities in Southern History." *Journal of Southern History, 52,* 4, 589–610.

Basso, Hamilton. (May 1935). "Huey Long and His Background." *Harper's Monthly,* vol. 170.

———. "The Kingfish: In Memoriam." *New Republic,* vol. 85, no. 1098, December 18, 1935, p. 177.

———. "Huey's Louisiana Heritage." *New Republic,* vol. 100, no. 1291, August 30, 1939, pp. 99–100.

———. "The Huey Long Legend." *Life,* December 9, 1946, pp. 106–21.

Bode, Ken. "Hero or Demagogue? The Two Faces of Huey Long on Film." *New Republic,* March 3, 1986, pp. 37–41.

Brinkley, Alan. (1981). "Huey Long, the Share Our Wealth Movement, and the Limits of Depression Dissidence." *Louisiana History, 22,* 2, 117–34.

———. (November 1984). "Comparative Biography as Political History: Huey Long and Father Coughlin." *History Teacher, 18,* 9–16.

Campbell, C. H. "Huey Long Chokes New Orleans." *Nation,* vol. 141, no. 3655, July 24, 1935, pp. 93–95.

Carter, Hodding. "Kingfish to Crawfish." *New Republic,* vol. 17, no. 999, January 24, 1934, pp. 302–5.

———. "The Kingfish on His Way." *New Republic,* vol. 81, no. 1042, November 21, 1934, pp. 40–42.

———. "How Come Huey Long?" *New Republic,* vol. 82, no. 1054, February 13, 1935, pp. 11–15.

———. (March 1935). "Louisiana Limelighter." *Review of Reviews, 91,* 3, 23–28.

———. (April 1949). "Huey Long: American Dictator." *American Mercury,* pp. 435–47.

"The Case of Governor Long." *New Republic,* vol. 59, no. 755, May 22, 1929, pp. 26–27.

Cassity, Michael J. (1973). "Huey Long: Barometer of Reform in the New Deal." *South Atlantic Quarterly, 72,* 2, 255–69.

Coad, George N. "I'm the Constitution in Louisiana." *Nation,* vol. 128, no. 3327, April 10, 1929, pp. 418–19.

Crown, James E. "Long at Home: Spurring on the Solons." *New York Times Magazine,* July 21, 1935, pp. 11–14.

Daniell, F. Raymond. (November 1934). "The Gentleman from Louisiana." *Current History,* 172–78.

———. "Huey's Heirs." *Saturday Evening Post,* vol. 210, no. 33, February 12, 1938, p. 5.

Davenport, Walter. "Yes, Your Excellency!" *Collier's,* December 13, 1930, pp. 22–23.

———. "How Huey Long Gets Away With It," *Collier's,* June 17, 1933, pp. 10–11.

———. "Catching up with Huey," *Collier's,* July 1, 1933, pp. 12, 42–46.

———. "Too High and Too Mighty," *Collier's,* January 19, 1935, p. 7.

———. "The Robes of the Kingfish," *Collier's,* November 23, 1935, p. 28.

"Demagogues: Johnson Lambasts Senator and Priest, Long Counters with Utopia." *Newsweek,* March 16, 1935, pp. 5–7.

"Democrats: Incredible Kingfish." *Time,* October 3, 1932, p. 11.

Dethloff, Henry C. (1964). "Huey P. Long: Interpretations." *Louisiana Studies, 3,* 2, 219–32.

———. (1978). "The Longs: Revolution or Populist Retrenchment?" *Louisiana History, 19,* 4, 401–12.

Deutsch, Hermann. "Huey Long of Louisiana." *New Republic,* vol. 68, no. 884, November 11, 1931, pp. 349–51.

———. "Hattie and Huey." *Saturday Evening Post,* October 15, 1932, pp. 6–7, 88–90, 92.

———. "Prelude to a Heterocrat." *Saturday Evening Post,* vol. 208, no. 10, September 7, 1935, pp. 5–11.

———. "Paradox in Pajamas." *Saturday Evening Post,* vol. 208, no. 14, October 5, 1935, pp. 14–18.

———. "Huey Long: The Last Phase." *Saturday Evening Post,* vol. 208, no. 15, October 12, 1935, pp. 27–31.

Dowie, William. (1986). *Regional Dimensions: Studies of Southeast Louisiana,* 4, 1, 1–13.

Gillette, Michael L. (1970). "Huey Long and the Chaco War." *Louisiana History,* 11, 4, 293–312.

Haas, Edward F. (1988). "Black Cat, Uncle Earl, Edwin and the Kingfish: The Wit of Modern Louisiana Politics." *Louisiana History,* 29, 3, 213–27.

———. (1991). "Huey Long and the Communists." *Louisiana History,* 32, 1, 29–46.

———. (February 1994). "Huey Pierce Long and Historical Speculation." *History Teacher,* 27, 2, 125–31.

Hair, William Ivy (1986). "Huey Long: A Historical Perspective." *Regional Dimensions: Studies of Southeast Louisiana,* 4, 1, 1–13.

Heleniak, Roman. (1969). "Local Reaction to the Great Depression in New Orleans." *Louisiana History,* 10, 4, 289–306.

"Homage to Huey." *Time,* vol. 37, no. 18, May 5, 1941, pp. 18–19.

Hoteling, Burton L. (March 1943). "Huey Pierce Long as Journalist and Propagandist." *Journalism Quarterly,* 20, 21.

"Huey Long." *New Republic,* vol. 84, no. 1085, September 18, 1935, pp. 146–47.

"Huey Long Invades the Middle West." *New Republic,* vol. 82, no. 1067, May 15, 1935.

"Huey Long: Through Washroom Window to Hearing." *Newsweek,* November 25, 1933, p. 9.

"Huey Long's Forty-Four Laws." *New Republic,* vol. 81, no. 1043, November 28, 1934, p. 63.

"Huey Proposes." *New Republic,* vol. 82, no. 1059, March 20, 1935, pp. 146–47.

Huie, William Bradford. "Gerald Smith's Bid for Power." *American Mercury,* August 1942.

Hutchinson, Paul. "Heretics of the Air." *Christian Century,* vol. 52, no. 14, April 3, 1935, pp. 431–33.

"Impeachment or Persecution in Louisiana." *New Republic,* vol. 58, no. 751, April 24, 1929, pp. 268–69.

Jeansonne, Glen. (Fall 1980). "Challenge to the New Deal: Huey P. Long and the Redistribution of National Wealth." *Louisiana History,* 21, 4, 331–39.

———. (1982). "Partisan Parson: An Oral History Account of the Louisiana Years of Gerald L. K. Smith." *Louisiana History,* 23, 2, 149–58.

———. (1986). "Huey P. Long, Robin Hood or Tyrant? A Critique of Huey Long." *Regional Dimensions: Studies of Southeast Louisiana,* 4, 1, 1–13.

———. (Fall 1989). "Apotheosis of Huey Long." *Biography,* 12, 283–301.

———. (1990). "Huey P. Long: A Political Contradiction." *Louisiana History,* 31, 4, 373–85.

———. (1992). "Huey Long and Racism." *Louisiana History, 33,* 3, 265–82.

———. (1994). "Huey P. Long, Gerald L. K. Smith and Leander Perez as Charismatic Leaders." *Louisiana History, 35,* 1, 5–21.

Jones, Ellis O. (April 1935). "The Truth About Huey Long." *Technocrat, 1,* 2.

Jones, Terry L. (1987). "An Administration Under Fire: The Long-Farley Affair of 1935." *Louisiana History, 28,* 1, 5–18.

Kent, Frank R. "Our Political Monstrosities." *Atlantic Monthly,* vol. 151, no. 4, April 1933, pp. 407–11.

King, Peter J. (March 1964). "Huey Long: The Louisiana Kingfish." *History Today, 14,* 3, 151–60.

"Kingfish Establishes Martial Law, Supplies Action, and Claims Victory." *Newsweek,* February 2, 1935, pp. 5–6.

Kurtz, Michael L. (1983). "Crime in Louisiana History: Myth and Reality." *Louisiana History, 24,* 4, 355–76.

———. (1986). "Longism and Louisiana Politics." *Regional Dimensions: Studies of Southeast Louisiana, 4,* 1, 1–13.

"Labor Notes, Huey Long and Labor." *Nation,* August 14, 1935, p. 192.

"Lawyer, Kingfish, Crawfish Investigates Plot." *Newsweek,* February 9, 1935, p. 11.

Lee, Rose. "Senator Long at Home." *New Republic,* vol. 79, no. 1017, May 30, 1934, pp. 66–68.

Leslie, J. Paul, Jr. (Winter 1972). "Louisiana Hayride Revisited." *Louisiana Studies, 11,* 4, 282–94.

Leuchtenburg, William E. (October/November 1985). "FDR and the Kingfish." *American Heritage, 36,* 6, 56–63.

Long, Huey P. "Our Blundering Government and Its Spokesman—Hugh Johnson." *Vital Speeches of the Day,* vol. 1, March 25, 1935, pp. 392–98.

Loria, Frank L. (1971). "Senator Long's Assassination." *Louisiana Historical Quarterly, 54,* 2, 7–17.

"Louisiana State University." (September 1937). *Scribner's Magazine,* 33–38.

Lovett, Robert M. "Huey Long Invades the Midwest." *New Republic,* vol. 83, no. 1067, May 15, 1935, pp. 10–12.

"The Man Who Understood Huey." *Saturday Evening Post,* vol. 212, August 26, 1939, p. 22.

McSween, Harold B. (Summer 1993). "Huey Long at His Centenary." *Virginia Quarterly Review, 29,* 3, 509–20.

"Medicine Gun Politics." *Commonweal,* vol. 22, no. 21, September 20, 1935, pp. 481–82.

Mencken, H. L. "The Glory of Louisiana." *Nation,* vol. 136, no. 3539, May 3, 1933, pp. 507–8.

———. "Why Not Gerald?" *Baltimore Evening Sun,* September 7, 1936.

Michie, Allan A. "Huey Long's Heritage." *Nation,* vol. 149, no. 5, July 29, 1939, pp. 120–23.

Moreau, John Adam. (1965). "Huey Long and His Chroniclers." *Louisiana History, 6,* 2, 121–39.

Morgan, Cecil. (April 1971). "Review of *Huey Long* by T. Harry Williams." *Tulane Law Review, 45,* 676–82.

"Mourners, Heirs, Foes." *Time,* vol. 26, no. 13, September 23, 1935, pp. 14–16.

Mugleston, William F. (1975). "Cornpone and Potlikker: A Moment of Relief in the Great Depression." *Louisiana History, 16,* 3, 279–88.

"Mystery in the Death of Huey Long." *Reader's Digest,* vol. 305, no. 209, September 1939, pp. 107–8.

"NRA: Huey Long's Filibuster Fails." *Newsweek,* June 22, 1935, pp. 7–8.

Nossiter, Adam. "Onetime Fascist, Modernist Once Huey Long Fan." *Baton Rouge Advocate,* January 31, 2005.

O'Conner, Stella. (1949). "The Charity Hospital at New Orleans: An Administrative and Financial History." *Louisiana Historical Quarterly, 31,* 1, 1–109.

Pleasant, John R., Jr. (1974). "Ruffin G. Pleasant and Huey P. Long in the Prison-Stripe Controversy." *Louisiana History, 15,* 4, 357–66.

"Poetic Kingfish." *Newsweek,* January 19, 1935, p. 8.

Pusateri, C. Joseph. (1976). "The Stormy Career of a Radio Maverick, W. K. Henderson of KWKH." *Louisiana History, 15,* 4, 389–408.

Rubin, Louis D. (1993). "Versions of the Kingfish." *Sewanee Review, 101,* 4.

Sanson, Jerry P. (1993). "Huey Long and Willie Stark: The Parallels of Myth and Reality." *North Louisiana Historical Association Journal, 24,* 3–11.

Scaramouche. (August 1933). "Huey Long: Clown and Knave of the U.S. Senate." *Real America, 1,* 6, 34–39.

Schott, Matthew W. (1986). "Huey Long: Progressive Backlash." *Louisiana History, 27,* 2, 133–46.

"Share the Wealth Wave." *Time,* April 1, 1935, pp. 15–17.

Simpich, Frederick. (September 1927). "The Great Mississippi Flood of 1927." *National Geographic,* 243–89.

Sindler, Allan P. (1955). "Bifactional Rivalry as an Alternative to Two Party Competition in Louisiana." *American Political Science Review, 44:* 635–47.

Smith, Gerald L. K. "How Come Huey Long?" *New Republic,* vol. 82, no. 1054, February 13, 1935, pp. 11–15.

Snyder, Robert E. (1975). "Huey Long and the Presidential Election of 1936." *Louisiana History, 16,* 2, 117–44.

———. (1976). "The Concept of Demagoguery: Huey Long and His Literary Critics." *Louisiana Studies, 15,* 1, 61–84.

———. (1977). "Huey Long and the Cotton-Holiday Plan of 1931." *Louisiana History, 18,* 2, 133–60.

Sokolsky, George E. "Huey Long." *Atlantic Monthly,* vol. 156, no. 5, November 1935, pp. 523–33.

"Square Dealers Attack Huey." *Newsweek,* January 26, 1935, p. 7.

Stolberg, Benjamin. "Dr. Huey and Mr. Long," *Nation,* vol. 141, September 18, 1935, pp. 344–46.

Swan, George Steven. (Summer 1984). "A Preliminary Comparison of Long's Louisiana and Duplessis' Quebec." *Louisiana History, 25,* 289–319.

Swing, Raymond Gram. "The Menace of Huey Long." *Nation,* vol 140, nos. 3627, 3628, 3629, January 9, 16, 23, 1935, pp. 36–39, 69–71, 98–100.

Thurber, James. "Talk of the Town: Rough on Rats." *The New Yorker,* vol. 8, no. 35, September 2, 1933, pp. 8–9.

"To Arms Louisiana." *Forum*, vol. 92, no. 4, October 1934, p. 256.

Towns, Stuart. (Summer 1966). "A Louisiana Medicine Show: The Kingfish Elects an Arkansas Senator." *Arkansas Historical Quarterly, 25.*

"Two Heavy Brickbats Hit Huey Long's University." *Newsweek*, January 5, 1935, p. 34.

"Undressed Governor." *Time*, June 6, 1930, p. 19.

Vaughn, Courtney. (1979). "The Legacy of Huey Long." *Louisiana History, 20, 1,* 93–101.

Whisenhunt, Donald W. (Summer 1974). "Huey Long and the Texas Cotton Acreage Control Law of 1931." *Louisiana Studies, 13,* 142–53.

Williams, T. Harry. (1960). "The Gentleman from Louisiana: Demagogue or Democrat." *Journal of Southern History, 26,* 3–21.

———. (Spring 1961). "The Politics of the Longs." *Georgia Review, 15,* 20–33.

———. (1973). "Huey, Lyndon, and Southern Radicalism." *Journal of American History, 60, 2,* 267–93.

Williams, T. Harry, and John Milton Price. (May 1970). "The Huey P. Long Papers at Louisiana State University." *Journal of Southern History, 36, 2,* 256–61.

Wingo, Barbara C. (1977). "The 1928 Presidential Election in Louisiana." *Louisiana History, 18, 4,* 405–36.

LETTERS, PAPERS, REMINISCENCES, AND MANUSCRIPT COLLECTIONS

Aswell, James B., papers, Louisiana and Lower Mississippi Valley Collections, Hill Memorial Library, Louisiana State University Libraries, Baton Rouge; hereafter LSU LLMVC.

Bozeman, Harley B. "Winn Parish as I Have Known It," series of 646 weekly columns published in *Winn Parish Enterprise* from October 2, 1956, to March 4, 1971. Six scrapbooks in Louisiana State Library, Baton Rouge.

———. papers, LSU LLMVC.

Christman, Henry, ed. (1985). *Kingfish to America, Share Our Wealth: Selected Senatorial Papers of Huey P. Long.* New York: Schocken.

Detro, Randall A., papers, LSU LLMVC.

Devol, Don, papers, LSU LLMVC.

Dugas, Claiborne J., papers, LSU LLMVC.

Federal Bureau of Investigation, "Huey P. Long," File #62-32509, 14 sections.

Fournet, John B., papers, LSU LLMVC.

French, George N., papers, LSU LLMVC.

Frey, Fred C., papers, LSU LLMVC.

Gilkison, Helen, papers, LSU LLMVC.

Harris, Thomas H. (1963). *The Memoirs of T. H. Harris: State Superintendent of Public Education in Louisiana, 1908–1940.* Baton Rouge: Louisiana State University Press.

Jennings-Heywood Oil Syndicate records, 1900–1970, LSU LLMVC.

Kemp, Bolivar E., papers, LSU LLMVC.

Leche, Richard, papers, LSU LLMVC.

Long, Huey P., papers, LSU LLMVC.

Long, Russell B. (1985). "Remembrances of Huey P. Long," typescript reminiscences, LSU, text entered into *Congressional Record*, U.S. Senate, September 10, 1985, pp. 11193–98.

McShane, Andrew, papers, New Orleans Public Library, New Orleans City Archives.

Morgan, Cecil, papers, Tulane University Special Collections, New Orleans.

Parker, John M., papers, Collection 44, Southwestern Archives, University of Louisiana, Lafayette.

Oge, John M., papers, LSU LLMVC.

Sanders, Jared Young, II, papers, LSU LLMVC.

Schwartz, Kurt S., papers, LSU LLMVC.

Tanner, Thomas J., papers, LSU LLMVC.

Uhler, John Earle, papers, LSU LLMVC.

Walmsley, T. Semmes, papers, New Orleans Public Library, New Orleans City Archives.

Weiss, Seymour, papers, LSU LLMVC.

Williams, T. Harry, papers, LSU LLMVC.

THESES AND DISSERTATIONS

Ader, Emile B. (1942). "An Analysis of the Campaign Techniques and Appeals of Huey P. Long." M.A. thesis, Tulane University.

Arnold, Charles LaRon. (1999). "Huey Long: Propagandist, Newspaper Publisher, Governor, and Senator." M.A. thesis, University of West Florida.

Banta, Brady Michael. (1981). "The Regulation and Conservation of Petroleum Resources in Louisiana, 1901–1940." Ph.D. dissertation, Louisiana State University.

Bormann, Ernest G. (1951). "An Analysis of the March 7, 1935, Radio Address of Senator Huey P. Long." M.A. thesis, University of Iowa.

———. (1953). "A Rhetorical Analysis of the National Radio Broadcasts of Senator Huey P. Long." Ph.D. dissertation, University of Iowa.

Faser, Karl Edward. (1965). "A Rhetorical Analysis of the Use of Invective by Huey Long." M.A. thesis, University of Oklahoma.

Field, Betty Marie. (1969). "The Campaigns of Huey Long, 1918–1928." M.A. thesis, Tulane University.

Goldsmith, Adolph Oliver. (1967). "A Study of the Objectivity of Treatment of Governor Huey P. Long by Six Louisiana Daily Newspapers During Long's First Eleven Months in Office." Ph.D. dissertation, University of Iowa.

Haberman, Frederick. (1935). "Persuasion in the Power of Huey Long." M.A. thesis, University of Wisconsin.

Hodges, James Curtis. (1940). "The Politics of Huey Long." M.A. thesis, Louisiana State University.

Lowery, Olan Buford. (1951). "An Analysis and Evaluation of Huey Long's 'Share Our Wealth' Speech, May 15, 1935." M.A. thesis, University of Iowa.

Martin, Margaret Ann. (1964). "Colonel Robert Ewing: Louisiana Journalist and Politician." M.A. thesis, Louisiana State University.

Minehan, Molly. (1962) "A Theoretical-Rhetorical Study in the Nature of Demagoguery: Huey Pierce Long, a Case Study." M.A. thesis, San Francisco State College.

Renwick, Edward F. (1967). "The Longs' Legislative Lieutenants." Ph.D. dissertation, University of Arizona.

Tyler, Pamela. (1989). "Silk Stockings and Ballot Boxes: Women of the Upper Class and New Orleans Politics, 1930–1955." Ph.D. dissertation, Tulane University.

LOUISIANA NEWSPAPERS

Alexandria Daily Town Talk
American Progress
Baton Rouge Advocate
Baton Rouge State-Times
Bienville Democrat
Bogalusa Enterprise
Bogalusa News
Donaldsonville Chief
Hammond Daily Courier
Hammond Vindicator
Houma Courier
Lafayette Daily Advertiser
Lafayette Tribune
Lake Charles American Press
Louisiana Progress
Monroe News-Star
Natchitoches Times
New Iberia Enterprise
New Orleans Morning Tribune
New Orleans States
New Orleans Times-Picayune
New Orleans Item
Shreveport Caucasian
Shreveport Times
Winnfield Comrade

FICTION

Basso, Hamilton. (1942). *Sun in Capricorn*. New York: Scribner's.
Dos Passos, John. (1943). *Number One*. Boston: Houghton Mifflin.
Langley, Adria Locke. (1945). *A Lion Is in the Streets*. New York: McGraw-Hill.
Lewis, Sinclair. (1936). *It Can't Happen Here*. Garden City, NY: Doubleday, Doran.
Long, Huey P. (1935). *My First Days in the White House*. Harrisburg, PA: Telegraph.
Uhler, John Earle. (1931). *Cane Juice*. New York: Century.
Warren, Robert Penn. (1946). *All the King's Men*. New York: Harcourt, Brace.

INDEX

ABOUT THE AUTHOR

A native of Williamsburg, Virginia, RICHARD D. WHITE, JR., is a Marjory B. Ourso Excellence in Teaching Professor at Louisiana State University and teaches in the university's Public Administration Institute. He received his PhD from Pennsylvania State University and was a National Security Research Fellow at Harvard University, where he taught public policy within the Institute of Politics. White is the author of *Roosevelt the Reformer: Theodore Roosevelt as Civil Service Commissioner, 1889–1895* (University of Alabama Press, 2003) and numerous scholarly articles. Prior to his academic career, White was a senior officer in the U.S. Coast Guard. He served eleven years at sea, including voyages to both the Antarctic and Arctic Oceans. His shoreside assignments included service in the White House as a special assistant to Vice President George Bush as well as at the U.S. State Department and the Central Intelligence Agency.

He lives in Baton Rouge with his wife, Cynthia.

ABOUT THE TYPE

This book was set in Scala, a typeface designed by Martin Majoor in 1991. It was originally designed for a music company in the Nether-lands and then was published by the international type house FSI FontShop. Its distinctive extended serifs add to the articulation of the letterforms to make it a very readable typeface.